English / French
Anglais / Français

THE OXFORD
Picture
Dictionary

NORMA SHAPIRO AND JAYME ADELSON-GOLDSTEIN

Translated by Techno-Graphics & Translations, Inc.

Oxford University Press

OXFORD
UNIVERSITY PRESS

198 Madison Avenue
New York, NY 10016 USA

Great Clarendon Street, Oxford OX2 6DP UK

Oxford University Press is a department of the University of Oxford.
It furthers the University's objective of excellence in research, scholarship,
and education by publishing worldwide in

Oxford New York

Auckland Cape Town Dar es Salaam Hong Kong Karachi
Kuala Lumpur Madrid Melbourne Mexico City Nairobi
New Delhi Shanghai Taipei Toronto

With offices in

Argentina Austria Brazil Chile Czech Republic France Greece
Guatemala Hungary Italy Japan Poland Portugal Singapore
South Korea Switzerland Thailand Turkey Ukraine Vietnam

OXFORD and OXFORD ENGLISH are registered trademarks of
Oxford University Press

© Oxford University Press 2005

Database right Oxford University Press (maker)

Library of Congress Cataloging-in-Publication Data

Shapiro, Norma.
   The Oxford picture dictionary : English/French =
anglais/français / Norma Shapiro and Jayme Adelson-Goldstein ;
translated by Techno-Graphics & Translations, Inc.
       p. cm.
   Includes bibliographical references and index.
   ISBN 978-0-19-439849-7
   1. Picture dictionaries, French. 2. Picture dictionaries,
English. 3. English language–Dictionaries–French.
   I. Adelson-Goldstein, Jayme. II. Title.

PC2629.S53 2005
443'.21–dc22

                                        2004061704

Executive Publisher: Janet Aitchison
Managing Editor: Stephanie Karras
Associate Editor: Ashli Totty
Editorial Assistant: Carla Mavrodin
Art Director: Lynn Luchetti
Design Project Manager: Maj-Britt Hagsted
Production Manager: Shanta Persaud
Production Controller: Eve Wong

Production Services by: Techno-Graphics and Translations, Inc.
Cover design by Silver Editions

ISBN: 978 0 19 439849 7

Printed in Hong Kong

10 9 8 7 6 5 4

ACKNOWLEDGMENTS

Illustrations by: David Aikins, Doug Archer, Craig Attebery, Garin Baker,
Sally Bensusen, Eliot Bergman, Mark Bischel, Dan Brown / Artworks NY, Roy
Douglas Buchman, George Burgos / Larry Dodge, Carl Cassler, Mary Chandler,
Robert Crawford, Jim DeLapine, Judy Francis, Graphic Chart and Map Co.,
Dale Gustafson, Biruta Akerbergs Hansen, Marcia Hartsock, C.M.I.,
David Hildebrand, The Ivy League of Artists, Inc. / Judy Degraffenreid,
The Ivy League of Artists, Inc. / Tom Powers, The Ivy League of Artists, Inc. /
John Rice, Pam Johnson, Ed Kurtzman, Narda Lebo, Scott A. MacNeill /
MACNEILL & MACINTOSH, Andy Lendway / Deborah Wolfe Ltd., Jeffrey Mangiat,
Suzanne Mogensen, Mohammad Mansoor, Tom Newsom, Melodye Benson Rosales,
Stacey Schuett, Rob Schuster, James Seward, Larry Taugher, Bill Thomson,
Anna Veltfort, Nina Wallace, Wendy Wassink-Ackison, Michael Wepplo,
Don Wieland

Thanks to Mike Mikos for his preliminary architectural sketches of
several pieces.

References

Boyer, Paul S., Clifford E. Clark, Jr., Joseph F. Kett, Thomas L. Purvis, Harvard
Sitkoff, Nancy Woloch *The Enduring Vision: A History of the American People*,
Lexington, Massachusetts: D.C. Heath and Co., 1990.

Grun, Bernard, *The Timetables of History: A Horizontal Linkage of People and Events*,
(based on Werner Stein's Kulturfahrplan) New York: A Touchstone Book,
Simon and Schuster, 1946, 1963, 1975, 1979.

Statistical Abstract of the United States: 1996, 116th Edition, Washington, DC:
US Bureau of the Census, 1996.

The World Book Encyclopedia, Chicago: World Book Inc., a Scott Fetzer Co.,
1988 Edition.

Toff, Nancy, Editor-in-Chief, *The People of North America* (Series), New York:
Chelsea House Publishers, Main Line Books, 1988.

Trager, James, *The People's Chronology*, A Year-by-Year Record of Human Events from
Prehistory to the Present, New York: Henry Holt Reference Book, 1992.

Acknowledgments

The publisher and authors would like to thank the following people for reviewing the manuscript and/or participating in focus groups as the book was being developed:

Ana Maria Aguilera, Lubie Alatriste, Ann Albarelli, Margaret Albers, Sherry Allen, Fiona Armstrong, Ted Auerbach, Steve Austen, Jean Barlow, Sally Bates, Sharon Batson, Myra Baum, Mary Beauparlant, Gretchen Bitterlin, Margrajean Bonilla, Mike Bostwick, Shirley Brod, Lihn Brown, Trish Brys-Overeem, Lynn Bundy, Chris Bunn, Carol Carvel, Leslie Crucil, Robert Denheim, Joshua Denk, Kay Devonshire, Thomas Dougherty, Gudrun Draper, Sara Eisen, Lynda Elkins, Ed Ende, Michele Epstein, Beth Fatemi, Andra R. Fawcett, Alice Fiedler, Harriet Fisher, James Fitzgerald, Mary Fitzsimmons, Scott Ford, Barbara Gaines, Elizabeth Garcia Grenados, Maria T. Gerdes, Penny Giacalone, Elliott Glazer, Jill Gluck de la Llata, Javier Gomez, Pura Gonzales, Carole Goodman, Joyce Grabowski, Maggie Grennan, Joanie Griffin, Sally Hansen, Fotini Haritos, Alice Hartley, Fernando Herrera, Ann Hillborn, Mary Hopkins, Lori Howard, Leann Howard, Pamela Howard, Rebecca Hubner, Jan Jarrell, Vicki Johnson, Michele Kagan, Nanette Kafka, Gena Katsaros, Evelyn Kay, Greg Keech, Cliff Ker, Gwen Kerner-Mayer, Marilou Kessler, Patty King, Linda Kiperman, Joyce Klapp, Susan Knutson, Sandy Kobrine, Marinna Kolaitis, Donna Korol, Lorraine Krampe, Karen Kuser, Andrea Lang, Nancy Lebow, Tay Lesley, Gale Lichter, Sandie Linn, Rosario Lorenzano, Louise Louie, Cheryl Lucas, Ronna Magy, Juanita Maltese, Mary Marquardsen, Carmen Marques Rivera, Susan McDowell, Alma McGee, Jerry McLeroy, Kevin McLure, Joan Meier, Patsy Mills, Judy Montague, Vicki Moore, Eneida Morales, Glenn Nadelbach, Elizabeth Neblett, Kathleen Newton, Yvonne Nishio, Afra Nobay, Rosa Elena Ochoa, Jean Owensby, Jim Park, John Perkins, Jane Pers, Laura Peskin, Maria Pick, Percy Pleasant, Selma Porter, Kathy Quinones, Susan Ritter, Martha Robledo, Maureen Rooney, Jean Rose, David Ross, Julietta Ruppert, Lorraine Ruston, Susan Ryan, Frederico Salas, Leslie Salmon, Jim Sandifer, Linda Sasser, Lisa Schreiber, Mary Segovia, Abe Shames, Debra Shaw, Stephanie Shipp, Pat Singh, Mary Sklavos, Donna Stark, Claire Cocoran Stehling, Lynn Sweeden, Joy Tesh, Sue Thompson, Christine Tierney, Laura Topete, Carmen Villanueva, Laura Webber, Renée Weiss, Beth Winningham, Cindy Wislofsky, Judy Wood, Paula Yerman.

A special thanks to Marna Shulberg and the students of the Saticoy Branch of Van Nuys Community Adult School.

We would also like to thank the following individuals and organizations who provided their expertise:

Carl Abato, Alan Goldman, Dr. Larry Falk, Caroll Gray, Henry Haskell, Susan Haskell, Los Angeles Fire Department, Malcolm Loeb, Barbara Lozano, Lorne Dubin, United Farm Workers.

Authors' Acknowledgments

Throughout our careers as English language teachers, we have found inspiration in many places—in the classroom with our remarkable students, at schools, conferences, and workshops with our fellow teachers, and with our colleagues at the ESL Teacher Institute. We are grateful to be part of this international community.

We would like to sincerely thank and acknowledge Eliza Jensen, the project's Senior Editor. Without Eliza, this book would not have been possible. Her indomitable spirit, commitment to clarity, and unwavering advocacy allowed us to realize the book we envisioned.

Creating this dictionary was a collaborative effort and it has been our privilege to work with an exceptionally talented group of individuals who, along with Eliza Jensen, make up the Oxford Picture Dictionary team. We deeply appreciate the contributions of the following people:

Lynn Luchetti, Art Director, whose aesthetic sense and sensibility guided the art direction of this book,

Susan Brorein, Senior Designer, who carefully considered the design of each and every page,

Klaus Jekeli, Production Editor, who pored over both manuscript and art to ensure consistency and accuracy, and

Tracy Hammond, Art Buyer, who skillfully managed thousands of pieces of art and reference material.

We also want to thank Susan Mazer, the talented artist who was by our side for the initial problem-solving and Mary Chandler who also lent her expertise to the project.

We have learned much working with Marjorie Fuchs, Lori Howard, and Renée Weiss, authors of the dictionary's ancillary materials. We thank them for their on-going contributions to the dictionary program.

We must make special mention of Susan Lanzano, Editorial Manager, whose invaluable advice, insights, and queries were an integral part of the writing process.

This book is dedicated to my husband, Neil Reichline, who has encouraged me to take the road less traveled, and to my sons, Eli and Alex, who have allowed me to sit at their baseball games with my yellow notepad. —NS

This book is lovingly dedicated to my husband, Gary and my daughter, Emily Rose, both of whom hugged me tight and let me work into the night. —JAG

A Letter to the Teacher

Welcome to The Oxford Picture Dictionary.

This comprehensive vocabulary resource provides you and your students with over 3,700 words, each defined by engaging art and presented in a meaningful context. *The Oxford Picture Dictionary* enables your students to learn and use English in all aspects of their daily lives. The 140 key topics cover home and family, the workplace, the community, health care, and academic studies. The topics are organized into 12 thematic units that are based on the curriculum of beginning and low-intermediate level English language coursework. The word lists of the dictionary include both single word entries and verb phrases. Many of the prepositions and adjectives are presented in phrases as well, demonstrating the natural use of words in conjunction with one another.

The Oxford Picture Dictionary uses a variety of visual formats, each suited to the topic being represented. Where appropriate, word lists are categorized and pages are divided into sections, allowing you to focus your students' attention on one aspect of a topic at a time.

Within the word lists:

- nouns, adjectives, prepositions, and adverbs are numbered,

- verbs are bolded and identified by letters, and

- targeted prepositions and adjectives within phrases are bolded.

The dictionary includes a variety of exercises and self-access tools that will guide your students toward accurate and fluent use of the new words.

- Exercises at the bottom of the pages provide vocabulary development through pattern practice, application of the new language to other topics, and personalization questions.

- An alphabetical index assists students in locating all words and topics in the dictionary.

- A phonetic listing for each word in the index and a pronunciation guide give students the key to accurate pronunciation.

- A verb index of all the verbs presented in the dictionary provides students with information on the present, past, and past participle forms of the verbs.

The Oxford Picture Dictionary is the core of *The Oxford Picture Dictionary Program* which includes a *Dictionary Cassette*, a *Teacher's Book* and its companion *Focused Listening Cassette, Beginning* and *Intermediate Workbooks, Classic Classroom Activities* (a photocopiable activity book), *Overhead Transparencies,* and *Read All About It 1* and *2.* Bilingual editions of *The Oxford Picture Dictionary* are available in Spanish, Chinese, Vietnamese, and many other languages.

TEACHING THE VOCABULARY

Your students' needs and your own teaching philosophy will dictate how you use *The Oxford Picture Dictionary* with your students. The following general guidelines, however, may help you adapt the dictionary's pages to your particular course and students. (For topic-specific, step-by-step guidelines and activities for presenting and practicing the vocabulary on each dictionary page see the *Oxford Picture Dictionary Teacher's Book.*)

Preview the topic

A good way to begin any lesson is to talk with students to determine what they already know about the topic. Some different ways to do this are:

- Ask general questions related to the topic;

- Have students brainstorm a list of words they know from the topic; or

- Ask questions about the picture(s) on the page.

Present the vocabulary

Once you've discovered which words your students already know, you are ready to focus on presenting the words they need. Introducing 10–15 new words in a lesson allows students to really learn the new words. On pages where the word lists are longer, and students are unfamiliar with many of the words, you may wish to introduce the words by categories or sections, or simply choose the words you want in the lesson.

Here are four different presentation techniques. The techniques you choose will depend on the topic being studied and the level of your students.

- Say each new word and describe or define it within the context of the picture.

- Demonstrate verbs or verb sequences for the students, and have volunteers demonstrate the actions as you say them.

- Use Total Physical Response commands to build comprehension of the vocabulary: *Put the pencil on your book. Put it on your notebook. Put it on your desk.*

- Ask a series of questions to build comprehension and give students an opportunity to say the new words:

▶ Begin with *yes/no* questions. *Is #16 chalk?* (yes)

▶ Progress to *or* questions. *Is #16 chalk or a marker?* (chalk)

▶ Finally ask *Wh* questions.

What can I use to write on this paper? (a marker / Use a marker.)

Check comprehension

Before moving on to the practice stage, it is helpful to be sure all students understand the target vocabulary. There are many different things you can do to check students' understanding. Here are two activities to try:

• Tell students to open their books and point to the items they hear you say. Call out target vocabulary at random as you walk around the room checking to see if students are pointing to the correct pictures.

• Make true/false statements about the target vocabulary. Have students hold up two fingers for true, three fingers for false. *You can write with a marker.* [two fingers] *You raise your notebook to talk to the teacher.* [three fingers]

Take a moment to review any words with which students are having difficulty before beginning the practice activities.

Practice the vocabulary

Guided practice activities give your students an opportunity to use the new vocabulary in meaningful communication. The exercises at the bottom of the pages are one source of guided practice activities.

• **Talk about...** This activity gives students an opportunity to practice the target vocabulary through sentence substitutions with meaningful topics.

e.g. **Talk about your feelings.**

I feel <u>happy</u> when I see my friends.

• **Practice...** This activity gives students practice using the vocabulary within common conversational functions such as making introductions, ordering food, making requests, etc.

e.g. **Practice asking for things in the dining room.**

Please pass <u>the platter</u>.

May I have <u>the creamer</u>?

Could I have <u>a fork</u>, please?

• **Use the new language.** This activity asks students to brainstorm words within various categories, or may ask them to apply what they have learned to another topic in the dictionary. For example, on *Colors*, page 12, students are asked to look at *Clothing I*, pages 64–65, and name the colors of the clothing they see.

• **Share your answers.** These questions provide students with an opportunity to expand their use of the target vocabulary in personalized discussion. Students can ask and answer these questions in whole class discussions, pair or group work, or they can write the answers as journal entries.

Further guided and communicative practice can be found in the *Oxford Picture Dictionary Teacher's Book* and in *Classic Classroom Activities.* The *Oxford Picture Dictionary Beginning* and *Intermediate Workbooks* and *Read All About It 1* and *2* provide your students with controlled and communicative reading and writing practice.

We encourage you to adapt the materials to suit the needs of your classes, and we welcome your comments and ideas. Write to us at:

Oxford University Press
ESL Department
198 Madison Avenue
New York, NY 10016

Jayme Adelson-Goldstein

Norma Shapiro

A Letter to the Student

Dear Student of English,

Welcome to *The Oxford Picture Dictionary*. The more than 3,700 words in this book will help you as you study English.

Each page in this dictionary teaches about a specific topic. The topics are grouped together in units. All pages in a unit have the same color and symbol. For example, each page in the Food unit has this symbol:

On each page you will see pictures and words. The pictures have numbers or letters that match the numbers or letters in the word lists. Verbs (action words) are identified by letters and all other words are identified by numbers.

How to find words in this book

- Use the Table of Contents, pages ix–xi.
  Look up the general topic you want to learn about.

- Use the Index, pages 173–205.
  Look up individual words in alphabetical (A–Z) order.

- Go topic by topic.
  Look through the book until you find something that interests you.

How to use the Index

When you look for a word in the index this is what you will see:

the word   the number (or letter) in the word list

apples [ăp′əlz] **50**–4

the pronunciation   the page number

If the word is on one of the maps, pages 122–125, you will find it in the Geographical Index on pages 206–208.

How to use the Verb Guide

When you want to know the past form of a verb or its past participle form, look up the verb in the verb guide. The regular verbs and their spelling changes are listed on pages 170–171. The simple form, past form, and past participle form of irregular verbs are listed on page 172.

Workbooks

There are two workbooks to help you practice the new words:
The Oxford Picture Dictionary Beginning and *Intermediate Workbooks*.

As authors and teachers we both know how difficult English can be (and we're native speakers!). When we wrote this book, we asked teachers and students from the U.S. and other countries for their help and ideas. We hope their ideas and ours will help you. Please write to us with your comments or questions at:

Oxford University Press
ESL Department
198 Madison Avenue
New York, NY 10016

We wish you success!

Jayme Adelson-Goldstein   *Norma Shapiro*

Lettre à l'étudiant(e)

Cher (chère) étudiant(e) de la langue anglaise,

The Oxford Picture Dictionary vous souhaite la bienvenue. Les quelques 3700 mots de ce livre vous aideront à étudier l'anglais.

Chaque page de ce dictionnaire traite d'un thème spécifique. Les thèmes sont regroupés en sections. Toutes les pages d'une section ont la même couleur et le même symbole. A titre d'exemple, chaque page de la section des aliments affiche ce symbole :

Chaque page affiche des images et des mots. Les images comportent des chiffres ou des lettres qui correspondent aux chiffres et aux lettres des listes de mots. Les verbes (mots relatifs à l'action) sont identifiés par des lettres et tous les autres mots sont identifiés par des chiffres.

Pour trouver des mots dans ce livre

- Utiliser la Table des matières, pages ix à xi.
  Rechercher le thème à étudier.

- Utiliser l'index, pages 173 à 205.
  Rechercher des mots spécifiques listés par ordre alphabétique (de A à Z).

- Rechercher par thème.
  Feuilleter le livre pour trouver quelque chose qui vous intéresse.

Utilisation de l'index

Voici comment se présente une recherche de mot dans l'index :

le mot   le chiffre (ou la lettre) dans la liste des mots

apples [ăp′əlz] **50**–4

la prononciation   le numéro de page

Si le mot figure sur une des cartes, page 122 à 125, vous le trouverez dans l'index des noms géographiques aux pages 206 à 208.

Utilisation du Guide des verbes

Pour trouver la forme du passé ou du participe passé d'un verbe, rechercher le verbe dans le guide des verbes. Les verbes réguliers et leur changement d'orthographe figurent dans la liste des pages 170 et 171. Les formes simple, passée et participe passé des verbes irréguliers figurent sur la liste de la page 172.

Cahiers d'exercices

Deux cahiers d'exercices vous aideront dans la pratique des mots nouveaux :
Les cahiers d'exercices de niveau débutant et intermédiaire dans *The Oxford Picture Dictionary Beginning* et *Intermediate Workbooks*.

En tant qu'auteurs et enseignants, nous savons que l'anglais peut être une matière difficile (bien que nous soyons nous-même de langue anglaise!). Lors de la rédaction de ce livre, nous avons sollicité l'aide et les idées d'enseignants et d'étudiants américains et étrangers. Nous espérons que leurs idées et les nôtres vous seront utiles. Veuillez nous faire parvenir vos commentaires ou vos questions à :

Oxford University Press
ESL Department
198 Madison Avenue
New York, NY 10016

Bonne réussite!

Jayme Adelson-Goldstein   *Norma Shapiro*

Contents   Table des matières

1. Everyday Language   Langage courant

A Classroom Une salle de classe		2–3
Personal Information Renseignements personnels		4
School L'école		5
Studying Etude		6–7
Everyday Conversation Conversation courante		8
The Telephone Le téléphone		9
Weather Climat		10
Describing Things Description de choses		11
Colors Couleurs		12
Prepositions Prépositions		13
Numbers and Measurements Nombres et mesures		14–15
Time L'heure		16–17
The Calendar Le calendrier		18–19
Money Argent		20
Shopping Faire des courses		21

2. People   Personnes

Age and Physical Description Age et description physique		22
Describing Hair Description des cheveux		23
Family La famille		24–25
Daily Routines Activités quotidiennes		26–27
Life Events Evénements de la vie		28–29
Feelings Sensations / sentiments		30–31
A Graduation Remise des diplômes		32–33

3. Housing   Logement

Places to Live Habitations		34
Finding a Home A la recherche d'un logement		35
Apartments Appartements		36–37
A House Une maison		38
A Yard Une cour		39
A Kitchen Une cuisine		40
A Dining Area Une salle à manger		41
A Living Room Un salon		42
A Bathroom Une salle de bains		43
A Bedroom Une chambre à coucher		44
A Children's Bedroom Une chambre d'enfants		45
Housework Tâches ménagères		46
Cleaning Supplies Accessoires de nettoyage		47
Household Problems and Repairs Problèmes et réparations domestiques		48–49

4. Food   Nourriture

Fruit Fruits		50
Vegetables Légumes		51
Meat and Poultry Viandes et volailles		52
Deli and Seafood Charcuterie et fruits de mer		53
The Market Le marché		54–55
Containers and Packaged Foods Contenants et aliments emballés		56
Weights and Measures Poids et mesures		57
Food Preparation Préparation des aliments		58
Kitchen Utensils Ustensiles de cuisine		59

Contents   Table des matières

Fast Food   Prêt-à-manger   60
A Coffee Shop Menu   Un menu de cafétéria   61
A Restaurant   Un restaurant   62–63

5. Clothing   Vêtements

Clothing I   Vêtements I   64–65
Clothing II   Vêtements II   66
Clothing III   Vêtements III   67
Shoes and Accessories   Chaussures et accessoires   68–69
Describing Clothes   Description de vêtements   70–71
Doing the Laundry   Faire la lessive   72
Sewing and Alterations   Couture et retouches   73

6. Health   Santé

The Body   Le corps   74–75
Personal Hygiene   Hygiène personnelle   76–77
Symptoms and Injuries   Symptômes et blessures   78
Illnesses and Medical Conditions   Maladies et état médical   79
Health Care   Soins de santé   80–81
Medical Emergencies   Urgences médicales   82
First Aid   Premiers soins   83
Clinics   Cliniques   84
Medical and Dental Exams   Examens médical et dentaire   85
A Hospital   Un hôpital   86–87

7. Community   Communauté

City Streets   Rues en ville   88–89
An Intersection   Un carrefour   90–91
A Mall   Un centre commercial   92–93
A Childcare Center   Garderie   94–95
U.S. Mail   Service de courrier des Etats-Unis   96
A Bank   Une banque   97
A Library   Une bibliothèque   98
The Legal System   Le système juridique   99
Crime   Crime   100
Public Safety   Sécurité publique   101
Emergencies and Natural Disasters   Urgences et désastres naturels   102–103

8. Transportation   Transport

Public Transportation   Transport public   104
Prepositions of Motion   Prépositions/expressions indiquant le mouvement   105
Cars and Trucks   Voitures et camions   106
Directions and Traffic Signs   Directions et panneaux de circulation   107
Parts of a Car and Car Maintenance   Voiture, pièces et entretien   108–109
An Airport   Un aéroport   110
A Plane Trip   Un voyage en avion   111

9. Areas of Study   Champs d'études

Types of Schools   Types d'écoles   112
English Composition   Composition anglaise   113
U.S. History   Histoire des E.-U.   114–115
U.S. Government and Citizenship   Gouvernement américain et citoyenneté   116

x

Geography   Géographie   117
Mathematics   Mathématiques   118
Science   Science   119
Music   Musique   120
More School Subjects   Autres matières scolaires   121
North America and Central America   Amérique du Nord et
    Amérique centrale   122–123
The World   Le monde   124–125
Energy and the Environment   Energie et environnement   126
The Universe   L'univers   127

10. Plants and Animals   Plantes et animaux

Trees and Plants   Arbres et plantes   128
Flowers   Fleurs   129
Marine Life, Amphibians, and Reptiles   Faune marine, amphibiens
    et reptiles   130–131
Birds, Insects, and Arachnids   Oiseaux, insectes et arachnides   132
Domestic Animals and Rodents   Animaux domestiques et rongeurs   133
Mammals   Mammifères   134–135

11. Work   Travail

Jobs and Occupations, A–H   Emplois et professions, A–H   136–137
Jobs and Occupations, H–W   Emplois et professions, H–W   138–139
Job Skills   Compétences professionnelles   140
Job Search   Recherche d'emploi   141
An Office   Un bureau   142–143
Computers   Ordinateurs   144
A Hotel   Un hôtel   145
A Factory   Une usine   146
Job Safety   La sécurité au travail   147
Farming and Ranching   A la ferme et au ranch   148
Construction   Construction   149
Tools and Building Supplies   Outils et fournitures pour le bâtiment   150–151

12. Recreation   Récréation

Places to Go   Endroits où aller   152
The Park and Playground   Le parc et le terrain de jeux   153
Outdoor Recreation   Activités de plein air   154
The Beach   La plage   155
Sports Verbs   Verbes se rapportant à des sports   156–157
Team Sports   Sports d'équipe   158
Individual Sports   Sports individuels   159
Winter Sports and Water Sports   Sports d'hiver et sports aquatiques   160
Sports Equipment   Articles de sport   161
Hobbies and Games   Passe-temps et jeux   162–163
Electronics and Photography   Électronique et photographie   164–165
Entertainment   Divertissements   166–167
Holidays   Jours fériés   168
A Party   Une réception   169
Verb Guide   Guide des verbes   170
Index   Index   173
Geographical Index   Index des noms géographiques   206
French Index   Index français   209

1. chalkboard
le tableau

2. screen
l'écran

3. student
l'étudiant

4. overhead projector
le rétroprojecteur

5. teacher
le professeur

6. desk
le pupitre

7. chair/seat
la chaise/le siège

A. Raise your hand.
Levez la main.

B. Talk to the teacher.
Parlez au professeur.

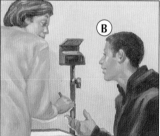

C. Listen to a cassette.
Écoutez une cassette.

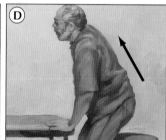

D. Stand up.
Levez-vous.

E. Sit down./Take a seat.
Assoyez-vous.

F. Point to the picture.
Pointez l'image.

G. Write on the board.
Écrivez au tableau.

H. Erase the board.
Effacez le tableau.

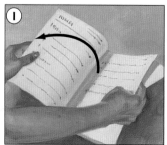

I. Open your book.
Ouvrez votre livre.

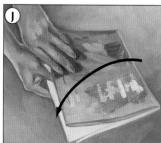

J. Close your book.
Fermez votre livre.

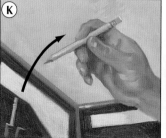

K. Take out your pencil.
Sortez votre crayon.

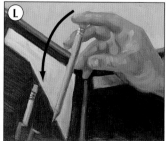

L. Put away your pencil.
Rangez votre crayon.

2

8. bookcase
la bibliothèque

9. globe
le globe terrestre

10. clock
l'horloge

11. cassette player
le lecteur de cassettes

12. map
la carte

13. pencil sharpener
le taille-crayon

14. bulletin board
le tableau d'affichage

15. computer
l'ordinateur

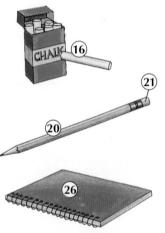

16. chalk
la craie

17. chalkboard eraser
la brosse feutrée

18. pen
le stylo

19. marker
le marqueur

20. pencil
le crayon

21. pencil eraser
la gomme

22. textbook
le livre

23. workbook
le cahier d'exercices

24. binder / notebook
le classeur / le cahier

25. notebook paper
les feuilles de cahier

26. spiral notebook
le carnet à spirale

27. ruler
la règle

28. dictionary
le dictionnaire

29. picture dictionary
le dictionnaire illustré

30. the alphabet
l'alphabet

31. numbers
les chiffres

Use the new language.

1. Name three things you can open.

2. Name three things you can put away.

3. Name three things you can write with.

Share your answers.

1. Do you like to raise your hand?

2. Do you ever listen to cassettes in class?

3. Do you ever write on the board?

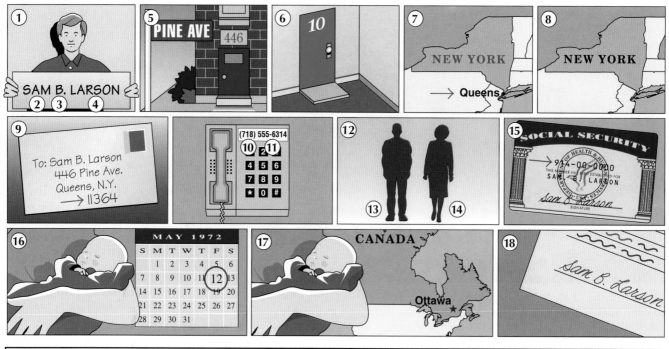

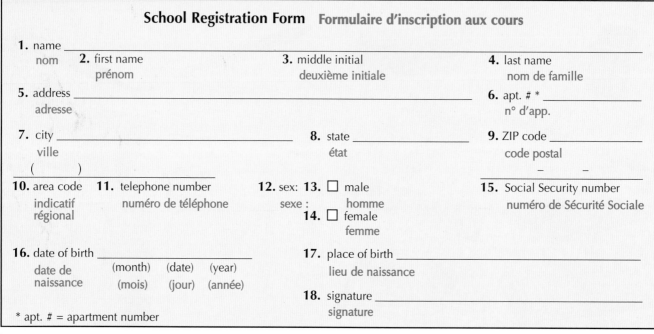

School Registration Form   Formulaire d'inscription aux cours

1. name _____
   nom   **2.** first name   **3.** middle initial   **4.** last name
            prénom   deuxième initiale   nom de famille

5. address _____   **6.** apt. # * _____
   adresse   n° d'app.

7. city _____   **8.** state _____   **9.** ZIP code _____
   ville   état   code postal
                                                            __ __
   (_____) _____

10. area code   **11.** telephone number   **12.** sex: **13.** ☐ male   **15.** Social Security number
   indicatif   numéro de téléphone   sexe :   homme   numéro de Sécurité Sociale
   régional   **14.** ☐ female
                                                                 femme

16. date of birth _____   **17.** place of birth _____
   date de   (month) (date) (year)   lieu de naissance
   naissance (mois) (jour) (année)
                                        18. signature _____
                                                signature

* apt. # = apartment number

A. Spell your name.
Épelez votre nom.

B. Fill out a form.
Remplissez un formulaire.

C. Print your name.
Écrivez votre nom en majuscules.

D. Sign your name.
Signez votre nom.

Talk about yourself.

My first name is _Sam_.

My last name is spelled _L-A-R-S-O-N_.

I come from _Ottawa_.

Share your answers.

1. Do you like your first name?
2. Is your last name from your mother? father? husband?
3. What is your middle name?

1. classroom
la salle de classe

2. teacher
le professeur

3. auditorium
la cour intérieure

4. cafeteria
la cafétéria

5. lunch benches
les bancs de déjeuner

6. library
la bibliothèque

7. lockers
les casiers

8. rest rooms
les toilettes

9. gym
le gymnase

10. bleachers
les gradins

11. track
la piste

12. field
le terrain

13. principal's office
le bureau du directeur

14. principal
le directeur

15. counselor's office
le bureau du conseiller

16. counselor
le conseiller

17. main office
le bureau principal

18. clerk
le préposé

More vocabulary

instructor: teacher

coach: gym teacher

administrator: principal or other school supervisor

Share your answers.

1. Do you ever talk to the principal of your school?

2. Is there a place for you to eat at your school?

3. Does your school look the same as or different from the one in the picture?

Dictionary work Usage du dictionnaire

A. Look up a word.
Chercher un mot.

B. Read the word.
Lire le mot.

C. Say the word.
Dire le mot.

D. Repeat the word.
Répéter le mot.

E. Spell the word.
Epeler le mot.

F. Copy the word.
Copier le mot.

Work with a partner Travail avec un partenaire

G. Ask a question.
Poser une question.

H. Answer a question.
Répondre à une question.

I. Share a book.
Partager un livre.

J. Help your partner.
Aider votre partenaire.

Work in a group Travail en groupe

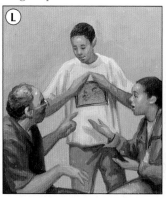
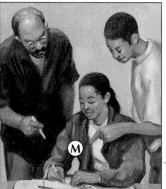

K. Brainstorm a list.
Collaborer à la création
d'une liste.

L. Discuss the list.
Discuter de la liste.

M. Draw a picture.
Faire un dessin.

N. Dictate a sentence.
Dicter une phrase.

Class work   Travail en classe

O. Pass out the papers.
Distribuer les devoirs.

P. Talk with each other.
Se **parler.**

Q. Collect the papers.
Recueillir les devoirs.

Follow directions   Suivre des instructions

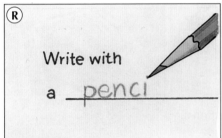

R. Fill in the blank.
Remplir l'espace blanc.

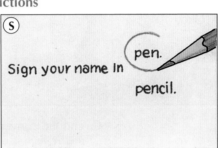

S. Circle the answer.
Entourer la réponse.

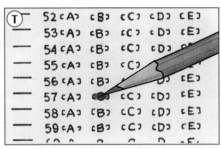

T. Mark the answer sheet.
Marquer / Annoter la feuille de réponses.

U. Cross out the word.
Biffer le mot.

V. Underline the word.
Souligner le mot.

W. Put the words **in order.**
Mettre les mots **en ordre.**

X. Match the items.
Faire correspondre les articles.

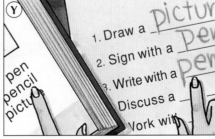

Y. Check your work.
Vérifier votre travail.

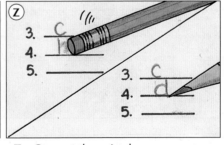

Z. Correct the mistake.
Corriger l'erreur.

Share your answers.

1. Do you like to work in groups?

2. Do you like to share books?

3. Do you like to answer questions?

4. Is it easy for you to talk with your classmates?

5. Do you always check your work?

6. Do you cross out your mistakes or erase them?

A. greet someone
saluer quelqu'un

B. begin a conversation
engager une conversation

C. end the conversation
mettre fin à la conversation

D. introduce yourself
se **présenter**

E. make sure you **understand**
s'**assurer** de **comprendre**

F. introduce your friend
présenter votre ami

G. compliment your friend
complimenter votre ami

H. thank your friend
remercier votre ami

I. apologize
s'**excuser**

Practice introductions.

Hi, I'm <u>Sam Jones</u> and this is my friend, <u>Pat Green</u>.

   Nice to meet you. I'm <u>Tomas Garcia</u>.

Practice giving compliments.

That's a great <u>sweater</u>, <u>Tomas</u>.

   Thanks <u>Pat</u>. I like your <u>shoes</u>.

Look at **Clothing I,** pages **64–65** for more ideas.

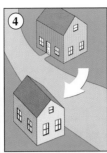

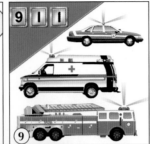

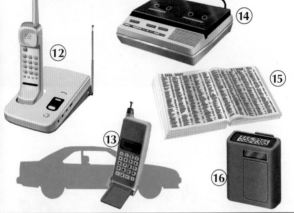

1. telephone / phone
   téléphone
2. receiver
   combiné
3. cord
   cordon
4. local call
   appel local
5. long-distance call
   appel interurbain
6. international call
   appel international
7. operator
   téléphoniste
8. directory assistance (411)
   assistance annuaire (411)
9. emergency service (911)
   service d'urgence (911)
10. phone card
    carte d'appel
11. pay phone
    téléphone public
12. cordless phone
    téléphone sans fil
13. cellular phone
    téléphone cellulaire
14. answering machine
    répondeur
15. telephone book
    annuaire téléphonique
16. pager
    téléavertisseur

Using a pay phone   Utilisation d'un téléphone public

A. **Pick up** the receiver.
   Décrocher le combiné.
B. **Listen** for the dial tone.
   Attendre la tonalité.
C. **Deposit** coins.
   Insérer des pièces.

D. **Dial** the number.
   Composer le numéro.
E. **Leave** a message.
   Laisser un message.
F. **Hang up** the receiver.
   Raccrocher le combiné.

More vocabulary

When you get a person or place that you didn't want to call, we say you have the **wrong number.**

Share your answers.

1. What kinds of calls do you make?
2. How much does it cost to call your country?
3. Do you like to talk on the telephone?

Weather Climat

Temperature
Température

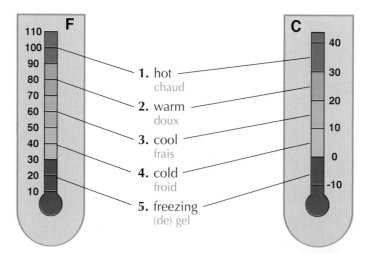

F

Degrees Fahrenheit

110 100 90 80 70 60 50 40 30 20 10

C

40 30 20 10 0 -10

Degrees Celsius

1. hot
chaud

2. warm
doux

3. cool
frais

4. cold
froid

5. freezing
(de) gel

6. sunny / clear	**7.** cloudy	**8.** raining	**9.** snowing
ensoleillé / clair	nuageux	pluvieux	neigeux

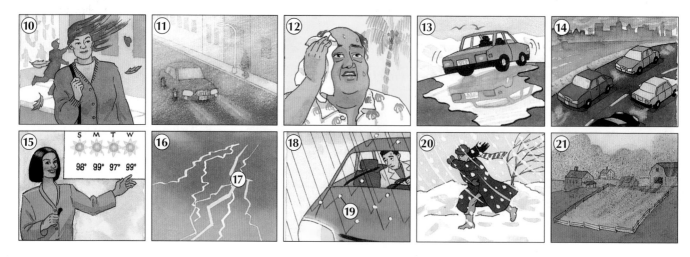

10. windy
venteux

11. foggy
brumeux

12. humid
humide

13. icy
glacial

14. smoggy
obscurci par le smog

15. heat wave
vague de chaleur

16. thunderstorm
orage

17. lightning
foudre

18. hailstorm
averse de grêle

19. hail
grêle

20. snowstorm
tempête de neige

21. dust storm
tempête de poussière

Language note: *it is, there is*

For **1–14** we use,   *It's <u>cloudy</u>.*

For **15–21** we use,   *There's <u>a heat wave</u>.*
There's <u>lightning</u>.

Talk about the weather.

Today it's <u>hot</u>. It's <u>98 degrees</u>.

Yesterday it was <u>warm</u>. It was <u>85 degrees</u>.

1. **little** hand
   petite main
2. **big** hand
   grosse main

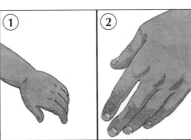

3. **fast** driver
   conducteur **rapide**
4. **slow** driver
   conducteur **lent**

5. **hard** chair
   chaise **dure**
6. **soft** chair
   chaise **moelleuse**

7. **thick** book/
   fat book
   livre **épais**
8. **thin** book
   livre **mince**

9. **full** glass
   verre **plein**
10. **empty** glass
    verre **vide**

11. **noisy** children/
    loud children
    enfants **bruyants**/
    enfants **tapageurs**
12. **quiet** children
    enfants **tranquilles**

13. **heavy** box
    boîte **lourde**
14. **light** box
    boîte **légère**

15. **neat** closet
    placard **bien rangé**
16. **messy** closet
    placard **en désordre**

17. **good** dog
    bon chien
18. **bad** dog
    mauvais chien

19. **expensive** ring
    bague **coûteuse**
20. **cheap** ring
    bague **bon marché**

21. **beautiful** view
    vue **magnifique**
22. **ugly** view
    vue **laide**

23. **easy** problem
    problème **simple**
24. **difficult** problem/
    hard problem
    problème **difficile**/
    problème **compliqué**

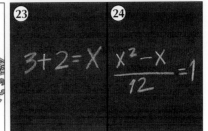

Use the new language.

1. Name three things that are thick.
2. Name three things that are soft.
3. Name three things that are heavy.

Share your answers.

1. Are you a slow driver or a fast driver?
2. Do you have a neat closet or a messy closet?
3. Do you like loud or quiet parties?

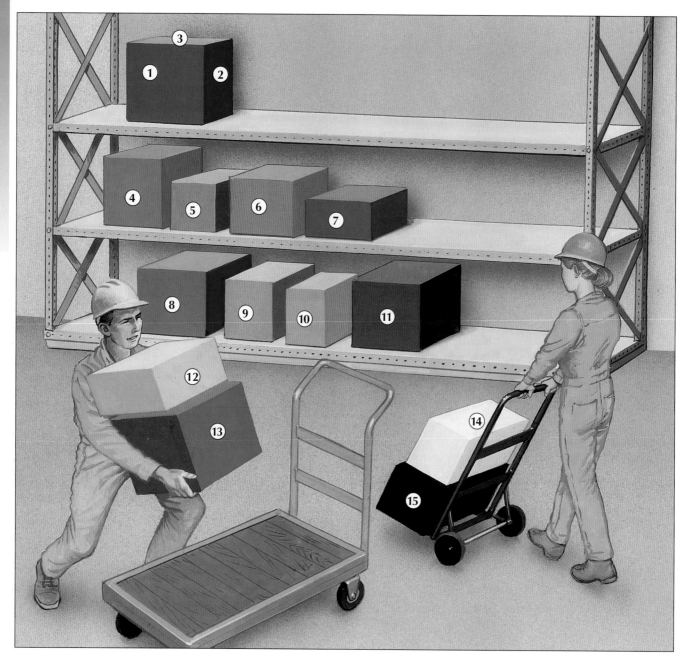

1. blue
bleu

2. dark blue
bleu foncé

3. light blue
bleu clair

4. turquoise
turquoise

5. gray
gris

6. orange
orange

7. purple
mauve

8. green
vert

9. beige
beige

10. pink
rose

11. brown
brun

12. yellow
jaune

13. red
rouge

14. white
blanc

15. black
noir

Use the new language.

Look at **Clothing I**, pages **64–65**.

Name the colors of the clothing you see.

That's a dark blue suit.

Share your answers.

1. What colors are you wearing today?

2. What colors do you like?

3. Is there a color you don't like? What is it?

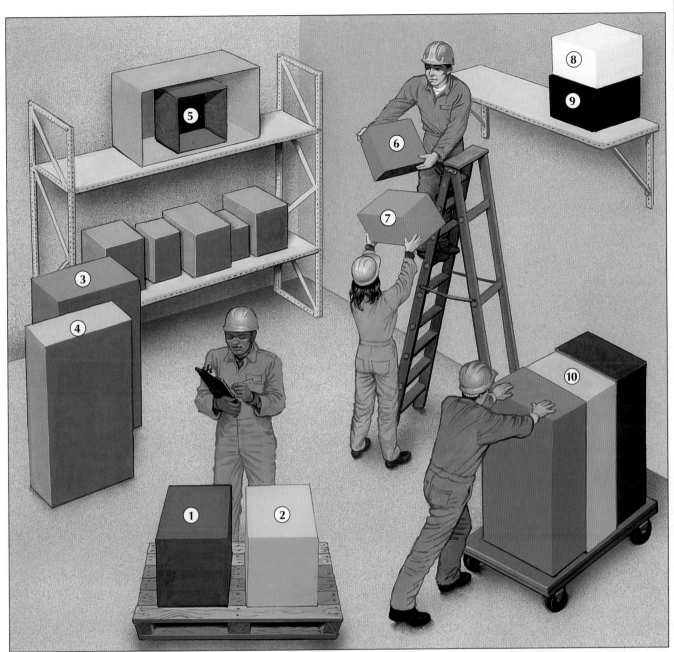

1. The red box is **next to** the yellow box, **on the left**.
   La boîte rouge est **à côté** de la boîte jaune, **à gauche**.

2. The yellow box is **next to** the red box, **on the right**.
   La boîte jaune est **à côté** de la boîte rouge, **à droite**.

3. The turquoise box is **behind** the gray box.
   La boîte turquoise est **derrière** la boîte grise.

4. The gray box is **in front of** the turquoise box.
   La boîte grise est **devant** la boîte turquoise.

5. The dark blue box is **in** the beige box.
   La boîte bleu foncé est **dans** la boîte beige.

6. The green box is **above** the orange box.
   La boîte verte est **au-dessus** de la boîte orange.

7. The orange box is **below** the green box.
   La boîte orange est **en dessous** de la boîte verte.

8. The white box is **on** the black box.
   La boîte blanche est **sur** la boîte noire.

9. The black box is **under** the white box.
   La boîte noire est **sous** la boîte blanche.

10. The pink box is **between** the purple box and the brown box.
    La boîte rose est **entre** la boîte mauve et la boîte brune.

More vocabulary

near: in the same area
*The white box is **near** the black box.*

far from: not near
*The red box is **far from** the black box.*

13

 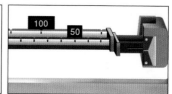

HOME	1 8
VISITOR	2 2

SAN DIEGO
235 miles

Cardinals   Cardinaux

0 zero
  zéro

1 one
  un

2 two
  deux

3 three
  trois

4 four
  quatre

5 five
  cinq

6 six
  six

7 seven
  sept

8 eight
  huit

9 nine
  neuf

10 ten
  dix

11 eleven
  onze

12 twelve
  douze

13 thirteen
  treize

14 fourteen
  quatorze

15 fifteen
  quinze

16 sixteen
  seize

17 seventeen
  dix-sept

18 eighteen
  dix-huit

19 nineteen
  dix-neuf

20 twenty
  vingt

21 twenty-one
  vingt et un

22 twenty-two
  vingt-deux

30 thirty
  trente

40 forty
  quarante

50 fifty
  cinquante

60 sixty
  soixante

70 seventy
  soixante-dix (septante)

80 eighty
  quatre-vingt(s) (octante)

90 ninety
  quatre-vingt-dix
  (nonante)

100 one hundred
  cent

101
  one hundred one
  cent un

1,000
  one thousand
  mille

1,001
  one thousand one
  mille un

10,000
  ten thousand
  dix mille

100,000
  one hundred thousand
  cent mille

1,000,000
  one million
  un million

1,000,000,000
  one billion
  un milliard

Ordinals   Ordinaux

1st first	1er premier
2nd second	2e deuxième
3rd third	3e troisième
4th fourth	4e quatrième
5th fifth	5e cinquième
6th sixth	6e sixième
7th seventh	7e septième

8th eighth
  8e huitième

9th ninth
  9e neuvième

10th tenth
  10e dixième

11th eleventh
  11e onzième

12th twelfth
  12e douzième

13th thirteenth
  13e treizième

14th fourteenth
  14e quatorzième

15th fifteenth
  15e quinzième

16th sixteenth
  16e seizième

17th seventeenth
  17e dix-septième

18th eighteenth
  18e dix-huitième

19th nineteenth
  19e dix-neuvième

20th twentieth
  20e vingtième

Roman numerals   Chiffres romains

I	= 1	VII	= 7	XXX	= 30
II	= 2	VIII	= 8	XL	= 40
III	= 3	IX	= 9	L	= 50
IV	= 4	X	= 10	C	= 100
V	= 5	XV	= 15	D	= 500
VI	= 6	XX	= 20	M	= 1,000

Fractions   Fractions

1. 1/8   one-eighth
un huitième

2. 1/4   one-fourth
un quart

3. 1/3   one-third
un tiers

4. 1/2   one-half
un demi

5. 3/4   three-fourths
trois quarts

6. 1   whole
entier

1 cup
3/4
2/3
1/2
1/3
1/4

Percents   Pourcentages

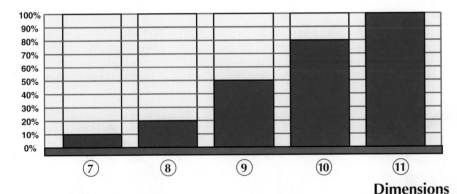

⑦   ⑧   ⑨   ⑩   ⑪

7. 10%   ten percent
10 %   dix pour cent

8. 20%   twenty percent
20 %   vingt pour cent

9. 50%   fifty percent
50 %   cinquante pour cent

10. 80%   eighty percent
80 %   quatre-vingts pour cent

11. 100%   one hundred percent
100 %   cent pour cent

Dimensions   Dimensions

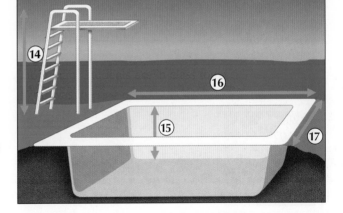

14. height
hauteur

15. depth
profondeur

16. length
longueur

17. width
largeur

Measurement   Mesure

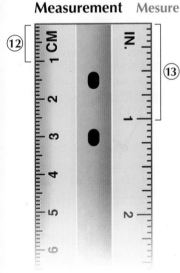

12. centimeter [cm]
centimètre [cm]

13. inch [in.]
pouce [po]

Equivalencies   Equivalences

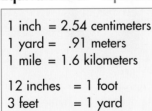

1 inch   = 2.54 centimeters
1 yard   = .91 meters
1 mile   = 1.6 kilometers

12 inches   = 1 foot
3 feet   = 1 yard
1,760 yards = 1 mile

More vocabulary

measure: to find the size or amount of something

count: to find the total number of something

Share your answers.

1. How many students are in class today?

2. Who was the first person in class today?

3. How far is it from your home to your school?

A.M.

P.M.

1. second
seconde

2. minute
minute

3. hour
heure

4. 1:00
one o'clock
une heure

5. 1:05
one-oh-five
une heure cinq
five after one
une heure cinq

6. 1:10
one-ten
une heure dix
ten after one
une heure dix

7. 1:15
one-fifteen
une heure quinze
a quarter after one
une heure quinze

8. 1:20
one-twenty
une heure vingt
twenty after one
une heure vingt

9. 1:25
one twenty-five
une heure vingt-cinq
twenty-five after one
une heure vingt-cinq

10. 1:30
one-thirty
une heure trente
half past one
une heure et demie

11. 1:35
one thirty-five
une heure trente-cinq
twenty-five to two
deux heures moins vingt-cinq

12. 1:40
one-forty
une heure quarante
twenty to two
deux heures moins vingt

13. 1:45
one forty-five
une heure quarante-cinq
a quarter to two
deux heures moins le quart

14. 1:50
one-fifty
une heure cinquante
ten to two
deux heures moins dix

15. 1:55
one fifty-five
une heure cinquante-cinq
five to two
deux heures moins cinq

Talk about the time.

What time is it? It's <u>10:00 a.m.</u>

What time do you wake up on weekdays? At <u>6:30 a.m.</u>

What time do you wake up on weekends? At <u>9:30 a.m.</u>

Share your answers.

1. How many hours a day do you study English?

2. You are meeting friends at 1:00. How long will you wait for them if they are late?

16. morning
matin

17. noon
midi

18. afternoon
après-midi

19. evening
soir

20. night
nuit

21. midnight
minuit

22. early
tôt

23. late
tard

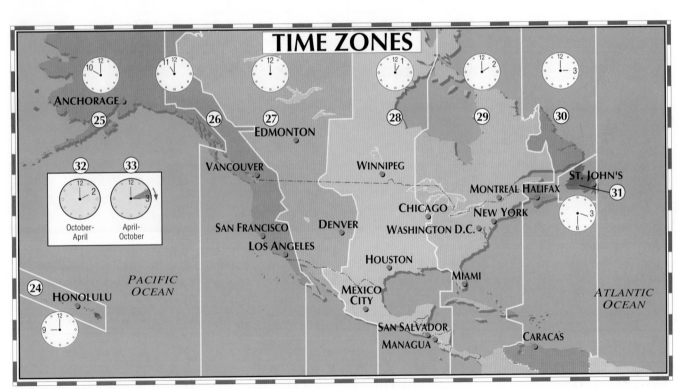

TIME ZONES

ANCHORAGE
25
26
EDMONTON
27
VANCOUVER
WINNIPEG
28
29
30
MONTREAL HALIFAX
ST. JOHN'S
31
CHICAGO
NEW YORK
WASHINGTON D.C.
SAN FRANCISCO
DENVER
LOS ANGELES
HOUSTON
MIAMI
PACIFIC
OCEAN
MEXICO
CITY
ATLANTIC
OCEAN
24
HONOLULU
SAN SALVADOR
MANAGUA
CARACAS

32 **33**
October-
April
April-
October

24. Hawaii-Aleutian time
heure d'Hawaï-des
Aléoutiennes

25. Alaska time
heure de l'Alaska

26. Pacific time
heure du Pacifique

27. mountain time
heure des Rocheuses

28. central time
heure du Centre

29. eastern time
heure de l'Est

30. Atlantic time
heure de l'Atlantique

31. Newfoundland time
heure de Terre-Neuve

32. standard time
heure normale

33. daylight saving time
heure d'été

More vocabulary

on time: not early and not late

*He's **on time**.*

Share your answers.

1. When do you watch television? study?
do housework?

2. Do you come to class on time? early? late?

Days of the week
Jours de la semaine

1. Sunday
dimanche

2. Monday
lundi

3. Tuesday
mardi

4. Wednesday
mercredi

5. Thursday
jeudi

6. Friday
vendredi

7. Saturday
samedi

8. year
année

9. month
mois

10. day
jour

11. week
semaine

12. weekdays
jours de semaine

13. weekend
weekend

14. date
date

15. today
aujourd'hui

16. tomorrow
demain

17. yesterday
hier

18. last week
la semaine dernière

19. this week
cette semaine

20. next week
la semaine prochaine

21. every day
chaque jour

22. once a week
une fois par semaine

23. twice a week
deux fois par semaine

24. three times a week
trois fois par semaine

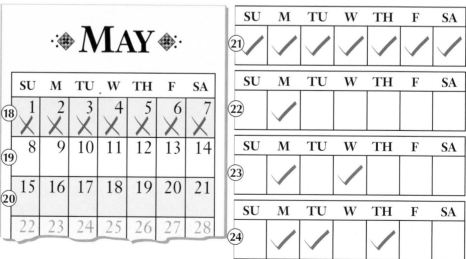

Talk about the calendar.

What's today's date? It's <u>March 10th</u>.

What day is it? It's <u>Tuesday</u>.

What day was yesterday? It was <u>Monday</u>.

Share your answers.

1. How often do you come to school?
2. How long have you been in this school?

2001

JAN ㉕						
SUN	MON	TUE	WED	THU	FRI	SAT
	1	2	3	4	5	6
7	8	9	10	11	12	13
14	15	16	17	18	19	20
21	22	23	24	25	26	27
28	29	30	31			

FEB ㉖						
SUN	MON	TUE	WED	THU	FRI	SAT
				1	2	3
4	5	6	7	8	9	10
11	12	13	14	15	16	17
18	19	20	21	22	23	24
25	26	27	28			

MAR ㉗						
SUN	MON	TUE	WED	THU	FRI	SAT
				1	2	3
4	5	6	7	8	9	10
11	12	13	14	15	16	17
18	19	20	21	22	23	24
25	26	27	28	29	30	31

APR ㉘						
SUN	MON	TUE	WED	THU	FRI	SAT
1	2	3	4	5	6	7
8	9	10	11	12	13	14
15	16	17	18	19	20	21
22	23	24	25	26	27	28
29	30					

MAY ㉙						
SUN	MON	TUE	WED	THU	FRI	SAT
		1	2	3	4	5
6	7	8	9	10	11	12
13	14	15	16	17	18	19
20	21	22	23	24	25	26
27	28	29	30	31		

JUN ㉚						
SUN	MON	TUE	WED	THU	FRI	SAT
					1	2
3	4	5	6	7	8	9
10	11	12	13	14	15	16
17	18	19	20	21	22	23
24	25	26	27	28	29	30

JUL ㉛						
SUN	MON	TUE	WED	THU	FRI	SAT
1	2	3	4	5	6	7
8	9	10	11	12	13	14
15	16	17	18	19	20	21
22	23	24	25	26	27	28
29	30	31				

AUG ㉜						
SUN	MON	TUE	WED	THU	FRI	SAT
			1	2	3	4
5	6	7	8	9	10	11
12	13	14	15	16	17	18
19	20	21	22	23	24	25
26	27	28	29	30	31	

SEP ㉝						
SUN	MON	TUE	WED	THU	FRI	SAT
						1
2	3	4	5	6	7	8
9	10	11	12	13	14	15
16	17	18	19	20	21	22
23/30	24	25	26	27	28	29

OCT ㉞						
SUN	MON	TUE	WED	THU	FRI	SAT
	1	2	3	4	5	6
7	8	9	10	11	12	13
14	15	16	17	18	19	20
21	22	23	24	25	26	27
28	29	30	31			

NOV ㉟						
SUN	MON	TUE	WED	THU	FRI	SAT
				1	2	3
4	5	6	7	8	9	10
11	12	13	14	15	16	17
18	19	20	21	22	23	24
25	26	27	28	29	30	

DEC ㊱						
SUN	MON	TUE	WED	THU	FRI	SAT
						1
2	3	4	5	6	7	8
9	10	11	12	13	14	15
16	17	18	19	20	21	22
23/30	24/31	25	26	27	28	29

Months of the year
Mois de l'année

25. January
janvier

26. February
février

27. March
mars

28. April
avril

29. May
mai

30. June
juin

31. July
juillet

32. August
août

33. September
septembre

34. October
octobre

35. November
novembre

36. December
décembre

Seasons
Saisons

37. spring
printemps

38. summer
été

39. fall
automne

40. winter
hiver

41. birthday
anniversaire

42. anniversary
anniversaire de mariage

43. legal holiday
jour férié

44. religious holiday
fête religieuse

45. appointment
rendez-vous

46. vacation
vacances

MARCH 21

JUNE 21

SEPT. 21

DEC. 21

JUNE 5
TIM!

MARCH 2
ANNIVERSARY

JULY 4
INDEPENDENCE DAY
STATE BANK
CLOSED – JULY 4

APRIL 4
EASTER SUNDAY

MAY 17
DOCTOR 4:30

AUGUST

Use the new language.

Look at the **ordinal numbers** on page **14**.

Use ordinal numbers to say the date.

It's June 5th. It's the fifth.

Talk about your birthday.

My birthday is in the winter.

My birthday is in January.

My birthday is on January twenty-sixth.

Coins   Pièces

1. $.01 = 1¢
a penny / 1 cent
1 cent

2. $.05 = 5¢
a nickel / 5 cents
5 cents

3. $.10 = 10¢
a dime / 10 cents
10 cents

4. $.25 = 25¢
a quarter / 25 cents
25 cents

5. $.50 = 50¢
a half dollar
50 cents

6. $1.00
a silver dollar
un dollar

Bills   Billets

7. $1.00
a dollar
un dollar

8. $5.00
five dollars
cinq dollars

9. $10.00
ten dollars
dix dollars

10. $20.00
twenty dollars
vingt dollars

11. $50.00
fifty dollars
cinquante dollars

12. $100.00
one hundred dollars
cent dollars

Ways to pay   Modes de paiement

13. cash
comptant

14. personal check
chèque personnel

15. credit card
carte de crédit

16. money order
mandat

17. traveler's check
chèque de voyage

More vocabulary

borrow: to get money from someone and return it later

lend: to give money to someone and get it back later

pay back: to return the money that you borrowed

Other ways to talk about money:

a dollar bill or a one

a five-dollar bill or a five

a ten-dollar bill or a ten

a twenty-dollar bill or a twenty

A. shop for
chercher (en faisant
des courses)

B. sell
vendre

C. pay for / **buy**
payer / acheter

D. give
donner

E. keep
garder

F. return
retourner

G. exchange
échanger

1. price tag
étiquette

2. regular price
prix courant

3. sale price
prix de vente

4. bar code
code à barres

5. receipt
reçu

6. price / cost
prix / coût

7. sales tax
taxe de vente

8. total
total

9. change
monnaie

More vocabulary

When you use a credit card to shop, you get a **bill** in the mail. Bills list, in writing, the items you bought and the total you have to pay.

Share your answers.

1. Name three things you pay for every month.

2. Name one thing you will buy this week.

3. Where do you like to shop?

1. **children**
   enfants

2. **baby**
   bébé

3. **toddler**
   enfant qui commence
   à marcher

4. **6-year-old boy**
   garçon de six ans

5. **10-year-old girl**
   fillette de 10 ans

6. **teenagers**
   adolescent(e)s

7. **13-year-old boy**
   garçon de 13 ans

8. **19-year-old girl**
   fille de 19 ans

9. **adults**
   adultes

10. **woman**
    femme

11. **man**
    homme

12. **senior citizen**
    personne âgée

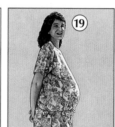

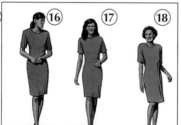

13. **young**
    jeune

14. **middle-aged**
    d'âge moyen

15. **elderly**
    âgé(e)

16. **tall**
    grand(e)

17. **average height**
    de taille moyenne

18. **short**
    petit(e)

19. **pregnant**
    enceinte

20. **heavyset**
    costaud(e)

21. **average weight**
    de poids moyen

22. **thin/slim**
    maigre/mince

23. **attractive**
    attrayant(e)

24. **cute**
    mignon(ne)

25. **physically challenged**
    handicapé(e)

26. **sight impaired/blind**
    malvoyant(e)/aveugle

27. **hearing impaired/deaf**
    malentendant(e)/sourd(e)

Talk about yourself and your teacher.

I am young, average height, and average weight.

My teacher is a middle-aged, tall, thin man.

Use the new language.

Turn to **Hobbies and Games,** pages **162–163.**

Describe each person on the page.

He's a heavyset, short, senior citizen.

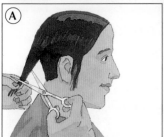
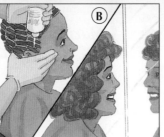

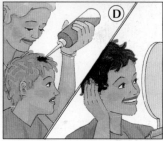

1. short hair
cheveux courts

2. shoulder-length hair
cheveux mi-longs

3. long hair
cheveux longs

4. part
raie

5. mustache
moustache

6. beard
barbe

7. sideburns
favoris / pattes

8. bangs
frange

9. straight hair
cheveux raides

10. wavy hair
cheveux ondulés

11. curly hair
cheveux frisés

12. bald
chauve

13. gray hair
cheveux gris

14. red hair
cheveux roux

15. black hair
cheveux noirs

16. blond hair
cheveux blonds

17. brown hair
cheveux bruns

18. brush
brosse

19. scissors
ciseaux

20. blow dryer
séchoir

21. rollers
rouleaux

22. comb
peigne

A. **cut** hair
couper les cheveux

B. **perm** hair
faire une **permanente**

C. **set** hair
faire une **mise en plis**

D. **color** hair / **dye** hair
colorer les cheveux /
teindre les cheveux

More vocabulary

hair stylist: a person who cuts, sets, and perms hair

hair salon: the place where a hair stylist works

Talk about your hair.

My hair is <u>long</u>, <u>straight</u>, and <u>brown</u>.

I have <u>long</u>, <u>straight</u>, <u>brown</u> hair.

When I was a child my hair was <u>short</u>, <u>curly</u>, and <u>blond</u>.

Tom Lee's Family

1. grandparents
grands-parents

Min *Lu*

2. grandmother
grand-mère

3. grandfather
grand-père

4. parents
parents

Rose *Chang*

Helen *Daniel*

Tom

5. mother
mère

6. father
père

10. aunt
tante

11. uncle
oncle

Lily *Alex*

Emily

8. sister
sœur

9. brother
frère

12. cousin
cousin

7. (Min and Lu's)
grandson
petit-fils
(de Min et Lu)

Berta *Mario*

*Ana Garcia's
Family*

13. mother-in-law
belle-mère

14. father-in-law
beau-père

Ana

Marta *Carlos*

Tito

20. (Tito's) wife
femme / conjointe
(de Tito)

15. sister-in-law
belle-sœur

16. brother-in-law
beau-frère

19. husband
mari / conjoint

Alice *Eddie*

Sara *Felix*

17. niece
nièce

18. nephew
neveu

21. daughter
fille

22. son
fils

More vocabulary

Lily and Emily are Min and Lu's **granddaughters.**

Daniel is Min and Lu's **son-in-law.**

Ana is Berta and Mario's **daughter-in-law.**

Share your answers.

1. How many brothers and sisters do you have?

2. What number son or daughter are you?

3. Do you have any children?

Lisa Smith's Family

23. married
marié(e)(s)

Carol   *Dan*

Lisa

24. divorced
divorcé(e)

25. single mother
mère célibataire

26. single father
père célibataire

Rick   *Carol*

27. remarried
remarié(e)(s)

Dan   *Sue*

Rick   *Carol*

28. stepfather
beau-père (adoptif)

David   *Mary*

29. half brother
demi-frère

30. half sister
demi-sœur

Lisa

Dan   *Sue*

31. stepmother
belle-mère (adoptive)

Kim   *Bill*

32. stepsister
demi-sœur

33. stepbrother
demi-frère

More vocabulary

Carol is Dan's **former wife.**

Sue is Dan's **wife.**

Dan is Carol's **former husband.**

Rick is Carol's **husband.**

Lisa is the **stepdaughter** of both Rick and Sue.

Daily Routines   Activités quotidiennes

6:00 A.M.

6:30 A.M.

7:00 A.M.

7:30 A.M.

8:00 A.M.

10:00 A.M.

4:30 P.M.

5:00 P.M.

A. wake up
s'**éveiller**

B. get up
se **lever**

C. take a shower
prendre une **douche**

D. get dressed
s'**habiller**

E. eat breakfast
prendre le petit-déjeuner

F. make lunch
préparer le déjeuner

G. take the children to school
emmener / accompagner les enfants
à l'école

H. take the bus to school
prendre l'autobus pour aller à l'école

I. drive to work / **go** to work
aller travailler (en voiture)

J. be in school
être à l'école

K. work
travailler

L. go to the market
aller au marché

M. leave work
quitter le travail

Grammar point: 3rd person singular

For **he** and **she**, we add **-s** or **-es** to the verb.

He/She wake**s** up.

He/She watch**es** TV.

These verbs are different (irregular):

be   He/She **is** in school at 10:00 a.m.

have   He/She **has** dinner at 6:30 p.m.

N. **clean** the house
nettoyer la maison

O. **pick up** the children
aller chercher les enfants

P. **cook** dinner
préparer le dîner

Q. **come** home / **get** home
revenir à la maison /
se rendre à la maison

R. **have** dinner
dîner

S. **watch** TV
regarder la télé

T. **do** homework
faire ses devoirs

U. **relax**
relaxer / se détendre

V. **read** the paper
lire le journal

W. **exercise**
faire de l'exercice

X. **go** to bed
aller se coucher

Y. **go** to sleep
s'endormir

Talk about your daily routine.

I take a shower in the morning.

I go to school in the evening.

I go to bed at 11 o'clock.

Share your answers.

1. Who makes dinner in your family?

2. Who goes to the market?

3. Who goes to work?

Life Events Evénements de la vie

A. be born
naître

B. start school
commencer l'école

C. immigrate
immigrer

D. graduate
obtenir son diplôme

E. learn to drive
apprendre à conduire

F. join the army
s'**enrôler** dans l'armée

G. get a job
trouver un emploi

H. become a citizen
obtenir sa citoyenneté

I. rent an apartment
louer un appartement

J. go to college
aller à l'université

K. fall in love
tomber amoureux

L. get married
se marier

Grammar point: past tense

start		immigrate	
learn		graduate	
join	+ed	move	+d
rent		retire	
travel		die	

These verbs are different (irregular):

be	— was	have	— had
get	— got	buy	— bought
become	— became		
go	— went		
fall	— fell		

28

1960

1967

M. have a baby
avoir un bébé

N. travel
voyager

1971

1971

O. buy a house
acheter une maison

P. move
déménager

1985

1997

Q. have a grandchild
avoir un petit-enfant

R. die
mourir

Registro Civil
Acta de Nacimiento

MARTÍN PEREZ DE LEÓN
01-05-25
JOSÉ PEREZ
RITA LEÓN
①

Los Angeles High School

Martin Perez

Rachid Hababi
Josephine R. Klee
Loretta Sommers
②

RESIDENT ALIEN
US Department of Justice-
Immigration and Naturalization Service
PEREZ, MARTIN
01-05-25
B043398414
10-28-40
Martin Perez
③

1. birth certificate
   certificat de naissance

2. diploma
   diplôme

3. Resident Alien card
   carte d'étranger résidant

DMV CALIFORNIA **DMV**
DRIVER LICENSE   CLASS: C
MO6178
EXPIRES: XX-XX-XX
PEREZ, MARTIN
Martin Perez
④

SOCIAL SECURITY
987-65-4321
PEREZ, MARTIN
Martin Perez
⑤

THE UNITED STATES OF AMERICA
No. 20779079
Certificate of Naturalization
INS Registration No. B04 398 414
Martin Perez
Henrietta J. Mulholland
⑥

4. driver's license
   permis de conduire

5. Social Security card
   carte de sécurité sociale

6. Certificate of Naturalization
   certificat de naturalisation

California State University
CSU
Martin Perez
Bachelor of Science
June 1964
With Honors
Sigmund G. Kaufmann
⑦

MAY 24 1955
CERTIFICATE of REGISTRY of MARRIAGE
| MARTIN | LEON | PEREZ | D1-0 |
| ROSA | MARÍA | LOPEZ | 11 |
⑧

PASSPORT
UNITED STATES OF AMERICA
PASSPORT
USA   PEREZ, MARTIN
01-05-25X   01-1
779876543   43-5-33
1-2-67
⑨

7. college degree
   diplôme universitaire

8. marriage license
   certificat de publication de
   bans (licence de mariage)

9. passport
   passeport

More vocabulary

When a husband dies, his wife becomes a **widow**.

When a wife dies, her husband becomes a **widower**.

When older people stop working, we say they **retire**.

Talk about yourself.

I was born in 1968.

I learned to drive in 1987.

I immigrated in 1990.

1. **hot**
   avoir chaud

2. **thirsty**
   avoir soif

3. **sleepy**
   avoir sommeil

4. **cold**
   avoir froid

5. **hungry**
   avoir faim

6. **full**
   être repu

7. **comfortable**
   être à l'aise

8. **uncomfortable**
   être mal à l'aise

9. **disgusted**
   être dégoûté(e)

10. **calm**
    être calme

11. **nervous**
    être nerveux (nerveuse)

12. **in pain**
    avoir mal

13. **worried**
    être inquiet(e)

14. **sick**
    être malade

15. **well**
    être bien

16. **relieved**
    être soulagé(e)

17. **hurt**
    être blessé(e) / peiné(e)

18. **lonely**
    se sentir seul(e)

19. **in love**
    être amoureux

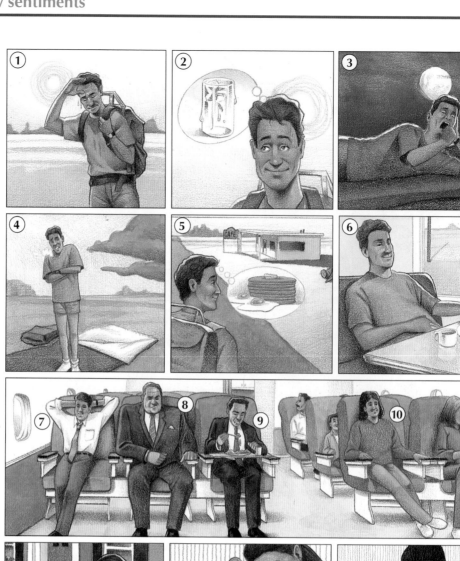

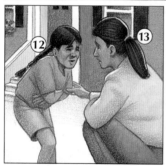

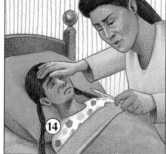

More vocabulary

furious: very angry

terrified: very scared

overjoyed: very happy

exhausted: very tired

starving: very hungry

humiliated: very embarrassed

Talk about your feelings.

I feel <u>happy</u> when I see <u>my friends</u>.

I feel <u>homesick</u> when I think about <u>my family</u>.

20. sad
triste

21. homesick
avoir le mal du pays

22. proud
fier (fière)

23. excited
excité(e)

24. scared
effrayé(e)

25. embarrassed
embarrassé(e)

26. bored
qui s'ennuie

27. confused
qui ne comprend
pas bien

28. frustrated
frustré(e)

29. angry
fâché(e)

30. upset
bouleversé(e)

31. surprised
surpris(e)

32. happy
heureux (heureuse)

33. tired
fatigué(e)

Use the new language.

Look at **Clothing I**, page **64**, and answer the questions.

1. How does the runner feel?

2. How does the man at the bus stop feel?

3. How does the woman at the bus stop feel?

4. How do the teenagers feel?

5. How does the little boy feel?

A Graduation   Remise des diplômes

The Ceremony

1. **graduating class**
   finissants

2. **gown**
   toge

3. **cap**
   cape

4. **stage**
   tribune

5. **podium**
   podium

6. **graduate**
   diplômé(e)

7. **diploma**
   diplôme

8. **valedictorian**
   élève qui prononce
   un discours d'adieu

9. **guest speaker**
   conférencier
   (conférencière) invité(e)

10. **audience**
    auditoire

11. **photographer**
    photographe

A. **graduate**
   obtenir son diplôme

B. **applaud / clap**
   applaudir

C. **cry**
   pleurer

D. **take** a picture
   prendre une photo

E. **give** a speech
   faire un discours

Talk about what the people in the pictures are doing.

She is
- taking a picture.
- giving a speech.
- smiling.
- laughing.

He is
- making a toast.
- clapping.

They are
- graduating.
- hugging.
- kissing.
- applauding.

The Party

12. caterer traiteur	**15.** banner bannière	**18.** gifts cadeaux	**H. laugh** rire
13. buffet buffet	**16.** dance floor piste de danse	**F. kiss** donner un **baiser**	**I. make a toast** porter un **toast**
14. guests invités	**17.** DJ (disc jockey) disc-jockey	**G. hug** serrer dans les bras	**J. dance** danser

Share your answers.

1. Did you ever go to a graduation? Whose?

2. Did you ever give a speech? Where?

3. Did you ever hear a great speaker? Where?

4. Did you ever go to a graduation party?

5. What do you like to eat at parties?

6. Do you like to dance at parties?

1. the city/an urban area
la ville/une zone urbaine

2. the suburbs
la banlieue

3. a small town
une petite ville

4. the country/a rural area
la campagne/une zone rurale

5. apartment building
immeuble à appartements

6. house
maison

7. townhouse
maison de ville

8. mobile home
mobile home

9. college dormitory
résidence universitaire

10. shelter
abri

11. nursing home
maison de retraite

12. ranch
ranch

13. farm
ferme

More vocabulary

duplex house: a house divided into two homes

condominium: an apartment building where each apartment is owned separately

co-op: an apartment building owned by the residents

Share your answers.

1. Do you like where you live?
2. Where did you live in your country?
3. What types of housing are there near your school?

Renting an apartment   Location d'un appartement

A. look for a new apartment
chercher un nouvel appartement

B. talk to the manager
parler au gérant

C. sign a rental agreement
signer un contrat de location

D. move in
emménager

E. unpack
déballer ses affaires

F. pay the rent
payer le loyer

Buying a house   Achat d'une maison

G. talk to the Realtor
parler à l'agent immobilier

H. make an offer
faire une offre

I. get a loan
obtenir un prêt

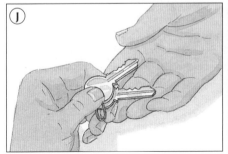

J. take ownership
prendre possession

K. arrange the furniture
disposer les meubles

L. pay the mortgage
payer l'emprunt-immobilier

More vocabulary

lease: a rental agreement for a specific period of time
utilities: gas, water, and electricity for the home

Practice talking to an apartment manager.

How much is the rent?
Are utilities included?
When can I move in?

Entrance

Laundry Room

Recreation Room

Garage

1. **first floor**
   rez-de-chaussée

2. **second floor**
   premier étage

3. **third floor**
   deuxième étage

4. **fourth floor**
   troisième étage

5. **roof garden**
   jardin sur le toit

6. **playground**
   terrain de jeux

7. **fire escape**
   escalier de secours

8. **intercom/speaker**
   interphone/haut-parleur

9. **security system**
   système de sécurité

10. **doorman**
    portier

11. **vacancy sign**
    affiche de disponibilité

12. **manager/superintendent**
    gérant/concierge

13. **security gate**
    barrière de sécurité

14. **storage locker**
    placard de rangement

15. **parking space**
    place de stationnement (parking)

More vocabulary

rec room: a short way of saying **recreation room**

basement: the area below the street level of an apartment or a house

Talk about where you live.

I live in Apartment 3 near the entrance.

I live in Apartment 11 on the second floor near the fire escape.

16. swimming pool piscine	**23.** fire exit sortie de secours	**30.** doorknob bouton de porte
17. balcony balcon	**24.** trash chute vide-ordures	**31.** key clé
18. courtyard cour	**25.** smoke detector détecteur de fumée	**32.** landlord propriétaire
19. air conditioner climatiseur	**26.** stairway escalier	**33.** tenant locataire
20. trash bin bac à ordures	**27.** peephole judas	**34.** elevator ascenseur
21. alley ruelle	**28.** door chain chaîne de sûreté	**35.** stairs marches
22. neighbor voisin	**29.** dead-bolt lock verrou	**36.** mailboxes boîtes aux lettres

Grammar point: *there is, there are*

singular: *there is*   plural: *there are*

There is a fire exit in the hallway.

There are mailboxes in the lobby.

Talk about apartments.

My apartment has <u>an elevator</u>, <u>a lobby</u>, and <u>a rec room</u>.

My apartment doesn't have <u>a pool</u> or <u>a garage</u>.

My apartment needs <u>air conditioning</u>.

37

1. floor plan plan d'étage	**7.** garage door porte de garage	**13.** steps marches	**19.** gutter gouttière
2. backyard arrière-cour	**8.** screen door porte moustiquaire	**14.** front walk trottoir	**20.** roof toit
3. fence clôture	**9.** porch light lampe de porte	**15.** front yard cour avant	**21.** chimney cheminée
4. mailbox boîte aux lettres	**10.** doorbell sonnette	**16.** deck terrasse	**22.** TV antenna antenne de télé
5. driveway allée	**11.** front door porte d'entrée	**17.** window fenêtre	
6. garage garage	**12.** storm door double porte	**18.** shutter volet	

More vocabulary

two-story house: a house with two floors

downstairs: the bottom floor

upstairs: the part of a house above the bottom floor

Share your answers.

1. What do you like about this house?

2. What's something you don't like about the house?

3. Describe the perfect house.

1. hedge
haie

2. hammock
hamac

3. garbage can
poubelle

4. leaf blower
souffleuse à feuilles

5. patio furniture
meubles de patio

6. patio
patio

7. barbecue grill
barbecue

8. sprinkler
arroseur

9. hose
tuyau d'arrosage

10. compost pile
tas de compost

11. rake
râteau

12. hedge clippers
cisailles à haie

13. shovel
pelle

14. trowel
truelle

15. pruning shears
coupe-branches

16. wheelbarrow
brouette

17. watering can
arrosoir

18. flowerpot
pot de fleurs

19. flower
fleur

20. bush
buisson

21. lawn
pelouse

22. lawn mower
tondeuse à gazon

A. weed the flower bed
désherber la plate-bande

B. water the plants
arroser les plantes

C. mow the lawn
tondre le gazon

D. plant a tree
planter un arbre

E. trim the hedge
tailler la haie

F. rake the leaves
râteler les feuilles

Talk about your yard and gardening.

I like to plant trees.

I don't like to weed.

I like/don't like to work in the yard/garden.

Share your answers.

1. What flowers, trees, or plants do you see in the picture? (Look at **Trees, Plants, and Flowers**, pages **128–129** for help.)

2. Do you ever use a barbecue grill to cook?

1. **cabinet**
   armoire

2. **paper towels**
   essuie-tout

3. **dish drainer**
   égouttoir à vaisselle

4. **dishwasher**
   lave-vaisselle

5. **garbage disposal**
   broyeur d'ordures

6. **sink**
   évier

7. **toaster**
   grille-pain

8. **shelf**
   tablette

9. **refrigerator**
   réfrigérateur

10. **freezer**
    congélateur

11. **coffeemaker**
    cafetière

12. **blender**
    mixeur

13. **microwave oven**
    four à micro-ondes

14. **electric can opener**
    ouvre-boîte électrique

15. **toaster oven**
    grille-pain four

16. **pot**
    casserole

17. **teakettle**
    théière

18. **stove**
    cuisinière

19. **burner**
    brûleur

20. **oven**
    four

21. **broiler**
    grilloir

22. **counter**
    comptoir

23. **drawer**
    tiroir

24. **pan**
    poêle

25. **electric mixer**
    batteur électrique

26. **food processor**
    robot culinaire

27. **cutting board**
    planche à découper

Talk about the location of kitchen items.

The toaster oven is *on the counter* *near the stove*.

The microwave is *above the stove*.

Share your answers.

1. Do you have a garbage disposal? a dishwasher? a microwave?

2. Do you eat in the kitchen?

1. china cabinet vaisselier	**8.** candlestick chandelier	**15.** pepper shaker poivrière
2. set of dishes service de vaisselle	**9.** vase vase	**16.** dining room chair chaise de salle à dîner
3. platter plat	**10.** tray plateau	**17.** dining room table table de salle à dîner
4. ceiling fan ventilateur de plafond	**11.** teapot théière	**18.** tablecloth nappe
5. light fixture luminaire	**12.** sugar bowl sucrier	**19.** napkin serviette
6. serving dish plateau de service	**13.** creamer pot à crème	**20.** place mat napperon
7. candle chandelle	**14.** saltshaker salière	**21.** fork fourchette

22. knife couteau	
23. spoon cuillère / cuiller	
24. plate assiette	
25. bowl bol	
26. glass verre	
27. coffee cup tasse à café	
28. mug grande tasse	

Practice asking for things in the dining room.

Please pass the platter.

May I have the creamer?

Could I have a fork, please?

Share your answers.

1. What are the women in the picture saying?

2. In your home, where do you eat?

3. Do you like to make dinner for your friends?

1. bookcase
bibliothèque

2. basket
panier

3. track lighting
rampe d'éclairage

4. lightbulb
ampoule

5. ceiling
plafond

6. wall
mur

7. painting
tableau

8. mantel
manteau

9. fireplace
foyer

10. fire
feu

11. fire screen
écran de cheminée

12. logs
bûches

13. wall unit
unité murale

14. stereo system
chaîne stéréo

15. floor lamp
lampe sur pied

16. drapes
tentures

17. window
fenêtre

18. plant
plante

19. sofa / couch
sofa / divan

20. throw pillow
coussin

21. end table
table d'extrémité

22. magazine holder
porte-journaux

23. coffee table
table de salon / table basse

24. armchair / easy chair
fauteuil

25. love seat
causeuse

26. TV (television)
télé (téléviseur)

27. carpet
tapis / moquette

Use the new language.

Look at **Colors,** page **12,** and describe this room.

There is a gray sofa and a gray armchair.

Talk about your living room.

In my living room I have a sofa, two chairs, and a coffee table.

I don't have a fireplace or a wall unit.

1. hamper
panier à linge

2. bathtub
baignoire

3. rubber mat
tapis de caoutchouc

4. drain
canalisation sanitaire

5. hot water
eau chaude

6. faucet
robinet

7. cold water
eau froide

8. towel rack
porte-serviettes

9. tile
tuile

10. showerhead
pommeau de douche

11. (mini)blinds
store (à lamelles)

12. bath towel
serviette de bain

13. hand towel
essuie-mains

14. washcloth
gant de toilette

15. toilet paper
papier hygiénique

16. toilet brush
balayette

17. toilet
cuvette

18. mirror
miroir

19. medicine cabinet
armoire à pharmacie

20. toothbrush
brosse à dents

21. toothbrush holder
porte-brosses à dents

22. sink
lavabo

23. soap
savon

24. soap dish
porte savon

25. wastebasket
corbeille à déchets

26. scale
pèse-personne

27. bath mat
tapis de bain

More vocabulary

half bath: a bathroom without a shower or bathtub

linen closet: a closet or cabinet for towels and sheets

stall shower: a shower without a bathtub

Share your answers.

1. Do you turn off the water when you brush your teeth?
wash your hair? shave?

2. Does your bathroom have a bathtub or a stall shower?

A Bedroom Une chambre à coucher

1. mirror
miroir

2. dresser/bureau
commode-coiffeuse/
commode

3. drawer
tiroir

4. closet
placard

5. curtains
rideaux

6. window shade
store

7. photograph
photographie

8. bed
lit

9. pillow
oreiller

10. pillowcase
taie d'oreiller

11. bedspread
couvre-lit

12. blanket
couverture

13. flat sheet
drap plat

14. fitted sheet
drap-housse

15. headboard
tête de lit

16. clock radio
radio-réveil

17. lamp
lampe

18. lampshade
abat-jour

19. light switch
interrupteur

20. outlet
prise

21. night table
table de nuit

22. dust ruffle
volant de lit

23. rug
carpette

24. floor
plancher

25. mattress
matelas

26. box spring
sommier

27. bed frame
cadre de lit

Use the new language.

Describe this room. (See **Describing Things**, page **11**, for help.)

I see a soft pillow and a beautiful bedspread.

Share your answers.

1. What is your favorite thing in your bedroom?

2. Do you have a clock in your bedroom? Where is it?

3. Do you have a mirror in your bedroom? Where is it?

1. bunk bed	**7.** bumper pad	**13.** diaper pail	**19.** cradle
lits superposés	bordure de protection	seau à couches	berceau
2. comforter	**8.** chest of drawers	**14.** dollhouse	**20.** coloring book
édredon	commode	maison de poupées	livre à colorier
3. night-light	**9.** baby monitor	**15.** blocks	**21.** crayons
veilleuse	moniteur de bébé	blocs	crayons
4. mobile	**10.** teddy bear	**16.** ball	**22.** puzzle
mobile	ours en peluche	balle	puzzle / casse-tête
5. wallpaper	**11.** smoke detector	**17.** picture book	**23.** stuffed animals
papier peint	détecteur de fumée	livre d'images	animaux en peluche
6. crib	**12.** changing table	**18.** doll	**24.** toy chest
lit d'enfant	table à langer	poupée	coffre à jouets

Talk about where items are in the room.

The dollhouse is near _the coloring book_.

The teddy bear is on _the chest of drawers_.

Share your answers.

1. Do you think this is a good room for children? Why?

2. What toys did you play with when you were a child?

3. What children's stories do you know?

A. dust the furniture épousseter les meubles	**G. make** the bed faire le lit	**M. wash** the dishes laver la vaisselle
B. recycle the newspapers recycler les journaux	**H. put away** the toys ranger les jouets	**N. dry** the dishes essuyer la vaisselle
C. clean the oven nettoyer le four	**I. vacuum** the carpet passer l'aspirateur sur le tapis	**O. wipe** the counter essuyer le comptoir
D. wash the windows laver les fenêtres	**J. mop** the floor laver le plancher	**P. change** the sheets changer les draps
E. sweep the floor balayer le plancher	**K. polish** the furniture polir les meubles	**Q. take out** the garbage sortir les ordures
F. empty the wastebasket vider la corbeille à papier	**L. scrub** the floor frotter le plancher	

Talk about yourself.

I wash the dishes every day.

I change the sheets every week.

I never dry the dishes.

Share your answers.

1. Who does the housework in your family?
2. What is your favorite cleaning job?
3. What is your least favorite cleaning job?

1. feather duster
plumeau

2. recycling bin
bac de recyclage

3. oven cleaner
nettoyant à four

4. rubber gloves
gants de caoutchouc

5. steel-wool soap pads
tampons à récurer en laine d'acier

6. rags
chiffons

7. stepladder
escabeau

8. glass cleaner
nettoyant à vitres

9. squeegee
raclette

10. broom
balai

11. dustpan
ramasse-poussière

12. trash bags
sacs à ordures

13. vacuum cleaner
aspirateur

14. vacuum cleaner attachments
accessoires d'aspirateur

15. vacuum cleaner bag
sac d'aspirateur

16. wet mop
serpillière

17. dust mop
vadrouille

18. furniture polish
encaustique pour meubles

19. scrub brush
brosse à récurer

20. bucket / pail
seau

21. dishwashing liquid
détergent à vaisselle

22. dish towel
linge à vaisselle

23. cleanser
détergent

24. sponge
éponge

Practice asking for the items.

I want to <u>wash the windows</u>.
Please hand me <u>the squeegee</u>.

I have to <u>sweep the floor</u>.
Can you get me <u>the broom</u>, please?

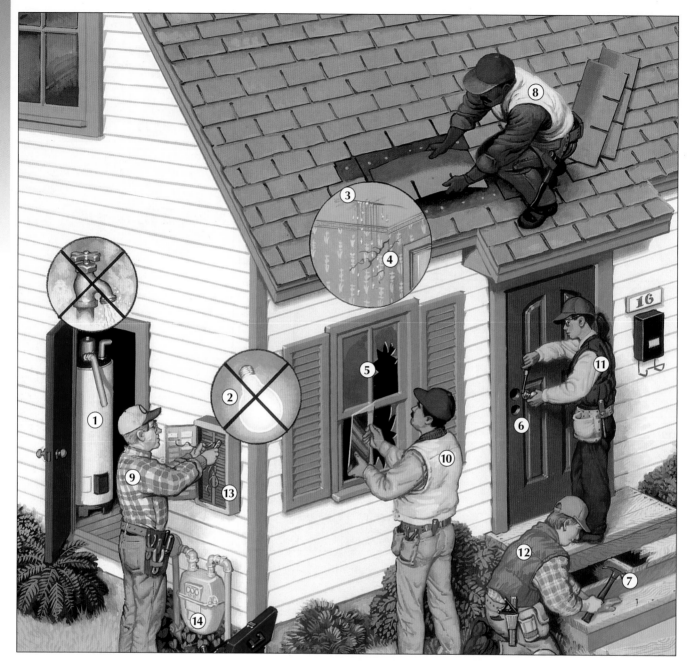

1. The water heater is **not working**.
   Le chauffe-eau **ne fonctionne pas**.

2. The power is **out**.
   Il y a une **panne** de courant.

3. The roof is **leaking**.
   Le toit **coule**.

4. The wall is **cracked**.
   Le mur est **fissuré**.

5. The window is **broken**.
   La fenêtre est **brisée**.

6. The lock is **broken**.
   La serrure est **cassée**.

7. The steps are **broken**.
   Les marches sont **cassées**.

8. roofer
   couvreur

9. electrician
   électricien

10. repair person
    réparateur

11. locksmith
    serrurier

12. carpenter
    charpentier

13. fuse box
    boîte à fusibles

14. gas meter
    compteur à gaz

Use the new language.

Look at **Tools and Building Supplies**, pages **150–151**.

Name the tools you use for household repairs.

I use a hammer and nails to fix a broken step.

I use a wrench to repair a dripping faucet.

15. The furnace is **broken**.
La chaudière est **cassée**.

16. The faucet is **dripping**.
Le robinet **coule**.

17. The sink is **overflowing**.
L'évier **déborde**.

18. The toilet is **stopped up**.
La cuvette est **bouchée**.

19. The pipes are **frozen**.
Les tuyaux sont **gelés**.

20. plumber
plombier

21. exterminator
exterminateur

Household pests
Insectes et animaux nuisibles

22. termite(s)
termite(s)

23. flea(s)
puce(s)

24. ant(s)
fourmi(s)

25. cockroach(es)
cafard(es) / blatte(s)

26. mice*
souris

27. rat(s)
rat(s)

*****Note:** *one mouse, two mice*

More vocabulary

fix: to repair something that is broken

exterminate: to kill household pests

pesticide: a chemical that is used to kill household pests

Share your answers.

1. Who does household repairs in your home?

2. What is the worst problem a home can have?

3. What is the most expensive problem a home can have?

TODAY
BANANAS 2lb/1.00
BLUEBERRIES 1.99 pint

1. grapes
raisins

2. pineapples
ananas

3. bananas
bananes

4. apples
pommes

5. peaches
pêches

6. pears
poires

7. apricots
abricots

8. plums
prunes

9. grapefruit
pamplemousses

10. oranges
oranges

11. lemons
citrons

12. limes
limes

13. tangerines
mandarines

14. avocadoes
avocats

15. cantaloupes
cantaloups

16. cherries
cerises

17. strawberries
fraises

18. raspberries
framboises

19. blueberries
myrtilles

20. papayas
papayes

21. mangoes
mangues

22. coconuts
noix de coco

23. nuts
noix

24. watermelons
pastèques

25. dates
dattes

26. prunes
pruneaux

27. raisins
raisins secs

28. not ripe
pas mûr

29. ripe
mûr

30. rotten
gâté

Language note: *a bunch of*

We say *a bunch of grapes* and *a bunch of bananas*.

Share your answers.

1. Which fruits do you put in a fruit salad?

2. Which fruits are sold in your area in the summer?

3. What fruits did you have in your country?

1. lettuce laitue	**9.** celery céleri	**17.** scallions échalotes	**25.** string beans haricots verts
2. cabbage choux	**10.** parsley persil	**18.** eggplants aubergines	**26.** mushrooms champignons
3. carrots carottes	**11.** spinach épinards	**19.** peas pois	**27.** corn maïs
4. zucchini courgettes	**12.** cucumbers concombres	**20.** artichokes artichauts	**28.** onions oignons
5. radishes radis	**13.** squash courges	**21.** potatoes pommes de terre	**29.** garlic ail
6. beets betteraves	**14.** turnips navets	**22.** yams patates douces	
7. sweet peppers poivrons	**15.** broccoli brocoli	**23.** tomatoes tomates	
8. chili peppers piments	**16.** cauliflower choux-fleurs	**24.** asparagus asperges	

Language note: *a bunch of, a head of*

We say *a bunch of carrots, a bunch of celery,* and *a bunch of spinach.*

We say *a head of lettuce, a head of cabbage,* and *a head of cauliflower.*

Share your answers.

1. Which vegetables do you eat raw? cooked?

2. Which vegetables need to be in the refrigerator?

3. Which vegetables don't need to be in the refrigerator?

MEAT

Beef   Bœuf

1. roast beef
   rôti de bœuf / rosbif

2. steak
   bifteck / steak

3. stewing beef
   bœuf à ragoût

4. ground beef
   bœuf haché

5. beef ribs
   côtes de bœuf

6. veal cutlets
   escalopes de veau

7. liver
   foie

8. tripe
   tripes

Pork   Porc

9. ham
   jambon

10. pork chops
    côtelettes de porc

11. bacon
    lard / bacon

12. sausage
    saucisses

Lamb   Agneau

13. lamb shanks
    jarrets d'agneau

14. leg of lamb
    gigot d'agneau

15. lamb chops
    côtelettes d'agneau

POULTRY

16. chicken
    poulet

17. turkey
    dindon

18. duck
    canard

19. breasts
    poitrines

20. wings
    ailes

21. thighs
    cuisses

22. drumsticks
    pilons

23. gizzards
    gésiers

24. **raw** chicken
    poulet **cru**

25. **cooked** chicken
    poulet **cuit**

More vocabulary

vegetarian: a person who doesn't eat meat

Meat and poultry without bones are called **boneless**.

Poultry without skin is called **skinless**.

Share your answers.

1. What kind of meat do you eat most often?

2. What kind of meat do you use in soup?

3. What part of the chicken do you like the most?

1. white bread
   pain blanc
2. wheat bread
   pain de blé
3. rye bread
   pain de seigle
4. smoked turkey
   dindon fumé
5. salami
   salami

6. pastrami
   pastrami
7. roast beef
   rôti de bœuf / rosbif
8. corned beef
   bœuf salé / bœuf en conserve
9. American cheese
   cheddar américain
10. cheddar cheese
    fromage cheddar

11. Swiss cheese
    fromage gruyère
12. jack cheese
    fromage jack
13. potato salad
    salade de pommes de terre
14. coleslaw
    salade de chou
15. pasta salad
    salade de pâtes

Fish Poisson

16. trout
    truite
17. catfish
    poisson-chat
18. whole salmon
    saumon entier
19. salmon steak
    darne de saumon

20. halibut
    flétan
21. filet of sole
    filet de sole

Shellfish Crustacés

22. crab
    crabe
23. lobster
    homard / langouste
24. shrimp
    crevettes
25. scallops
    pétoncles

26. mussels
    moules
27. oysters
    huîtres
28. clams
    palourdes
29. **fresh** fish
    poisson **frais**
30. **frozen** fish
    poisson **surgelé**

Practice ordering a sandwich.

I'd like <u>roast beef</u> and <u>American cheese</u> on <u>rye bread</u>.

Tell what you want on it.

Please put <u>tomato</u>, <u>lettuce</u>, <u>onions</u>, and <u>mustard</u> on it.

Share your answers.

1. Do you like to eat fish?
2. Do you buy fresh or frozen fish?

1. bottle return
retour de bouteilles
consignées

2. meat and poultry section
rayon des viandes et
volailles

3. shopping cart
caddie

4. canned goods
conserves

5. aisle
allée

6. baked goods
produits cuisinés

7. shopping basket
panier de provisions

8. manager
gérant

9. dairy section
rayon des produits laitiers

10. pet food
aliments pour animaux

11. produce section
rayon des fruits et
légumes

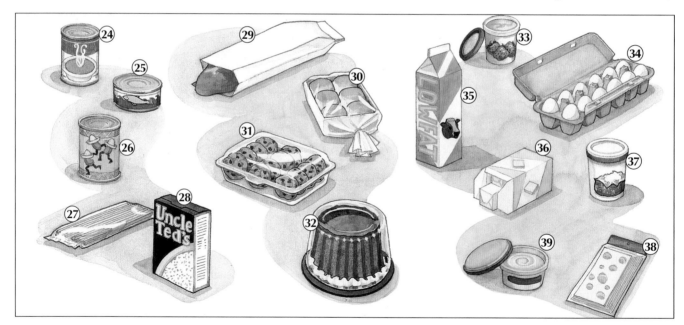

24. soup
soupe

25. tuna
thon

26. beans
fèves

27. spaghetti
spaghetti

28. rice
riz

29. bread
pain

30. rolls
petits pains

31. cookies
biscuits

32. cake
gâteau

33. yogurt
yaourt / yogourt

34. eggs
œufs

35. milk
lait

36. butter
beurre

37. sour cream
crème aigre

38. cheese
fromage

39. margarine
margarine

12. frozen foods
aliments surgelés

13. baking products
produits de cuisson

14. paper products
produits de papier

15. beverages
boissons

16. snack foods
grignotines

17. checkstand
comptoir de caisse

18. cash register
caisse

19. checker
caissier / caissière

20. line
queue

21. bagger
emballeur

22. paper bag
sac de papier

23. plastic bag
sac de plastique

40. potato chips
chips

41. candy bar
friandise

42. gum
chewing-gum

43. frozen vegetables
légumes surgelés

44. ice cream
crème glacée

45. flour
farine

46. spices
épices

47. cake mix
mélange à gâteaux

48. sugar
sucre

49. oil
huile

50. apple juice
jus de pomme

51. instant coffee
café instantané

52. soda
boisson gazeuse

53. bottled water
eau en bouteille

54. plastic wrap
film alimentaire

55. aluminum foil
papier aluminium

1. bottle
bouteille

2. jar
bocal

3. can
boîte de conserve

4. carton
carton

5. container
contenant

6. box
boîte

7. bag
sac

8. package
emballage

9. six-pack
pack de six

10. loaf
pain

11. roll
petit pain

12. tube
tube

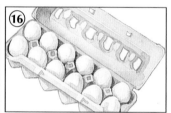

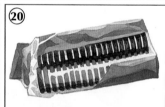

13. a bottle of soda
une bouteille de boisson gazeuse

14. a jar of jam
un bocal de confiture

15. a can of soup
une boîte de soupe

16. a carton of eggs
un carton d'œufs

17. a container of cottage cheese
un contenant de fromage cottage

18. a box of cereal
une boîte de céréales

19. a bag of flour
un sac de farine

20. a package of cookies
un paquet de biscuits

21. a six-pack of soda
un pack de six boissons gazeuses

22. a loaf of bread
un pain

23. a roll of paper towels
un rouleau d'essuie-tout

24. a tube of toothpaste
un tube de dentifrice

Grammar point: *How much? How many?*
Some foods can be counted: *one apple, two apples.*
How many apples do you need? I need ***two*** apples.

Some foods cannot be counted, like liquids, grains, spices, or dairy foods. For these, count containers: *one box of rice, two boxes of rice.*

How much rice do you need? I need ***two boxes.***

A

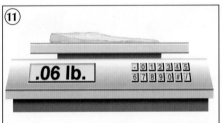

B

3.25 lb.

C

1 cup = 237 milliliters

A. Measure the ingredients.
Mesurer les ingrédients.

B. Weigh the food.
Peser les aliments.

C. Convert the measurements.
Convertir les mesures.

Liquid measures   *Mesures de liquides*

(1)   1 fl. oz.

(2)   1 c.

(3)   1 pt.

(4)   1 qt.

(5)   1 gal.

Dry measures   *Mesures de matières sèches*

(6)   1 tsp.

(7)   1 TBS.

(8)   1/4 c.

(9)   1/2 c.

(10)   1 c.

Weight   *Poids*

(11)   **.06 lb.**

(12)   **1.00 lb.**

1. a fluid ounce of water
une once liquide d'eau

2. a cup of oil
une tasse d'huile

3. a pint of yogurt
un demi-litre de yogourt

4. a quart of milk
un litre de lait

5. a gallon of apple juice
un gallon de jus de pomme

6. a teaspoon of salt
une cuillerée à café de sel

7. a tablespoon of sugar
une cuillerée à soupe de sucre

8. a 1/4 cup of brown sugar
un quart de tasse de cassonade

9. a 1/2 cup of raisins
une demi-tasse de raisins secs

10. a cup of flour
une tasse de farine

11. an ounce of cheese
une once de fromage

12. a pound of roast beef
une livre de rôti de bœuf / de rosbif

VOLUME
1 fl. oz. = 30 milliliters (ml.)
1 c. = 237 ml.
1 pt. = .47 liters (l.)
1 qt. = .95 l.
1 gal. = 3.79 l.

EQUIVALENCIES	
3 tsp. = 1 TBS.	2 c. = 1 pt.
2 TBS. = 1 fl. oz.	2 pt. = 1 qt.
8 fl. oz. = 1 c.	4 qt. = 1 gal.

WEIGHT
1 oz. = 28.35 grams (g.)
1 lb. = 453.6 g.
2.205 lbs. = 1 kilogram
1 lb. = 16 oz.

Scrambled eggs   Œufs brouillés

A. Break 3 eggs.
Casser trois (3) œufs.

B. Beat well.
Battre vigoureusement.

C. Grease the pan.
Graisser le poêlon.

D. Pour the eggs into the pan.
Verser les œufs dans le poêlon.

E. Stir.
Remuer.

F. Cook until done.
Faire cuire jusqu'à la consistance désirée.

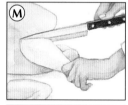

Vegetable casserole   Ragoût de légumes

G. Chop the onions.
Hacher les oignons.

H. Sauté the onions.
Faire sauter les oignons.

I. Steam the broccoli.
Faire cuire le brocoli à la vapeur.

J. Grate the cheese.
Râper le fromage.

K. Mix the ingredients.
Mélanger les ingrédients.

L. Bake at 350° for 45 minutes.
Faire cuire au four à 350 °F (175 °C) pendant 45 minutes.

Chicken soup   Soupe au poulet

M. Cut up the chicken.
Couper le poulet.

N. Peel the carrots.
Eplucher les carottes.

O. Slice the carrots.
Trancher les carottes.

P. Boil the chicken.
Faire bouillir le poulet.

Q. Add the vegetables.
Ajouter les légumes.

R. Simmer for 1 hour.
Faire mijoter pendant une (1) heure.

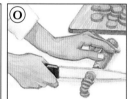

Five ways to cook chicken   Cinq façons de faire cuire du poulet

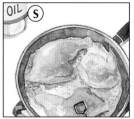

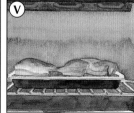

S. fry
friture

T. barbecue / grill
barbecue / grill

U. roast
rôti

V. broil
grillé

W. stir-fry
sauté

Talk about the way you prepare these foods.

I _fry_ eggs.

I _bake_ potatoes.

Share your answers.

1. What are popular ways in your country to make rice? vegetables? meat?

2. What is your favorite way to cook chicken?

1. can opener
ouvre-boîte

2. grater
râpe

3. plastic storage
container
contenant de plastique

4. steamer
cuit-vapeur

5. frying pan
poêle à frire

6. pot
casserole

7. ladle
louche

8. double boiler
bain-marie

9. wooden spoon
cuiller de bois

10. garlic press
presse-ail

11. casserole dish
cocotte

12. carving knife
couteau à découper

13. roasting pan
rôtissoire / lèchefrite

14. roasting rack
grille

15. vegetable peeler
éplucheur / économe

16. paring knife
couteau à éplucher

17. colander
passoire

18. kitchen timer
minuteur

19. spatula
spatule

20. eggbeater
batteur à œufs

21. whisk
fouet

22. strainer
tamis

23. tongs
pinces

24. lid
couvercle

25. saucepan
casserole

26. cake pan
moule à gâteau

27. cookie sheet
tôle à biscuits

28. pie pan
moule à tarte

29. pot holders
poignées / maniques

30. rolling pin
rouleau à pâtisserie

31. mixing bowl
saladier

Talk about how to use the utensils.

You use a peeler to peel potatoes.

You use a pot to cook soup.

Use the new language.

Look at **Food Preparation**, page **58**.

Name the different utensils you see.

1. hamburger
   hamburger
2. french fries
   frites
3. cheeseburger
   cheeseburger /
   hamburger au fromage
4. soda
   boisson gazeuse
5. iced tea
   thé glacé
6. hot dog
   hot-dog
7. pizza
   pizza

8. green salad
   salade verte
9. taco
   taco
10. nachos
    nachos
11. frozen yogurt
    yogourt glacé
12. milk shake
    milk-shake
13. counter
    comptoir
14. muffin
    muffin

15. doughnut
    beignet
16. salad bar
    buffet de crudités
17. lettuce
    laitue
18. salad dressing
    vinaigrette
19. booth
    box
20. straw
    paille
21. sugar
    sucre

22. sugar substitute
    succédané de sucre
23. ketchup
    ketchup
24. mustard
    moutarde
25. mayonnaise
    mayonnaise
26. relish
    relish / achards
A. **eat**
   manger
B. **drink**
   boire

More vocabulary

donut: doughnut (spelling variation)

condiments: relish, mustard, ketchup, mayonnaise, etc.

Share your answers.

1. What would you order at this restaurant?
2. Which fast foods are popular in your country?
3. How often do you eat fast food? Why?

Breakfast

Lunch

Dinner

Desserts

Beverages

1. **scrambled eggs**
   œufs brouillés

2. **sausage**
   saucisses

3. **toast**
   toasts

4. **waffles**
   gaufres

5. **syrup**
   sirop

6. **pancakes**
   crêpes

7. **bacon**
   lard / bacon

8. **grilled cheese sandwich**
   sandwich au fromage grillé

9. **chef's salad**
   salade du chef

10. **soup of the day**
    soupe du jour

11. **mashed potatoes**
    purée de pommes de terre

12. **roast chicken**
    poulet rôti

13. **steak**
    bifteck / steak

14. **baked potato**
    pomme de terre au four

15. **pasta**
    pâtes

16. **garlic bread**
    pain à l'ail

17. **fried fish**
    poisson frit

18. **rice pilaf**
    riz pilaf

19. **cake**
    gâteau

20. **pudding**
    pudding

21. **pie**
    tarte

22. **coffee**
    café

23. **decaf coffee**
    café déca

24. **tea**
    thé

Practice ordering from the menu.

I'd like <u>a grilled cheese sandwich</u> and <u>some soup</u>.

I'll have <u>the chef's salad</u> and <u>a cup of decaf coffee</u>.

Use the new language.

Look at **Fruit,** page **50.**

Order a slice of pie using the different fruit flavors.

Please give me a slice of <u>apple</u> pie.

1. hostess
hôtesse

2. dining room
salle à dîner

3. menu
menu

4. server / waiter
serveur

5. patron / diner
client / dîneur

A. set the table
mettre la table

B. seat the customer
faire asseoir le client

C. pour the water
verser l'eau

D. order from the menu
choisir dans le menu

E. take the order
prendre la commande

F. serve the meal
servir le repas

G. clear the table
débarrasser la table

H. carry the tray
porter le plateau

I. pay the check
payer l'addition

J. leave a tip
laisser un pourboire

More vocabulary

eat out: to go to a restaurant to eat

take out: to buy food at a restaurant and take it home to eat

Practice giving commands.

Please <u>set the table</u>.

I'd like you to <u>clear the table</u>.

It's time to <u>serve the meal</u>.

6. server / waitress
serveur / serveuse

7. dessert tray
plateau à desserts

8. bread basket
corbeille à pain

9. busperson
aide-serveur /
aide-serveuse

10. kitchen
cuisine

11. chef
chef / cuisinier / cuisinière

12. dishroom
plonge

13. dishwasher
plongeur

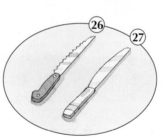

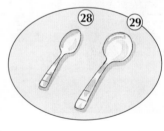

14. place setting
couvert

15. dinner plate
grande assiette

16. bread-and-butter plate
assiette à pain

17. salad plate
assiette à salade

18. soup bowl
bol à soupe

19. water glass
verre à eau

20. wine glass
verre à vin

21. cup
tasse

22. saucer
soucoupe

23. napkin
serviette

24. salad fork
fourchette à salade

25. dinner fork
fourchette de table

26. steak knife
couteau à viande

27. knife
couteau

28. teaspoon
petite cuiller / cuillère

29. soupspoon
cuiller à soupe

Talk about how you set the table in your home.

The glass is on the right.

The fork goes on the left.

The napkin is next to the plate.

Share your answers.

1. Do you know anyone who works in a restaurant? What does he or she do?

2. In your opinion, which restaurant jobs are hard? Why?

1. **three-piece suit**
   costume trois pièces

2. **suit**
   costume

3. **dress**
   robe

4. **shirt**
   chemise

5. **jeans**
   jeans

6. **sports coat**
   manteau sport

7. **turtleneck**
   col roulé

8. **slacks / pants**
   pantalon

9. **blouse**
   blouse

10. **skirt**
    jupe

11. **pullover sweater**
    tricot / pullover

12. **T-shirt**
    T-shirt

13. **shorts**
    short

14. **sweatshirt**
    survêtement

15. **sweatpants**
    pantalon d'entraînement

More vocabulary:

outfit: clothes that look nice together

When clothes are popular, they are **in fashion**.

Talk about what you're wearing today and what you wore yesterday.

I'm wearing <u>a gray sweater</u>, <u>a red T-shirt</u>, and <u>blue jeans</u>.

Yesterday I wore <u>a green pullover sweater</u>, <u>a white shirt</u>, and <u>black slacks</u>.

16. jumpsuit
combinaison-pantalon

17. uniform
uniforme

18. jumper
robe-chasuble

19. maternity dress
robe maternité / robe de grossesse

20. knit shirt
chemise de tricot / chemise à mailles

21. overalls
salopette

22. tunic
tunique

23. leggings
jambières

24. vest
gilet

25. split skirt
jupe avec une fente sur le devant

26. sports shirt
chemise sport

27. cardigan sweater
cardigan

28. tuxedo
smoking

29. evening gown
robe du soir

Use the new language.

Look at **A Graduation**, pages 32–33.

Name the clothes you see.

The man at the podium is wearing a suit.

Share your answers.

1. Which clothes in this picture are in fashion now?

2. Who is the best-dressed person in this line? Why?

3. What do you wear when you go to the movies?

1. hat
chapeau

2. overcoat
pardessus

3. leather jacket
veste de cuir

4. wool scarf / muffler
écharpe de laine /
cache-nez

5. gloves
gants

6. cap
casquette

7. jacket
veste

8. parka
parka

9. mittens
moufles / mitaines

10. ski cap
casquette norvégienne

11. tights
collant

12. earmuffs
protège-oreilles

13. down vest
gilet en duvet

14. ski mask
masque de ski

15. down jacket
veste en duvet

16. umbrella
parapluie

17. raincoat
imperméable

18. poncho
poncho

19. rain boots
bottes de pluie

20. trench coat
trench-coat

21. sunglasses
lunettes de soleil

22. swimming trunks
maillot de bain

23. straw hat
chapeau de paille

24. windbreaker
coupe-vent

25. cover-up
cache-maillot

26. swimsuit / bathing suit
maillot de bain / costume de bain

27. baseball cap
casquette de base-ball

Use the new language.

Look at **Weather**, page **10**.

Name the clothing for each weather condition.

Wear a jacket when it's windy.

Share your answers.

1. Which is better in the rain, an umbrella or a poncho?

2. Which is better in the cold, a parka or a down jacket?

3. Do you have more summer clothes or winter clothes?

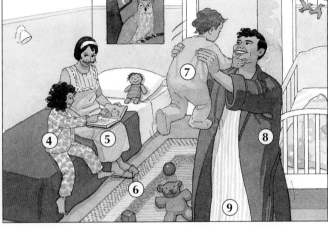

1. leotard
justaucorps

2. tank top
débardeur

3. bike shorts
shorts de vélo

4. pajamas
pyjama

5. nightgown
robe de nuit

6. slippers
pantoufles

7. blanket sleeper
dormeuse molletonnée /
pyjama-couverture /
dors-bien ouverture

8. bathrobe
peignoir de bain

9. nightshirt
chemise de nuit

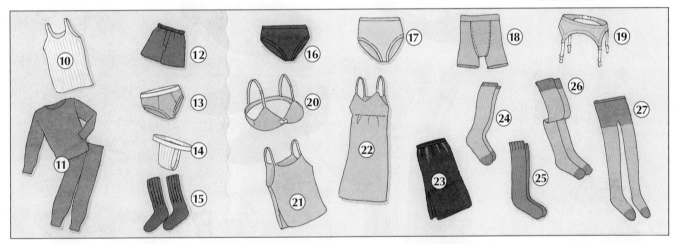

10. undershirt
maillot de corps / tricot de corps /
gilet de corps

11. long underwear
caleçon-combinaison

12. boxer shorts
caleçon boxeur

13. briefs
caleçons

14. athletic supporter / jockstrap
coquille

15. socks
chaussettes

16. (bikini) panties
slip

17. briefs / underpants
caleçon / petite culotte

18. girdle
gaine

19. garter belt
porte-jarretelles

20. bra
soutien-gorge

21. camisole
camisole

22. full slip
combinaison

23. half slip
jupon

24. knee-highs
mi-bas

25. kneesocks
bas-genoux

26. stockings
bas

27. pantyhose
collant

More vocabulary

lingerie: underwear or sleepwear for women

loungewear: clothing (sometimes sleepwear) people
wear around the home

Share your answers.

1. What do you wear when you exercise?

2. What kind of clothing do you wear for sleeping?

Shoes and Accessories   Chaussures et accessoires

1. salesclerk
vendeur (vendeuse)

2. suspenders
bretelles

3. shoe department
rayon des chaussures

4. silk scarves*
écharpes de soie

5. hats
chapeaux

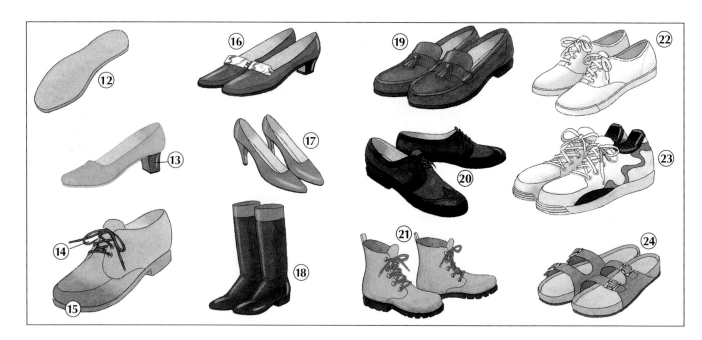

12. sole
semelle

13. heel
talon

14. shoelace
lacet

15. toe
bout

16. pumps
escarpins

17. high heels
talon aiguille / talon haut

18. boots
bottes

19. loafers
mocassins

20. oxfords
souliers de ville / souliers lacés

21. hiking boots
bottes de randonnée

22. tennis shoes
chaussures de tennis

23. athletic shoes
chaussures athlétiques

24. sandals
sandales

*Note: *one scarf, two scarves*

Talk about the shoes you're wearing today.

I'm wearing a pair of <u>white sandals</u>.

Practice asking a salesperson for help.

Could I try on these <u>sandals</u> in size <u>10</u>?

Do you have any <u>silk scarves</u>?

Where are <u>the hats</u>?

6. purses / handbags
sacs à main / sacoches

7. display case
vitrine

8. jewelry
bijoux

9. necklaces
colliers

10. ties
cravates

11. belts
ceintures

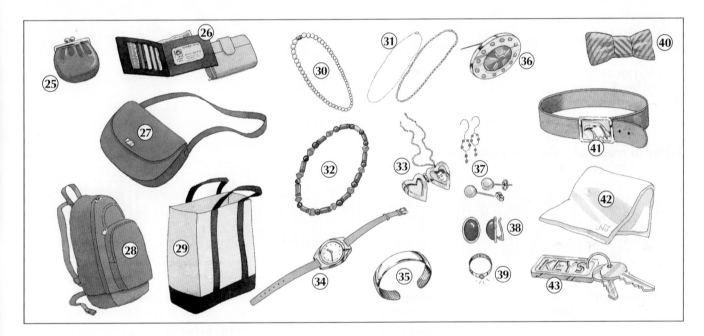

25. change purse
porte-monnaie

26. wallet
portefeuille

27. shoulder bag
sac à bandoulière

28. backpack / bookbag
sac à dos

29. tote bag
fourre-tout

30. string of pearls
collier de perles

31. chain
chaîne

32. beads
perles

33. locket
médaillon

34. (wrist)watch
montre-bracelet

35. bracelet
bracelet

36. pin
broche

37. pierced earrings
boucles d'oreilles pour
oreilles percées

38. clip-on earrings
boucles d'oreilles

39. ring
bague

40. bow tie
noeud papillon

41. belt buckle
boucle de ceinture

42. handkerchief
mouchoir

43. key chain
porte-clé

Share your answers.

1. Which of these accessories are usually worn by
women? by men?

2. Which of these do you wear every day?

3. Which of these would you wear to a job interview?
Why?

4. Which accessory would you like to receive as a
present? Why?

Describing Clothes Description de vêtements

Sizes Tailles

1. extra small
très petit

2. small
petit

3. medium
moyen

4. large
grand

5. extra large
très grand

Patterns Motifs

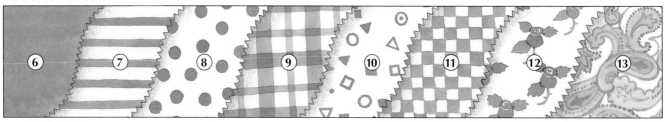

6. solid green
vert uni

7. striped
rayé

8. polka-dotted
à pois

9. plaid
écossais

10. print
imprimé

11. checked
à carreaux

12. floral
fleuri

13. paisley
cachemire

Types of material Types de matériaux

14. wool sweater
chandail / pull de **laine**

15. silk scarf
écharpe de **soie**

16. cotton T-shirt
T-shirt de **coton**

17. linen jacket
veste de **lin**

18. leather boots
bottes de **cuir**

19. nylon stockings*
bas de **nylon**

Problems Problèmes

     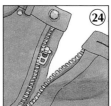 

20. too small
trop petit

21. too big
trop grand

22. stain
tache

23. rip / tear
déchirure

24. broken zipper
fermeture éclair **cassée**

25. missing button
bouton **manquant**

*****Note:** Nylon, polyester, rayon, and plastic are synthetic materials.

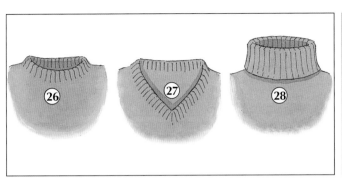

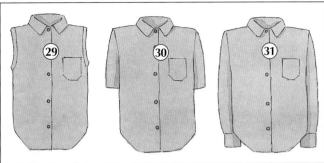

26. crewneck sweater
chandail / pull **à col rond**

27. V-neck sweater
chandail / pull **à col en v**

28. turtleneck sweater
chandail / pull **à col roulé**

29. sleeveless shirt
chemise **sans manches**

30. short-sleeved shirt
chemise **à manches courtes**

31. long-sleeved shirt
chemise **à manches longues**

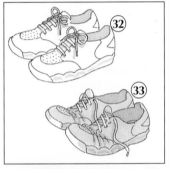

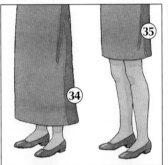

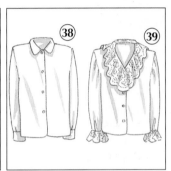

32. new shoes
chaussures **neuves**

33. old shoes
vieilles chaussures

34. long skirt
jupe **longue**

35. short skirt
jupe **courte**

36. formal dress
tenue **de soirée**

37. casual dress
tenue **décontractée**

38. plain blouse
blouse **simple**

39. fancy blouse
blouse **fantaisie**

40. light jacket
veste **légère**

41. heavy jacket
veste **épaisse**

42. loose pants / **baggy** pants
pantalon **ample**

43. tight pants
pantalon **serré**

44. wide tie
cravate **large**

45. narrow tie
cravate **étroite**

46. low heels
talons **courts**

47. high heels
talons **hauts**

Talk about yourself.

I like <u>long-sleeved</u> shirts and <u>baggy</u> pants.

I like <u>short skirts</u> and <u>high heels</u>.

I usually wear <u>plain</u> clothes.

Share your answers.

1. What type of material do you usually wear in the summer? in the winter?

2. What patterns do you see around you?

3. Are you wearing casual or formal clothes?

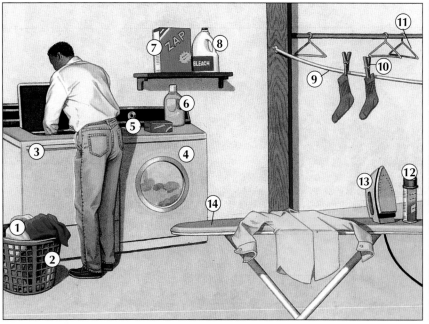
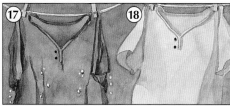
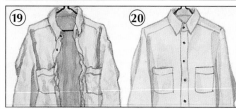
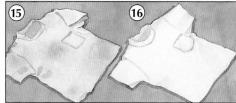

1. **laundry**
   lessive

2. **laundry basket**
   panier de lessive

3. **washer**
   lave-linge / laveuse

4. **dryer**
   sèche-linge / sécheuse

5. **dryer sheets**
   assouplisseur textile en feuilles / voiles sèche-linge

6. **fabric softener**
   produit assouplissant / adoucissant

7. **laundry detergent**
   détergent à lessive

8. **bleach**
   eau de javel

9. **clothesline**
   corde à linge

10. **clothespin**
    pince à linge

11. **hanger**
    cintre

12. **spray starch**
    amidon

13. **iron**
    fer à repasser

14. **ironing board**
    planche à repasser

15. **dirty** T-shirt
    T-shirt **sale**

16. **clean** T-shirt
    T-shirt **propre**

17. **wet** T-shirt
    T-shirt **mouillé**

18. **dry** T-shirt
    T-shirt **sec**

19. **wrinkled** shirt
    chemise **froissée**

20. **ironed** shirt
    chemise **repassée**

A. **Sort** the laundry.
   Trier la lessive.

B. **Add** the detergent.
   Ajouter le détergent.

C. **Load** the washer.
   Remplir le lave-linge / la laveuse.

D. **Clean** the lint trap.
   Nettoyer le filtre à charpie / filtre à air.

E. **Unload** the dryer.
   Vider le sèche-linge / la sécheuse.

F. **Fold** the laundry.
   Plier la lessive.

G. **Iron** the clothes.
   Repasser les vêtements.

H. **Hang up** the clothes.
   Suspendre les vêtements.

More vocabulary

dry cleaners: a business that cleans clothes using chemicals, not water and detergent

wash in cold water only

no bleach

line dry

dry-clean only, do not wash

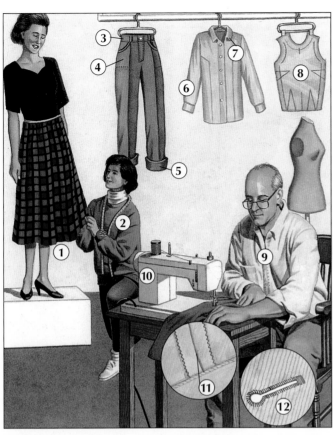

A. **sew** by hand
coudre à la main

B. **sew** by machine
coudre à la machine

C. **lengthen**
rallonger

D. **shorten**
raccourcir

E. **take in**
rabattre

F. **let out**
allonger

1. hemline
ourlet

2. dressmaker
couturière

3. waistband
ceinture montée

4. pocket
poche

5. cuff
revers

6. sleeve
manche

7. collar
col

8. pattern
motif

9. tailor
tailleur

10. sewing machine
machine à coudre

11. seam
couture

12. buttonhole
boutonnière

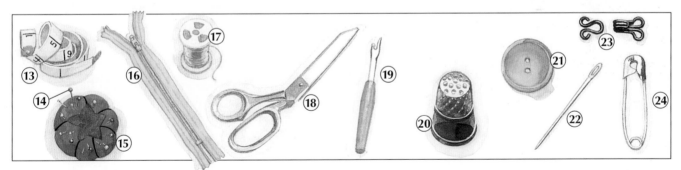

13. tape measure
mètre à ruban

14. pin
épingle

15. pin cushion
coussin à épingles

16. zipper
fermeture éclair

17. spool of thread
bobine de fil

18. (pair of) scissors
(paire de) ciseaux

19. seam ripper
découseur

20. thimble
dé à coudre

21. button
bouton

22. needle
aiguille

23. hook and eye
agrafe et porte

24. safety pin
épingle de sûreté

More vocabulary

pattern maker: a person who makes patterns

garment worker: a person who works in a clothing factory

fashion designer: a person who makes original clothes

Share your answers.

1. Do you know how to use a sewing machine?

2. Can you sew by hand?

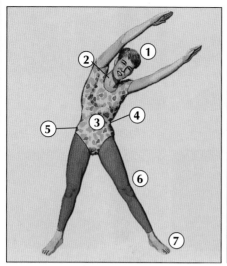

1. head
tête

2. neck
cou

3. abdomen
abdomen

4. waist
taille

5. hip
hanche

6. leg
jambe

7. foot
pied

8. hand
main

9. arm
bras

10. shoulder
épaule

11. back
dos

12. buttocks
fesses / postérieur

13. chest
poitrine

14. breast
sein

15. elbow
coude

16. thigh
cuisse

17. knee
genou

18. calf
mollet

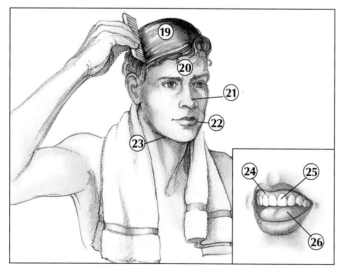

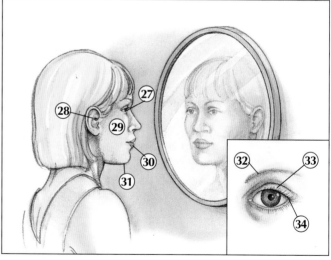

The face
Le visage

19. hair
cheveux

20. forehead
front

21. nose
nez

22. mouth
bouche

23. jaw
mâchoire

24. gums
gencives

25. teeth
dents

26. tongue
langue

27. eye
œil

28. ear
oreille

29. cheek
joue

30. lip
lèvre

31. chin
menton

32. eyebrow
sourcil

33. eyelid
paupière

34. eyelashes
cils

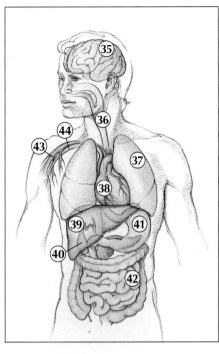

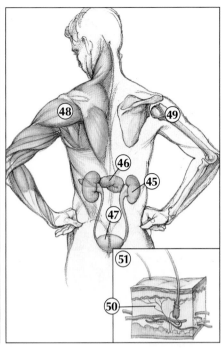

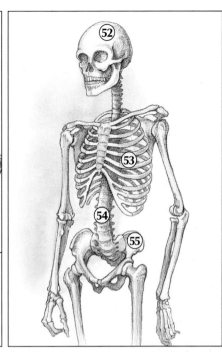

Inside the body
L'intérieur du corps

35. brain
cerveau

36. throat
gorge

37. lung
poumon

38. heart
cœur

39. liver
foie

40. gallbladder
vésicule biliaire

41. stomach
estomac

42. intestines
intestins

43. artery
artère

44. vein
veine

45. kidney
rein

46. pancreas
pancréas

47. bladder
vessie

48. muscle
muscle

49. bone
os

50. nerve
nerf

51. skin
peau

The skeleton
Le squelette

52. skull
crâne

53. rib cage
cage thoracique

54. spinal column
colonne vertébrale

55. pelvis
bassin

PHALLIC
PHALLUS

PHALANXES

PHALANX
PHALANXES

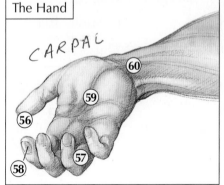

The Hand

CARPAL

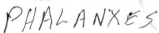

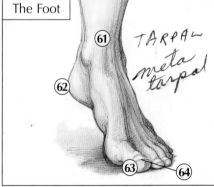

The Foot

TARPAL
meta
tarpal

The Senses

56. thumb
pouce

57. fingers
doigts

58. fingernail
ongle

59. palm
paume

60. wrist
poignet

61. ankle
cheville

62. heel
talon

63. toe
orteil

64. toenail
ongle de pied

A. see
voir

B. hear
entendre

C. smell
sentir

D. taste
goûter

E. touch
toucher

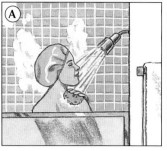

A. take a shower
prendre une douche

B. bathe / take a bath
prendre un bain

C. use deodorant
utiliser un déodorant

D. put on sunscreen
mettre de l'écran solaire

1. shower cap
bonnet de douche

2. soap
savon

3. bath powder / talcum powder
poudre de bain / poudre de talc

4. deodorant
déodorant

5. perfume / cologne
parfum / eau de Cologne

6. sunscreen
écran solaire

7. body lotion
lotion pour le corps

8. moisturizer
hydratant

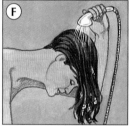
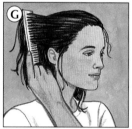

E. wash…hair
laver…
les cheveux

F. rinse…hair
rincer…
les cheveux

G. comb…hair
peigner…
les cheveux

H. dry…hair
sécher…
les cheveux

I. brush…hair
brosser…
les cheveux

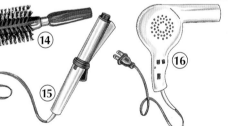

9. shampoo
shampooing

10. conditioner
après-shampooing

11. hair gel
gel cheveux

12. hair spray
fixatif capillaire

13. comb
peigne

14. brush
brosse

15. curling iron
fer à friser

16. blow dryer
séchoir à main

17. hair clip
pince à cheveux

18. barrette
barrette

19. bobby pins
pinces à cheveux

J. brush…teeth
brosser…les dents

K. floss…teeth
**passer la soie dentaire
entre**…les dents

L. gargle
se gargariser

M. shave
se raser

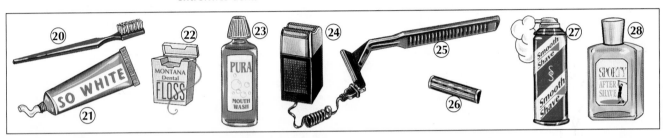

20. toothbrush
brosse à dents

21. toothpaste
pâte dentifrice

22. dental floss
soie dentaire

23. mouthwash
rince-bouche

24. electric shaver
rasoir électrique

25. razor
rasoir

26. razor blade
lame de rasoir

27. shaving cream
crème de rasage

28. aftershave
(lotion) après-rasage

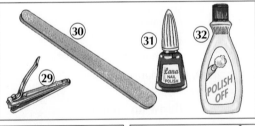

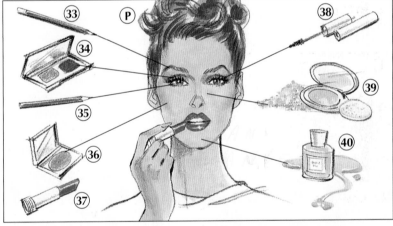

N. cut…nails
se couper…
les ongles

O. polish…nails
se polir…
les ongles

P. put on…makeup
se mettre du…maquillage

29. nail clipper
coupe-ongles

30. emery board
lime émeri

31. nail polish
vernis à ongles

32. nail polish remover
dissolvant de vernis à ongles

33. eyebrow pencil
crayon à sourcils

34. eye shadow
ombre à paupières

35. eyeliner
eye-liner

36. blush / rouge
fard à joues / rouge

37. lipstick
rouge à lèvres

38. mascara
rimmel / fard à cils

39. face powder
poudre pour le visage

40. foundation
fond de teint

More vocabulary

A product without perfume or scent is **unscented.**

A product that is better for people with allergies is
hypoallergenic.

Share your answers.

1. What is your morning routine if you stay home?
if you go out?

2. Do women in your culture wear makeup? How old
are they when they begin to use it?

77

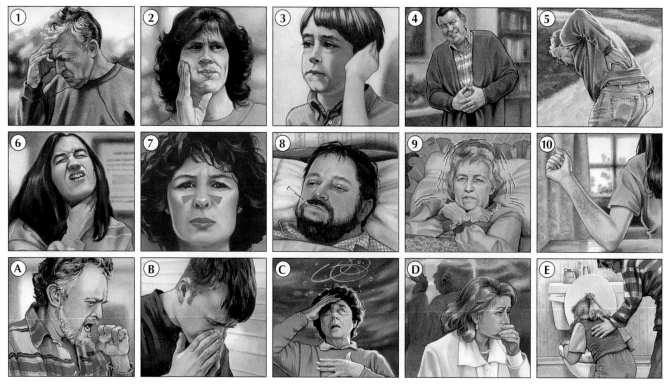

1. **headache**
   mal de tête

2. **toothache**
   mal de dents

3. **earache**
   mal d'oreille

4. **stomachache**
   mal d'estomac

5. **backache**
   mal de dos

6. **sore throat**
   mal de gorge

7. **nasal congestion**
   congestion nasale

8. **fever / temperature**
   fièvre / température

9. **chills**
   frissons

10. **rash**
    éruption cutanée

A. **cough**
   tousser

B. **sneeze**
   éternuer

C. **feel dizzy**
   se sentir étourdi

D. **feel nauseous**
   avoir la nausée

E. **throw up / vomit**
   vomir

11. **insect bite**
    morsure d'insecte

12. **bruise**
    ecchymose

13. **cut**
    coupure

14. **sunburn**
    coup de soleil

15. **blister**
    ampoule

16. **swollen finger**
    doigt enflé

17. **bloody nose**
    nez qui saigne / ensanglanté

18. **sprained ankle**
    entorse

Use the new language.

Look at **Health Care**, pages **80–81**.

Tell what medication or treatment you would use for each health problem.

Share your answers.

1. For which problems would you go to a doctor? use medication? do nothing?

2. What do you do for a sunburn? for a headache?

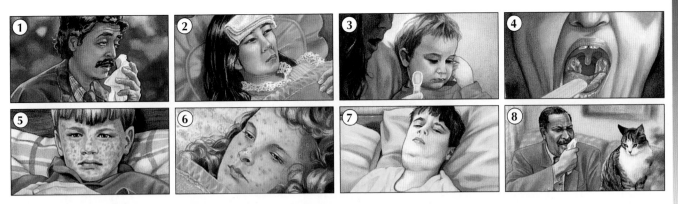

Common illnesses and childhood diseases Maladies communes et maladies de l'enfance

1. cold
rhume

2. flu
grippe

3. ear infection
infection de l'oreille

4. strep throat
angine streptococcique

5. measles
rougeole

6. chicken pox
varicelle

7. mumps
oreillons

8. allergies
allergies

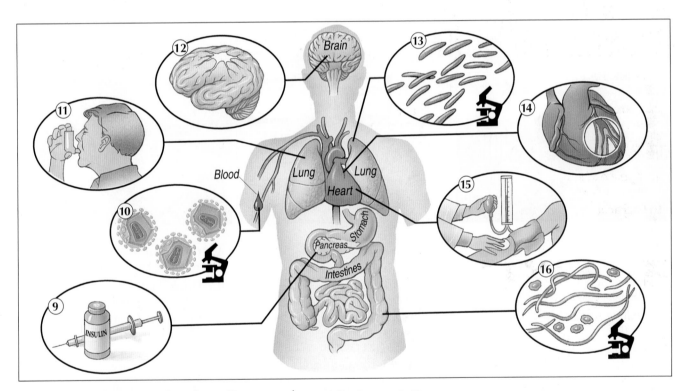

Medical conditions and serious diseases État médical et maladies graves

9. diabetes
diabète

10. HIV (human immunodeficiency virus)
VIH (virus de l'immunodéficience humaine)

11. asthma
asthme

12. brain cancer
cancer du cerveau

13. TB (tuberculosis)
TB (tuberculose)

14. heart disease
maladie cardiaque

15. high blood pressure
hypertension

16. intestinal parasites
parasites intestinaux

More vocabulary

AIDS (acquired immunodeficiency syndrome): a medical condition that results from contracting the HIV virus

influenza: flu

hypertension: high blood pressure

infectious disease: a disease that is spread through air or water

Share your answers.

Which diseases on this page are infectious?

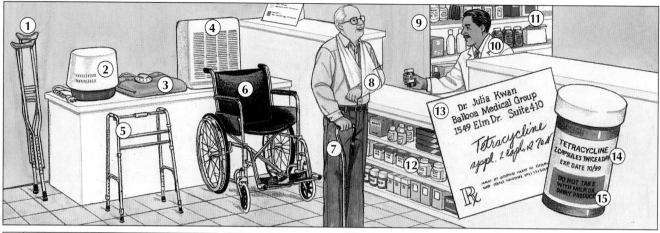

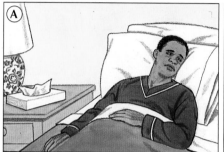

1. **crutches**
   béquilles

2. **humidifier**
   humidificateur

3. **heating pad**
   bouillotte

4. **air purifier**
   purificateur d'air

5. **walker**
   ambulateur

6. **wheelchair**
   fauteuil roulant

7. **cane**
   cane

8. **sling**
   écharpe

9. **pharmacy**
   pharmacie

10. **pharmacist**
    pharmacien/pharmacienne

11. **prescription medication**
    médicament d'ordonnance/
    médicament prescrit

12. **over-the-counter medication**
    médicament sans ordonnance

13. **prescription**
    prescription

14. **prescription label**
    étiquette de prescription/
    étiquette d'ordonnance

15. **warning label**
    étiquette d'avertissement

A. **Get** bed rest.
   Rester au lit.

B. **Drink** fluids.
   Boire des liquides.

C. **Change** your diet.
   Changer de régime.

D. **Exercise.**
   Faire de l'exercice.

E. **Get** an injection.
   Prendre une injection.

F. **Take** medicine.
   Prendre un médicament.

More vocabulary

dosage: how much medicine you take and how many times a day you take it

expiration date: the last day the medicine can be used

treatment: something you do to get better

Staying in bed, drinking fluids, and getting physical therapy are treatments.

An injection that stops a person from getting a serious disease is called **an immunization** or **a vaccination.**

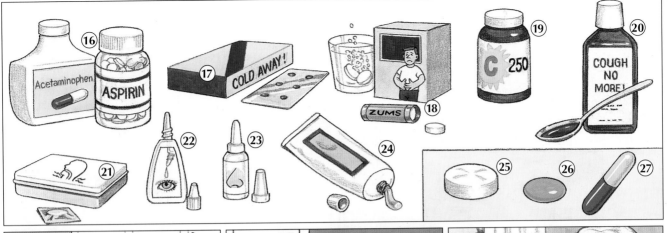

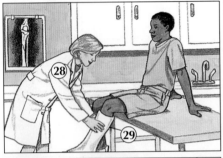

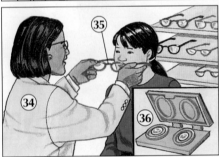

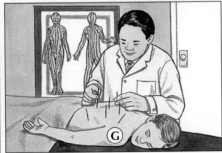

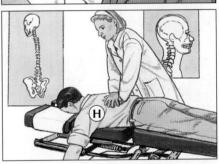

16. pain reliever
analgésique

17. cold tablets
comprimés contre le rhume

18. antacid
antiacide

19. vitamins
vitamines

20. cough syrup
sirop contre la toux

21. throat lozenges
pastilles pour la gorge

22. eyedrops
gouttes pour les yeux

23. nasal spray
pulvérisation nasale

24. ointment
onguent

25. tablet
comprimé

26. pill
pilule

27. capsule
capsule

28. orthopedist
orthopédiste

29. cast
plâtre

30. physical therapist
physiothérapeute

31. brace
appareil orthopédique

32. audiologist
audiologiste

33. hearing aid
appareil auditif

34. optometrist
optométriste

35. (eye)glasses
lunettes

36. contact lenses
verres de contact

G. Get acupuncture.
Subir un traitement d'acupuncture.

H. Go to a chiropractor.
Aller chez un chiropracteur/
chiropraticien.

Share your answers.

1. What's the best treatment for a headache? a sore throat? a stomachache? a fever?

2. Do you think vitamins are important? Why or why not?

3. What treatments are popular in your culture?

A. **be injured / be hurt**
être blessé(e)

B. **be** unconscious
être inconscient

C. **be** in shock
être en état de choc

D. **have** a heart attack
avoir une crise cardiaque

E. **have** an allergic reaction
avoir une réaction allergique

F. **get** an electric shock
subir un choc électrique

G. **get** frostbite
avoir des gelures / engelures

H. **burn** (your)self
se brûler

I. **drown**
se noyer

J. **swallow** poison
avaler du poison

K. **overdose** on drugs
faire une overdose / surdose de drogues

L. **choke**
s'étouffer

M. **bleed**
saigner

N. **can't breathe**
ne pas pouvoir respirer

O. **fall**
tomber

P. **break** a bone
se casser un os

Grammar point: past tense

burn	—	burned	choke	—	choked
drown	—	drowned	be	—	was, were
swallow	—	swallowed	have	—	had
overdose	—	overdosed	get	—	got

bleed	—	bled
can't	—	couldn't
fall	—	fell
break	—	broke

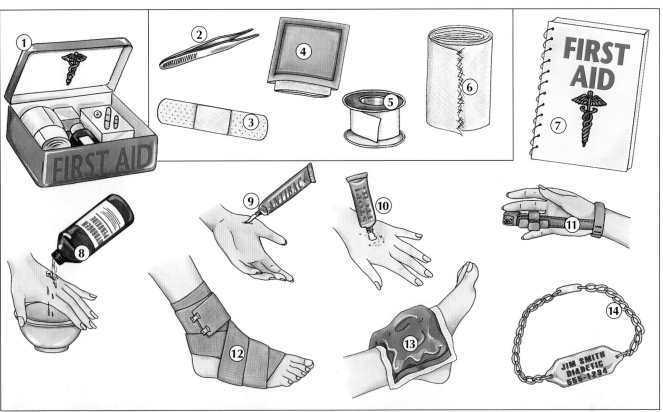

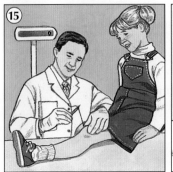

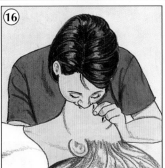

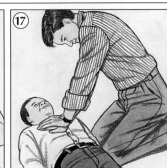

1. **first aid kit**
   trousse de premiers soins

2. **tweezers**
   pince à épiler

3. **adhesive bandage**
   pansement adhésif

4. **sterile pad**
   compresse stérile

5. **tape**
   ruban

6. **gauze**
   gaze

7. **first aid manual**
   manuel de premiers soins

8. **hydrogen peroxide**
   eau oxygénée

9. **antibacterial ointment**
   onguent antibactérien

10. **antihistamine cream**
    crème antihistaminique

11. **splint**
    attelle

12. **elastic bandage**
    bandage élastique

13. **ice pack**
    poche de glace

14. **medical emergency bracelet**
    bracelet d'urgence médicale

15. **stitches**
    points de suture

16. **rescue breathing**
    respiration artificielle

17. **CPR (cardiopulmonary resuscitation)**
    RCR (réanimation cardio-respiratoire)

18. **Heimlich maneuver**
    manœuvre de Heimlich

Important Note: Only people who are properly trained should give stitches or do CPR.

Share your answers.

1. Do you have a First Aid kit in your home? Where can you buy one?

2. When do you use hydrogen peroxide? an elastic support bandage? antihistamine cream?

3. Do you know first aid? Where did you learn it?

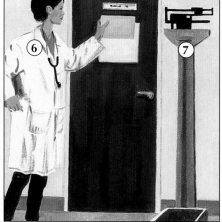
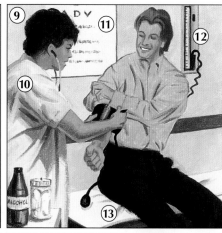

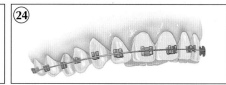

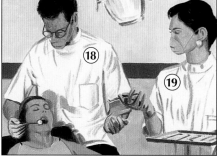

Medical clinic   Clinique médicale

1. **waiting room**
   salle d'attente

2. **receptionist**
   réceptionniste

3. **patient**
   patient(e)

4. **insurance card**
   carte d'assurance

5. **insurance form**
   formulaire d'assurance

6. **doctor**
   docteur

7. **scale**
   balance

8. **stethoscope**
   stéthoscope

9. **examining room**
   salle d'examen

10. **nurse**
    infirmier / infirmière

11. **eye chart**
    échelle d'acuité visuelle

12. **blood pressure gauge**
    indicateur de pression artérielle

13. **examination table**
    table d'examen

14. **syringe**
    seringue

15. **thermometer**
    thermomètre

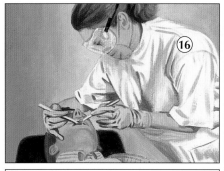

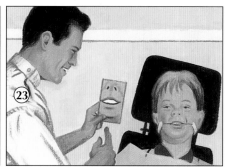

Dental clinic   Clinique dentaire

16. **dental hygienist**
    hygiéniste dentaire

17. **tartar**
    tartre

18. **dentist**
    dentiste

19. **dental assistant**
    assistant(e) dentaire

20. **cavity**
    carie

21. **drill**
    fraise

22. **filling**
    obturation

23. **orthodontist**
    orthodontiste

24. **braces**
    appareil orthodontique

Can I come in on the 5th?

Yes. Come in at 2:00.

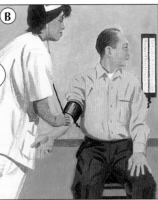

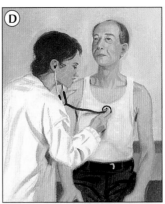

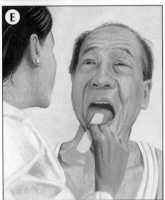

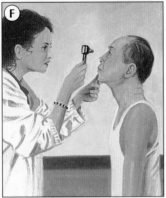

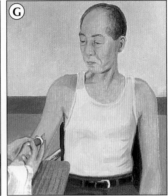

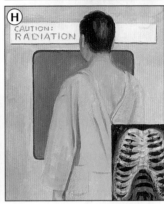

A. **make** an appointment
prendre un rendez-vous

B. **check**…blood pressure
vérifier…la pression artérielle

C. **take**…temperature
prendre…la température

D. **listen** to…heart
écouter…le cœur

E. **look** in…throat
examiner…la gorge

F. **examine**…eyes
examiner…les yeux

G. **draw**…blood
prélever…du sang

H. **get** an X ray
faire faire une radio/radiographie

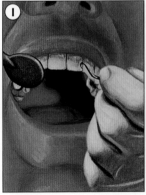

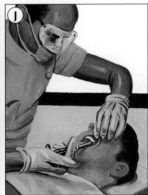

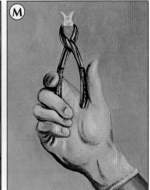

I. **clean**…teeth
nettoyer…les dents

J. **give**…a shot of anesthetic
donner…une injection d'anesthésique

K. **drill** a tooth
percer une dent

L. **fill** a cavity
boucher une carie

M. **pull** a tooth
arracher une dent

More vocabulary

get a checkup: to go for a medical exam

extract a tooth: to pull out a tooth

Share your answers.

1. What is the average cost of a medical exam in your area?

2. Some people are nervous at the dentist's office. What can they do to relax?

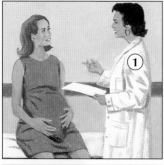

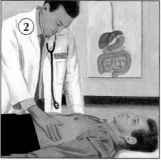

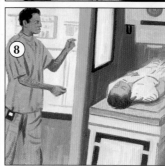

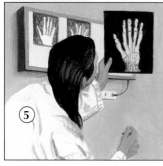
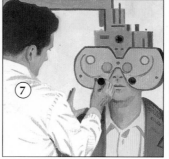
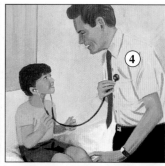

Hospital staff Personnel de l'hôpital

1. obstetrician
obstétricien(ne)

2. internist
interne

3. cardiologist
cardiologue

4. pediatrician
pédiatre

5. radiologist
radiologue

6. psychiatrist
psychiatre

7. ophthalmologist
ophtalmologiste / ophtalmologue /
oculiste

8. X-ray technician
technicien en radiologie

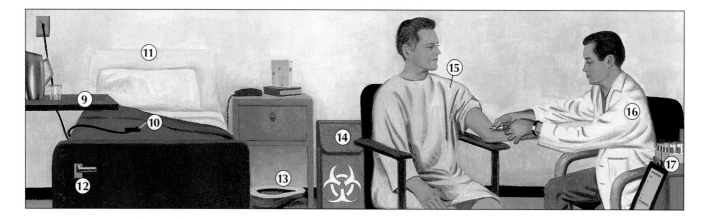

Patient's room Chambre du patient

9. bed table
table de chevet

10. call button
bouton d'appel

11. hospital bed
lit d'hôpital

12. bed control
commande de lit

13. bedpan
bassin de lit / bassine

14. medical waste disposal
dispositif d'évacuation des
déchets médicaux

15. hospital gown
chemise d'hôpital

16. lab technician
technicien de laboratoire

17. blood work / blood test
analyse sanguine

More vocabulary

nurse practitioner: a nurse licensed to give
medical exams

specialist: a doctor who only treats specific
medical problems

gynecologist: a specialist who examines and
treats women

nurse midwife: a nurse practitioner who examines
pregnant women and delivers babies

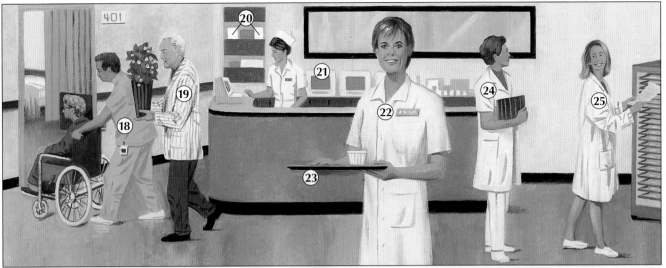

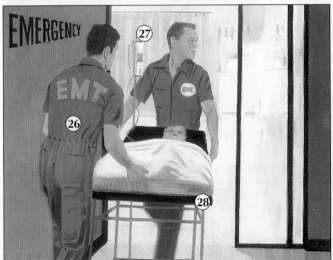

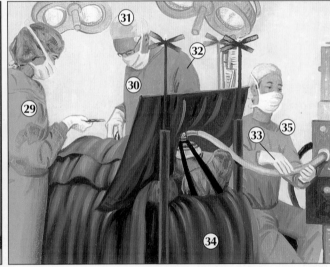

Nurse's station
Station / poste d'infirmier(ère)

18. orderly
aide soignant(e) / préposé(e) aux soins

19. volunteer
bénévole

20. medical charts
fiches médicales

21. vital signs monitor
moniteur de contrôle des
signes vitaux

22. RN (registered nurse)
infirmier(ière) diplômé(e)

23. medication tray
plateau à médicaments

24. LPN (licensed practical nurse) /
LVN (licensed vocational nurse)
infirmier(ière) auxiliaire autorisé(e) /
infirmier(ière) professionnell(e)
autorisé(e)

25. dietician
diététicien(ne)

Emergency room
Salle d'urgence

26. emergency medical technician
(EMT)
technicien d'urgence médicale

27. IV (intravenous drip)
I.V. (goutte-à-goutte intraveineux)

28. stretcher / gurney
civière / brancard / civière roulante

Operating room
Salle d'opération

29. surgical nurse
infirmier(ière) en chirurgie

30. surgeon
chirurgien(ne)

31. surgical cap
bonnet de chirurgien(ne)

32. surgical gown
blouse de chirurgien(ne)

33. latex gloves
gants de latex

34. operating table
table d'opération

35. anesthesiologist
anesthésiste

Practice asking for the hospital staff.

Please get the nurse. I have a question for her.
Where's the anesthesiologist? I need to talk to her.
I'm looking for the lab technician. Have you seen him?

Share your answers.

1. Have you ever been to an emergency room? Who
helped you?

2. Have you ever been in the hospital? How long did
you stay?

1. **fire station**
   caserne de pompiers

2. **coffee shop**
   café-restaurant

3. **bank**
   banque

4. **car dealership**
   concession d'automobiles

5. **hotel**
   hôtel

6. **church**
   église

7. **hospital**
   hôpital

8. **park**
   parc

9. **synagogue**
   synagogue

10. **theater**
    théâtre

11. **movie theater**
    cinéma

12. **gas station**
    station-service

13. **furniture store**
    magasin de meubles

14. **hardware store**
    quincaillerie

15. **barber shop**
    salon de coiffure / barbier

More vocabulary

skyscraper: a very tall office building

downtown / city center: the area in a city with the city hall, courts, and businesses

Practice giving your destination.

I'm going to go <u>downtown</u>.

I have to go to <u>the post office</u>.

16. bakery
boulangerie

17. city hall
hôtel de ville / mairie

18. courthouse
tribunal / palais de justice

19. police station
poste de police

20. market
marché

21. health club
club de (re)mise en forme /
club de santé

22. motel
motel

23. mosque
mosquée

24. office building
immeuble de bureaux

25. high-rise building
immeuble de grande hauteur /
gratte-ciel

26. parking garage
stationnement / parc de stationnement

27. school
école

28. library
bibliothèque

29. post office
poste

Practice asking for and giving the locations of buildings.

Where's <u>the post office</u>?

   It's on <u>Oak Street</u>.

Share your answers.

1. Which of the places in this picture do you go to every week?

2. Is it good to live in a city? Why or why not?

3. What famous cities do you know?

1. Laundromat
blanchisserie

2. drugstore / pharmacy
pharmacie

3. convenience store
dépanneur / commerce de proximité

4. photo shop
magasin de photo

5. parking space
place de stationnement

6. traffic light
feu de signalisation /
feu de circulation

7. pedestrian
piéton

8. crosswalk
passage pour piétons

9. street
rue

10. curb
bord du trottoir

11. newsstand
kiosque à journaux

12. mailbox
boîte aux lettres

13. drive-thru window
service au volant / service à l'auto

14. fast food restaurant
restaurant-minute / prêt-à-manger

15. bus
autobus

A. **cross** the street
traverser la rue

B. **wait** for the light
attendre le changement de feu /
de lumière

C. **drive** a car
conduire une automobile

More vocabulary

neighborhood: the area close to your home

do errands: to make a short trip from your home to buy
or pick up something

Talk about where to buy things.

You can buy <u>newspapers</u> at <u>a newsstand</u>.

You can buy <u>donuts</u> at <u>a donut shop</u>.

You can buy <u>food</u> at <u>a convenience store</u>.

16. bus stop
    arrêt d'autobus

17. corner
    coin

18. parking meter
    parc-mètre / parcomètre

19. motorcycle
    moto

20. donut shop
    beignerie

21. public telephone
    téléphone public

22. copy center / print shop
    centre de reprographie

23. streetlight
    réverbère

24. dry cleaners
    nettoyeur / teinturerie / pressing

25. nail salon
    centre de manucure

26. sidewalk
    trottoir

27. garbage truck
    camion à ordures

28. fire hydrant
    bouche d'incendie

29. sign
    panneau de signalisation

30. street vendor
    vendeur ambulant

31. cart
    chariot

D. **park** the car
   stationner l'auto

E. **ride** a bicycle
   rouler en vélo

Share your answers.

1. Do you like to do errands?

2. Do you always like to go to the same stores?

3. Which businesses in the picture are also in your neighborhood?

4. Do you know someone who has a small business? What kind?

5. What things can you buy from a street vendor?

A Mall Un centre commercial

1. music store
magasin de musique

2. jewelry store
bijouterie

3. candy store
confiserie

4. bookstore
librairie

5. toy store
magasin de jouets

6. pet store
animalerie

7. card store
magasin de cartes

8. optician
opticien

9. travel agency
agence de voyage

10. shoe store
magasin de chaussures

11. fountain
fontaine

12. florist
fleuriste

More vocabulary

beauty shop: hair salon

men's store: a store that sells men's clothing

dress shop: a store that sells women's clothing

Talk about where you want to shop in this mall.

Let's go to <u>the card store</u>.

I need to buy <u>a card</u> for Maggie's birthday.

13. department store grand magasin	**17.** maternity shop boutique de maternité	**21.** escalator escalier mécanique
14. food court aire de restauration	**18.** electronics store magasin d'électronique	**22.** information booth kiosque d'information
15. video store club vidéo	**19.** directory tableau d'information	
16. hair salon salon de coiffure	**20.** ice cream stand stand de crème glacée	

Practice asking for and giving the location of different shops.

Where's <u>the maternity shop</u>?

  It's on <u>the first floor</u>, next to <u>the hair salon</u>.

Share your answers.

1. Do you like shopping malls? Why or why not?

2. Some people don't go to the mall to shop.
Name some other things you can do in a mall.

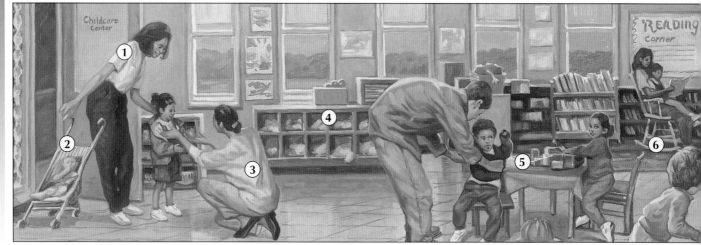

1. parent
parent

2. stroller
poussette

3. childcare worker
éducatrice (éducateur) en garderie

4. cubby
casier de rangement

5. toys
jouets

6. rocking chair
berceuse

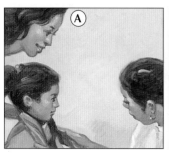

A. drop off
déposer

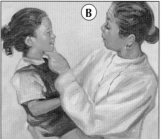

B. hold
tenir

C. nurse
allaiter

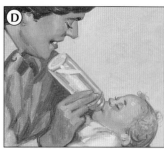

D. feed
nourrir

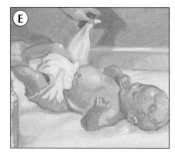

E. change diapers
changer les couches

F. read a story
lire une histoire

G. pick up
soulever

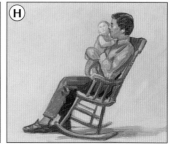

H. rock
bercer

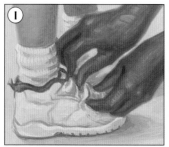

I. tie shoes
attacher les lacets
(des souliers)

J. dress
habiller

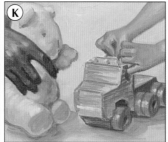

K. play
jouer

L. take a nap
faire une sieste

7. high chair
chaise haute

8. bib
bavette

9. changing table
table à langer

10. potty seat
pot

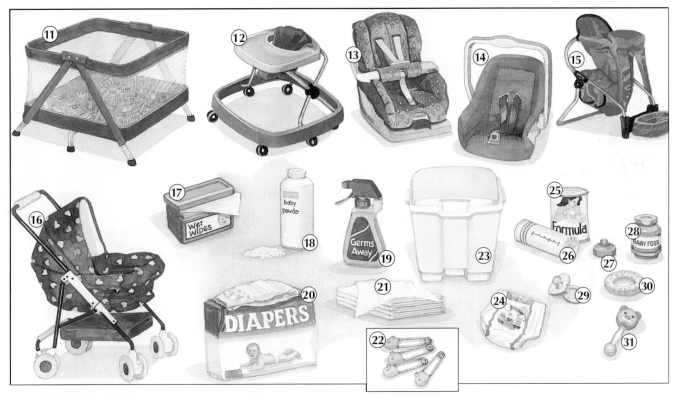

11. playpen
parc

12. walker
trotte-bébé / marchette

13. car safety seat
siège de sécurité pour enfant

14. baby carrier
porte-bébé

15. baby backpack
sac à dos pour bébé

16. carriage
poussette

17. wipes
serviettes humides pour bébés

18. baby powder
poudre pour bébés

19. disinfectant
désinfectant

20. disposable diapers
couches jetables

21. cloth diapers
couches lavables

22. diaper pins
épingles à couche

23. diaper pail
seau à couches

24. training pants
culottes de propreté

25. formula
lait maternisé

26. bottle
biberon

27. nipple
tétine

28. baby food
aliments pour bébés

29. pacifier
sucette

30. teething ring
anneau de bébé qui perce ses dents

31. rattle
hochet

1. envelope
enveloppe

2. letter
lettre

3. postcard
carte postale

4. greeting card
carte de vœux

5. package
paquet

6. letter carrier
facteur

7. return address
adresse de retour

8. mailing address
adresse postale

9. postmark
cachet de la poste

10. stamp/postage
timbre

11. certified mail
envoi certifié

12. priority mail
courrier prioritaire

13. air letter/aerogramme
aérogramme

14. ground post/
parcel post
colis postal

15. Express Mail/
overnight mail
courrier express/
livraison le lendemain

A. **address** a postcard
adresser une carte postale

B. **send** it/**mail** it
l'**envoyer**/l'**expédier**
par courrier

C. **deliver** it
le/la **livrer**

D. **receive** it
le/la **recevoir**

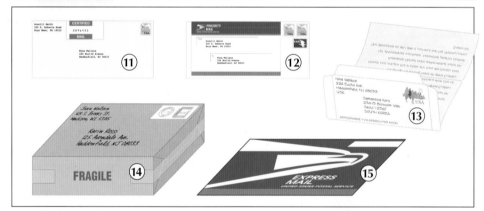

Emily Rose
1543 Oak Lane
Springvale, CA 91254
⑦

SPRINGVALE
5-7-99
CA
⑨

USA
⑩

Alyson Shepard
249 Courtney Drive
Newton, NY 10043
⑧

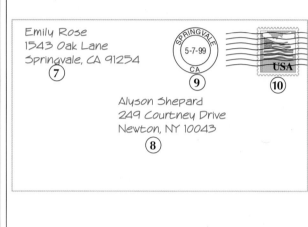

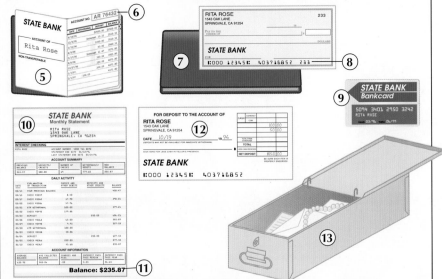

1. teller
   caissier (caissière)
2. vault
   chambre forte
3. ATM (automated teller machine)
   guichet automatique
4. security guard
   garde de sécurité

5. passbook
   livret
6. savings account number
   numéro de compte d'épargne
7. checkbook
   chéquier
8. checking account number
   numéro de compte de chèque
9. ATM card
   carte de retrait
10. monthly statement
    relevé mensuel
11. balance
    solde
12. deposit slip
    bordereau de dépôt
13. safe-deposit box
    coffre-fort

Using the ATM machine *Utilisation du guichet automatique*

A. **Insert** your ATM card.
   Introduire votre carte de retrait.
B. **Enter** your PIN number.*
   Saisir le code confidentiel.
C. **Make** a deposit.
   Faire un dépôt.
D. **Withdraw** cash.
   Retirer de l'argent.
E. **Transfer** funds.
   Transférer des fonds.
F. **Remove** your ATM card.
   Retirer la carte de retrait.

*PIN: personal identification number

More vocabulary

overdrawn account: When there is not enough money in an account to pay a check, we say the account is overdrawn.

Share your answers.

1. Do you use a bank?
2. Do you use an ATM card?
3. Name some things you can put in a safe-deposit box.

1. **reference librarian**
   bibliothécaire des
   ouvrages de référence

2. **reference desk**
   service de consultation

3. **atlas**
   atlas

4. **microfilm reader**
   lecteur de microfilm

5. **microfilm**
   microfilm

6. **periodical section**
   section des périodiques

7. **magazine**
   magazine

8. **newspaper**
   journal

9. **online catalog**
   catalogue en ligne

10. **card catalog**
    catalogue sur fiches

11. **media section**
    section des médias

12. **audiocassette**
    audiocassette

13. **videocassette**
    vidéocassette

14. **CD (compact disc)**
    disque compact

15. **record**
    disque

16. **checkout desk**
    comptoir
    d'enregistrement

17. **library clerk**
    bibliothécaire

18. **encyclopedia**
    encyclopédie

19. **library card**
    carte de bibliothèque

20. **library book**
    livre de bibliothèque

21. **title**
    titre

22. **author**
    auteur

More vocabulary

check a book out: to borrow a book from the library

nonfiction: real information, history or true stories

fiction: stories from the author's imagination

Share your answers.

1. Do you have a library card?

2. Do you prefer to buy books or borrow them from
   the library?

A. arrest a suspect
arrêter un suspect

1. police officer
agent de police

2. handcuffs
menottes

B. hire a lawyer / **hire** an attorney
embaucher un avocat

3. guard
gardien

4. defense attorney
avocat de la défense

C. appear in court
se présenter en cour

5. defendant
accusé

6. judge
juge

D. stand trial
subir un procès

7. courtroom
salle d'audience

8. jury
jury

9. evidence
preuves

10. prosecuting attorney
procureur

11. witness
témoin

12. court reporter
greffier de la cour

13. bailiff
huissier

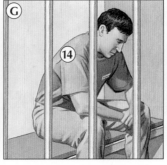

E. give the verdict*
rendre un verdict

F. sentence the defendant
condamner l'accusé

G. go to jail / **go** to prison
aller en prison

14. convict
détenu(e)

H. be released
être relâché

*****Note:** There are two possible verdicts, "guilty" and "not guilty."

Share your answers.

1. What are some differences between the legal system in the United States and the one in your country?

2. Do you want to be on a jury? Why or why not?

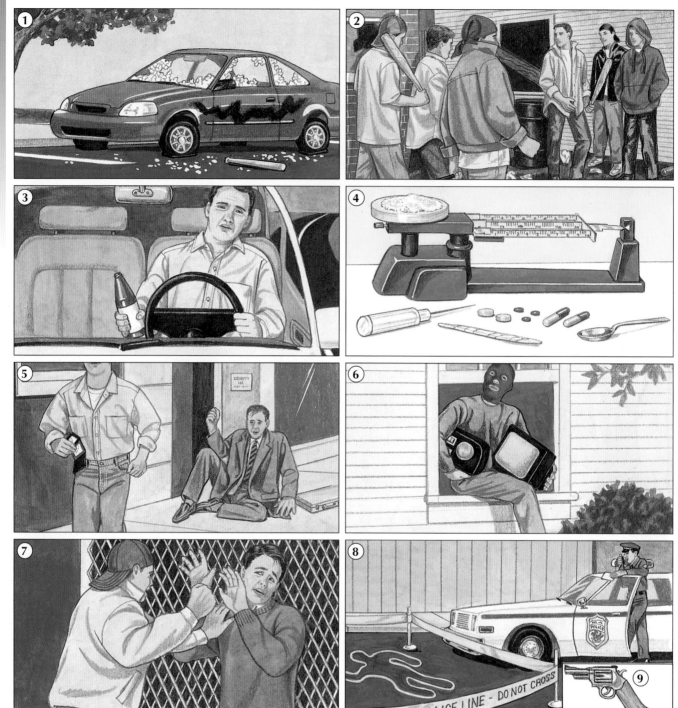

1. **vandalism**
   vandalisme

2. **gang violence**
   violence des gangs

3. **drunk driving**
   conduite en état d'ivresse

4. **illegal drugs**
   drogues illégales

5. **mugging**
   vol et agression

6. **burglary**
   cambriolage

7. **assault**
   agression

8. **murder**
   meurtre

9. **gun**
   pistolet

More vocabulary

commit a crime: to do something illegal

criminal: someone who commits a crime

victim: someone who is hurt or killed by someone else

Share your answers.

1. Is there too much crime on TV? in the movies?

2. Do you think people become criminals from watching crime on TV?

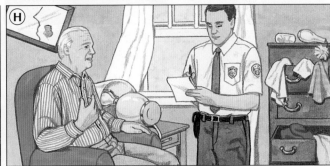

A. **Walk** with a friend.
Marcher avec un ami.

B. **Stay** on well-lit streets.
Aller dans les rues bien éclairées.

C. **Hold** your purse close to your body.
Garder son sac près du corps.

D. **Protect** your wallet.
Protéger son portefeuille.

E. **Lock** your doors.
Verrouiller vos portes.

F. **Don't open** your door to strangers.
Ne pas ouvrir la porte à des étrangers.

G. **Don't drink** and **drive**.
Ne pas boire et conduire.

H. **Report** crimes to the police.
Signaler les crimes à la police.

More vocabulary

Neighborhood Watch: a group of neighbors who watch for criminals in their neighborhood

designated drivers: people who don't drink alcoholic beverages so that they can drive drinkers home

Share your answers.

1. Do you feel safe in your neighborhood?

2. Look at the pictures. Which of these things do you do?

3. What other things do you do to stay safe?

1. lost child
enfant perdu

2. car accident
accident d'automobile

3. airplane crash
écrasement d'avion

4. explosion
explosion

5. earthquake
tremblement de terre

6. mudslide
coulée de boue

7. fire
incendie

8. firefighter
pompier

9. fire truck
camion de pompiers

Practice reporting a fire.

This is <u>Lisa Broad</u>. There is a fire.

The address is <u>323 Oak Street</u>.

Please send someone quickly.

Share your answers.

1. Can you give directions to your home if there is a fire?

2. What information do you give to the other driver if you are in a car accident?

10. drought
sécheresse

11. blizzard
blizzard

12. hurricane
ouragan

13. tornado
tornade

14. volcanic eruption
éruption volcanique

15. tidal wave
raz-de-marée

16. flood
inondation

17. search and rescue team
équipe de recherche et sauvetage

Share your answers.

1. Which disasters are common in your area? Which never happen?

2. What can you do to prepare for emergencies?

3. Do you have emergency numbers near your telephone?

4. What organizations will help you in an emergency?

1. bus stop
arrêt d'autobus

2. route
trajet

3. schedule
horaire

4. bus
autobus

5. fare
tarif

6. transfer
transfert

7. passenger
passager

8. bus driver
chauffeur d'autobus

9. subway
métro

10. track
rails

11. token
jeton

12. fare card
carte d'abonnement

13. train station
gare

14. ticket
ticket

15. platform
passerelle

16. conductor
conducteur

17. train
train

18. taxi / cab
taxi

19. taxi stand
station de taxis

20. taxi driver
chauffeur de taxi

21. meter
compteur

22. taxi license
licence de taxi

23. ferry
ferry

More vocabulary

hail a taxi: to get a taxi driver's attention by raising your hand

miss the bus: to arrive at the bus stop late

Talk about how you and your friends come to school.

I take _the bus_ to school.

You take _the train_.

We take _the subway_.

He _drives_ to school.

She _walks_ to school.

They _ride_ bikes.

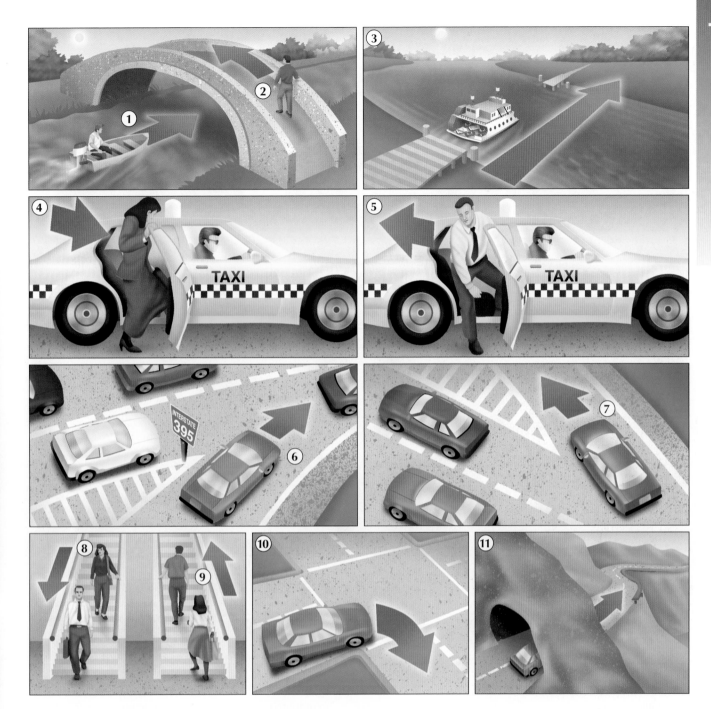

1. **under** the bridge
   sous le pont

2. **over** the bridge
   sur le pont

3. **across** the water
   traversée de la voie fluviale

4. **into** the taxi
   dans le taxi

5. **out of** the taxi
   hors du taxi

6. **onto** the highway
   sur l'autoroute

7. **off** the highway
   quitter l'autoroute

8. **down** the stairs
   au bas de l'escalier

9. **up** the stairs
   en haut de l'escalier

10. **around** the corner
    autour du coin

11. **through** the tunnel
    à travers le tunnel

Grammar point: *into, out of, on, off*

We say, *get **into** a taxi or a car.*

But we say, *get **on** a bus, a train, or a plane.*

We say, *get **out of** a taxi or a car.*

But we say, *get **off** a bus, a train, or a plane.*

Cars and Trucks Voitures et camions

1. subcompact
sous-compacte

2. compact
compacte

3. midsize car
voiture moyenne

4. full-size car
grosse voiture

5. convertible
décapotable

6. sports car
voiture de sport

7. pickup truck
camionnette

8. station wagon
familiale/break

9. SUV (sports utility
vehicle)
véhicule utilitaire sport

10. minivan
mini-fourgonnette/
monospace

11. camper
camping-car

12. dump truck
camion à benne

13. tow truck
dépanneuse

14. moving van
fourgon de
déménagement

15. tractor trailer/semi
camion semi-remorque

16. cab
cabine

17. trailer
remorque

More vocabulary

make: the name of the company that makes the car

model: the style of car

Share your answers.

1. What is your favorite kind of car?

2. What kind of car is good for a big family? for a
single person?

Directions Trajet

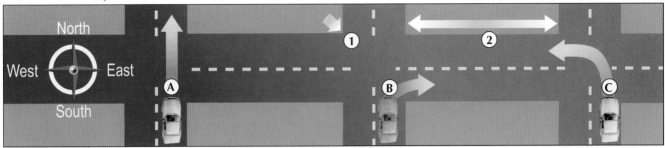

A. go straight
aller tout droit

B. turn right
tourner à droite

C. turn left
tourner à gauche

1. corner
coin

2. block
pâté

Signs Panneaux

3. stop
stop / arrêt

4. do not enter / wrong way
ne pas entrer / sens interdit

5. speed limit
limite de vitesse

6. one way
voie à sens unique

7. U-turn OK
demi-tour autorisé

8. no outlet / dead end
sans issue / cul-de-sac

9. right turn only
tourner à droite seulement

10. pedestrian crossing
passages pour piétons

11. railroad crossing
passage à niveau

12. no parking
stationnement interdit

13. school crossing
passage pour écoliers

14. handicapped parking
stationnement pour
personnes handicapées

More vocabulary

right-of-way: the right to go first

yield: to give another person or car the right-of-way

Share your answers.

1. Which traffic signs are the same in your country?

2. Do pedestrians have the right-of-way in your city?

3. What is the speed limit in front of your school?
your home?

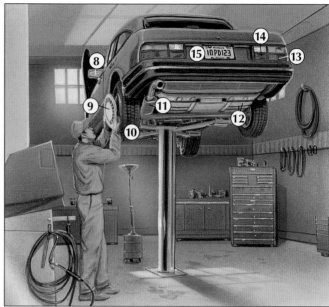

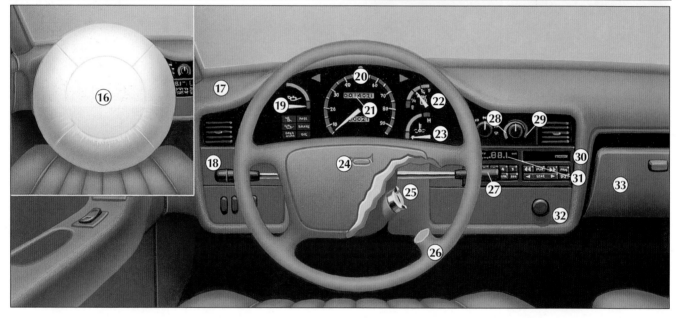

1. rearview mirror
rétroviseur

2. windshield
pare-brise

3. windshield wipers
essuie-glaces

4. turn signal
clignotant

5. headlight
phare

6. hood
capot

7. bumper
pare-chocs

8. sideview mirror
rétroviseur extérieur
(latéral)

9. hubcap
enjoliveur de roue

10. tire
pneu

11. muffler
silencieux

12. gas tank
réservoir d'essence

13. brake light
feu de frein

14. taillight
feu arrière

15. license plate
plaque d'immatriculation

16. air bag
coussin gonflable

17. dashboard
tableau de bord

18. turn signal
clignotant

19. oil gauge
jauge d'huile

20. speedometer
compteur de vitesse

21. odometer
odomètre/compteur
kilométrique

22. gas gauge
jauge d'essence

23. temperature gauge
indicateur de température
du moteur

24. horn
klaxon

25. ignition
allumage

26. steering wheel
volant

27. gearshift
levier de vitesses

28. air conditioning
climatiseur

29. heater
appareil de chauffage

30. tape deck
platine-cassettes

31. radio
radio

32. cigarette lighter
allume-cigares

33. glove compartment
coffre à gant

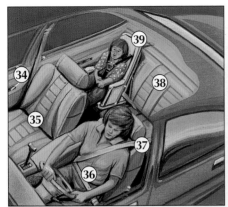
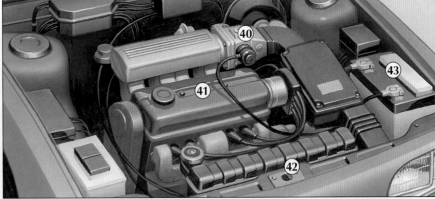

34. lock
    verrou

35. front seat
    siège avant

36. seat belt
    ceinture de sécurité

37. shoulder harness
    harnais d'épaule

38. backseat
    siège arrière

39. child safety seat
    siège de sécurité pour enfant

40. fuel injection system
    système d'injection de carburant

41. engine
    moteur

42. radiator
    radiateur

43. battery
    batterie

44. emergency brake
    frein

45. clutch*
    embrayage

46. brake pedal
    pédale de frein

47. accelerator / gas pedal
    pédale d'accélérateur

48. stick shift
    levier de vitesse au plancher

49. trunk
    coffre

50. lug wrench
    démonte-roue

51. jack
    cric

52. jumper cables
    câbles de démarrage

53. spare tire
    pneu de secours

54. The car needs **gas**.
    La voiture a besoin d'**essence**.

55. The car needs **oil**.
    La voiture a besoin d'**huile**.

56. The radiator needs **coolant**.
    Le radiateur a besoin de **liquide de refroidissement**.

57. The car needs **a smog check**.
    La voiture a besoin d'un **contrôle de smog**.

58. The battery needs **recharging**.
    La batterie a besoin d'être **rechargée**.

59. The tires need **air**.
    Les pneus ont besoin de **pression**.

*Note: Standard transmission cars have a clutch; automatic transmission cars do not.

1. airline terminal
aérogare

2. airline representative
représentant de compagnie aérienne

3. check-in counter
comptoir d'enregistrement

4. arrival and departure monitors
écrans d'arrivée et de départ

5. gate
porte (d'embarquement)

6. boarding area
zone d'embarquement

7. control tower
tour de contrôle

8. helicopter
hélicoptère

9. airplane
avion

10. overhead compartment
compartiment à bagages

11. cockpit
poste de pilotage

12. pilot
pilote

13. flight attendant
agent(e) de bord

14. oxygen mask
masque d'oxygène

15. airsickness bag
sac vomitoire

16. tray table
tablette

17. baggage claim area
zone de récupération des bagages

18. carousel
carrousel

19. luggage carrier
porte-bagages

20. customs
douanes

21. customs officer
douanier (douanière)

22. declaration form
formulaire de déclaration

23. passenger
passager

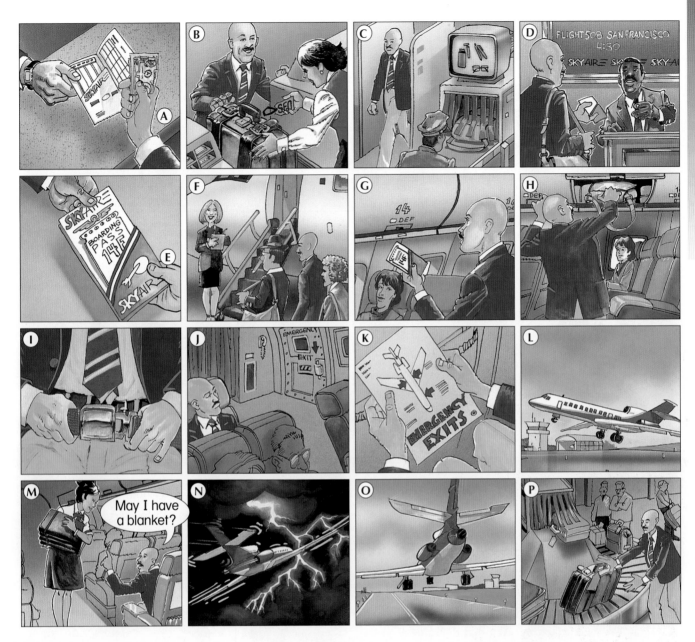

A. **buy** your ticket
   acheter votre billet

B. **check** your bags
   enregistrer vos bagages

C. **go through** security
   passer au contrôle de sécurité

D. **check in** at the gate
   se présenter à la porte
   d'embarquement

E. **get** your boarding pass
   recevoir une carte d'embarquement

F. **board** the plane
   monter à bord de l'avion

G. **find** your seat
   chercher le siège

H. **stow** your carry-on bag
   ranger les bagages à main

I. **fasten** your seat belt
   mettre la ceinture de sécurité

J. **look for** the emergency exit
   repérer la sortie de secours

K. **look at** the emergency card
   examiner la carte de mesures de
   sécurité

L. **take off / leave**
   décoller

M. **request** a blanket
   demander une couverture

N. **experience** turbulence
   traverser une zone de turbulence

O. **land / arrive**
   atterrir / arriver

P. **claim** your baggage
   chercher vos bagages

More vocabulary

destination: the place the passenger is going

departure time: the time the plane takes off

arrival time: the time the plane lands

direct flight: a plane trip between two cities with no stops

stopover: a stop before reaching the destination,
sometimes to change planes

1. public school
école publique

2. private school
école privée

3. parochial school
école paroissiale

4. preschool
établissement préscolaire

5. elementary school
école élémentaire /
primaire

6. middle school /
junior high school
collège

7. high school
lycée

8. adult school
centre d'éducation (de formation)
des adultes / centre de formation
continue (permanente)

9. vocational school / trade school
école professionnelle /
école de métiers

10. college / university
collège / université

Note: In the U.S. most children begin school at age 5 (in kindergarten)
and graduate from high school at 17 or 18.

More vocabulary

When students graduate from a college or university
they receive a **degree**:

Bachelor's degree—usually 4 years of study

Master's degree—an additional 1–3 years of study

Doctorate—an additional 3–5 years of study

community college: a two-year college where students
can get an Associate of Arts degree

graduate school: a school in a university where students
study for their master's degrees and doctorates

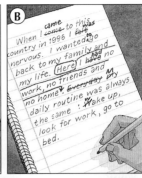

> I like that part about your family.

1. writing assignment
devoir de rédaction

A. Write a first draft.
Rédiger une version
préliminaire.

B. Edit your paper.
Corriger le texte.

C. Get feedback.
Recevoir des
commentaires.

D. Rewrite your paper.
Rédiger au propre.

E. Turn in your paper.
Rendre la rédaction.

2. paper / composition
rédaction / composition

My life in the U.S.

I arrived in this country in 1996. My family did not come with me. I was homesick, nervous, and a little excited. I had no job and no friends here. I lived with my aunt and my daily routine was always the same: get up, look for a job, go to bed. At night I remembered my mother's words to me, "Son, you can always come home!" I was homesick and scared, but I did not go home.

I started to study English at night. English is a difficult language and many times I was too tired to study. One teacher, Mrs. Armstrong, was very kind to me. She showed me many

3. title
titre

4. sentence
phrase

5. paragraph
paragraphe

Punctuation Ponctuation

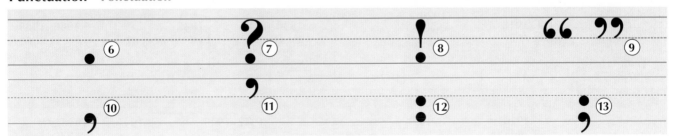

6. period
point

7. question mark
point d'interrogation

8. exclamation mark
point d'exclamation

9. quotation marks
guillemets

10. comma
virgule

11. apostrophe
apostrophe

12. colon
deux points

13. semicolon
point virgule

Exploration

War

Immigration

Historical and Political Events Evénements historiques et politiques	**1492 →** French, Spanish, English explorers Explorateurs français, espagnols et anglais	**1607–1750** Colonies along Atlantic coast founded by Northern Europeans Colonies le long de la côte atlantique fondées par les nord-européens	**1619** 1st African slave sold in Virginia Premier esclave africain vendu en Virginie **1653** 1st Indian reservation in Virginia Première réserve indienne en Virginie

Before 1700 Avant 1700 | **1700**

Immigration* Immigration	**1607** 1st English in Virginia Premiers Anglais en Virginie	**1610** Spanish at Santa Fe Les Espagnols à Santa Fé	

Population**
Population | Before 1700: Native American: 1,000,000+
Avant 1700   Amérindiens/Autochtones d'Amérique du Nord : 1 000 000+ | 1700: colonists: 250,000
colons : 250 000

1803 Louisiana Purchase Achat de la Louisiane	**1812** War of 1812 Guerre de 1812	**1820** Missouri Compromise Compromis du Missouri	**1830** Indian Removal Act Loi sur le Déplacement des Indiens	**1835–1838** Cherokee Trail of Tears Chemin des larmes des Cherokee	**1846–1848** U.S. war with Mexico Guerre des Etats-Unis contre le Mexique

1800 | 1810 | 1820 | 1830 | 1840

1815 →
Irish
Irlandais

1800: citizens and free blacks: 5,300,000
citoyens et noirs affranchis : 5 300 000 | slaves: 450,000
esclaves : 450 000

1903 1st *Model A* Ford car Premier *modèle A* de Ford	**1927** 1st sound pictures Premières images sonores	**1929** stock market crashes krach boursier	**1939–1945** World War II Deuxième guerre mondiale	**1945** United Nations Nations Unies

1st air flight
Premier vol en avion | **1914–1918**
World War I
Première Guerre mondiale | **1920**
women get vote
les femmes obtiennent le droit de vote | **1930–1940**
The Depression
La grande dépression | **1945**
1st atomic bomb
Première bombe atomique | **1948–1985**
The Cold War
La Guerre Froide

1900 | 1910 | 1920 | 1930 | 1940

1910 →
Mexicans
Mexicains | **1924**
U.S. closes borders
Les Etats-Unis ferment les frontières | **1942–1945**
Japanese internment
Internement des japonais | **1945 →**
Puerto Ricans
Porto-ricains | **1948**
WW II refugees immigrate
Immigration des réfugiés de la Seconde Guerre mondi

1900: 75,994,000

*Immigration dates indicate a time when large numbers of that group first began to immigrate to the U.S.
**All population figures before 1790 are estimates. Figures after 1790 are based on the official U.S. census.

Movement

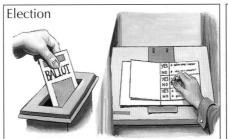

Election

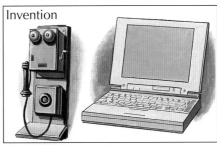

Invention

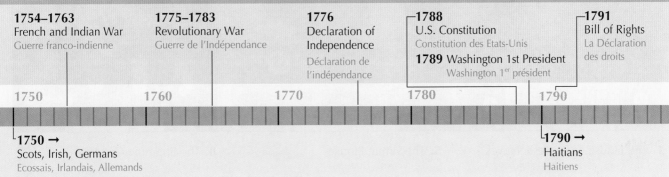

1754–1763
French and Indian War
Guerre franco-indienne

1775–1783
Revolutionary War
Guerre de l'Indépendance

1776
Declaration of Independence
Déclaration de l'indépendance

1788
U.S. Constitution
Constitution des Etats-Unis

1789 Washington 1st President
Washington 1er président

1791
Bill of Rights
La Déclaration des droits

1750   1760   1770   1780   1790

1750 →
Scots, Irish, Germans
Ecossais, Irlandais, Allemands

1790 →
Haitians
Haitiens

1750: Native American: 1,000,000 +
Autochtones d'Amérique du Nord : 1 000 000 +

colonists and free blacks: 1,171,000
colons et noirs affranchis : 1 171 000

slaves: 200,000
esclaves : 200 000

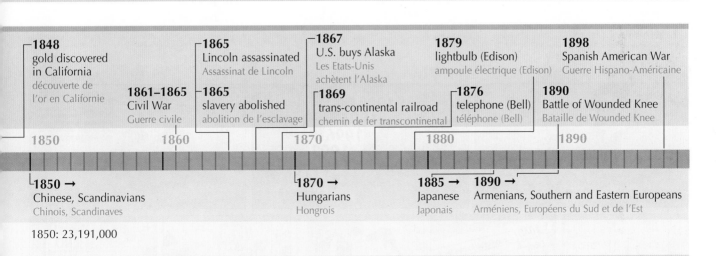

1848
gold discovered in California
découverte de l'or en Californie

1861–1865
Civil War
Guerre civile

1865
Lincoln assassinated
Assassinat de Lincoln

1865
slavery abolished
abolition de l'esclavage

1867
U.S. buys Alaska
Les Etats-Unis achètent l'Alaska

1869
trans-continental railroad
chemin de fer transcontinental

1879
lightbulb (Edison)
ampoule électrique (Edison)

1876
telephone (Bell)
téléphone (Bell)

1898
Spanish American War
Guerre Hispano-Américaine

1890
Battle of Wounded Knee
Bataille de Wounded Knee

1850   1860   1870   1880   1890

1850 →
Chinese, Scandinavians
Chinois, Scandinaves

1870 →
Hungarians
Hongrois

1885 →
Japanese
Japonais

1890 →
Armenians, Southern and Eastern Europeans
Arméniens, Européens du Sud et de l'Est

1850: 23,191,000

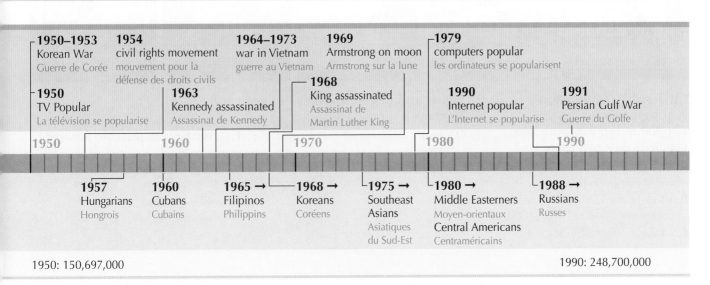

1950–1953
Korean War
Guerre de Corée

1950
TV Popular
La télévision se popularise

1954
civil rights movement
mouvement pour la défense des droits civils

1963
Kennedy assassinated
Assassinat de Kennedy

1964–1973
war in Vietnam
guerre au Vietnam

1968
King assassinated
Assassinat de Martin Luther King

1969
Armstrong on moon
Armstrong sur la lune

1979
computers popular
les ordinateurs se popularisent

1990
Internet popular
L'Internet se popularise

1991
Persian Gulf War
Guerre du Golfe

1950   1960   1970   1980   1990

1957
Hungarians
Hongrois

1960
Cubans
Cubains

1965 →
Filipinos
Philippins

1968 →
Koreans
Coréens

1975 →
Southeast Asians
Asiatiques du Sud-Est

1980 →
Middle Easterners
Moyen-orientaux
Central Americans
Centraméricains

1988 →
Russians
Russes

1950: 150,697,000

1990: 248,700,000

BRANCHES OF GOVERNMENT

Legislative

Executive

Judicial

1. The House of Representatives
   La Chambre des Représentants

2. congresswoman / congressman
   membre du Congrès

3. The Senate
   Le Sénat

4. senator
   sénateur / sénatrice

5. The White House
   La Maison Blanche

6. president
   président

7. vice president
   vice-président

8. The Supreme Court
   La Cour suprême

9. chief justice
   président de la Court Suprême

10. justices
    juges

Citizenship application requirements
Conditions requises pour une demande de citoyenneté

A. **be** 18 years old
   être âgé de 18 ans

B. **live** in the U.S. for five years
   vivre aux Etats-Unis pendant cinq ans

C. **take** a citizenship test
   passer l'examen de citoyenneté

Rights and responsibilities
Droits et responsabilités

D. **vote**
   voter

E. **pay** taxes
   payer les impôts

F. **register** with Selective Service*
   s'inscrire au Service Sélectif

G. **serve** on a jury
   siéger sur un jury

H. **obey** the law
   respecter les lois

*Note: All males 18 to 26 who live in the U.S. are required to register with Selective Service.

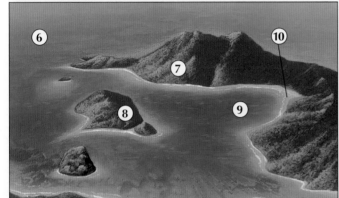

1. rain forest
forêt pluviale

2. waterfall
cascade

3. river
rivière

4. desert
désert

5. sand dune
dune de sable

6. ocean
océan

7. peninsula
péninsule

8. island
île

9. bay
baie

10. beach
plage

11. forest
forêt

12. shore
rivage

13. lake
lac

14. mountain peak
sommet de montagne

15. mountain range
chaîne de montagnes

16. hills
collines

17. canyon
canyon

18. valley
vallée

19. plains
plaines

20. meadow
pré

21. pond
étang

More vocabulary

a body of water: a river, lake, or ocean

stream/creek: a very small river

Talk about where you live and where you like to go.

I live in a valley. There is a lake nearby.

I like to go to the beach.

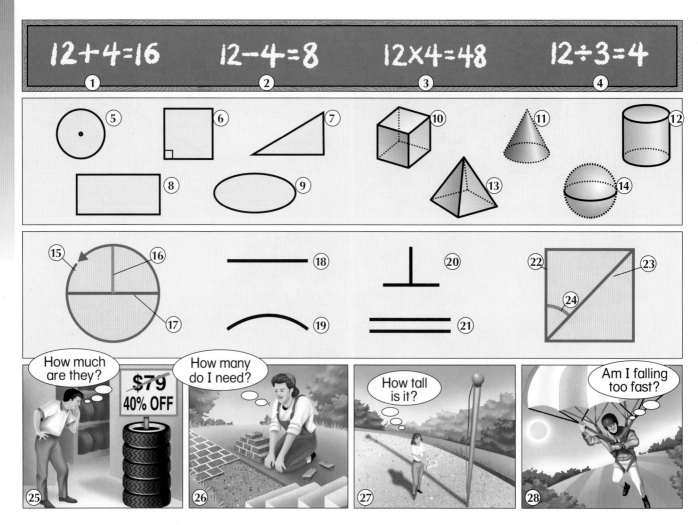

Operations
Opérations

1. addition
addition

2. subtraction
soustraction

3. multiplication
multiplication

4. division
division

Shapes
Formes

5. circle
cercle

6. square
carré

7. triangle
triangle

8. rectangle
rectangle

9. oval / ellipse
ovale / ellipse

Solids
Solides

10. cube
cube

11. cone
cône

12. cylinder
cylindre

13. pyramid
pyramide

14. sphere
sphère

Parts of a circle
Parties d'un cercle

15. circumference
circonférence

16. radius
rayon

17. diameter
diamètre

Lines
Lignes

18. straight
droite

19. curved
courbe

20. perpendicular
perpendiculaire

21. parallel
parallèle

Parts of a square
Parties d'un carré

22. side
côté

23. diagonal
diagonale

24. angle
angle

Types of math
Types de mathématiques

25. algebra
algèbre

26. geometry
géométrie

27. trigonometry
trigonométrie

28. calculus
calcul

More vocabulary

total: the answer to an addition problem

difference: the answer to a subtraction problem

product: the answer to a multiplication problem

quotient: the answer to a division problem

pi (π): the number when you divide the circumference of a circle by its diameter (approximately = 3.14)

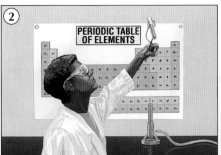

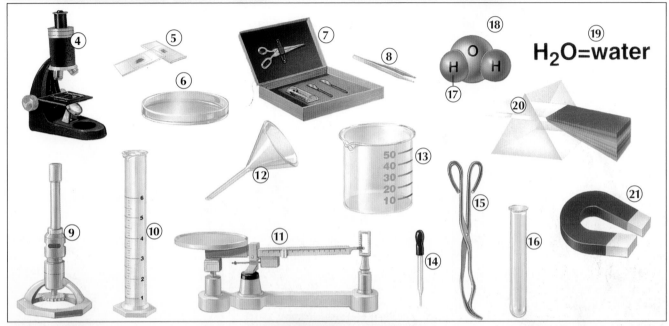

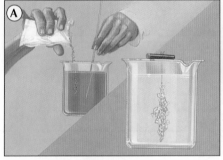

H₂O=water

1. biology
   biologie

2. chemistry
   chimie

3. physics
   physique

4. microscope
   microscope

5. slide
   règle

6. petri dish
   boîte de Pétri

7. dissection kit
   trousse à dissection

8. forceps
   forceps

9. Bunsen burner
   brûleur Bensen / bec Bensen

10. graduated cylinder
    cylindre gradué / éprouvette graduée

11. balance
    balance

12. funnel
    entonnoir

13. beaker
    bécher

14. dropper
    compte-gouttes

15. crucible tongs
    pince à creusets

16. test tube
    éprouvette

17. atom
    atome

18. molecule
    molécule

19. formula
    formule

20. prism
    prisme

21. magnet
    aimant

A. **do** an experiment
   faire une expérience

B. **observe**
   observer

C. **record** results
   enregistrer les résultats

A. **play** an instrument
jouer d'un instrument

B. **sing** a song
chanter une chanson

1. orchestra
orchestre

2. rock band
groupe de rock

Woodwinds

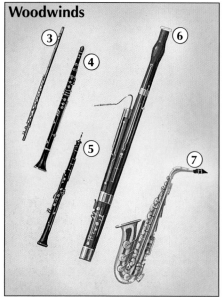

Strings

Brass

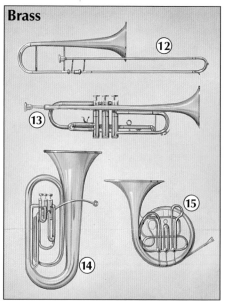

Percussion

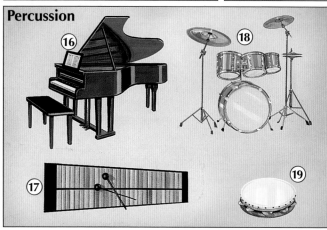

Other Instruments

3. flute
flûte

4. clarinet
clarinette

5. oboe
hautbois

6. bassoon
basson

7. saxophone
saxophone

8. violin
violon

9. cello
violoncelle

10. bass
contrebasse

11. guitar
guitare

12. trombone
trombone

13. trumpet / horn
trompette

14. tuba
tuba

15. French horn
cor d'harmonie / cor
français

16. piano
piano

17. xylophone
xylophone

18. drums
batterie

19. tambourine
tambourine

20. electric keyboard
clavier électrique

21. accordion
accordéon

22. organ
orgue

STUDENT DRIVER

Profit Margin

It's a chair.

C'est une chaise.

1. art
art

2. business education
études commerciales (de commerce)

3. chorus
chorale

4. computer science
informatique

5. driver's education
cours de conduite

6. economics
économie

7. English as a second language
Anglais en tant que seconde langue

8. foreign language
langue étrangère

9. home economics
économie domestique

10. industrial arts/shop
arts industriels/atelier

11. PE (physical education)
éducation physique

12. theater arts
arts de la scène

More vocabulary

core course: a subject students have to take

elective: a subject students choose to take

Share your answers.

1. What are your favorite subjects?

2. In your opinion, what subjects are most important? Why?

3. What foreign languages are taught in your school?

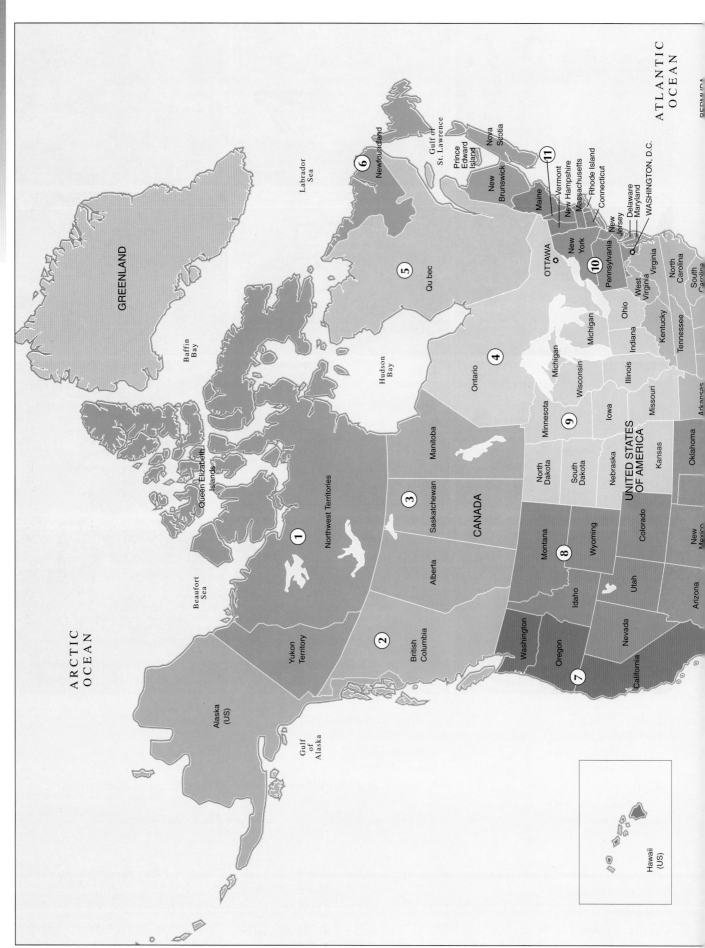

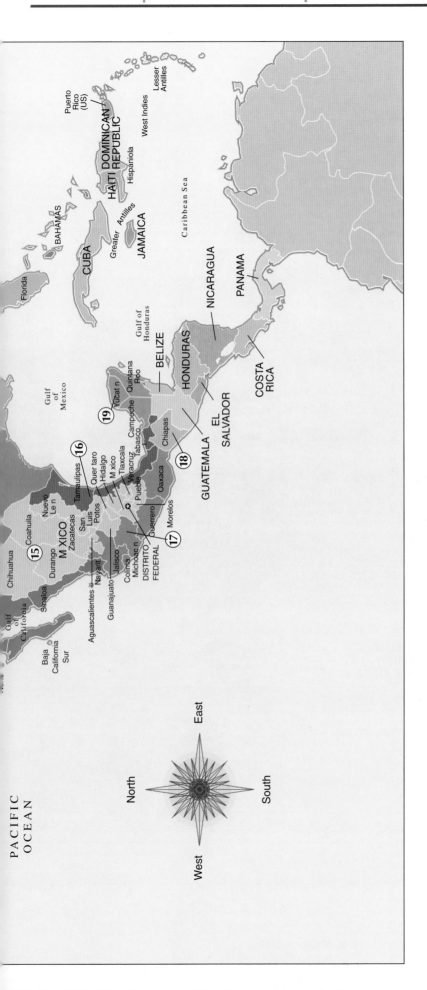

Regions of Mexico
Régions du Mexique

14. The Pacific Northwest
Le nord-ouest du Pacifique

15. The Plateau of Mexico
Le plateau mexicain

16. The Gulf Coastal Plain
La plaine côtière de Golfe

17. The Southern Uplands
Les hautes terres du sud

18. The Chiapas Highlands
Les hautes terres du Chiapas

19. The Yucatan Peninsula
La péninsule du Yucatan

Regions of the United States
Régions des Etats-Unis

7. The Pacific States/the West Coast
Les états du Pacifique/la côte ouest

8. The Rocky Mountain States
Les états des Rocheuses

9. The Midwest
Le Midwest

10. The Mid-Atlantic States
Les états du centre du littoral de l'Atlantique

11. New England
Nouvelle-Angleterre

12. The Southwest
Le sud-ouest

13. The Southeast/the South
Le sud-est/le sud

Regions of Canada
Régions du Canada

1. Northern Canada
Nord du Canada

2. British Columbia
Colombie britannique

3. The Prairie Provinces
Les provinces des Prairies

4. Ontario
Ontario

5. Québec
Québec

6. The Atlantic Provinces
Les provinces de l'Atlantique

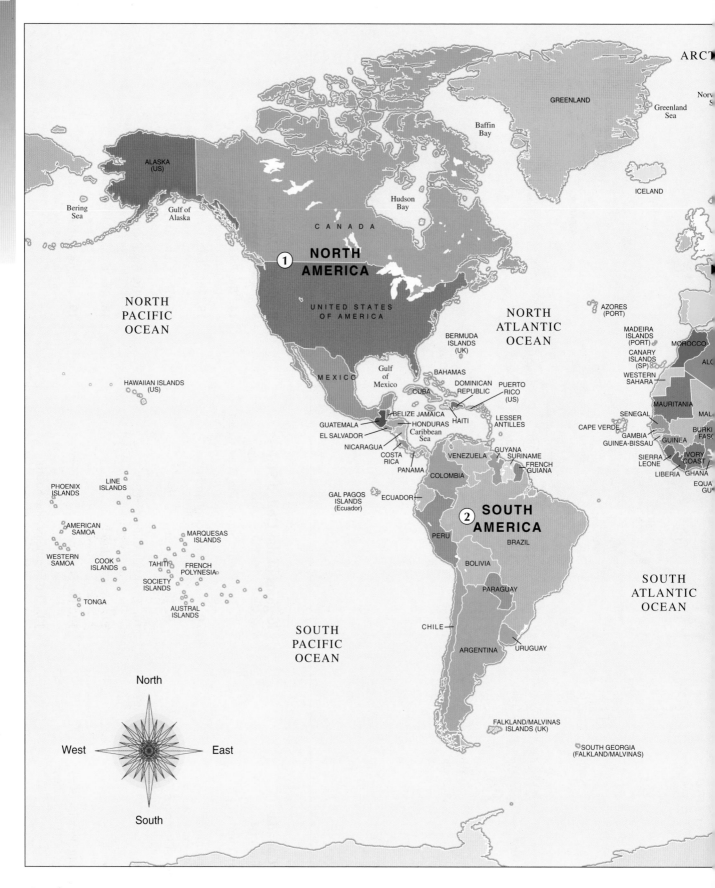

Continents
Continents

1. North America
Amérique du Nord

2. South America
Amérique du Sud

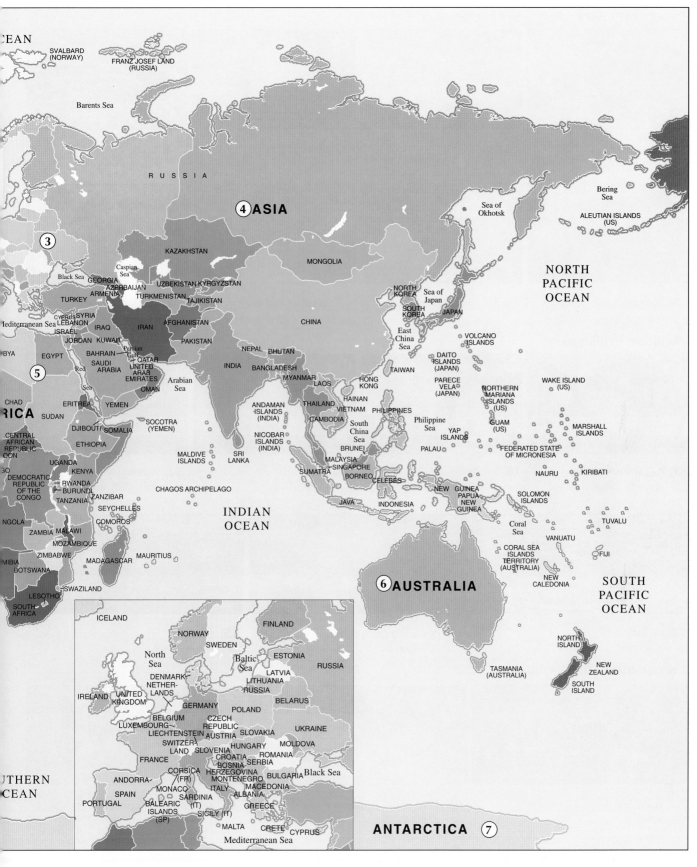

3. Europe
Europe

4. Asia
Asie

5. Africa
Afrique

6. Australia
Australie

7. Antarctica
Antarctique

Energy and the Environment   Energie et environnement

Energy resources   Ressources énergétiques

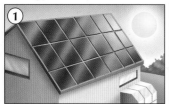

1. solar energy
énergie solaire

2. wind
vent

3. natural gas
gaz naturel

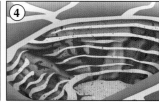

4. coal
charbon

5. hydroelectric power
énergie hydroélectrique

6. oil / petroleum
pétrole

7. geothermal energy
énergie géothermique

8. nuclear energy
énergie nucléaire

Pollution   Pollution

9. hazardous waste
déchets dangereux

10. air pollution / smog
pollution de l'air / smog

11. acid rain
pluie acide

12. water pollution
pollution de l'eau

13. radiation
radiation

14. pesticide poisoning
pollution par les pesticides

15. oil spill
marée noire

Conservation   Conservation

A. recycle
recycler

B. save water / **conserve** water
économiser l'eau / **conserver** l'eau

C. save energy / **conserve** energy
économiser l'énergie /
conserver l'énergie

Share your answers.

1. How do you heat your home?

2. Do you have a gas stove or an electric stove?

3. What are some ways you can save energy when it's cold?

4. Do you recycle? What products do you recycle?

5. Does your market have recycling bins?

The Solar System

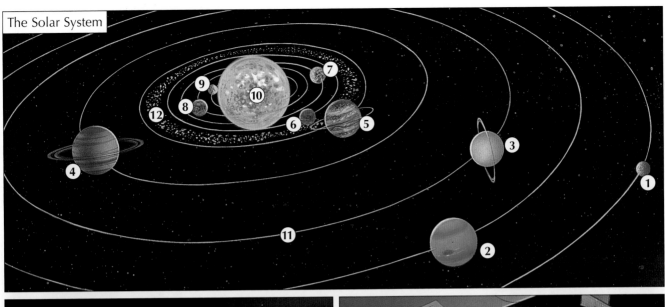

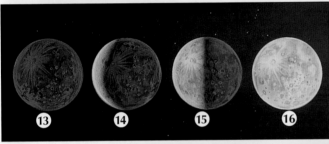

The planets
Les planètes

1. Pluto
Pluton

2. Neptune
Neptune

3. Uranus
Uranus

4. Saturn
Saturne

5. Jupiter
Jupiter

6. Mars
Mars

7. Earth
Terre

8. Venus
Vénus

9. Mercury
Mercure

10. sun
soleil

11. orbit
orbite

12. asteroid belt
ceinture d'astéroïdes /
anneau d'astéroïdes

13. new moon
nouvelle lune

14. crescent moon
croissant de lune

15. quarter moon
quart de lune

16. full moon
pleine lune

17. astronaut
astronaute

18. space station
station spatiale

19. observatory
observatoire

20. astronomer
astronome

21. telescope
télescope

22. space
espace

23. star
étoile

24. constellation
constellation

25. comet
comète

26. galaxy
galaxie

More vocabulary

lunar eclipse: when the earth is between the sun and
the moon

solar eclipse: when the moon is between the earth and
the sun

Share your answers.

1. Do you know the names of any constellations?

2. How do you feel when you look up at the night sky?

3. Is the night sky in the U.S. the same as in your country?

Parts of a tree Parties d'un arbre

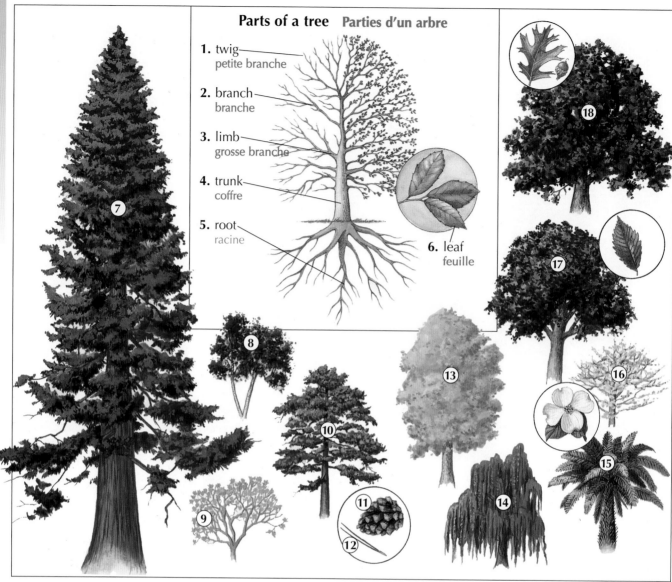

1. twig
petite branche

2. branch
branche

3. limb
grosse branche

4. trunk
coffre

5. root
racine

6. leaf
feuille

7. redwood
séquoia

8. birch
bouleau

9. magnolia
magnolier

10. pine
pin

11. pinecone
pomme de pin

12. needle
aiguille de pin

13. maple
érable

14. willow
saule

15. palm
palmier

16. dogwood
cornouiller

17. elm
orme

18. oak
chêne

Plants Plantes

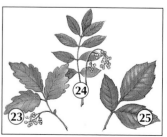

19. holly
houx

20. berries
baies

21. cactus
cactus

22. vine
vigne

23. poison oak
chêne vénéneux

24. poison sumac
sumac lustré

25. poison ivy
sumac vénéneux

Parts of a flower Parties d'une fleur

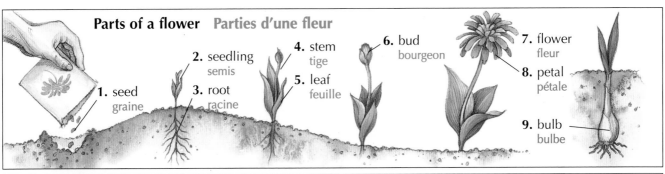

1. seed
graine

2. seedling
semis

3. root
racine

4. stem
tige

5. leaf
feuille

6. bud
bourgeon

7. flower
fleur

8. petal
pétale

9. bulb
bulbe

10. sunflower tournesol	**15.** rose rose	**20.** iris iris	**25.** crocus crocus
11. tulip tulipe	**16.** gardenia gardénia	**21.** jasmine jasmin	**26.** daffodil jonquille
12. hibiscus hibiscus	**17.** orchid orchidée	**22.** violet violette	**27.** bouquet bouquet
13. marigold souci	**18.** carnation œillet	**23.** poinsettia poinsettia	**28.** thorn épine
14. daisy marguerite	**19.** chrysanthemum chrysanthème	**24.** lily lis	**29.** houseplant plante d'intérieur

Parts of a fish   Parties d'un poisson   **Sea animals**   Animaux marins

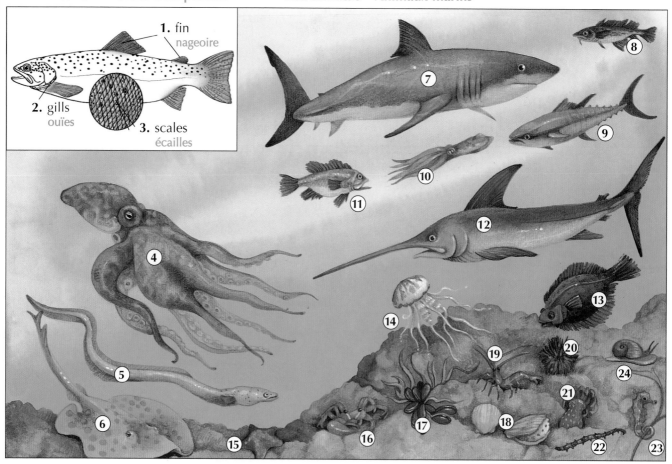

1. fin   nageoire
2. gills   ouïes
3. scales   écailles

4. octopus
poulpe / pieuvre

5. eel
anguille

6. ray
raie

7. shark
requin

8. cod
morue

9. tuna
thon

10. squid
calmar

11. bass
perche (eau douce) / bar (eau salée)

12. swordfish
poisson-épée / espadon

13. flounder
flet / poisson plat

14. jellyfish
méduse

15. starfish
étoile de mer

16. crab
crabe

17. mussel
moule

18. scallop
pétoncle / coquille Saint-Jacques

19. shrimp
crevette

20. sea urchin
oursin

21. sea anemone
anémone de mer

22. worm
ver

23. sea horse
hippocampe

24. snail
escargot

Amphibians   Amphibiens

25. frog
grenouille

26. newt
triton

27. salamander
salamandre

28. toad
crapaud

Sea mammals Mammifères marins

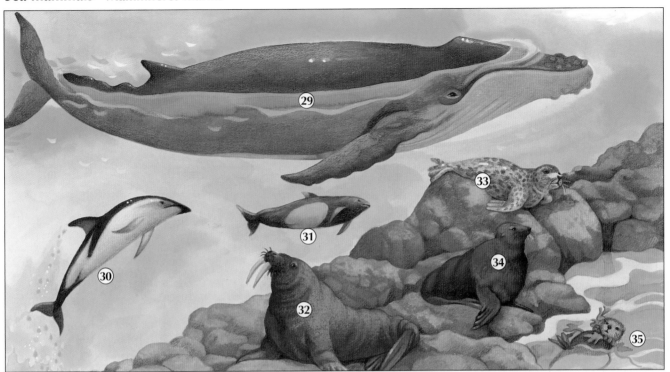

29. whale
baleine

30. dolphin
dauphin

31. porpoise
marsouin

32. walrus
morse

33. seal
phoque

34. sea lion
otarie

35. otter
loutre

Reptiles Reptiles

36. alligator
alligator

37. crocodile
crocodile

38. rattlesnake
crotale / serpent à sonnettes

39. garter snake
thamnophis

40. cobra
cobra

41. lizard
lézard

42. turtle
tortue

Birds, Insects, and Arachnids Oiseaux, insectes et arachnides

Parts of a bird Parties d'un oiseau

1. beak/bill
   bec
2. wing
   aile
3. nest
   nid
4. claw
   griffe/serre
5. feather
   plume

6. owl
   hibou/chouette
7. blue jay
   geai bleu
8. sparrow
   moineau

9. woodpecker
   pic
10. eagle
    aigle
11. hummingbird
    oiseau-mouche/colibri

12. penguin
    pingouin
13. duck
    canard
14. goose
    oie

15. peacock
    paon
16. pigeon
    pigeon
17. robin
    rouge-gorge/
    merle américain

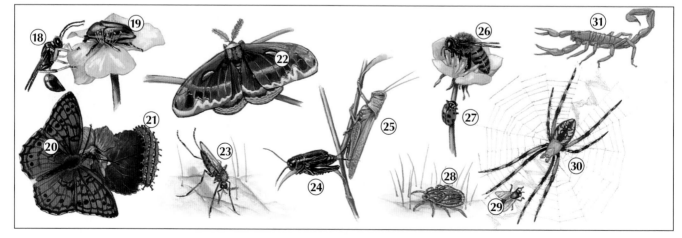

18. wasp
    guêpe
19. beetle
    scarabée/coléoptère
20. butterfly
    papillon
21. caterpillar
    chenille

22. moth
    papillon de nuit
23. mosquito
    moustique
24. cricket
    cricket/grillon
25. grasshopper
    sauterelle

26. honeybee
    abeille
27. ladybug
    coccinelle
28. tick
    tique

29. fly
    mouche
30. spider
    araignée
31. scorpion
    scorpion

Farm animals Animaux de la ferme

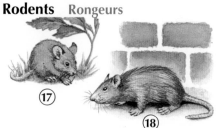

1. goat chèvre	**3.** cow vache	**5.** hen poule	**7.** sheep mouton
2. donkey âne	**4.** horse cheval	**6.** rooster coq	**8.** pig cochon

Pets Animaux de compagnie

9. cat chat	**11.** dog chien	**13.** rabbit lapin	**15.** parakeet perruche
10. kitten chaton	**12.** puppy chiot	**14.** guinea pig cochon d'Inde	**16.** goldfish poisson rouge

Rodents Rongeurs

17. mouse souris	**19.** gopher gaufre / gauphre	**21.** squirrel écureuil
18. rat rat	**20.** chipmunk tamia	**22.** prairie dog chien de prairie

More vocabulary

Wild animals live, eat, and raise their young away from people, in the forests, mountains, plains, etc.

Domesticated animals work for people or live with them.

Share your answers.

1. Do you have any pets? any farm animals?

2. Which of these animals are in your neighborhood? Which are not?

1. moose
élan / orignal

2. mountain lion
cougar / puma

3. coyote
coyote

4. opossum
opossum

5. wolf
loup

6. buffalo / bison
bison

7. bat
chauve-souris

8. armadillo
tatou

9. beaver
castor

10. porcupine
porc-épic

11. bear
ours

12. skunk
mouffette

13. raccoon
raton laveur

14. deer
chevreuil / cerf

15. fox
renard

16. antler
ramure / bois

17. hoof
sabot

18. whiskers
moustaches

19. coat / fur
fourrure

20. paw
patte

21. horn
corne

22. tail
queue

23. quill
piquant

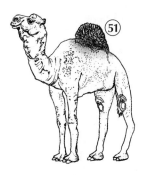

24. anteater
tamanoir

25. leopard
léopard

26. llama
lama

27. monkey
singe

28. chimpanzee
chimpanzé

29. rhinoceros
rhinocéros

30. gorilla
gorille

31. hyena
hyène

32. baboon
babouin

33. giraffe
girafe

34. zebra
zèbre

35. antelope
antilope

36. lion
lion

37. tiger
tigre

38. camel
chameau

39. panther
panthère

40. orangutan
orang-outan

41. panda
panda

42. elephant
éléphant

43. hippopotamus
hippopotame

44. kangaroo
kangourou

45. koala
koala

46. platypus
ornithorynque

47. trunk
trompe

48. tusk
défense

49. mane
crinière

50. pouch
poche

51. hump
bosse

Jobs and Occupations, A–H   Emplois et professions, A–H

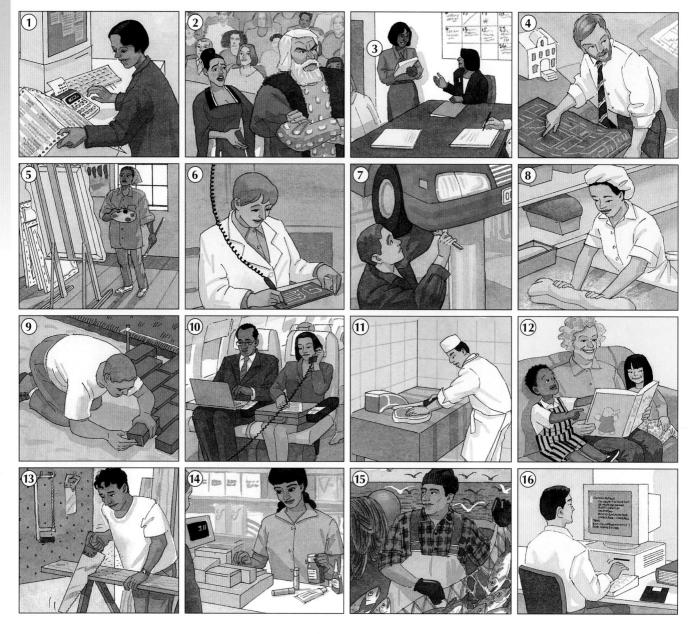

1. **accountant**
   comptable

2. **actor**
   acteur (actrice)

3. **administrative assistant**
   adjoint(e) administratif (ve)

4. **architect**
   architecte

5. **artist**
   artiste

6. **assembler**
   monteur (monteuse)

7. **auto mechanic**
   mécanicien (mécanicienne) auto

8. **baker**
   boulanger (boulangère)

9. **bricklayer**
   maçon

10. **businessman/businesswoman**
    homme (femme) d'affaires

11. **butcher**
    boucher (bouchère)

12. **caregiver/baby-sitter**
    gardienne/baby-sitter

13. **carpenter**
    charpentier

14. **cashier**
    caissier (caissière)

15. **commercial fisher**
    pêcheur commercial

16. **computer programmer**
    programmeur (programmeuse)
    informatique

Use the new language.

1. Who works outside?

2. Who works inside?

3. Who makes things?

4. Who uses a computer?

5. Who wears a uniform?

6. Who sells things?

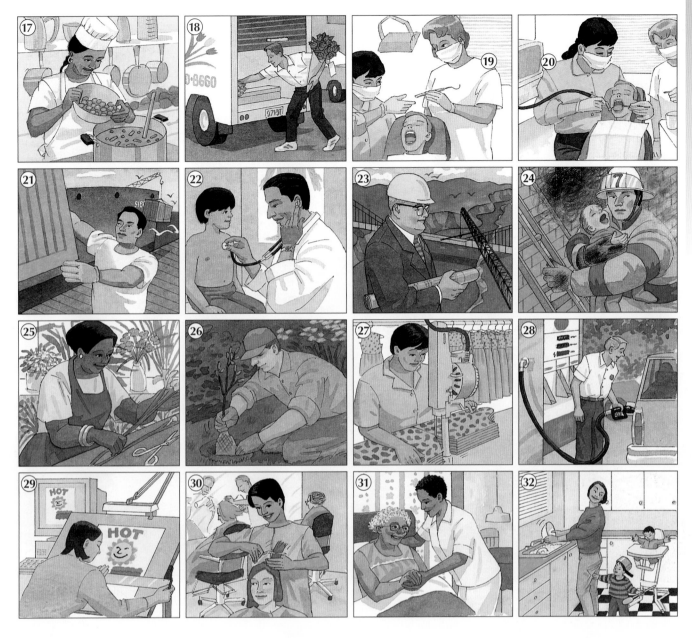

17. cook
cuisinier (cuisinière)

18. delivery person
livreur (livreuse)

19. dental assistant
assistant(e) dentaire

20. dentist
dentiste

21. dockworker
docker

22. doctor
docteur

23. engineer
ingénieur

24. firefighter
pompier

25. florist
fleuriste

26. gardener
jardinier (jardinière)

27. garment worker
confectionneur (confectionneuse)
de vêtements

28. gas station attendant
pompiste

29. graphic artist
graphiste

30. hairdresser
coiffeur (coiffeuse)

31. home attendant
aide familial(e)

32. homemaker
femme d'intérieur

Share your answers.

1. Do you know people who have some of these jobs? What do they say about their work?

2. Which of these jobs are available in your city?

3. For which of these jobs do you need special training?

33. housekeeper
homme (bonne) à tout faire

34. interpreter / translator
interprète / traducteur (traductrice)

35. janitor / custodian
concierge / gardien (gardienne)

36. lawyer
avocat(e)

37. machine operator
opérateur (opératrice) de machine

38. messenger / courier
messager (messagère)

39. model
mannequin

40. mover
déménageur

41. musician
musicien (musicienne)

42. nurse
infirmier (infirmière)

43. painter
peintre

44. police officer
policier (policière)

45. postal worker
postier (postière)

46. printer
imprimeur

47. receptionist
réceptionniste

48. repair person
réparateur (réparatrice)

Talk about each of the jobs or occupations.

She's a housekeeper. She works in a hotel.

He's an interpreter. He works for the government.

She's a nurse. She works with patients.

49. reporter
journaliste

50. salesclerk / salesperson
vendeur (vendeuse)

51. sanitation worker
éboueur

52. secretary
secrétaire

53. server
serveur (serveuse)

54. serviceman / servicewoman
militaire

55. stock clerk
commis aux stocks

56. store owner
propriétaire de magasin

57. student
étudiant(e)

58. teacher / instructor
enseignant(e) / instructeur

59. telemarketer
télé-vendeur (vendeuse)

60. travel agent
agent de voyage

61. truck driver
conducteur (conductrice) de camions

62. veterinarian
vétérinaire

63. welder
soudeur (soudeuse)

64. writer / author
écrivain / auteur

Talk about your job or the job you want.

What do you do?

I'm a salesclerk. I work in a store.

What do you want to do?

I want to be a veterinarian. I want to work with animals.

139

A. **assemble** components
monter des éléments

B. **assist** medical patients
aider des malades

C. **cook**
cuisiner

D. **do** manual labor
faire des travaux manuels

E. **drive** a truck
conduire un camion

F. **operate** heavy machinery
conduire de la machinerie lourde

G. **repair** appliances
réparer des appareils ménagers

H. **sell** cars
vendre des voitures

I. **sew** clothes
coudre des vêtements

J. **speak** another language
parler une langue étrangère

K. **supervise** people
encadrer des personnes

L. **take care** of children
prendre soin d'enfants

M. **type**
taper à la machine

N. **use** a cash register
utiliser une caisse enregistreuse

O. **wait on** customers
servir des clients

P. **work** on a computer
travailler à l'ordinateur

More vocabulary

act: to perform in a play, movie, or TV show

fly: to pilot an airplane

teach: to instruct, to show how to do something

Share your answers.

1. What job skills do you have? Where did you learn them?

2. What job skills do you want to learn?

A. talk to friends
parler à des amis

B. look at a job board
lire le tableau d'affichage
des offres d'emploi

C. look for a help wanted sign
chercher les panneaux
offrant des emplois

D. look in the classifieds
consulter les petites annonces

E. call for information
appeler pour obtenir de l'information

F. ask about the hours
s'enquérir / demander à propos
des heures (de travail)

G. fill out an application
remplir une demande d'emploi

H. go on an interview
se présenter à une entrevue

I. talk about your experience
parler de son expérience

J. ask about benefits
s'enquérir / demander à propos
des avantages sociaux

K. inquire about the salary
s'enquérir à propos du salaire

L. get hired
être engagé

141

1. **desk**
   bureau

2. **typewriter**
   machine à écrire

3. **secretary**
   secrétaire

4. **microcassette transcriber**
   transcripteur à microcassette

5. **stacking tray**
   corbeilles empilables

6. **desk calendar**
   calendrier éphéméride

7. **desk pad**
   sous-main

8. **calculator**
   calculatrice

9. **electric pencil sharpener**
   taille-crayons électrique

10. **file cabinet**
    meuble classeur

11. **file folder**
    chemise

12. **file clerk**
    préposé au classement

13. **supply cabinet**
    armoire de rangement des
    fournitures de bureau

14. **photocopier**
    photocopieuse

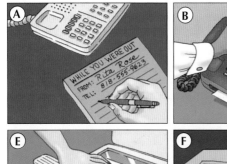

A. **take** a message
   prendre un message

B. **fax** a letter
   faxer une lettre

C. **transcribe** notes
   transcrire des notes

D. **type** a letter
   taper une lettre

E. **make** copies
   faire des photocopies

F. **collate** papers
   collationner des feuilles

G. **staple**
   agrafer

H. **file** papers
   classer des papiers

Practice taking messages.

Hello. My name is <u>Sara Scott</u>. Is <u>Mr. Lee</u> in?

Not yet. Would you like to leave a message?

Yes. Please ask <u>him</u> to call me at <u>555-4859</u>.

Share your answers.

1. Which office equipment do you know how to use?
2. Which jobs does a file clerk do?
3. Which jobs does a secretary do?

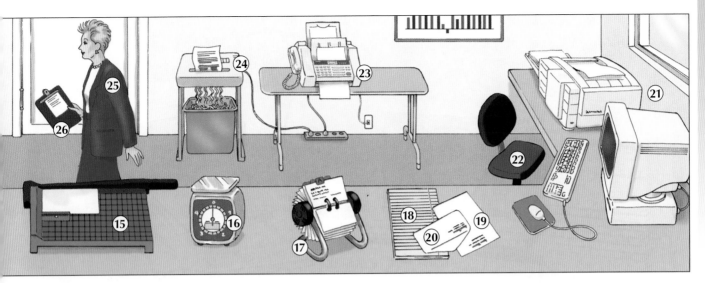

15. paper cutter
massicot

16. postal scale
pèse-lettre

17. rotary card file
fichier rotatif

18. legal pad
bloc format légal

19. letterhead paper
papier à en-tête

20. envelope
enveloppe

21. computer workstation
poste de travail informatique

22. swivel chair
siège pivotant

23. fax machine
télécopieur

24. paper shredder
destructeur de documents

25. office manager
chef de bureau

26. clipboard
écritoire à pince

27. appointment book
carnet de rendez-vous

28. stapler
agrafeuse

29. staple
agrafe

30. organizer
organiseur

31. typewriter cartridge
ruban cartouche de
machine à écrire

32. mailer
pochette matelassée

33. correction fluid
liquide correcteur

34. Post-it notes
papillons adhésifs

35. label
étiquette

36. notepad
bloc-notes

37. glue
colle

38. rubber cement
colle au caoutchouc

39. clear tape
ruban adhésif transparent

40. rubber stamp
tampon de caoutchouc

41. ink pad
tampon encreur

42. packing tape
ruban d'emballage

43. pushpin
clou à dessin

44. paper clip
trombone

45. rubber band
élastique

Use the new language.

1. Which items keep things together?

2. Which items are used to mail packages?

3. Which items are made of paper?

Share your answers.

1. Which office supplies do students use?

2. Where can you buy them?

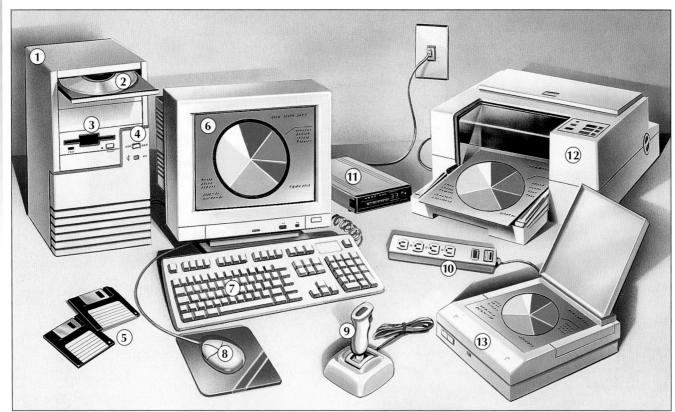

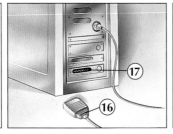

Hardware
Matériel

1. CPU (central processing unit)
UC (unité centrale)

2. CD-ROM disc
disque compact ROM

3. disk drive
unité de disques

4. power switch
interrupteur de tension

5. disk / floppy
disquette

6. monitor / screen
moniteur / écran

7. keyboard
clavier

8. mouse
souris

9. joystick
manche à balais

10. surge protector
parasurtenseur

11. modem
modem

12. printer
imprimante

13. scanner
scanner

14. laptop
ordinateur portatif

15. trackball
boule roulante

16. cable
câble

17. port
porte d'accès

18. motherboard
carte mère

19. slot
fente

20. hard disk drive
unité de disque dur

Software
Logiciels

21. program / application
programme / application

22. user's manual
manuel de l'utilisateur

More vocabulary

data: information that a computer can read

memory: how much data a computer can hold

speed: how fast a computer can work with data

Share your answers.

1. Can you use a computer?

2. How did you learn? in school? from a book? by yourself?

1. valet parking
service de garage des voitures

2. doorman
portier

3. lobby
hall

4. bell captain
chef chasseur

5. bellhop
chasseur

6. luggage cart
chariot à bagages

7. gift shop
boutique de cadeaux

8. front desk
réception

9. desk clerk
réceptionniste

10. guest room
chambre

11. guest
client(e)

12. room service
service aux chambres

13. hall
hall

14. housekeeping cart
chariot de ménage

15. housekeeper
femme de ménage

16. pool
piscine

17. pool service
nettoyage de la piscine

18. ice machine
machine à glaçons

19. meeting room
salle de réunion

20. ballroom
salle de danse

More vocabulary

concierge: the hotel worker who helps guests find restaurants and interesting places to go

service elevator: an elevator for hotel workers

Share your answers.

1. Does this look like a hotel in your city? Which one?

2. Which hotel job is the most difficult?

3. How much does it cost to stay in a hotel in your city?

1. front office
   bureau de direction

2. factory owner
   propriétaire de l'usine

3. designer
   concepteur

4. time clock
   pointeuse

5. line supervisor
   agent de maîtrise

6. factory worker
   travailleur (travailleuse)

7. parts
   pièces

8. assembly line
   chaîne de montage

9. warehouse
   entrepôt

10. order puller
    préposé aux commandes

11. hand truck
    chariot à main

12. conveyor belt
    transporteur à courroie

13. packer
    emballeur (emballeuse)

14. forklift
    chariot élévateur

15. shipping clerk
    préposé à l'expédition

16. loading dock
    plate-forme de chargement

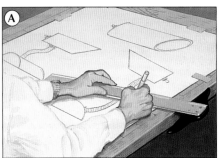

A.   design
conception

B.   manufacture
fabrication

C.   ship
expédition

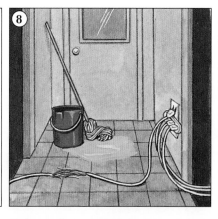

1. electrical hazard
risque électrique

2. flammable
inflammable

3. poison
poison

4. corrosive
corrosif

5. biohazard
risque biologique

6. radioactive
risque de radioactivité

7. hazardous materials
matières dangereuses

8. dangerous situation
situation dangereuse

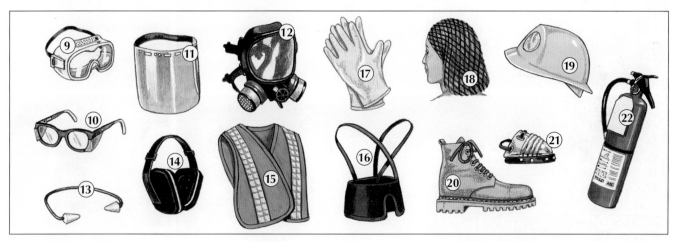

9. safety goggles
lunettes de sécurité

10. safety glasses
lunettes de sûreté

11. safety visor
visière de sécurité

12. respirator
masque respiratoire

13. earplugs
protège-tympans

14. safety earmuffs
serre-tête de sécurité

15. safety vest
gilet de sécurité

16. back support
support lombaire

17. latex gloves
gants de latex

18. hair net
filet à cheveux

19. hard hat
casque

20. safety boot
chaussures de sécurité

21. toe guard
embout protecteur

22. fire extinguisher
extincteurs

23. careless
imprudent

24. careful
prudent

Crops Récoltes

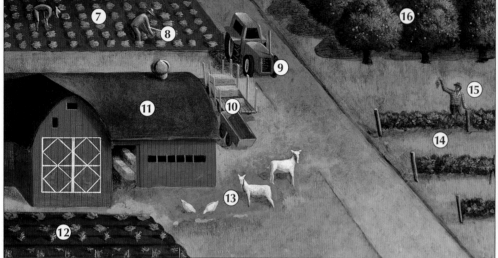

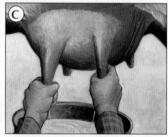

1. rice
   riz

2. wheat
   blé

3. soybeans
   soja

4. corn
   maïs

5. alfalfa
   luzerne

6. cotton
   coton

7. field
   champ

8. farmworker
   ouvrier (ouvrière) agricole

9. tractor
   tracteur

10. farm equipment
    matériel agricole

11. barn
    grange

12. vegetable garden
    jardin potager

13. livestock
    bétail

14. vineyard
    vignoble

15. farmer / grower
    fermier (fermière) /
    producteur (productrice)

16. orchard
    verger

17. corral
    corral

18. hay
    foin

19. fence
    barrière

20. hired hand
    ouvrier (ouvrière) engagé(e)

21. steers / cattle
    bœufs / bétail

22. rancher
    cow-boy

A. **plant**
   planter

B. **harvest**
   récolter

C. **milk**
   traire

D. **feed**
   donner à manger

1. **construction worker**
   ouvrier (ouvrière) du bâtiment

2. **ladder**
   échelle

3. **I beam / girder**
   poutre en I / poutrelle

4. **scaffolding**
   échafaudage

5. **cherry picker**
   engin élévateur à nacelle

6. **bulldozer**
   bulldozer

7. **crane**
   grue

8. **backhoe**
   pelle rétrocaveuse

9. **jackhammer / pneumatic drill**
   marteau pneumatique

10. **concrete**
    béton

11. **bricks**
    briques

12. **trowel**
    truelle

13. **insulation**
    isolation

14. **stucco**
    stuc

15. **window pane**
    vitre

16. **plywood**
    contreplaqué

17. **wood / lumber**
    bois / bois de charpente

18. **drywall**
    placoplâtre

19. **shingles**
    bardeaux

20. **pickax**
    pioche

21. **shovel**
    pelle

22. **sledgehammer**
    marteau de forgeron

A. **paint**
   peindre

B. **lay** bricks
   poser des briques

C. **measure**
   mesurer

D. **hammer**
   marteler

1. **hammer**
   marteau
2. **mallet**
   maillet
3. **ax**
   hache

4. **handsaw**
   scie à main
5. **hacksaw**
   scie à métaux
6. **C-clamp**
   serre-joints en C

7. **pliers**
   pinces
8. **electric drill**
   perceuse électrique
9. **power sander**
   ponceuse à moteur

10. **circular saw**
    scie circulaire
11. **blade**
    lame
12. **router**
    toupie

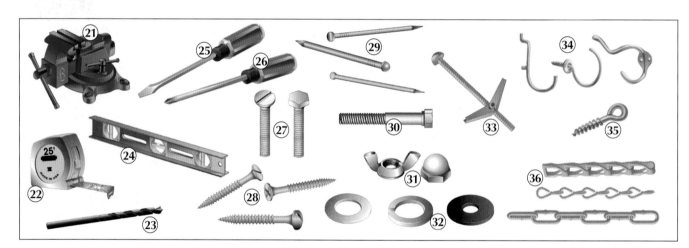

21. **vise**
    étau
22. **tape measure**
    mètre à ruban
23. **drill bit**
    foret
24. **level**
    niveau

25. **screwdriver**
    tournevis
26. **Phillips screwdriver**
    tournevis Phillips
27. **machine screw**
    vis à métaux
28. **wood screw**
    vis à bois

29. **nail**
    clou
30. **bolt**
    boulon
31. **nut**
    écrou
32. **washer**
    rondelle

33. **toggle bolt**
    boulon de scellement
34. **hook**
    crochet
35. **eye hook**
    crochet à œillet
36. **chain**
    chaîne

Use the new language.

1. Which tools are used for plumbing?

2. Which tools are used for painting?

3. Which tools are used for electrical work?

4. Which tools are used for working with wood?

13. wire
fil

14. extension cord
rallonge (électrique)

15. yardstick
mètre

16. pipe
tuyau

17. fittings
raccords

18. wood
bois

19. spray gun
pistolet à peinture

20. paint
peinture

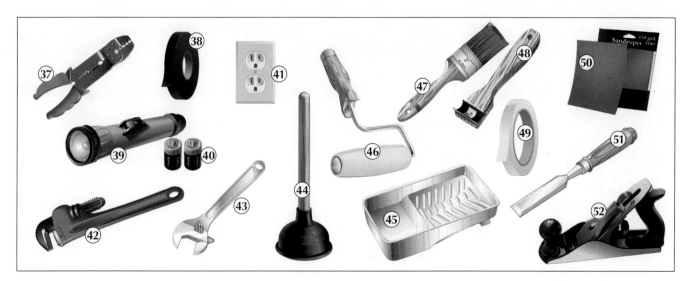

37. wire stripper
pince à dénuder

38. electrical tape
chaterton

39. flashlight
lampe de poche

40. battery
pile

41. outlet
prise de courant

42. pipe wrench
clé à tuyau

43. wrench
clé

44. plunger
débouchoir à ventouse

45. paint pan
bac à peinture

46. paint roller
rouleau

47. paintbrush
brosse

48. scraper
grattoir

49. masking tape
ruban à masquer

50. sandpaper
papier de verre

51. chisel
burin

52. plane
rabot

Use the new language.

Look at **Household Problems and Repairs,** pages **48–49.**

Name the tools you use to fix the problems you see.

Share your answers.

1. Which tools do you have in your home?
2. Which tools can be dangerous to use?

1. zoo
   jardin zoologique

2. animals
   animaux

3. zookeeper
   gardien(ne) de zoo

4. botanical gardens
   jardins botaniques

5. greenhouse
   serre

6. gardener
   jardinier (jardinière)

7. art museum
   musée d'art

8. painting
   tableau

9. sculpture
   sculpture

10. the movies
    cinéma

11. seat
    siège

12. screen
    écran

13. amusement park
    foire

14. puppet show
    spectacle de marionnettes

15. roller coaster
    montagnes russes

16. carnival
    carnaval

17. rides
    manèges

18. game
    jeu

19. county fair
    fête régionale/foire régionale

20. first place/first prize
    première place/premier prix

21. exhibition
    exposition

22. swap meet/flea market
    marché aux puces

23. booth
    baraque foraine

24. merchandise
    marchandise

25. baseball game
    match de base-ball

26. stadium
    stade

27. announcer
    annonceur

Talk about the places you like to go.

I like <u>animals</u>, so I go to <u>the zoo</u>.

I like <u>rides</u>, so I go to <u>carnivals</u>.

Share your answers.

1. Which of these places is interesting to you?
2. Which rides do you like at an amusement park?
3. What are some famous places to go to in your country?

1. ball field
terrain de base-ball

2. bike path
piste cyclable

3. cyclist
cycliste

4. bicycle/bike
bicyclette/vélo

5. jump rope
corde à sauter

6. duck pond
mare aux canards

7. tennis court
court de tennis

8. picnic table
table de pique-nique

9. tricycle
tricycle

10. bench
banc

11. water fountain
fontaine

12. swings
balançoires

13. slide
toboggan

14. climbing apparatus
cage à poules

15. sandbox
bac à sable

16. seesaw
jeu de bascule

A. **pull** the wagon
tirer le wagonnet

B. **push** the swing
pousser la balançoire

C. **climb** on the bars
grimper sur les barres

D. **picnic/have** a picnic
pique-niquer/faire un pique-nique

1. camping
   camping

2. boating
   canotage

3. canoeing
   canoë/kayak

4. rafting
   rafting

5. fishing
   pêche

6. hiking
   randonnées

7. backpacking
   randonnées avec sac à dos

8. mountain biking
   faire du vélo tout terrain

9. horseback riding
   faire de l'équitation

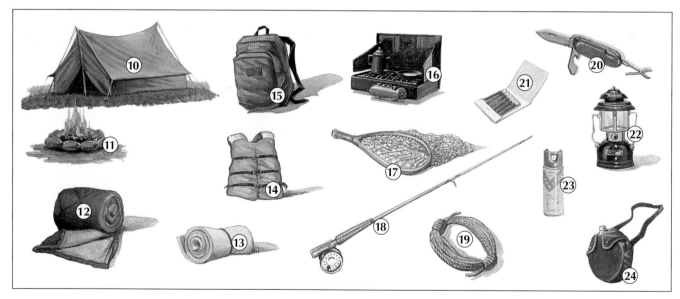

10. tent
    tente

11. campfire
    feu de camp

12. sleeping bag
    sac de couchage

13. foam pad
    matelas de mousse

14. life vest
    gilet de sauvetage

15. backpack
    sac à dos

16. camping stove
    réchaud de camping

17. fishing net
    épuisette

18. fishing pole
    canne à pêche

19. rope
    corde

20. multi-use knife
    couteau suisse

21. matches
    allumettes

22. lantern
    lanterne

23. insect repellent
    produit anti-insecte

24. canteen
    bidon

1. ocean/water
   océan/eau

2. fins
   palmes

3. diving mask
   masque de plongée

4. sailboat
   voilier

5. surfboard
   planche de surf

6. wave
   vague

7. wet suit
   combinaison de plongée

8. scuba tank
   bouteille de plongée

9. beach umbrella
   parasol de plage

10. sand castle
    château de sable

11. cooler
    glacière

12. shade
    ombre

13. sunscreen/sunblock
    crème solaire/écran solaire

14. beach chair
    chaise de plage

15. beach towel
    serviette de plage

16. pier
    jetée

17. sunbather
    personne prenant un bain de soleil

18. lifeguard
    maître nageur

19. lifesaving device
    matériel de sauvetage

20. lifeguard station
    poste de secours

21. seashell
    coquillage

22. pail/bucket
    seau

23. sand
    sable

24. rock
    pierre

More vocabulary

seaweed: a plant that grows in the ocean

tide: the level of the ocean. The tide goes in and out every twelve hours.

Share your answers.

1. Are there any beaches near your home?

2. Do you prefer to spend more time on the sand or in the water?

3. Where are some of the world's best beaches?

A. walk marcher	**E. catch** attraper	**I. shoot** tirer	**L. kick** botter
B. jog faire du jogging	**F. pitch** lancer	**J. jump** sauter	**M. tackle** plaquer
C. run courir	**G. hit** frapper	**K. dribble / bounce** dribbler / faire rebondir le ballon	
D. throw lancer	**H. pass** passer		

Practice talking about what you can do.

I can <u>swim</u>, but I can't <u>dive</u>.

I can <u>pass the ball</u> well, but I can't <u>shoot</u> too well.

Use the new language.

Look at **Individual Sports**, page **159**.

Name the actions you see people doing.

The man in number 18 is riding a horse.

N. serve
servir

O. swing
frapper une balle
avec un swing

P. exercise / work out
faire de l'exercice /
s'entraîner

Q. stretch
s'étirer

R. bend
se pencher

S. dive
plonger

T. swim
nager

U. ski
skier

V. skate
faire du patin / patiner

W. ride
se promener / aller
(à pied, en vélo,
à cheval, en voiture)

X. start
démarrer / commencer

Y. race
courir

Z. finish
passer le fil d'arrivée

Share your answers.

1. What do you like to do?

2. What do you have difficulty doing?

3. How often do you exercise? Once a week? Two or three times a week? More? Never?

4. Which is more difficult, throwing a ball or catching it?

1. **score**
   score

2. **coach**
   entraîneur

3. **team**
   équipe

4. **fan**
   supporter

5. **player**
   joueur

6. **official / referee**
   officiel / arbitre

7. **basketball court**
   terrain de basket

8. **basketball**
   basket-ball

9. **baseball**
   base-ball

10. **softball**
    soft-ball

11. **football**
    football américain

12. **soccer**
    football

13. **ice hockey**
    hockey sur glace

14. **volleyball**
    volley-ball

15. **water polo**
    water-polo

More vocabulary

captain: the team leader

umpire: in baseball, the name for referee

Little League: a baseball league for children

win: to have the best score

lose: the opposite of win

tie: to have the same score as the other team

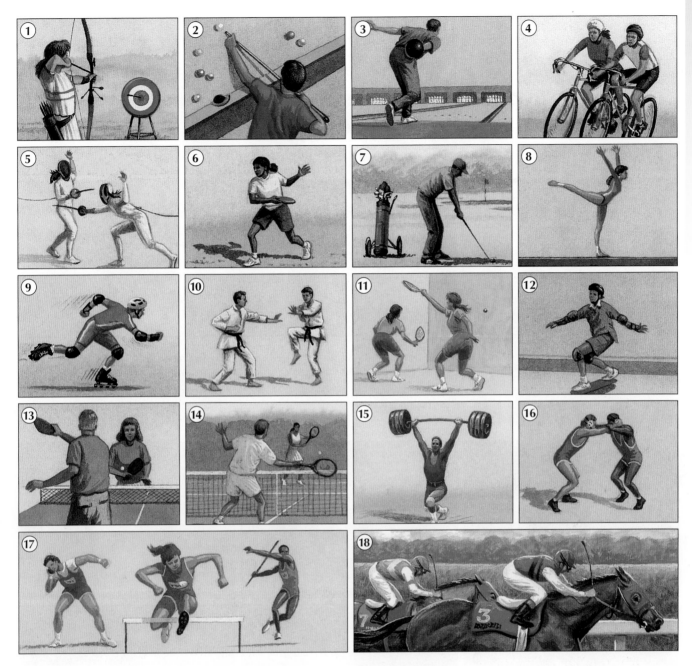

1. archery
   tir à l'arc

2. billiards / pool
   billard

3. bowling
   bowling

4. cycling / biking
   cyclisme

5. fencing
   escrime

6. flying disc*
   frisbee / disque volant

7. golf
   golf

8. gymnastics
   gymnastique

9. inline skating
   patinage avec patins
   à roues alignées

10. martial arts
    arts martiaux

11. racquetball
    racquetball

12. skateboarding
    faire du skateboard / de
    la planche à roulettes

13. table tennis /
    Ping-Pong™
    tennis de table /
    Ping-Pong^MC

14. tennis
    tennis

15. weightlifting
    haltérophilie

16. wrestling
    lutte

17. track and field
    athlétisme

18. horse racing
    hippisme

*Note: one brand is Frisbee®
(Mattel, Inc.)

Talk about sports.

Which sports do you like?

   I like <u>tennis</u> but I don't like <u>golf</u>.

Share your answers.

1. Which sports are good for children to learn? Why?

2. Which sport is the most difficult to learn? Why?

3. Which sport is the most dangerous? Why?

1. downhill skiing
ski alpin

2. snowboarding
faire du surf des neiges

3. cross-country skiing
ski de randonnée

4. ice skating
patinage sur glace

5. figure skating
patinage artistique

6. sledding
faire de la luge

7. waterskiing
ski nautique

8. sailing
faire de la voile

9. surfing
faire du surf

10. sailboarding
faire de la planche à voile

11. snorkeling
plongée en apnée

12. scuba diving
plongée sous-marine

Use the new language.
Look at **The Beach,** page **155.**
Name the sports you see.

Share your answers.

1. Which sports are in the Winter Olympics?

2. Which sports do you think are the most exciting to watch?

1. golf club
club de golf

2. tennis racket
raquette de tennis

3. volleyball
balle de volley-ball

4. basketball
balle de basket-ball

5. bowling ball
boule de bowling

6. bow
arc

7. arrow
flèche

8. target
cible

9. ice skates
patins à glace

10. inline skates
patins à roues alignées

11. hockey stick
crosse de hockey

12. soccer ball
ballon de football

13. shin guards
jambières

14. baseball bat
batte de base-ball

15. catcher's mask
masque d'attrapeur

16. uniform
uniforme

17. glove
gant

18. baseball
balle de base-ball

19. weights
haltères

20. football helmet
casque de
football américain

21. shoulder pads
épaulettes

22. football
ballon de
football américain

23. snowboard
surf des neiges

24. skis
skis

25. ski poles
bâtons de ski

26. ski boots
chaussures de ski

27. flying disc*
frisbee / disque volant

*Note: one brand is Frisbee®
(Mattel, Inc.)

Share your answers.

1. Which sports equipment is used for safety reasons?

2. Which sports equipment is heavy?

3. What sports equipment do you have at home?

Use the new language.

Look at **Individual Sports,** page **159.**

Name the sports equipment you see.

A. collect things
collectionner des objets

B. play games
jouer à des jeux

C. build models
construire des
modèles réduits

D. do crafts
faire des bricolages

1. video game system
   jeux vidéos

2. cartridge
   cartouche

3. board game
   jeu de société

4. dice
   dés

5. checkers
   jeu de dames

6. chess
   jeu d'échecs

7. model kit
   modèle réduit

8. glue
   colle

9. acrylic paint
   peinture acrylique

10. figurine
    figurine

11. baseball card
    carte de base-ball

12. stamp collection
    collection de timbres

13. coin collection
    collection de pièces
    de monnaie

14. clay
    argile

15. doll making kit
    kit de confection de poupée

16. woodworking kit
    kit de menuisier

Talk about how much time you spend on your hobbies.

I *do crafts* all the time.

I *play chess* sometimes.

I never *build models*.

Share your answers.

1. How often do you play video games? Often?
   Sometimes? Never?

2. What board games do you know?

3. Do you collect anything? What?

E. paint
peindre

F. knit
tricoter

G. pretend
faire semblant

H. play cards
jouer aux cartes

17. yarn
fil

18. knitting needles
aiguilles à tricoter

19. embroidery
broderie

20. crochet
crochet

21. easel
chevalet

22. canvas
toile

23. paintbrush
pinceau

24. oil paint
peinture à l'huile

25. watercolor
aquarelle

26. clubs
trèfles

27. diamonds
carreaux

28. spades
pics

29. hearts
cœurs

30. paper doll
poupée de papier

31. action figure
figurine

32. model trains
modèles réduits de train

Share your answers.

1. Do you like to play cards? Which games?

2. Did you pretend a lot when you were a child? What did you pretend to be?

3. Is it important to have hobbies? Why or why not?

4. What's your favorite game?

5. What's your hobby?

1. clock radio
   radio réveil

2. portable radio-cassette player
   combiné radio-lecteur de cassettes
   portatif

3. cassette recorder
   magnétophone à cassettes

4. microphone
   micro

5. shortwave radio
   radio à ondes courtes

6. TV (television)
   TV (télévision)

7. portable TV
   téléviseur portable

8. VCR (videocassette recorder)
   magnétoscope

9. remote control
   télécommande

10. videocassette
    cassette vidéo

11. speakers
    haut-parleurs

12. turntable
    tourne-disque

13. tuner
    syntonisateur

14. CD player
    lecteur de disques compacts

15. personal radio-cassette player
    baladeur

16. headphones
    écouteurs

17. adapter
    adaptateur

18. plug
    fiche

19. video camera
caméra vidéo

20. tripod
trépied

21. camcorder
caméscope

22. battery pack
bloc-piles

23. battery charger
chargeur de piles

24. 35 mm camera
appareil-photo de 35 mm

25. zoom lens
zoom

26. film
film

27. camera case
étui à appareil-photo

28. screen
écran

29. carousel slide projector
projecteur de diapositives

30. slide tray
carrousel

31. slides
diapositives

32. photo album
album de photos

33. out of focus
flou

34. overexposed
surexposé

35. underexposed
sous-exposé

A. **record**
enregistrer

B. **play**
jouer

C. **fast forward**
avance rapide

D. **rewind**
rembobiner

E. **pause**
pause

F. **stop** and **eject**
arrêt et éjection

Entertainment   Divertissement

Types of entertainment   Types de divertissement

1. film / movie
film

2. play
pièce de théâtre

3. television program
émission de télévision

4. radio program
émission de radio /
radiophonique

5. stand-up comedy
monologue comique

6. concert
concert

7. ballet
ballet

8. opera
opéra

Types of stories   Types d'histoires

9. western
western

10. comedy
comédie

11. tragedy
drame

12. science fiction story
science-fiction

13. action story /
adventure story
action / aventure

14. horror story
horreur

15. mystery
mystère

16. romance
amour

Types of TV programs Types de programmes télé

17. news
nouvelles

18. sitcom (situation comedy)
comédie de situation

19. cartoon
dessin animé

20. talk show
causerie

21. soap opera
feuilleton à l'eau de rose

22. nature program
programme sur la nature

23. game show / quiz show
jeu-questionnaire / jeu-concours

24. children's program
émission pour enfants

25. shopping program
émission sur le shopping

26. serious book
livre **sérieux**

27. funny book
livre **drôle**

28. sad book
livre **triste**

29. boring book
livre **ennuyeux**

30. interesting book
livre **intéressant**

1. New Year's Day
Nouvel an

2. parade
parade

3. confetti
confettis

4. Valentine's Day
Saint-Valentin

5. card
carte

6. heart
cœur

7. Independence Day / 4th of July
Fête de l'Indépendance / 4 juillet

8. fireworks
feu d'artifice

9. flag
drapeau

10. Halloween
Halloween

11. jack-o'-lantern
feu follet

12. mask
masque

13. costume
costume

14. candy
bonbon

15. Thanksgiving
Action de grâce

16. feast
fête

17. turkey
dinde

18. Christmas
Noël

19. ornament
ornement

20. Christmas tree
arbre de Noël

A. **plan** a party
planifier une réception

B. **invite** the guests
convier les invités

C. **decorate** the house
décorer la maison

D. **wrap** a gift
emballer un cadeau

E. **hide**
se cacher

F. **answer** the door
ouvrir la porte

G. **shout** "surprise!"
crier « surprise ! »

H. **light** the candles
allumer les bougies

I. **sing** "Happy Birthday"
chanter « joyeux anniversaire »

J. **make** a wish
faire un vœu

K. **blow out** the candles
souffler les bougies

L. **open** the presents
ouvrir les cadeaux

Practice inviting friends to a party.

I'd love for you to come to my party <u>next week</u>.

Could <u>you and your friend</u> come to my party?

Would <u>your friend</u> like to come to a party I'm giving?

Share your answers.

1. Do you celebrate birthdays? What do you do?

2. Are there birthdays you celebrate in a special way?

3. Is there a special birthday song in your country?

Verb Guide

Verbs in English are either regular or irregular in the past tense and past participle forms.

Regular Verbs

The regular verbs below are marked 1, 2, 3, or 4 according to four different spelling patterns. (See page 172 for the **irregular verbs** which do not follow any of these patterns.)

Spelling Patterns for the Past and the Past Participle	*Example*		
1. Add **-ed** to the end of the verb.	**ASK**	→	**ASKED**
2. Add **-d** to the end of the verb.	**LIVE**	→	**LIVED**
3. Double the final consonant and add **-ed** to the end of the verb.	**DROP**	→	**DROPPED**
4. Drop the final y and add **-ied** to the end of the verb.	**CRY**	→	**CRIED**

The Oxford Picture Dictionary List of Regular Verbs

act (1)	collect (1)	exercise (2)
add (1)	color (1)	experience (2)
address (1)	comb (1)	exterminate (2)
answer (1)	commit (3)	fasten (1)
apologize (2)	compliment (1)	fax (1)
appear (1)	conserve (2)	file (2)
applaud (1)	convert (1)	fill (1)
arrange (2)	cook (1)	finish (1)
arrest (1)	copy (4)	fix (1)
arrive (2)	correct (1)	floss (1)
ask (1)	cough (1)	fold (1)
assemble (2)	count (1)	fry (4)
assist (1)	cross (1)	gargle (2)
bake (2)	cry (4)	graduate (2)
barbecue (2)	dance (2)	grate (2)
bathe (2)	design (1)	grease (2)
board (1)	deposit (1)	greet (1)
boil (1)	deliver (1)	grill (1)
borrow (1)	dial (1)	hail (1)
bounce (2)	dictate (2)	hammer (1)
brainstorm (1)	die (2)	harvest (1)
breathe (2)	discuss (1)	help (1)
broil (1)	dive (2)	hire (2)
brush (1)	dress (1)	hug (3)
burn (1)	dribble (2)	immigrate (2)
call (1)	drill (1)	inquire (2)
carry (4)	drop (3)	insert (1)
change (2)	drown (1)	introduce (2)
check (1)	dry (4)	invite (2)
choke (2)	dust (1)	iron (1)
chop (3)	dye (2)	jog (3)
circle (2)	edit (1)	join (1)
claim (1)	eject (1)	jump (1)
clap (3)	empty (4)	kick (1)
clean (1)	end (1)	kiss (1)
clear (1)	enter (1)	knit (3)
climb (1)	erase (2)	land (1)
close (2)	examine (2)	laugh (1)
collate (2)	exchange (2)	learn (1)

lengthen (1)
listen (1)
live (2)
load (1)
lock (1)
look (1)
mail (1)
manufacture (2)
mark (1)
match (1)
measure (2)
milk (1)
miss (1)
mix (1)
mop (3)
move (2)
mow (1)
need (1)
nurse (2)
obey (1)
observe (2)
open (1)
operate (2)
order (1)
overdose (2)
paint (1)
park (1)
pass (1)
pause (2)
peel (1)
perm (1)
pick (1)
pitch (1)
plan (3)
plant (1)
play (1)
point (1)
polish (1)
pour (1)
pretend (1)
print (1)
protect (1)

pull (1)
push (1)
race (2)
raise (2)
rake (2)
receive (2)
record (1)
recycle (2)
register (1)
relax (1)
remove (2)
rent (1)
repair (1)
repeat (1)
report (1)
request (1)
return (1)
rinse (2)
roast (1)
rock (1)
sauté (2)
save (2)
scrub (3)
seat (1)
sentence (2)
serve (2)
share (2)
shave (2)
ship (3)
shop (3)
shorten (1)
shout (1)
sign (1)
simmer (1)
skate (2)
ski (1)
slice (2)
smell (1)
sneeze (2)
sort (1)
spell (1)
staple (2)

start (1)
stay (1)
steam (1)
stir (3)
stir-fry (4)
stop (3)
stow (1)
stretch (1)
supervise (2)
swallow (1)
tackle (2)
talk (1)
taste (2)
thank (1)
tie (2)
touch (1)
transcribe (2)
transfer (3)
travel (1)
trim (3)
turn (1)
type (2)
underline (2)
unload (1)
unpack (1)
use (2)
vacuum (1)
vomit (1)
vote (2)
wait (1)
walk (1)
wash (1)
watch (1)
water (1)
weed (1)
weigh (1)
wipe (2)
work (1)
wrap (3)
yield (1)

Verb Guide

Irregular Verbs

These verbs have irregular endings in the past and/or the past participle.

The Oxford Picture Dictionary List of Irregular Verbs

simple	past	past participle	simple	past	past participle
be	was	been	leave	left	left
beat	beat	beaten	lend	lent	lent
become	became	become	let	let	let
begin	began	begun	light	lit	lit
bend	bent	bent	make	made	made
bleed	bled	bled	pay	paid	paid
blow	blew	blown	picnic	picnicked	picnicked
break	broke	broken	put	put	put
build	built	built	read	read	read
buy	bought	bought	rewind	rewound	rewound
catch	caught	caught	rewrite	rewrote	rewritten
come	came	come	ride	rode	ridden
cut	cut	cut	run	ran	run
do	did	done	say	said	said
draw	drew	drawn	see	saw	seen
drink	drank	drunk	sell	sold	sold
drive	drove	driven	send	sent	sent
eat	ate	eaten	set	set	set
fall	fell	fallen	sew	sewed	sewn
feed	fed	fed	shoot	shot	shot
feel	felt	felt	sing	sang	sung
find	found	found	sit	sat	sat
fly	flew	flown	speak	spoke	spoken
get	got	gotten	stand	stood	stood
give	gave	given	sweep	swept	swept
go	went	gone	swim	swam	swum
hang	hung	hung	swing	swung	swung
have	had	had	take	took	taken
hear	heard	heard	teach	taught	taught
hide	hid	hidden	throw	threw	thrown
hit	hit	hit	wake	woke	woken
hold	held	held	wear	wore	worn
keep	kept	kept	withdraw	withdrew	withdrawn
lay	laid	laid	write	wrote	written

Index

Two numbers are shown after words in the index: the first refers to the page where the word is illustrated and the second refers to the item number of the word on that page. For example, cool [kōōl] **10**-3 means that the word *cool* is item number 3 on page 10. If only the bold page number appears, then that word is part of the unit title or subtitle, or is found somewhere else on the page. A bold number followed by ◆ means the word can be found in the exercise space at the bottom of that page.

Words or combinations of words that appear in **bold** type are used as verbs or verb phrases. Words used as other parts of speech are shown in ordinary type. So, for example, **file** (in bold type) is the verb *file*, while file (in ordinary type) is the noun *file*. Words or phrases in small capital letters (for example, HOLIDAYS) form unit titles.

Phrases and other words that form combinations with an individual word entry are often listed underneath it. Rather than repeating the word each time it occurs in combination with what is listed under it, the word is replaced by three dots (...), called an ellipsis. For example, under the word *bus*, you will find ...driver and ...stop meaning *bus driver* and *bus stop*. Under the word *store* you will find shoe... and toy..., meaning *shoe store* and *toy store*.

Pronunciation Guide

The index includes a pronunciation guide for all the words and phrases illustrated in the book. This guide uses symbols commonly found in dictionaries for native speakers. These symbols, unlike those used in pronunciation systems such as the International Phonetic Alphabet, tend to use English spelling patterns and so should help you to become more aware of the connections between written English and spoken English.

Consonants

[b] as in back [băk]	[k] as in key [kē]	[sh] as in shoe [shōō]
[ch] as in cheek [chēk]	[l] as in leaf [lēf]	[t] as in tape [tāp]
[d] as in date [dāt]	[m] as in match [măch]	[th] as in three [thrē]
[dh] as in this [dhĭs]	[n] as in neck [nĕk]	[v] as in vine [vīn]
[f] as in face [fās]	[ng] as in ring [rĭng]	[w] as in wait [wāt]
[g] as in gas [găs]	[p] as in park [pärk]	[y] as in yams [yămz]
[h] as in half [hăf]	[r] as in rice [rīs]	[z] as in zoo [zōō]
[j] as in jam [jăm]	[s] as in sand [sănd]	[zh] as in measure [mĕzh/ər]

Vowels

[ā] as in bake [bāk]	[ĭ] as in lip [lĭp]	[ow] as in cow [kow]
[ă] as in back [băk]	[ï] as in near [nïr]	[oy] as in boy [boy]
[ä] as in car [kär] or box [bäks]	[ō] as in cold [kōld]	[ŭ] as in cut [kŭt]
[ē] as in beat [bēt]	[ö] as in short [shört]	[ü] as in curb [kürb]
[ĕ] as in bed [bĕd]	or claw [klö]	[ə] as in above [ə bŭv/]
[ë] as in bear [bër]	[ōō] as in cool [kōōl]	
[ī] as in line [līn]	[ŏŏ] as in cook [kŏŏk]	

All the pronunciation symbols used are alphabetical except for the schwa [ə]. The schwa is the most frequent vowel sound in English. If you use the schwa appropriately in unstressed syllables, your pronunciation will sound more natural.

Vowels before [r] are shown with the symbol [¨] to call attention to the special quality that vowels have before [r]. (Note that the symbols [ä] and [ö] are also used for vowels not followed by [r], as in *box* or *claw*.) You should listen carefully to native speakers to discover how these vowels actually sound.

Stress

This index follows the system for marking stress used in many dictionaries for native speakers.

1. Stress is not marked if a word consisting of a single syllable occurs by itself.

2. Where stress is marked, two levels are distinguished:

   a bold accent [/] is placed after each syllable with primary (or strong) stress, a light accent [/] is placed after each syllable with secondary (or weaker) stress.

In phrases and other combinations of words, stress is indicated for each word as it would be pronounced within the whole phrase or other unit. If a word consisting of a single syllable is stressed in the combinations listed below it, the accent mark indicating the degree of stress it has in the phrases (primary or secondary) is shown in parentheses. A hyphen replaces any part of a word or phrase that is omitted. For example, bus [bŭs(/–)] shows that the word *bus* is said with primary stress in the combinations shown below it. The word ...driver [–drī/vər], listed under *bus*, shows that *driver* has secondary stress in the combination *bus driver*: [bŭs/ drī/vər].

Syllable Boundaries

Syllable boundaries are indicated by a single space or by a stress mark.

Note: The pronunciations shown in this index are based on patterns of American English. There has been no attempt to represent all of the varieties of American English. Students should listen to native speakers to hear how the language actually sounds in a particular region.

Index

abdomen [ăb/də mən] **74**–3
above [ə bŭv/] **13**–6
accelerator [ĭk sĕl/ə rā/tər] **109**– 47
ACCESSORIES [ĭk sĕs/ə rēz] **68–69**
accident [ăk/sə dənt] **102**–2
accordion [ə kör/dē ən] **120**–21
accountant [ə kown/tnt] **136**–1
acid rain [ăs/əd rān] **126**–11
across [ə krös/] **105**–3
acrylic paint [ə krĭl/ĭk pānt/] **162**– 9
act [ăkt] **140** ✦
action [ăk/shən]
   ...figure [–fĭg/yər] **163**–31
   ...story [–stör/ē] **166**–13
actor [ăk/tər] **136**–2
acupuncture [ăk/yə pŭngk/chər] **81**–G
adapter [ə dăp/tər] **164**–18
add [ăd] **58**–Q, **72**–B
addition [ə dĭsh/ən] **118**–1
address [ə drĕs/] **96**–A
address [ə drĕs/, ă/drĕs] **4**–5, **96**–7,8
adhesive bandage [əd hē/sĭv băn/dĭj] **83**–3
administrative assistant [əd mĭn/ə strā/tĭv ə sĭs/tənt] **136**–3
administrator [əd mĭn/ə strā/tər] **5** ✦
adults [ə dŭlts/, ăd/ŭlts] **22**–9
adult school [ə dŭlt/ skool/, ăd/ŭlt–] **112**–8
adventure story [əd vĕn/chər stör/ē] **166**–13
aerogramme [ĕr/ə grăm/] **96**–13
afternoon [ăf/tər noon/] **17**–18
aftershave [ăf/tər shāv/] **77**–28
AGE AND PHYSICAL DESCRIPTION [āj/ ən fĭz/ĭ kəl dĭ skrĭp/shən] **22**
AIDS (acquired immunodeficiency syndrome) [ādz] **79** ✦
air [ĕr(/–)] **109**–59
   ...bag [–băg/] **108**–16
   ...conditioner [–kən dĭsh/ə nər] **37**–19
   ...conditioning [–kən dĭsh/ə nĭng] **108**–28
   ...letter [–lĕt/ər] **96**–13
   ...pollution [–pə loo/shən] **126**–10
   ...purifier [–pyoor/ə fī ər] **80**–4
airline [ĕr/līn/]
   ...representative [–rĕp rĭ zĕn/tə tĭv] **110**–2
   ...terminal [–tür/mə nəl] **110**–1
airplane [ĕr/plān/] **110**–9
   ...crash [–krăsh/] **102**–3
AIRPORT [ĕr/pört/] **110**
airsickness bag [ĕr/sĭk/nəs băg/] **110**–15
aisle [īl] **54**–5
Alaska time [ə lăs/kə tīm/] **17**–25
alfalfa [ăl făl/fə] **148**–5
algebra [ăl/jə brə] **118**–25
allergies [ăl/ər jēz] **79**–8
alley [ăl/ē] **37**–21
alligator [ăl/ə gā/tər] **131**–36
alphabet [ăl/fə bĕt/] **3**–30
ALTERATIONS [öl/tə rā/shənz] **73**
aluminum foil [ə loo/mə nəm foyl/] **55**–55
a.m. [ā/ĕm/] **16** ✦
American cheese [ə mĕr/ə kən chēz/] **53**–9
AMPHIBIANS [ăm fĭb/ē ənz] **130–131**
amusement park [ə myooz/mənt pärk/] **152**–13
anesthesiologist [ăn/əs thē/zē äl/ə jĭst] **87**–35
angle [ăng/gəl] **118**–24
angry [ăng/grē] **31**–29
animals [ăn/ə məlz] **152**–2
ANIMALS, DOMESTIC [də mĕs/tĭk ăn/ə məlz] **133**

ankle [ăng/kəl] **75**–61, **78**–18
anniversary [ăn/ə vür/sə rē] **19**– 42
announcer [ə nown/sər] **152**–27
answer [ăn/sər]
   ...a question [–ə kwĕs/chən] **6**–H
   ...the door [–dhə dör/] **169**–F
answering machine [ăn/sə rĭng mə shēn/] **9**–14
answer sheet [ăn/sər shēt/] **7**–T
antacid [ănt ăs/əd] **81**–18
anteater [ănt/ē/tər] **135**–24
antelope [ăn/tə lōp/] **135**–35
antibacterial ointment [ăn/tē băk tïr/ē əl oynt/mənt] **83**–9
antihistamine cream [ăn/tĭ hĭs/tə mēn krēm/] **83**–10
antler [ănt/lər] **134**–16
ants [ănts] **49**–24
apartment [ə pärt/mənt]
   ...building [–bĭl/dĭng] **34**–5
   ...number [–nŭm/bər] **4**–6
APARTMENTS [ə pärt/mənts] **36–37**
apologize [ə päl/ə jīz/] **8**–I
apostrophe [ə päs/trə fē] **113**–11
appear in court [ə pïr/ ĭn kört/] **99**–C
applaud [ə plöd/] **32**–B
apple juice [ăp/əl joos/] **55**–50, **57**–5
apples [ăp/əlz] **50**–4
application [ăp/lə kā/shən] **144**–21
appointment [ə poynt/mənt] **19**– 45, **85**
   ...book [–book/] **143**–27
apricots [ăp/rə kăts/] **50**–7
April [ā/prəl] **19**–28
archery [är/chə rē] **159**–1
architect [är/kə tĕkt/] **136**–4
area [ĕr/ē ə] **34**–(1, 4)
area code [ĕr/ē ə kōd/] **4**–10
arm [ärm] **74**–9
armadillo [är/mə dĭl/ō] **134**–8
armchair [ärm/chër/] **42**–24
around [ə rownd/] **105**–10
arrange [ə rānj/] **35**–K
arrest [ə rĕst/] **99**–A
arrival and departure monitors [ə rī/vəl ən dĭ pär/chər män/ə tərz] **110**–4
arrival time [ə rī/vəl tīm/] **111** ✦
arrive [ə rīv/] **111**–O
arrow [ăr/ō] **161**–7
art [ärt] **121**–1
artery [är/tə rē] **75**–43
artichokes [är/tə chōks/] **51**–20
artist [är/tĭst] **136**–5
art museum [ärt/ myoo zē/əm] **152**–7
ask [ăsk(/–)]
   ...about benefits [–ə bowt/ bĕn/ə fĭts] **141**–J
   ...about the hours [–ə bowt/ dhē ow/ərz] **141**–F
   ...a question [–ə kwĕs/chən] **6**–G
asparagus [ə spăr/ə gəs] **51**–24
assault [ə sölt/] **100**–7
assemble [ə sĕm/bəl] **140**–A
assembler [ə sĕm/blər] **136**–6
assembly line [ə sĕm/blē līn/] **146**–8
assist [ə sĭst/] **140**–B
Associate of Arts (AA) [ə sō/shē ĭt əv ärts/, –sē ĭt–] / [ā/ā/] **112** ✦
asteroid belt [ăs/tə royd bĕlt/] **127**–12
asthma [ăz/mə] **79**–11
astronaut [ăs/trə nöt/] **127**–17
astronomer [ə strän/ə mər] **127**–20

athletic [ăth lĕt/ĭk]
...shoes [–shōoz/] **68**–23
...supporter [–sə pör/tər] **67**–14
Atlantic time [ət lăn/tĭk tīm/] **17**–30
atlas [ăt/ləs] **98**–3
ATM (automated teller machine) [ā/tē/ĕm/] **97**–3
ATM card [ā/tē/ĕm/ kärd/] **97**–9
atom [ăt/əm] **119**–17
attorney [ə tür/nē] **99**–4
attractive [ə trăk/tĭv] **22**–23
audience [ö/dē əns] **32**–10
audiocassette [ö/dē ō kə sĕt/] **98**–12
audiologist [ö/dē äl/ə jĭst] **81**–32
auditorium [ö/də tör/ē əm] **5**–3
August [ö/gəst] **19**–32
aunt [ănt] **24**–10
author [ö/thər] **98**–22, **139**–64
automatic transmission
  [ö/tə măt/ĭk trănz mĭsh/ən, –trăns–] **109**
auto mechanic [ö/tō mə kăn/ĭk] **136**–7
average [ăv/rĭj]
...height [–hīt/] **22**–17
...weight [–wāt/] **22**–21
avocadoes [ä/və kä/dōz, ăv/ə–] **50**–14
ax [ăks] **150**–3
baboon [bă bōon/] **135**–32
baby [bā/bē] **22**–2
...backpack [–băk/păk/] **95**–15
...carrier [–kăr/ē ər] **95**–14
...food [–fōod/] **95**–28
...monitor [–măn/ə tər] **45**–9
...powder [–pow/dər] **95**–18
baby-sitter [bā/bē sĭt/ər] **136**–12
Bachelor's degree [băch/lərz də grē/] **112** ✦
back [băk(/–)] **74**–11
...support [–sə pört/] **147**–16
backache [băk/āk/] **78**–5
backhoe [băk/hō/] **149**–8
backpack [băk/păk/] **69**–28, **95**–15, **154**–15
backpacking [băk/păk/ĭng] **154**–7
backseat [băk/sēt/] **109**–38
backyard [băk/yärd/] **38**–2
bacon [bā/kən] **52**–11, **61**–7
bad [băd] **11**–18
bag [băg] (market) **55**–22, 23, **56**–7, 19 (purse) **69**–27, 28, 29
baggage claim area [băg/ĭj klăm/ ĕr/ē ə] **110**–17
bagger [băg/ər] **55**–21
baggy [băg/ē] **71**–42
bag of flour [băg/ əv flow/ər] **56**–19
bags (luggage) [băgz] **111**–B
bailiff [bā/ləf] **99**–13
bake [bāk] **58**–L
baked [bākt(/–)]
...goods [–gōodz/] **54**–6
...potato [–pə tā/tō] **61**–14
baker [bā/kər] **136**–8
bakery [bā/kə rē] **89**–16
baking products [bā/kĭng präd/ŭkts] **55**–13
balance [băl/əns] (bank) **97**–11, (science) **119**–11
balcony [băl/kə nē] **37**–17
bald [böld] **23**–12
ball [böl] **45**–16, **161**–3, 4, 5, 12, 18, 22
ballet [bă lā/] **166**–7
ball field [böl/ fēld/] **153**–1
ballroom [böl/rōom/] **145**–20

bananas [bə năn/əz] **50**–3
bandage [băn/dĭj] **83**–3, 12
bangs [băngz] **23**–8
BANK [băngk] **97**
bank [băngk] **88**–3
banner [băn/ər] **33**–15
barbecue [bär/bĭ kyōo/] **58**–T
barbecue grill [bär/bĭ kyōo grĭl/] **39**–7
barber shop [bär/bər shäp/] **88**–15
bar code [bär/ kōd/] **21**–4
barn [bärn] **148**–11
barrette [bə rĕt/] **76**–18
baseball [bās/böl/] **158**–9, **161**–18
...bat [–băt/] **161**–14
...cap [–kăp/] **66**–27
...card [–kärd/] **162**–11
...game [–gām/] **152**–25
basement [bās/mənt] **36** ✦
basket [băs/kət] **42**–2
basketball [băs/kət böl/] **158**–8, **161**–4
...court [–kört/] **158**–7
bass (fish) [băs] **130**–11
bass (instrument) [bās] **120**–10
bassoon [bə sōon/] **120**–6
bat [băt] (animal) **134**–7, (baseball) **161**–14
bath [băth(/–)]
...mat [–măt/] **43**–27
...powder [–pow/dər] **76**–3
...towel [–tow/əl] **43**–12
bathe [bādh] **76**–B
bathing suit [bā/dhĭng sōot/] **66**–26
bathrobe [băth/rōb/] **67**–8
BATHROOM [băth/rōom/] **43**
bathtub [băth/tŭb/] **43**–2
battery [băt/ə rē] (car) **109**–43, (flashlight) **151**–40
...charger [–chär/jər] **165**–23
...pack [–păk/] **165**–22
bay [bā] **117**–9
be [bē]
...18 years old [–ā/tēn/ yïrz/ ōld/] **116**–A
...**born** [–börn/] **28**–A
...**hurt** [–hürt/] **82**–A
...**injured** [–ĭn/jərd/] **82**–A
...in school [–ĭn skōol/] **26**–J
...in shock [–ĭn shäk/] **82**–C
...**released** [–rĭ lēst/] **99**–H
...unconscious [–ŭn kän/shəs] **82**–B
BEACH [bēch] **155**
beach [bēch(/–)] **117**–10
...chair [–chër/] **155**–14
...towel [–tow/əl] **155**–15
...umbrella [–ŭm brĕl/ə] **155**–9
beads [bēdz] **69**–32
beak [bēk] **132**–1
beaker [bē/kər] **119**–13
beam [bēm] **149**–3
beans [bēnz] **51**–25, **54**–26
bear [bër] **134**–11
beard [bïrd] **23**–6
beat [bēt] **58**–B
beautiful [byōo/tə fəl] **11**–21
beauty shop [byōo/tē shäp/] **92** ✦
beaver [bē/vər] **134**–9
become a citizen [bĭ kŭm/ ə sĭt/ə zən] **28**–H
bed [bĕd(/–)] **44**–8

Index

...control [–kən trōl/] **86**–12
...frame [–frām/] **44**–27
...table [–tā/bəl] **86**–9
bedpan [bĕd/păn/] **86**–13
BEDROOM [bĕd/rōōm/] **44**
bedspread [bĕd/sprĕd/] **44**–11
Beef [bēf] **52**
beef ribs [bēf/ rĭbz/] **52**–5
beetle [bēt/l] **132**–19
beets [bēts] **51**–6
begin [bĭ gĭn/] **8**–B
behind [bĭ hīnd/] **13**–3
beige [bāzh] **12**–9
bell captain [bĕl/ kăp/tən] **145**–4
bellhop [bĕl/häp/] **145**–5
below [bĭ lō/] **13**–7
belt buckle [bĕlt/ bŭk/əl] **69**–41
belts [bĕlts] **69**–11
bench [bĕnch] **153**–10
bend [bĕnd] **157**–R
berries [bĕr/ēz] **128**–20
between [bĭ twēn/] **13**–10
beverages [bĕv/rə jəz] **55**–15, **61**
bib [bĭb] **95**–8
bicycle [bī/sĭ kəl] **153**–4
big [bĭg] **11**–2
bike [bīk(/–)] **153**–4
...path [–păth/] **153**–2
...shorts [–shörts/] **67**–3
biking [bī/kĭng] **159**–4
bikini panties [bə kē/nē păn/tēz] **67**–16
bill (bird) [bĭl] **132**–1
bill (invoice) [bĭl] **21** ✦
billiards [bĭl/yərdz] **159**–2
billion [bĭl/yən] **14**
bills (paper money) [bĭlz] **20, 20** ✦
bin [bĭn] **37**–20
binder [bīn/dər] **3**–24
biohazard [bī/ō hăz/ərd] **147**–5
biology [bī äl/ə jē] **119**–1
birch [bürch] **128**–8
BIRDS, INSECTS, AND ARACHNIDS
[bürdz/ ĭn/sĕkts ən ə răk/nĭdz] **132**
birth certificate [bürth/ sər tĭf/ə kət] **29**–1
birthday [bürth/dā/] **19**–41, **169**–I
bison [bī/sən] **134**–6
black [blăk(/–)] **12**–15
...hair [–hër/] **23**–15
bladder [blăd/ər] **75**–47
blade [blād] **150**–11
blanket [blăng/kət] **44**–12
...sleeper [–slē/pər] **67**–7
bleach [blēch] **72**–8
bleachers [blē/chərz] **5**–10
bleed [blēd] **82**–M
blender [blĕn/dər] **40**–12
blind [blīnd] **22**–26
blinds [blīndz] **43**–11
blister [blĭs/tər] **78**–15
blizzard [blĭz/ərd] **103**–11
block [bläk] **107**–2
blocks [bläks] **45**–15
blond [bländ] **23**–16
blood [blŭd(/–)] **79**–15
...pressure gauge [–prĕsh/ər gāj/] **84**–12

...test [–tĕst/] **86**–17
...work [–würk/] **86**–17
bloody nose [blŭd/ē nōz/] **78**–17
blouse [blows] **64**–9
blow dryer [blō/ drī/ər] **23**–20, **76**–16
blow out [blō/ owt/] **169**–K
blue [blōō] **12**–1
blueberries [blōō/bĕr/ēz] **50**–19
blue jay [blōō/ jā/] **132**–7
blush [blŭsh] **77**–36
board game [börd/ gām/] **162**–3
boarding area [bör/dĭng ër/ē ə] **110**–6
board the plane [börd/ dhə plān/] **111**–F
boating [bō/tĭng] **154**–2
bobby pins [bäb/ē pĭnz/] **76**–19
BODY [bäd/ē] **74**–75
body lotion [bäd/ē lō/shən] **76**–7
body of water [bäd/ē əv wö/tər] **117** ✦
boil [boyl] **58**–P
bolt [bōlt] **37**–29, **150**–30, 33
bone [bōn] (body) **75**–49, (broken) **82**–P
boneless [bōn/ləs] **52** ✦
bookbag [bŏŏk/băg/] **69**–28
bookcase [bŏŏk/kās/] **3**–8, **42**–1
bookstore [bŏŏk/stör/] **92**–4
booth [bōōth] **60**–19, **152**–23
boots [bōōts] **68**–18
bored [börd] **31**–26
boring [bör/ĭng] **167**–29
borrow [bär/ō, bör/ō] **20** ✦
botanical gardens [bə tăn/ĭ kəl gär/dnz] **152**–4
bottle [bät/l] **56**–1, **95**–26
...of soda [–əv sō/də] **56**–13
bottled water [bät/ld wö/tər] **55**–53
bottle return [bät/l rĭ türn/] **54**–1
bounce [bowns] **156**–K
bouquet [bō kā/, bōō–] **129**–27
bow [bō] **161**–6
bowl [bōl] **41**–25
bowling [bō/lĭng] **159**–3
...ball [–böl/] **161**–5
bow tie [bō/ tī/] **69**–40
box [bäks(/–)] **56**–6
...of cereal [–əv sïr/ē əl] **56**–18
...spring [–sprĭng/] **44**–26
boxer shorts [bäk/sər shörts/] **67**–12
boy [boy] **22**–4, 7
bra [brä] **67**–20
brace [brās] **81**–31
bracelet [brās/lət] **69**–35, **83**–14
braces [brā/səz] **84**–24
brain [brān(/–)] **75**–35
...cancer [–kăn/sər] **79**–12
brainstorm [brān/störm/] **6**–K
brake [brāk(/–)]
...light [–līt/] **108**–13
...pedal [–pĕd/l] **109**–46
branch [brănch] **128**–2
Branches of government [brăn/chəz əv gŭv/ər mənt] **116**
Brass [brăs] **120**
bread [brĕd(/–)] **53**–1, 2, 3, **54**–29
...basket [–băs/kət] **63**–8
bread-and-butter plate [brĕd/ n bŭt/ər plāt/] **63**–16
break [brāk(/–)]
...a bone [–ə bōn/] **82**–P

...three eggs [–thrē′ ĕgz′] **58**–A
Breakfast [brĕk′fəst] **61**
breast (body) [brĕst] **74**–14
breasts (chicken) [brĕsts] **52**–19
bricklayer [brĭk′lā′ər] **136**–9
bricks [brĭks] **149**–11
bridge [brĭj] **105**–2
briefs [brēfs] **67**–13, 17
broccoli [bräk′ə lē] **51**–15, **58**–I
broil [broyl] **58**–V
broiler [broy′lər] **40**–21
broken [brō′kən] **48**–5, 6, 7, **49**–15, **70**–24
broom [brōōm] **47**–10
brother [brŭdh′ər] / [–brŭdh′ər] **24**–9
    half... [hăf′–] **25**–29
brother-in-law [brŭdh′ər ĭn lö′] **24**–16
brown [brown(′–)] **12**–11
    ...hair [–hër′] **23**–17
bruise [brōōz] **78**–12
brush [brŭsh(′–)]
    ...hair [–hër′] **76**–I
    ...teeth [–tēth′] **77**–J
brush [(–)brŭsh(′)] **23**–18, **76**–14
    paint... [pānt′–] **151**–47, **163**–23
    scrub... [skrŭb′–] **47**–19
    toilet... [toy′lət–] **43**–16
bucket [bŭk′ət] **47**–20, **155**–22
buckle [bŭk′əl] **69**–41
bud [bŭd] **129**–6
buffalo [bŭf′ə lō] **134**–6
buffet [bə fā′] **33**–13
building [bĭl′dĭng] **34**–5
BUILDING SUPPLIES [bĭl′dĭng sə plīz′] **150–151**
build models [bĭld′ mäd′lz] **162**–C
bulb [bŭlb] **129**–9
bulldozer [bŏŏl′dō′zər] **149**–6
bulletin board [bŏŏl′ə tn börd′] **3**–14
bumper [bŭm′pər] **108**–7
bumper pad [bŭm′pər păd′] **45**–7
bunk [bŭngk] **45**–1
Bunsen burner [bŭn′sən bür′nər] **119**–9
bureau [byŏŏr′ō] **44**–2
burglary [bür′glə rē] **100**–6
burner [bür′nər] **40**–19
burn (your)self [bürn′ (yər)sĕlf′] **82**–H
bus [bŭs(′–)] **90**–15, **104**–4
    ...driver [–drī′vər] **104**–8
    ...stop [–stäp′] **91**–16, **104**–1
bush [bŏŏsh] **39**–20
business education [bĭz′nəs ĕj ə kā′shən] **121**–2
businessman [bĭz′nəs măn′] **136**–10
businesswoman [bĭz′nəs wŏŏm′ən] **136**–10
busperson [bŭs′pür′sən] **63**–9
butcher [bŏŏch′ər] **136**–11
butter [bŭt′ər] **54**–36
butterfly [bŭt′ər flī′] **132**–20
buttocks [bŭt′əks] **74**–12
button [bŭt′n] **73**–21
buttonhole [bŭt′n hōl′] **73**–12
buy [bī(′–)] **21**–C
    ...a house [–ə hows′] **29**–O
    ...your ticket [–yər tĭk′ət] **111**–A
Buying a house [bī′ĭng ə hows′] **35**
cab [kăb] **104**–18, **106**–16
cabbage [kăb′ĭj] **51**–2

cabinet [kăb′ə nət] **40**–1
cable [kā′bəl] **144**–16
cactus [kăk′təs] **128**–21
cafeteria [kăf′ə tïr′ē ə] **5**–4
cake [kāk(′–)] **54**–32, **61**–19
    ...mix [–mīks′] **55**–47
    ...pan [–păn′] **59**–26
calculator [kăl′kyə lā′tər] **142**–8
calculus [kăl′kyə ləs] **118**–28
CALENDAR [kăl′ən dər] **18–19**
calf [kăf] **74**–18
call [köl] **141**–E
call button [köl′ bŭt′n] **86**–10
calm [käm] **30**–10
camcorder [kăm′kör′dər] **165**–21
camel [kăm′əl] **135**–38
camera [kăm′rə] **165**–19, 24, 27
    ...case [–kās′] **165**–27
camisole [kăm′ə sōl′] **67**–21
camper [kăm′pər] **106**–11
campfire [kămp′fīr′] **154**–11
camping [kăm′pĭng] **154**–1
    ...stove [–stōv′] **154**–16
can [kăn(′–)] **56**–3
    ...of soup [–əv sōōp′] **56**–15
    ...opener [–ō′pə nər] **40**–14, **59**–1
cancer [kăn′sər] **79**–12
candle [kăn′dl] **41**–7
candles [kăn′dlz] **169**–H, K
candlestick [kăn′dl stĭk′] **41**–8
candy [kăn′dē] **55**–41, **168**–14
    ...bar [–băr′] **55**–41
    ...store [–stör′] **92**–3
cane [kān] **80**–7
canned goods [kănd′ gŏŏdz′] **54**–4
canoeing [kə nōō′ĭng] **154**–3
cantaloupes [kăn′tə lōps′] **50**–15
can't breathe [kănt′ brēdh′] **82**–N
canteen [kăn tēn′] **154**–24
canvas [kăn′vəs] **163**–22
canyon [kăn′yən] **117**–17
cap [kăp] (graduation) **32**–3, (clothing) **66**–6
capsule [kăp′səl] **81**–27
captain [kăp′tən] **158** ✦
car [kär(′–)]
    ...accident [–ăk′sə dənt] **102**–2
    ...dealership [–dē′lər shĭp′] **88**–4
    ...safety seat [–sāf′tē sēt′] **95**–13
card [kärd(′–)] **96**–4, **168**–5
    ...catalog [–kăt′l ög, –äg] **98**–10
    ...store [–stör′] **92**–7
cardigan sweater [kär′də gən swĕt′ər] **65**–27
Cardinals [kärd′nəlz] **14**
cardiologist [kär′dē äl′ə jĭst] **86**–3
cards [kärdz] **163**–H
careful [kër′fəl] **147**–24
caregiver [kër′gĭv′ər] **136**–12
careless [kër′ləs] **147**–23
CAR MAINTENANCE [kär′ mān′tn əns] **108–109**
carnation [kär nā′shən] **129**–18
carnival [kär′nə vəl] **152**–16
carousel [kăr′ə sĕl′] **110**–18
carousel slide projector [kăr′ə sĕl′ slīd′ prə jĕk′tər] **165**–29
carpenter [kär′pən tər] **48**–12, **136**–13
carpet [kär′pət] **42**–27

Index

carriage [kăr/ĭj] **95**–16
carrots [kăr/əts] **51**–3
carry [kăr/ē] **62**–H
carry-on bag [kăr/ē än băg/, –ön–] **111**–H
CARS AND TRUCKS [kärz/ ən trŭks/] **106**
cart [kärt] **54**–3, **91**–31
carton [kär/tn] **56**–4
...of eggs [–əv ĕgz/] **56**–16
cartoon [kär tōōn/] **167**–19
cartridge [kär/trĭj] / [–kär/trĭj] **162**–2
typewriter... [tīp/rī/tər–] **143**–31
carving knife [kär/vĭng nīf/] **59**–12
cash [kăsh(/–)] **20**–13, **97**–D
...register [–rĕj/ə stər] **55**–18, **140**–N
cashier [kă shïr/] **136**–14
casserole dish [kăs/ə rōl dĭsh/] **59**–11
cassette [kə sĕt/]
...player [–plā/ər] **3**–11, **164**–2, 15
...recorder [–rĭ kör/dər] **164**–3
cast [kăst] **81**–29
casual [kăzh/ōō əl] **71**–37
cat [kăt] **133**–9
catch [kăch] **156**–E
catcher's mask [kăch/ərz măsk/] **161**–15
caterer [kā/tər ər] **33**–12
caterpillar [kăt/ə pĭl/ər, kăt/ər–] **132**–21
catfish [kăt/fĭsh/] **53**–17
cattle [kăt/l] **148**–21
cauliflower [kö/lĭ flow/ər, kä/–] **51**–16
cavity [kăv/ə tē] **84**–20
C-clamp [sē/klămp/] **150**–6
CD (compact disc) [sē/dē/] **98**–14
...player [–plā/ər] **164**–14
...ROM disc [–räm/ dĭsk/] **144**–2
ceiling [sē/lĭng] **42**–5
...fan [–făn/] **41**–4
celery [sĕl/ə rē] **51**–9
cello [chĕl/ō] **120**–9
cellular phone [sĕl/yə lər fōn/] **9**–13
Celsius [sĕl/sē əs] **10**
cent [sĕnt] **20**–1
centimeter (cm) [sĕn/tə mē/tər] **15**–12
CENTRAL AMERICA [sĕn/trəl ə mĕr/ə kə] **122**–123
central time [sĕn/trəl tīm/] **17**–28
cents [sĕnts] **20**–2, 3, 4
cereal [sïr/ē əl] **56**–18
Ceremony [sĕr/ə mō/nē] **32**
Certificate of Naturalization
[sər tĭf/ə kət əv năch/rə lə zā/shən] **29**–6
certified mail [sür/tə fīd/ māl] **96**–11
chain [chān] (hardware) **37**–28, **150**–36, (jewelry) **69**–31
chair [(–)chër(/)] **2**–7
dining room... [dī/nĭng rōōm/–] **41**–16
easy... [ē/zē–] **42**–24
high... [hī/–] **95**–7
rocking... [räk/ĭng–] **94**–6
swivel... [swĭv/əl–] **143**–22
chalk [chök] **3**–16
chalkboard [chök/börd/] **2**–1
...eraser [–ī rā/sər] **3**–17
change [chānj(/–)] **21**–9
...purse [–pürs/] **69**–25
change [chānj(/–)]
...diapers [–dī/pərz] **94**–E
...the sheets [–dhə shĕts/] **46**–P

...your diet [–yər dī/ət] **80**–C
changing table [chān/jĭng tā/bəl] **45**–12, **95**–9
cheap [chēp] **11**–20
check [chĕk(/–)]
...blood pressure [–blŭd/ prĕsh/ər] **85**–B
...your bags [–yər băgz/] **111**–B
...your work [–yər würk/] **7**–Y
checkbook [chĕk/bŏŏk/] **97**–7
checked [chĕkt] **70**–11
checker [chĕk/ər] **55**–19
checkers [chĕk/ərz] **162**–5
check in [chĕk/ ĭn/] **111**–D
check-in counter [chĕk/ĭn kown/tər] **110**–3
checking account number [chĕk/ĭng ə kownt/ nŭm/bər] **97**–8
check out [chĕk/ owt/] **98** ✦
checkout desk [chĕk/owt dĕsk/] **98**–16
checkstand [chĕk/stănd/] **55**–17
cheddar cheese [chĕd/ər chēz/] **53**–10
cheek [chēk] **74**–29
cheese [chēz] **53**–9, 10, 11, 12, **54**–38
cheeseburger [chēz/bür/gər] **60**–3
chef [shĕf] **63**–11
chef's salad [shĕfs/ săl/əd] **61**–9
chemistry [kĕm/ə strē] **119**–2
cherries [chĕr/ēz] **50**–16
cherry picker [chĕr/ē pĭk/ər] **149**–5
chess [chĕs] **162**–6
chest (body) [chĕst] **74**–13
chest of drawers [chĕst/ əv drörz/] **45**–8
chicken [chĭk/ən] **52**–16, **61**–12
...soup [–sōōp/] **58**
chicken pox [chĭk/ən päks/] **79**–6
Chief Justice [chēf/ jŭs/təs] **116**–9
CHILDCARE CENTER [chīld/kër sĕn/tər] **94**–95
childcare worker [chīld/kër wür/kər] **94**–3
Childhood diseases [chīld/hŏŏd dĭ zē/zəz] **79**
children [chĭl/drən] **11**–11, 12, **22**–1
CHILDREN'S BEDROOM [chĭl/drənz bĕd/rōōm] **45**
children's program [chĭl/drənz prō/grăm] **167**–24
child safety seat [chīld/ sāf/tē sēt/] **109**–39
chili peppers [chĭl/ē pĕp/ərz] **51**–8
chills [chĭlz] **78**–9
chimney [chĭm/nē] **38**–21
chimpanzee [chĭm/păn zē/] **135**–28
chin [chĭn] **74**–31
china cabinet [chī/nə kăb/ə nət] **41**–1
chipmunk [chĭp/mŭngk/] **133**–20
chiropractor [kī/rə prăk/tər] **81**–H
chisel [chĭz/əl] **151**–51
choke [chōk] **82**–L
chop [chäp] **58**–G
chorus [kör/əs] **121**–3
Christmas [krĭs/məs] **168**–18
...tree [–trē/] **168**–20
chrysanthemum [krĭ săn/thə məm] **129**–19
church [chürch] **88**–6
cigarette lighter [sĭg/ə rĕt/ lī/tər, sĭg/ə rĕt–] **108**–32
circle [sür/kəl] **7**–5
circle [sür/kəl] **118**–5
circular saw [sür/kyə lər sö/] **150**–10
circumference [sər kŭm/frəns] **118**–15
Citizen application requirements
[sĭt/ə zən ăp/lə kā/shən rĭ kwīr/mənts] **116**
CITIZENSHIP [sĭt/ə zən shĭp/] **116**
city [sĭt/ē] **4**–7, **34**–1

...center [–sĕn/tər] **88** ✦
...hall [–höl/] **89**–17
CITY STREETS [sĭt/ē strēts/] **88**–**89**
claim your baggage [klām/ yər băg/ĭj] **111**–P
clams [klămz] **53**–28
clap [klăp] **32**–B
clarinet [klăr/ə nĕt/] **120**–4
CLASSROOM [klăs/rōōm/] **2**–**3**
classroom [klăs/rōōm/] **5**–1
Class work [klăs/ würk/] **7**
claw [klö] **132**–4
clay [klā] **162**–14
clean [klēn] (household) **27**–N, **46**–C, **72**–D, (teeth) **85**–I
clean [klēn] **72**–16
CLEANING SUPPLIES [klē/nĭng sə plīz/] **47**
cleanser [klĕn/zər] **47**–23
clear [klïr(/–)] **10**–6
...tape [–tāp/] **143**–39
clear [klïr] **62**–G
clear [klïr] **10**–6
clerk [(–)klürk(/)] **5**–18
desk... [dĕsk/–] **145**–8
file... [fīl/–] **142**–12
library... [lī/brër ē–] **98**–17
shipping... [shĭp/ĭng–] **146**–15
stock... [stäk/–] **139**–55
climb [klīm] **153**–C
climbing apparatus [klī/mĭng ăp ə răt/əs] **153**–14
CLINICS [klĭn/ĭks] **84**
clipboard [klĭp/börd/] **143**–26
clip-on earrings [klĭp/än ïr/ĭngz, –ön–] **69**–38
clock [kläk(/–)] **3**–10
...radio [–rā/dē ō] **44**–16, **164**–1
close [klōz] **2**–J
closet [kläz/ət] **11**–15, 16, **43** ✦, **44**–4
cloth diapers [klöth/ dī/pərz] **95**–21
clothesline [klōz/līn/] **72**–9
clothespin [klōz/pĭn/] **72**–10
CLOTHING I, II, III [klō/dhĭng] **64**–**67**
cloudy [klow/dē] **10**–7
clubs [klŭbz] **163**–26
clutch [klŭch] **109**–45
coach [kōch] **5** ✦, **158**–2
coal [kōl] **126**–4
coat [kōt] (clothing) **66**, (animal) **134**–19
cobra [kō/brə] **131**–40
cockpit [käk/pĭt/] **110**–11
cockroaches [käk/rō/chəz] **49**–25
coconuts [kō/kə nŭts/] **50**–22
cod [käd] **130**–8
coffee [kö/fē] **55**–51, **61**–22
...cup [–kŭp/] **41**–27
...shop [–shäp/] **88**–2
...table [–tā/bəl] **42**–23
instant... [ĭn/stənt–] **55**–51
coffeemaker [kö/fē mā/kər] **40**–11
COFFEE SHOP MENU [kö/fē shäp/ mĕn/yōō] **61**
coin collection [koyn/ kə lĕk/shən] **162**–13
Coins [koynz] **20**
colander [käl/ən dər] **59**–17
cold [kōld] (weather) **10**–4, (feeling) **30**–4
cold (illness) [kōld(/–)] **79**–1
...tablets [–tăb/ləts] **81**–17
cold water [kōld/ wö/tər] **43**–7
coleslaw [kōl/slö/] **53**–14

collar [käl/ər] **73**–7
collate [kō/lāt/, kə lāt/] **142**–F
collect [kə lĕkt/]
...the papers [–dhə pā/pərz] **7**–Q
...things [–thĭngz/] **162**–A
collection [kə lĕk/shən] **162**–12, 13
college [käl/ĭj] **112**–10
...degree [–də grē/] **29**–7
...dormitory [–dör/mə tör/ē] **34**–9
community... [kə myōō/nə tē–] **112** ✦
cologne [kə lōn/] **76**–5
colon [kō/lən] **113**–12
color hair [kŭl/ər hër/] **23**–D
coloring book [kŭl/ə rĭng bŏŏk/] **45**–20
COLORS [kŭl/ərz] **12**
comb...hair [kōm/ hër/] **76**–G
comb [kōm] **23**–22, **76**–13
comedy [käm/ə dē] **166**–10
come home [kŭm/ hōm/] **27**–Q
comet [käm/ət] **127**–25
comfortable [kŭmf/tə bəl, –tər–] **30**–7
comforter [kŭm/fər tər] **45**–2
comma [käm/ə] **113**–10
commercial fisher [kə mür/shəl fĭsh/ər] **136**–15
commit a crime [kə mĭt/ ə krīm/] **100** ✦
Common illnesses and childhood diseases
[käm/ən ĭl/nə səz ən chĭld/hŏŏd dĭ zē/zəz] **79**
community college [kə myōō/nə tē käl/ĭj] **112** ✦
compact [käm/păkt] **106**–2
compact disc (CD) [käm/păkt dĭsk/] **98**–14
compliment [käm/plə mĕnt/] **8**–G
components [kəm pō/nənts] **140**–A
composition [käm/pə zĭsh/ən] **113**–2
compost pile [käm/pōst pīl/] **39**–10
computer [kəm pyōō/tər] **3**–15
...programmer [–prō/grăm ər] **136**–16
...science [–sī/əns] **121**–4
...workstation [–würk/stā/shən] **143**–21
COMPUTERS [kəm pyōō/tərz] **144**
concert [kän/sərt] **166**–6
concierge [kän/sē ërzh/, kōn/–] **145** ✦
concrete [käng/krēt, kän krēt/] **149**–10
condiments [kän/də mənts] **60** ✦
conditioner [kən dĭsh/ə nər] **76**–10
condominium [kän/də mĭn/ē əm] **34** ✦
conductor [kən dŭk/tər] **104**–16
cone [kōn] **118**–11
confetti [kən fĕt/ē] **168**–3
confused [kən fyōōzd/] **31**–27
congestion [kən jĕs/chən] **78**–7
Congressman [käng/grəs mən] **116**–2
Congresswoman [käng/grəs wŏŏm/ən] **116**–2
Conservation [kän/sər vā/shən] **126**
conserve [kən sürv/] **126**–B, C
constellation [kän/stə lā/shən] **127**–24
CONSTRUCTION [kən strŭk/shən] **149**
construction worker [kən strŭk/shən wür/kər] **149**–1
contact lenses [kän/tăkt lĕn/zəz] **81**–36
container [kən tā/nər] **56**–5, **59**–3
...of cottage cheese [–əv kät/ĭj chēz/] **56**–17
CONTAINERS AND PACKAGED FOODS
[kən tā/nərz ən păk/ĭjd fōōdz/] **56**
Continents [kän/tə nənts] **124**
control tower [kən trōl/ tow/ər] **110**–7
convenience store [kən vēn/yəns stör/] **90**–3

Index

CONVERSATION, EVERYDAY [ĕv/rē dā/ kän/vər sā/shən] **8**
convertible [kən vür/tə bəl] **106**–5
convert the measurements
   [kən vürt/ dhə mĕzh/ər mənts] **57**–C
conveyor belt [kən vā/ər bĕlt/] **146**–12
convict [kən vĭkt/] **99**–14
cook [kŏŏk] **27**–P, **58**–F, **140**–C
cook [kŏŏk] **137**–17
cooked chicken [kŏŏkt/ chĭk/ən] **52**–25
cookies [kŏŏk/ēz] **54**–31, **56**–20
cookie sheet [kŏŏk/ē shēt/] **59**–27
cool [kōōl] **10**–3
coolant [kōō/lənt] **109**–56
cooler [kōō/lər] **155**–11
co-op [kō/äp/] **34** ✦
copy [käp/ē] **6**–F
copy center [käp/ē sĕn/tər] **91**–22
cord [körd] **9**–3, **151**–14
cordless phone [körd/ləs fōn/] **9**–12
core course [kör/ körs/] **121** ✦
corn [körn] **51**–27, **148**–4
corned beef [körnd/ bēf/] **53**–8
corner [kör/nər] **91**–17, **105**–10, **107**–1
corral [kə răl/] **148**–17
correct [kə rĕkt/] **7**–Z
correction fluid [kə rĕk/shən flōō/əd] **143**–33
corrosive [kə rō/sĭv] **147**–4
cost [köst] **21**–6
costume [käs/tōōm] **168**–13
cottage cheese [kät/ĭj chēz/] **56**–17
cotton [kät/n] **70**–16, **148**–6
couch [kowch] **42**–19
cough [köf] **78**–A
cough syrup [köf/ sĭr/əp, –sür/–] **81**–20
counselor [kown/slər] **5**–16
counselor's office [kown/slərz ö/fəs] **5**–15
count [kownt] **15** ✦
counter [kown/tər] **40**–22, **46**–O, **60**–13, **80**–12, **110**–3
country [kŭn/trē] **34**–4
county fair [kown/tē fër/] **152**–19
courier [kür/ē ər, kŏŏr/–] **138**–38
court [kört(/–)] **99**–C
   ...reporter [–rĭ pör/tər] **99**–12
courthouse [kört/hows/] **89**–18
courtroom [kört/rōōm/] **99**–7
courtyard [kört/yärd/] **37**–18
cousin [kŭz/ən] **24**–12
cover-up [kŭv/ər ŭp/] **66**–25
cow [kow] **133**–3
coyote [kī ō/tē, kī/ōt/] **134**–3
CPR (cardiopulmonary resuscitation) [sē/pē/är/] **83**–17
CPU (central processing unit) [sē/pē/yōō/] **144**–1
crab [krăb] **53**–22, **130**–16
cracked [krăkt] **48**–4
cradle [krād/l] **45**–19
crane [krān] **149**–7
crash [krăsh] **102**–3
crayons [krā/änz] **45**–21
creamer [krē/mər] **41**–13
credit card [krĕd/ət kärd/] **20**–15
creek [krēk, krĭk] **117** ✦
crescent moon [krĕs/ənt mōōn/] **127**–14
crewneck sweater [krōō/nĕk/ swĕt/ər] **71**–26
crib [krĭb] **45**–6
cricket [krĭk/ət] **132**–24

CRIME [krīm] **100**
criminal [krĭm/ə nəl] **100** ✦
crochet [krō shā/] **163**–20
crocodile [kräk/ə dīl/] **131**–37
crocus [krō/kəs] **129**–25
Crops [kräps] **148**
cross-country skiing [krös/kŭn/trē skē/ĭng] **160**–3
cross out [krös/ owt/] **7**–U
cross the street [krös/ dhə strēt/] **90**–A
crosswalk [krös/wök/] **90**–8
crucible tongs [krōō/sə bəl tängz/, –töngz/] **119**–15
crutches [krŭch/əz] **80**–1
cry [krī] **32**–C
cubby [kŭb/ē] **94**–4
cube [kyōōb] **118**–10
cucumbers [kyōō/kŭm bərz] **51**–12
cuff [kŭf] **73**–5
cup [kŭp(/–)] **63**–21
   ...of flour [–əv flow/ər] **57**–10
   ...of oil [–əv oyl/] **57**–2
curb [kürb] **90**–10
curling iron [kür/lĭng ī/ərn] **76**–15
curly [kür/lē] **23**–11
curtains [kür/tnz] **44**–5
curved [kürvd] **118**–19
custodian [kŭ stō/dē ən] **138**–35
customs [kŭs/təmz] **110**–20
   ...officer [–ö/fə sər] **110**–21
cut [kŭt] **23**–A, **77**–N
cut [kŭt] **78**–13
cute [kyōōt] **22**–24
cutting board [kŭt/ĭng börd/] **40**–27
cut up [kŭt/ ŭp/] **58**–M
cycling [sī/klĭng] **159**–4
cyclist [sī/klĭst] **153**–3
cylinder [sĭl/ən dər] **118**–12
daffodil [dăf/ə dĭl] **129**–26
DAILY ROUTINES [dā/lē rōō tēnz/] **26**–**27**
dairy section [dër/ē sĕk/shən] **54**–9
daisy [dā/zē] **129**–14
dance [dăns] **33**–J
dance floor [dăns/ flör/] **33**–16
dangerous situation [dān/jər əs sĭch/ōō ā/shən] **147**–8
dark blue [därk/ blōō/] **12**–2
dashboard [dăsh/börd/] **108**–17
data [dā/tə, dăt/ə] **144** ✦
date [dāt(/–)] **18**–14
   ...of birth [–əv bürth/] **4**–16
dates (fruit) [dāts] **50**–25
daughter [dö/tər] **24**–21
daughter-in-law [dö/tər ĭn lö/] **24** ✦
day [dā] **18**–10
daylight saving time [dā/līt/ sā/vĭng tīm/] **17**–33
Days of the week [dāz/ əv dhə wēk/] **18**
dead-bolt lock [dĕd/bōlt/ läk/] **37**–29
dead end [dĕd/ĕnd/] **107**–8
deaf [dĕf] **22**–27
decaf coffee [dē/kăf/ kö/fē] **61**–23
December [dĭ sĕm/bər] **19**–36
deck [dĕk] **38**–16
declaration form [dĕk/lə rā/shən förm/] **110**–22
decorate [dĕk/ə rāt/] **169**–C
deer [dïr] **134**–14
defendant [dĭ fĕn/dənt] **99**–5
defense attorney [dĭ fĕns/ ə tür/nē] **99**–4

degree [də grē′] **29**–7, **112** ✦
degrees [də grēz′]
   ...Celsius [–sĕl′sē əs] **10**
   ...Fahrenheit [–făr′ən hīt′] **10**
DELI AND SEAFOOD [dĕl′ē ən sē′fōod′] **53**
deliver [də lĭv′ər] **96**–C
delivery person [də lĭv′ə rē pür′sən] **137**–18
dental [dĕn′təl]
   ...assistant [–ə sĭs′tənt] **84**–19, **137**–19
   ...floss [–flös′, –fläs′] **77**–22
   ...hygienist [–hī jē′nĭst, –jĕn′ĭst] **84**–16
Dental clinic [dĕn′təl klĭn′ĭk] **84**
DENTAL EXAMS [dĕn′təl ĭg zămz′] **85**
dentist [dĕn′tĭst] **84**–18, **137**–20
deodorant [dē ō′dər ənt] **76**–4
department store [dĭ pärt′mənt stör′] **93**–13
departure time [dĭ pär′chər tīm′] **111** ✦
deposit [dĭ päz′ət] **9**–C
deposit [dĭ päz′ət] **97**–C
   ...slip [–slĭp′] **97**–12
depth [dĕpth] **15**–15
DESCRIBING CLOTHES [dĭ skrī′bĭng klōz′] **70**–**71**
DESCRIBING HAIR [dĭ skrī′bĭng hër′] **23**
DESCRIBING THINGS [dĭ skrī′bĭng thĭngz′] **11**
desert [dĕz′ərt] **117**–4
design [dĭ zīn′] **146**–A
designated drivers [dĕz′ĭg nā′təd drī′vərz] **101** ✦
designer [dĭ zī′nər] **146**–3
desk [dĕsk′–] **2**–6, **142**–1
   ...calendar [–kăl′ən dər] **142**–6
   ...clerk [–klürk′] **145**–9
   ...pad [–păd′] **142**–7
dessert tray [dĭ zürt′ trā′] **63**–7
destination [dĕs′tə nā′shən] **111** ✦
diabetes [dī′ə bē′tēz, –təs] **79**–9
diagonal [dī ăg′ə nəl, –ăg′nəl] **118**–23
dial [dī′əl] **9**–D
dial tone [dī′əl tōn′] **9**–B
diameter [dī ăm′ə tər] **118**–17
diamonds [dī′məndz] **163**–27
diaper [dī′pər]
   ...pail [–pāl′] **45**–13, **95**–23
   ...pins [–pĭnz′] **95**–22
dice [dīs] **162**–4
dictate [dĭk′tāt] **6**–N
dictionary [dĭk′shə nër′ē] **3**–28
Dictionary work [dĭk′shə nër ē würk′] **6**
die [dī] **29**–R
dietician [dī′ə tĭsh′ən] **87**–25
difference [dĭf′rəns] **118** ✦
difficult [dĭf′ĭ kŭlt′] **11**–24
dime [dīm] **20**–3
Dimensions [də mĕn′shənz] **15**
diner [dī′nər] **62**–5
DINING AREA [dī′nĭng ër′ē ə] **41**
dining room [dī′nĭng rōom′] **62**–2
   ...chair [–chër′] **41**–16
   ...table [–tā′bəl] **41**–17
dinner [dĭn′ər]
   ...fork [–förk′] **63**–25
   ...plate [–plāt′] **63**–15
diploma [də plō′mə] **29**–2, **32**–7
direct flight [də rĕkt′ flīt′, dī–] **111** ✦
Directions [də rĕk′shənz, dī–] **107**

DIRECTIONS AND TRAFFIC SIGNS
   [də rĕk′shənz ən trăf′ĭk sīnz′, dī–] **107**
directory [də rĕk′tə rē, dī–] **9**–8, **93**–19
directory assistance (411) [də rĕk′tə rē ə sĭs′təns, dī–] **9**–8
dirty [dür′tē] **72**–15
discuss [dĭ skŭs′] **6**–L
disgusted [dĭ skŭs′təd] **30**–9
dish [dĭsh′–]
   ...drainer [–drā′nər] **40**–3
   ...towel [–tow′əl] **47**–22
dishroom [dĭsh′rōom′] **63**–12
dishwasher [dĭsh′wä′shər, –wö′–] (machine) **40**–4, (person) **63**–13
dishwashing liquid [dĭsh′wä′shĭng lĭk′wəd, –wö′–] **47**–21
disinfectant [dĭs′ən fĕk′tənt] **95**–19
disk [dĭsk′–] **144**–5
   ...drive [–drīv′] **144**–3
display case [dĭ splā′ kās′] **69**–7
disposable diapers [dĭ spō′zə bəl dī′pərz] **95**–20
dissection kit [dĭ sĕk′shən kĭt′, dī–] **119**–7
dive [dīv] **157**–5
diving mask [dī′vĭng măsk′] **155**–3
division [də vĭzh′ən] **118**–4
divorced [də vörst′] **25**–24
DJ (disc jockey) [dē′jā′] / [dĭsk′ jäk′ē] **33**–17
do [dōo′–]
   ...an experiment [–ən ĭk spër′ə mənt] **119**–A
   ...crafts [–krăfts′] **162**–A
   ...errands [–ĕr′əndz] **90** ✦
   ...homework [–hōm′würk′] **27**–T
   ...manual labor [–măn′yōo əl lā′bər] **140**–D
dockworker [däk′wür′kər] **137**–21
doctor [däk′tər] **84**–6, **137**–22
Doctorate [däk′tər ət] **112** ✦
dog [dög] **11**–17, 18, **133**–11
dogwood [dög′wōod′] **128**–16
DOING THE LAUNDRY [dōo′ĭng dhə lön′drē] **72**–2
doll [däl] **45**–18
dollar [däl′ər] **20**–7
dollhouse [däl′hows′] **45**–14
doll making kit [däl′ mā′kĭng kĭt′] **162**–15
dolphin [däl′fən, döl′–] **131**–30
DOMESTIC ANIMALS AND RODENTS
   [də mĕs′tĭk ăn′ə məlz ən rōd′nts] **133**
domesticated animals [də mĕs′tə kā′təd ăn′ə məlz] **133** ✦
donkey [däng′kē, dŭng′–, döng′–] **133**–2
do not enter [dōo′ nät′ ĕn′tər] **107**–4
do not wash [dōo′ nät′ wäsh′, –wösh′] **72** ✦
don't [dōnt′–]
   ...**drink** and **drive** [–drĭngk′ ən drīv′] **101**–G
   ...**open** [–ō′pən] **101**–F
donut shop [dō′nŭt shäp′] **91**–20
doorbell [dör′bĕl′] **38**–10
door chain [dör′ chān′] **37**–28
doorknob [dör′näb′] **37**–30
doorman [dör′măn′] **36**–10, **145**–2
dosage [dō′sĭj] **80** ✦
double boiler [dŭb′əl boy′lər] **59**–8
doughnut [dō′nŭt] **60**–15, **60** ✦
down (feathers) [down′–]
   ...jacket [–jăk′ət] **66**–15
   ...vest [–vĕst′] **66**–13
down (preposition) [down] **105**–8
downhill skiing [down′hĭl′ skē′ĭng] **160**–1
downstairs [down′stërz′] **38** ✦

Index

downtown [down/town/] **88** ✦
drain [drān] **43**–4
drapes [drāps] **42**–16
draw a picture [drö/ ə pĭk/chər] **6**–M
draw blood [drö/ blŭd/] **85**–G
drawer [drör] **40**–23, **44**–3
dress [(–)drĕs(/)] **64**–3
   maternity... [mə tür/nə tē–] **65**–19
dress [drĕs] **94**–J
dresser [drĕs/ər] **44**–2
dressmaker [drĕs/mā/kər] **73**–2
dress shop [drĕs/ shäp/] **92** ✦
dribble [drĭb/əl] **156**–K
drill [drĭl(/–)] **84**–21, **150**–8, 23
   ...bit [–bĭt/] **150**–23
drill a tooth [drĭl/ ə tooth/] **85**–K
drink [drĭngk(/–)] / [–drĭngk/] **60**–B
   ...fluids [–floo/ədz] **80**–B
   don't... [dōnt/–] **101**–G
dripping [drĭp/ĭng] **49**–16
drive [drīv] **26**–I, **90**–C, **140**–E
drive (computer) [drīv] **144**–3, 20
driver's [drī/vərz]
   ...education [–ĕj/ə kā/shən] **121**–5
   ...license [–lī/səns] **29**–4
drive-thru window [drīv/throo/ wĭn/dō] **90**–13
driveway [drīv/wā/] **38**–5
drop off [dräp/ öf/] **94**–A
dropper [dräp/ər] **119**–14
drought [drowt] **103**–10
drown [drown] **82**–I
drugs [drŭgz] **100**–4
drugstore [drŭg/stör/] **90**–2
drums [drŭmz] **120**–8
drumsticks [drŭm/stĭks/] **52**–22
drunk driving [drŭngk/ drī/vĭng] **100**–3
dry [drī(/–)]
   ...hair [–hër/] **76**–H
   ...the dishes [–dhə dĭsh/əz] **46**–N
dry [drī] **72**–18
dry-clean [drī/klēn/] **72** ✦
dry cleaners [drī/ klē/nərz] **72** ✦, **91**–24
dryer [drī/ər] **72**–4
   ...sheets [–shēts/] **72**–5
Dry measures [drī/ mĕzh/ərz] **57**
drywall [drī/wöl/] **149**–18
duck [dŭk(/–)] **52**–18, **132**–13
   ...pond [–pänd/] **153**–6
dump truck [dŭmp/ trŭk/] **106**–12
duplex house [doo/plĕks hows/] **34** ✦
dust [dŭst] **46**–A
dust [dŭst(/–)]
   ...mop [–mäp/] **47**–17
   ...ruffle [–rŭf/əl] **44**–22
   ...storm [–störm/] **10**–21
dustpan [dŭst/păn/] **47**–11
dye hair [dī/ hër/] **23**–D
eagle [ē/gəl] **132**–10
ear [ïr(/–)] **74**–28
   ...infection [–ĭn fĕk/shən] **79**–3
earache [ïr/āk/] **78**–3
early [ür/lē] **17**–22
earmuffs [ïr/mŭfs/] (outdoor) **66**–12, (safety) **147**–14
earplugs [ïr/plŭgz/] **147**–13
earrings [ïr/ĭngz] **69**–37

Earth [ürth] **127**–7
earthquake [ürth/kwāk/] **102**–5
easel [ē/zəl] **163**–21
east [ēst] **107, 123, 124**
eastern time [ē/stərn tīm/] **17**–29
easy [ē/zē] **11**–23
   ...chair [–chër/] **42**–24
eat [ēt(/–)] **60**–B
   ...breakfast [–brĕk/fəst] **26**–E
eat out [ēt/ owt/] **62** ✦
eclipse [ĭ klĭps/]
   lunar... [loo/nər–] **127** ✦
   solar... [sō/lər–] **127** ✦
economics [ĕk/ə näm/ĭks, ē/kə–] **121**–6
edit [ĕd/ət] **113**–B
eel [ēl] **130**–5
eggbeater [ĕg/bē/tər] **59**–20
eggplants [ĕg/plănts/] **51**–18
eggs [(–)ĕgz(/)] **54**–34
   scrambled... [skrăm/bəld–] **61**–1
eight [āt] **14**
eighteen [ā/tēn/] **14**
eighteenth [ā/tēnth/] **14**
eighth [ātth, āth] **14, 15**–1
eighty [ā/tē] **14, 15**–10
eject [ĭ jĕkt/] **165**–F
elastic bandage [ĭ lăs/tĭk băn/dĭj] **83**–12
elbow [ĕl/bō] **74**–15
elderly [ĕl/dər lē] **22**–15
Election [ĭ lĕk/shən] **115**
elective [ĭ lĕk/tĭv] **121** ✦
electric [ĭ lĕk/trĭk]
   ...can opener [–kăn/ ō/pə nər] **40**–14
   ...drill [–drĭl/] **150**–8
   ...keyboard [–kē/börd/] **120**–20
   ...mixer [–mĭk/sər] **40**–25
   ...pencil sharpener [–pĕn/səl shär/pə nər] **142**–9
   ...shaver [–shā/vər] **77**–24
electrical [ĭ lĕk/trĭ kəl] **151**–38
   ...hazard [–hăz/ərd] **147**–1
   ...tape [–tāp/] **151**–38
electrician [ĭ lĕk trĭsh/ən] **48**–9
ELECTRONICS AND PHOTOGRAPHY
   [ĭ lĕk trän/ĭks ən fə täg/rə fē] **164–165**
electronics store [ĭ lĕk trän/ĭks stör/] **93**–18
elementary school [ĕl/ə mĕn/trē skool/] **112**–5
elephant [ĕl/ə fənt] **135**–42
elevator [ĕl/ə vā/tər] **37**–34, **145** ✦
eleven [ĭ lĕv/ən] **14**
eleventh [ĭ lĕv/ənth] **14**
ellipse [ĭ lĭps/] **118**–9
elm [ĕlm] **128**–17
embarrassed [ĭm băr/əst] **31**–25
embroidery [ĭm broy/də rē] **163**–19
EMERGENCIES AND NATURAL DISASTERS [ĭ mür/jən sēz ən
   năch/rəl dĭ zăs/tərz, –năch/ər əl–] **102–103**
emergency [ĭ mür/jən sē]
   ...brake [–brāk/] **109**–44
   ...card [–kärd/] **111**–K
   ...exit [–ĕg/zət, –ĕk/sət] **111**–J
   ...medical technician (EMT)
      [–mĕd/ĭ kəl tĕk nĭsh/ən] / [ē/ĕm/tē/] **87**–26
   ...service (911) [–sür/vəs] **9**–9
Emergency room [ĭ mür/jən sē room/] **87**
emery board [ĕm/ə rē börd/, ĕm/rē–] **77**–30

empty [ĕmp/tē] **46**–F
empty [ĕmp/tē] **11**–10
encyclopedia [ĭn sī/klə pē/dē ə] **98**–18
end table [ĕnd/ tā/bəl] **42**–21
end the conversation [ĕnd/ dhə kän/vər sā/shən] **8**–C
ENERGY AND THE ENVIRONMENT
[ĕn/ər jē ən dhē ĭn vī/rən mənt, –vī/ərn–] **126**
Energy resources [ĕn/ər jē rē/sör səz, –rī sör/səz] **126**
engine [ĕn/jən] **109**–41
engineer [ĕn/jə nïr/] **137**–23
English as a second language
[ĭng/glĭsh əz ə sĕk/ənd lăng/gwĭj] **121**–7
ENGLISH COMPOSITION [ĭng/glĭsh käm/pə zĭsh/ən] **113**
ENTERTAINMENT [ĕn/tər tān/mənt] **166**–**167**
enter your PIN number [ĕn/tər yər pĭn/ nŭm/bər] **97**–B
entrance [ĕn/trəns] **36**✦
Entryway [ĕn/trē wā/] **37**
envelope [ĕn/və lōp/] **96**–1, **143**–20
ENVIRONMENT [ĭn vī/rən mənt, –vī/ərn–] **126**
Equivalents [ĭ kwĭv/ə lənts] **15**
erase [ĭ rās/] **2**–H
eraser [ĭ rā/sər] **3**–21
escalator [ĕs/kə lā/tər] **93**–21
evening [ēv/nĭng] **17**–19
...gown [–gown/] **65**–29
every day [ĕv/rē dā/] **18**–21
EVERYDAY CONVERSATION [ĕv/rē dā/ kän/vər sā/shən] **8**
evidence [ĕv/ə dəns] **99**–9
examination table [ĭg zăm/ə nā/shən tā/bəl] **84**–13
examine [ĭg zăm/ən] **85**–F
examining room [ĭg zăm/ə nĭng rōōm/] **84**–9
exchange [ĭks chānj/] **21**–G
excited [ĭk sī/təd] **31**–23
exclamation mark [ĕk/sklə mā/shən märk/] **113**–8
Excuse me. [ĭk skyōōz/ mē] **8**
Executive [ĭg zĕk/yə tĭv] **116**
exercise [ĕk/sər sīz/] **27**–W, **80**–D, **157**–P
exhausted [ĭg zö/stəd] **30**✦
exhibition [ĕk/sə bĭsh/ən] **152**–21
expensive [ĭk spĕn/sĭv] **11**–19
experience turbulence [ĭk spïr/ē əns tür/byə ləns] **111**–N
expiration date [ĕk/spə rā/shən dāt/] **80**✦
Exploration [ĕk/splə rā/shən] **114**
explosion [ĭk splō/zhən] **102**–4
Express Mail [ĭk sprĕs/ māl/] **96**–15
extension cord [ĭk stĕn/shən körd/] **151**–14
exterminate [ĭk stür/mə nāt/] **49**✦
exterminator [ĭk stür/mə nā/tər] **49**–21
extra [ĕk/strə]
...large [–lärj/] **70**–5
...small [–smöl/] **70**–1
extract a tooth [ĭk străkt/ ə tōōth/] **85**✦
eye [ī(/–)] / [–ī/] **73**–23, **74**–27
...chart [–chärt/] **84**–11
...glasses [–glăs/əz] **81**–35
...hook [–hōōk/] **150**–35
...shadow [–shăd/ō] **77**–34
hook and... [hōōk/ ən–] **73**–23
eyebrow [ī/brow/] **74**–32
...pencil [–pĕn/səl] **77**–33
eyedrops [ī/dräps/] **81**–22
eyelashes [ī/lăsh/əz] **74**–34
eyelid [ī/lĭd/] **74**–33
eyeliner [ī/lī/nər] **77**–35
fabric softener [făb/rĭk sö/fə nər] **72**–6

Face [fās] **74, 77**
face powder [fās/ pow/dər] **77**–39
FACTORY [făk/tə rē, –trē] **146**
factory [făk/tə rē, –trē]
...owner [–ō/nər] **146**–2
...worker [–wür/kər] **146**–6
fall [föl] **82**–O
fall [föl] **19**–39
fall in love [föl/ ĭn lŭv/] **28**–K
FAMILY [făm/lē, făm/ə lē] **24**–**25**
fan [făn] (appliance) **41**–4, (person) **158**–4
fancy [făn/sē] **71**–39
fare [fër(/–)] **104**–5
...card [–kärd/] **104**–12
far from [fär/ frŭm/, –frəm] **13**✦
farm [färm(/–)] **34**–13
...equipment [–ĭ kwĭp/mənt] **148**–10
Farm animals [färm/ ăn/ə məlz] **133**
farmer [fär/mər] **148**–15
FARMING AND RANCHING [fär/mĭng ən răn/chĭng] **148**
farmworker [färm/wür/kər] **148**–8
fashion designer [făsh/ən dĭ zī/nər] **73**✦
fast [făst] **11**–3
fasten your seat belt [făs/ən yər sēt/ bĕlt/] **111**–I
FAST FOOD [făst/ fōōd/] **60**
fast food restaurant [făst/ fōōd/ rĕs/tə rənt, –ränt] **90**–14
fast forward [făst/ för/wərd] **165**–C
fat [făt] **11**–7
father [fä/dhər] **24**–6
father-in-law [fä/dhər ĭn lö/] **24**–14
faucet [fö/sət] **43**–6, **49**–16
fax [făks] **142**–B
fax machine [făks/ mə shēn/] **143**–23
feast [fēst] **168**–16
feather [fĕdh/ər] **132**–5
...duster [–dŭs/tər] **47**–1
February [fĕb/yōō ër/ē, fĕb/rōō–] **19**–26
feed [fēd] **94**–D, **148**–D
feel [fēl(/–)]
...dizzy [–dĭz/ē] **78**–C
...nauseous [–nö/shəs, –zē əs] **78**–D
FEELINGS [fē/lĭngz] **30**–**31**
feet [fēt] **15**✦
female [fē/māl/] **4**–14
fence [fĕns] **38**–3, **148**–19
fencing [fĕn/sĭng] **159**–5
ferry [fĕr/ē] **104**–23
fever [fē/vər] **78**–8
fiction [fĭk/shən] **98, 166**
field [fēld] (school) **5**–12, (farm) **148**–7, (sports) **159**–17
fifteen [fĭf/tēn/] **14**
fifteenth [fĭf/tēnth/] **14**
fifth [fĭfth] **14**
fifty [fĭf/tē] **14**
...dollars [–däl/ərz] **20**–11
...percent [–pər sĕnt/] **15**–9
figure skating [fĭg/yər skā/tĭng] **160**–5
figurine [fĭg/yə rēn/] **162**–10
file [fīl] **142**–H
file [fīl(/–)]
...cabinet [–kăb/ə nət] **142**–10
...clerk [–klürk/] **142**–12
...folder [–fōl/dər] **142**–11
filet of sole [fĭ lā/ əv sōl/] **53**–21
fill a cavity [fĭl/ ə kăv/ə tē] **85**–L

fill in the blank [fĭl′ ĭn dhə blăngk′] **7**–R
fill out [fĭl′ owt′] / [fĭl′ owt′–]
...a form [–ə förm′] **4**–B
...an application [–ən ăp′lə kā′shən] **141**–G
filling [fĭl′ĭng] **84**–22
film [fĭlm] (camera) **165**–26, (movie) **166**–1
fin [fĭn] **130**–1
find your seat [fīnd′ yər sēt′] **111**–G
FINDING A HOME [fīn′dĭng ə hōm′] **35**
fingernail [fĭng′gər nāl′] **75**–58
fingers [fĭng′gərz] **75**–57
finish [fĭn′ĭsh] **157**–Z
fins [fĭnz] **155**–2
fire [fīr(′–)] **42**–10, **102**–7
...escape [–ĭ skāp′] **36**–7
...exit [–ĕg′zət, –ĕk′sət] **37**–23
...extinguisher [–ĭk stĭng′gwĭ shər] **147**–22
...hydrant [–hī′drənt] **91**–28
...screen [–skrēn′] **42**–11
...station [–stā′shən] **88**–1
...truck [–trŭk′] **102**–9
firefighter [fīr′fī′tər] **102**–8, **137**–24
fireplace [fīr′plās′] **42**–9
fireworks [fīr′würks′] **168**–8
first [fürst(′–)] **14**
...draft [–drăft′] **113**–A
...floor [–flör′] **36**–1
...name [–nām′] **4**–2
...place [–plās′] **152**–20
...prize [–prīz′] **152**–20
FIRST AID [fürst′ ād′] **83**
first aid [fürst′ ād′]
...kit [–kĭt′] **83**–1
...manual [–măn′yōō əl] **83**–7
Fish [fĭsh] **53**
fish [fĭsh] **61**–17, **130**–12, 14, 15
fishing [fĭsh′ĭng] **154**–5
...net [–nĕt′] **154**–17
...pole [–pōl′] **154**–18
fitted sheet [fĭt′əd shēt′] **44**–14
fittings [fĭt′ĭngz] **151**–17
five [fīv(′–)] **14**–5, 20
...after one [–ăf′tər wŭn′] **16**–5
...to two [tə tōō′] **16**–15
Five ways to cook chicken [fīv′ wāz′ tə kōōk′ chĭk′ən] **58**
fix [fĭks] **49** ✦
flag [flăg] **168**–9
flammable [flăm′ə bəl] **147**–2
flashlight [flăsh′līt′] **151**–39
flat sheet [flăt′ shēt′] **44**–13
flea market [flē′ mär′kət] **152**–22
fleas [flēz] **49**–23
flight attendant [flīt′ ə tĕn′dənt] **110**–13
flood [flŭd] **103**–16
floor [flör(′–)] / [–flör′] **44**–24
...lamp [–lămp′] **42**–15
...plan [–plăn′] **38**–1
dance... [dăns′–] **33**–16
floppy [fläp′ē] **144**–5
floral [flör′əl] **70**–12
florist [flör′ĭst] **92**–12, **137**–25
floss [flös, fläs] **77**–K
flounder [flown′dər] **130**–13
flour [flow′ər] **55**–45, **57**–10
flower [flow′ər] **39**–19, **129**–7

...bed [–bĕd′] **39**–A
...pot [–pät′] **39**–18
Parts of a... [pärts′ əv ə–] **129**
FLOWERS [flow′ərz] **129**
flu [flōō] **79**–2
fluid ounce [flōō′əd owns′] **57**–1
flute [flōōt] **120**–3
fly [flī] **140** ✦
fly [flī] **132**–29
flying disc [flī′ĭng dĭsk′] **159**–6, **161**–27
foam pad [fōm′ păd′] **154**–13
foggy [fö′gē, fäg′ē–] **10**–11
fold [fōld] **72**–F
Follow directions [fäl′ō də rek′shənz, –dī–] **7**
food [fōōd(′–)]
...court [–kört′] **93**–14
...processor [–prä′sĕ sər] **40**–26
FOOD PREPARATION [fōōd′ prĕp ə rā′shən] **58**
Foot [fōōt] **75**
foot [fōōt] (measurement) **15** ✦, (body) **74**–7
football [fōōt′böl′] **158**–11, **161**–22
...helmet [–hĕl′mət] **161**–20
forceps [för′səps, –sĕps] **119**–8
forehead [för′əd, –hĕd′, fär′–] **74**–20
foreign language [för′ən lăng′gwĭj, fär′–] **121**–8
forest [för′əst, fär′–] **117**–11
fork [förk] **41**–21, **63**–24, 25, ✦
forklift [förk′lĭft′] **146**–14
form [(–)förm(′)]
declaration... [dĕk′lə rā′shən–] **110**–22
registration... [rĕj′ə strā′shən–] **4**
formal [för′məl] **71**–36
former husband [för′mər hŭz′bənd] **25** ✦
former wife [för′mər wīf′] **25** ✦
formula [för′myə lə] **95**–25, **119**–19
forty [för′tē] **14**, **16**–12
foundation [fown dā′shən] **77**–40
fountain [fown′tn] / [–fown′tn] **92**–11
water... [wö′tər–] **153**–11
four [för] **14**
fourteen [för′tēn′] **14**
fourteenth [för′tēnth′] **14**
fourth [förth(′–)] **14**, **15**–2
...floor [–flör′] **36**–4
fox [fäks] **134**–15
Fractions [frăk′shənz] **15**
freezer [frē′zər] **40**–10
freezing [frē′zĭng] **10**–5
french fries [frĕnch′ frīz′] **60**–2
French horn [frĕnch′ hörn′] **120**–15
fresh [frĕsh] **53**–29
Friday [frī′dā, –dē] **18**–6
fried [frīd] **61**–17
frog [frög, fräg] **130**–25
front... [frŭnt(′–)]
...desk [–dĕsk′] **145**–8
...door [–dör′] **38**–11
...office [–ö′fəs] **146**–1
...seat [–sēt′] **109**–35
...walk [–wök′] **38**–14
...yard [–yärd′] **38**–15
frozen [frō′zən]
...fish [–fĭsh′] **53**–30
...foods [–fōōdz′] **55**–12
...vegetables [–vĕj′tə bəlz] **55**–43

...yogurt [–yō/gərt] **60**–11
FRUIT [fro͞ot] **50**
frustrated [frŭs/trā/təd] **31**–28
fry [frī] **58**–5
frying pan [frī/ĭng păn/] **59**–5
fuel injection system [fyo͞o/əl ĭn jĕk/shən sĭs/təm] **109**–40
full [fo͝ol] (not empty) **11**–9, (satisfied) **30**–6
full [fo͝ol(/–)]
...moon [–mo͞on/] **127**–16
...slip [–slĭp/] **67**–22
full-size car [fo͝ol/sīz/ kär/] **106**–4
funnel [fŭn/əl] **119**–12
funny [fŭn/ē] **167**–27
fur [für] **134**–19
furious [fyo͝or/ē əs] **30** ✦
furniture [für/nĭ chər] / [–für/nĭ chər] **35**–K
...polish [–päl/ĭsh] **47**–18
...store [–stör/] **88**–13
patio... [păt/ē ō–] **39**–5
fuse box [fyo͞oz/ bäks/] **48**–13
galaxy [găl/ək sē] **127**–26
gallbladder [göl/blăd/ər] **75**–40
gallon [găl/ən] **57**–5
game [gām(/–)] **152**–18
...show [–shō/] **167**–23
GAMES [gām(/–)] **162**–163
gang violence [găng/ vī/ə ləns] **100**–2
garage [gə räzh/, –räj/] / [–gə räzh/, –räj/] **36, 38**–6
...door [–dör/] **38**–7
garbage [gär/bĭj] **46**–Q
...can [–kăn/] **39**–3
...disposal [–dĭ spō/zəl] **40**–5
...truck [–trŭk/] **91**–27
garden [gär/dn] (vegetable) **148**–12, (botanical) **152**–4
gardener [gärd/nər, gär/dn ər] **137**–26, **152**–6
gardenia [gär dēn/yə] **129**–16
gargle [gär/gəl] **77**–L
garlic [gär/lĭk] **51**–29
...bread [–brĕd/] **61**–16
...press [–prĕs/] **59**–10
garment worker [gär/mənt wür/kər] **73** ✦, **137**–27
garter belt [gär/tər bĕlt/] **67**–19
garter snake [gär/tər snāk/] **131**–39
gas [găs(/–)] / [–găs/] **109**–54
...gauge [–gāj/] **108**–22
...meter [–mē/tər] **48**–14
...pedal [–pĕd/l] **109**–47
...station [–stā/shən] **88**–12, **137**–28
...station attendant [–stā/shən ə tĕn/dənt] **137**–28
...tank [–tăngk/] **108**–12
natural... [năch/rəl–, năch/ər əl–] **126**–3
gate [gāt] (garage) **36**, (airport) **110**–5, **111**–D
gauge [gāj] **84**–12, **108**–19, 22, 23
gauze [göz] **83**–6
gearshift [gïr/shĭft/] **108**–27
GEOGRAPHY [jē äg/rə fē] **117**
geometry [jē äm/ə trē] **118**–26
geothermal energy [jē/ō thür/məl ĕn/ər jē] **126**–7
get [gĕt(/–)]
...a checkup [–ə chĕk/ŭp/] **85** ✦
...acupuncture [–ăk/yə pŭngk/chər] **81**–G
...a job [–ə jäb/] **28**–G
...a loan [–ə lōn/] **35**–I
...an electric shock [–ən ĭ lĕk/trĭk shäk/] **82**–F
...an injection [–ən ĭn jĕk/shən] **80**–E
...an X ray [–ən ĕks/ rā/] **85**–H
...bed rest [–bĕd/ rĕst/] **80**–A
...feedback [–fēd/băk/] **113**–C
...frostbite [–fröst/bīt/] **82**–G
...home [–hōm/] **27**–Q
...your boarding pass [–yər bör/dĭng păs/] **111**–E
get dressed [gĕt/ drĕst/] **26**–D
get hired [gĕt/ hīrd/] **141**–L
get married [gĕt/ măr/ēd] **28**–L
get up [gĕt/ ŭp/] **26**–B
gift [gĭft(/–)] **169**–D
...shop [–shäp/] **145**–7
gifts [gĭfts] **33**–18
gills [gĭlz] **130**–2
giraffe [jə răf/] **135**–33
girder [gür/dər] **149**–3
girdle [gür/dl] **67**–18
girl [gürl] **22**–5, 8
give [gĭv(/–)] **21**–D
...a shot of anesthetic [–ə shät/ əv ăn/əs thet/ĭk] **85**–J
...a speech [–ə spēch/] **32**–E
...the verdict [–dhə vür/dĭkt] **99**–E
gizzards [gĭz/ərdz] **52**–23
glass [glăs(/–)] **11**–9, 10, **41**–26, **63**–19, 20, ✦
...cleaner [–klē/nər] **47**–8
glasses [glăs/əz] **81**–35
globe [glōb] **3**–9
glove [glŭv(/–)] **161**–17
...compartment [–kəm pärt/mənt] **108**–33
gloves [glŭvz] **66**–5
glue [glo͞o] **143**–37, **162**–8
go [gō(/–)]
...on an interview [–än ən ĭn/tər vyo͞o/, –ön–] **141**–H
...straight [–strāt/] **107**–A
...through security [–thro͞o sĭ kyo͝or/ə tē] **111**–C
...to a chiropractor [–to͞o ə kī/rə präk/tər] **81**–H
...to bed [–tə bĕd/] **27**–X
...to college [–tə käl/ĭj] **28**–J
...to jail [–tə jāl/] **99**–G
...to prison [–tə prĭz/ən] **99**–G
...to sleep [–tə slēp/] **27**–Y
...to the market [–tə dhə mär/kət] **26**–L
...to work [–tə würk/] **26**–I
goat [gōt] **133**–1
goggles [gäg/əlz] **147**–9
goldfish [gōld/fĭsh/] **133**–16
golf [gälf(/–), gölf(/–)] **159**–7
...club [–klŭb/] **161**–1
good [go͝od] **11**–17
good-bye [go͝od bī/, gə–] **8**
goose [go͞os] **132**–14
gopher [gō/fər] **133**–19
gorilla [gə rĭl/ə] **135**–30
gown [gown] **32**–2, **65**–29
graduate [grăj/o͞o āt/] **28**–D, **32**–A
graduate [grăj/o͞o ət] **32**–6
...school [–sko͞ol/] **112** ✦
graduated cylinder [grăj/o͞o ā/təd sĭl/ən dər] **119**–10
graduating class [grăj/o͞o ā/tĭng klăs/] **32**–1
GRADUATION [grăj/o͞o ā/shən] **32**–33
grams [grămz] **57** ✦
grandchild [grăn/chīld/, grănd/–] **29**–Q
granddaughters [grăn/dö/tərz] **24** ✦
grandfather [grăn/fä/dhər, grănd/–] **24**–3
grandmother [grăn/mŭdh/ər, grănd/–] **24**–2

Index

grandparents [grăn/pĕr/ənts, grănd/–] **24**–1
grandson [grăn/sŭn/, grănd/–] **24**–7
grapefruit [grāp/frōōt/] **50**–9
grapes [grāps] **50**–1
graphic artist [grăf/ĭk är/tĭst] **137**–29
grasshopper [grăs/häp/ər] **132**–25
grate [grāt] **58**–J
grater [grā/tər] **59**–2
gray [grā(/–)] **12**–5
...hair [–hër/] **23**–13
grease [grēs] **58**–C
green [grēn] **12**–8
greenhouse [grēn/hows/] **152**–5
green salad [grēn/ săl/əd] **60**–8
greeting card [grē/tĭng kärd/] **96**–4
greet someone [grēt/ sŭm/wŭn] **8**–A
grill [grĭl] **58**–T
grilled cheese sandwich [grĭld/ chēz/ săn/wĭch, –sănd/–] **61**–8
ground beef [grownd/ bēf/] **52**–4
ground post [grownd/ pōst/] **96**–14
grower [grō/ər] **148**–15
guard [gärd] **97**–4, **99**–3
guest [gĕst(/–)] **32**–9, **145**–11
...room [–rōōm/] **145**–10
...speaker [–spē/kər] **32**–9
guests [gĕsts] **33**–14, **169**–B
guilty [gĭl/tē] **99**
guinea pig [gĭn/ē pĭg/] **133**–14
guitar [gĭ tär/] **120**–11
gum [gŭm] **55**–42
gums [gŭmz] **74**–24
gun [gŭn] **100**–9
gurney [gûr/nē] **87**–28
gutter [gŭt/ər] **38**–19
gym [jĭm] **5**–9
gymnastics [jĭm năs/tĭks] **159**–8
gynecologist [gī/nə kăl/ə jĭst] **86** ✦
hacksaw [hăk/sö/] **150**–5
hail [hāl] **10**–19
hail a taxi [hāl/ ə tăk/sē] **104** ✦
hailstorm [hāl/störm/] **10**–18
hair [hër(/–)] **23**, **74**–19
...clip [–klĭp/] **76**–17
...gel [–jĕl/] **76**–11
...net [–nĕt/] **147**–18
...salon [–sə län/] **23** ✦, **93**–16
...spray [–sprā/] **76**–12
...stylist [–stī/lĭst] **23** ✦
hairdresser [hër/drĕs/ər] **137**–30
half [hăf(/–)] **15**–4, **16**–10, **20**–5
...bath [–băth/] **43** ✦
...brother [–brŭdh/ər] **25**–29
...cup of raisins [–kŭp/ əv rā/zənz] **57**–9
...past one [–păst/ wŭn/] **16**
...sister [–sĭs/tər] **25**–30
...slip [–slĭp/] **67**–23
halibut [hăl/ə bət] **53**–20
hall [höl] **89**–17, **145**–13
Halloween [hăl/ə wēn/, häl/–] **168**–10
Hallway [höl/wā/] **37**
ham [hăm] **52**–9
hamburger [hăm/bür/gər] **60**–1
hammer [hăm/ər] **149**–D
hammer [hăm/ər] **150**–1
hammock [hăm/ək] **39**–2

hamper [hăm/pər] **43**–1
Hand [hănd] **75**
hand [hănd(/–)] **2**, **11**, **74**–8
...towel [–tow/əl] **43**–13
...truck [–trŭk/] **146**–11
handbags [hănd/băgz/] **69**–6
handcuffs [hănd/kŭfs/] **99**–2
handicapped parking [hăn/dē kăpt pär/kĭng] **107**–14
handkerchief [hăng/kər chĭf, –chēf/] **69**–42
handsaw [hănd/sö/] **150**–4
hanger [hăng/ər] **72**–11
hang up [hăng/ ŭp/] / [hăng/ ŭp/–]
...the clothes [–dhə klōz/] **72**–H
...the receiver [–dhə rĭ sē/vər] **9**–F
happy [hăp/ē] **31**–32
Happy Birthday [hăp/ē bürth/dā] **169**
hard [härd] (surface) **11**–5, (difficult) **11**–24
hard [härd(/–)]
...disk drive [–dĭsk/ drīv/] **144**–20
...hat [–hăt/] **147**–19
Hardware [härd/wër/] **144**
hardware [härd/wër/] **150**
...store [–stör/] **88**–14
harvest [här/vəst] **148**–B
hat [hăt] **66**–1
hats [hăts] **68**–5
have [hăv(/–)]
...a baby [–ə bā/bē] **29**–M
...a grandchild [–ə grăn/chīld/, grănd/–] **29**–Q
...a heart attack [–ə härt/ ə tăk/] **82**–D
...an allergic reaction [–ən ə lür/jĭk rē ăk/shən] **82**–E
...a picnic [–ə pĭk/nĭk] **153**–D
...dinner [–dĭn/ər] **27**–R
Hawaii-Aleutian time [hə wī/ē ə lōō/shən tīm/] **17**–24
hay [hā] **148**–18
hazardous [hăz/ər dəs]
...materials [–mə tïr/ē əlz] **147**–7
...waste [–wāst/] **126**–9
head [hĕd] **74**–1
headache [hĕd/āk/] **78**–1
headboard [hĕd/börd/] **44**–15
headlight [hĕd/līt/] **108**–5
headphones [hĕd/fōnz/] **164**–16
HEALTH CARE [hĕlth/ kër/] **80**–**81**
health [hĕlth(/–)]
...club [–klŭb/] **89**–21
...insurance card [–ĭn shōōr/əns kärd/] **84**
hear [hïr] **75**–B
hearing aid [hïr/ĭng ād/] **81**–33
hearing impaired [hïr/ĭng ĭm përd/] **22**–27
heart (symbol) [härt] **168**–6
heart (body) [härt(/–)] **75**–38, **79**–14
...disease [–dĭ zēz/] **79**–14
listen to... [lĭs/ən tə–] **85**–D
hearts [härts] **163**–29
heater [hē/tər] **48**–1, **108**–29
heating pad [hē/tĭng păd/] **80**–3
heat wave [hēt/ wāv/] **10**–15
heavy [hĕv/ē] **11**–13, **71**–41
...machinery [–mə shē/nə rē] **140**–F
heavyset [hĕv/ē sĕt/] **22**–20
hedge [hĕj(/–)] **39**–1
...clippers [–klĭp/ərz] **39**–12
heel [hēl] (shoe) **68**–13, (foot) **75**–62
height [hīt] **15**–14, **22**

Heimlich maneuver [hīm/līk mə noo/vər] **83**–18
helicopter [hĕl/ə käp/tər] **110**–8
hello [hə lō/, hĕ–] **8**
help [hĕlp] **6**–J
help wanted sign [hĕlp/ wän/təd sīn/, –wön/–] **141**–C
hemline [hĕm/līn/] **73**–1
hen [hĕn] **133**–5
Hi! [hī] **8**
hibiscus [hī bĭs/kəs, hĭ–] **129**–12
hide [hīd] **169**–E
high [hī(/–)]
  ...chair [–chër/] **95**–7
  ...heels [–hēlz/] **68**–17, **71**–47
high blood pressure [hī/ blŭd/ prĕsh/ər] **79**–15
high-rise building [hī/rīz/ bĭl/dĭng] **89**–25
high school [hī/ skool/] **112**–7
hiking [hī/kĭng] **154**–6
  ...boots [–boots/] **68**–21
hills [hĭlz] **117**–16
hip [hĭp] **74**–5
hippopotamus [hĭp/ə pät/ə məs] **135**–43
hire [hīr] **99**–B
hired hand [hīrd/ hănd/] **148**–20
hit [hĭt] **156**–G
HIV (human immunodeficiency virus) [ăch/ī/vē/]
  [hyoo/mən ĭm/yə nō dĭ fĭsh/ən sē vī/rəs] **79**–10
HOBBIES AND GAMES [häb/ēz ən gāmz/] **162**–**163**
hockey stick [häk/ē stĭk/] **161**–11
hold [hōld] **94**–B, **101**–C
holiday [häl/ə dā/] **19**–43, 44
HOLIDAYS [häl/ə dāz/] **168**
holly [häl/ē] **128**–19
home [hōm(/–)]
  ...attendant [–ə tĕn/dənt] **137**–31
  ...economics [–ĕk/ə näm/ĭks, –ē/kə–] **121**–9
homemaker [hōm/mā/kər] **137**–32
homesick [hōm/sĭk/] **31**–21
honeybee [hŭn/ē bē/] **132**–26
hood [hood] **108**–6
hoof [hoof] **134**–17
hook [hook(/–)] **150**–34, 35
  ...and eye [–ən ī/] **73**–23
horn [hörn] (car) **108**–24, (music) **120**–13, (animal) **134**–21
horror story [hör/ər stör/ē, här/–] **166**–14
horse [hörs(/–)] **133**–4
  ...racing [–rā/sĭng] **159**–18
horseback riding [hörs/băk rī/dĭng] **154**–9
hose [hōz] **39**–9
HOSPITAL [häs/pĭ tl] **86**–**87**
hospital [häs/pĭ tl] **88**–7
  ...bed [–bĕd/] **86**–11
  ...gown [–gown/] **86**–15
Hospital staff [häs/pĭ tl stăf/] **86**
hostess [hō/stəs] **62**–1
hot [hät] (weather) **10**–1, (feeling) **30**–1
hot dog [hät/ dög/] **60**–6
HOTEL [hō tĕl/] **145**
hotel [hō tĕl/] **88**–5
hot water [hät/ wö/tər] **43**–5
hour [ow/ər] **16**–3
HOUSE [hows] **38**
house [(–)hows(/)] **34**–6
  buy a... [bī/ ə–] **29**–O
  clean the... [klēn/ dhə–] **27**–N
Household Pests [hows/hōld/ pĕsts/] **49**

HOUSEHOLD PROBLEMS AND REPAIRS
  [hows/hōld/ präb/ləmz ən rĭ përz/] **48**–**49**
housekeeper [hows/kē/pər] **138**–33, **145**–15
housekeeping cart [hows/kē/pĭng kärt/] **145**–14
House of Representatives [hows/ əv rĕp/rĭ zĕn/tə tĭvz] **116**–1
houseplant [hows/plănt/] **129**–29
HOUSEWORK [hows/würk/] **46**
hubcap [hŭb/kăp/] **108**–9
hug [hŭg] **33**–G
humid [hyoo/məd] **10**–12
humidifier [hyoo mĭd/ə fī/ər] **80**–2
humiliated [hyoo mĭl/ē ā/təd] **30** ✦
hummingbird [hŭm/ĭng bürd/] **132**–11
hump [hŭmp] **135**–51
hundred [hŭn/drəd] **14**
hungry [hŭng/grē] **30**–5
hurricane [hür/ə kān/] **103**–12
hurt [hürt] (feeling) **30**–17, (medical) **82**–A
husband [hŭz/bənd] **24**–19
hydrant [hī/drənt] **91**–28
hydroelectric power [hī/drō ĭ lĕk/trĭk pow/ər] **126**–5
hydrogen peroxide [hī/drə jən pə räk/sīd] **83**–8
hyena [hī ē/nə] **135**–31
hygienist [hī jē/nĭst, –jĕn/ĭst] **84**–16
hypertension [hī/pər tĕn/shən] **79** ✦
hypoallergenic [hī/pō ăl/ər jĕn/ĭk] **77** ✦
I beam [ī/ bēm/] **149**–3
ice [īs(/–)]
  ...hockey [–häk/ē] **158**–13
  ...machine [–mə shēn/] **145**–18
  ...pack [–păk/] **83**–13
  ...skates [–skāts/] **161**–9
  ...skating [–skā/tĭng] **160**–4
ice cream [īs/ krēm/] **55**–44
ice cream stand [īs/ krēm stănd/] **93**–20
iced tea [īst/ tē/] **60**–5
icy [ī/sē] **10**–13
ignition [ĭg nĭsh/ən] **108**–25
illegal drugs [ĭ lē/gəl drŭgz/] **100**–4
ILLNESSES AND MEDICAL CONDITIONS
  [ĭl/nə səz ən mĕd/ĭ kəl kən dĭsh/ənz] **79**
immigrate [ĭm/ə grāt/] **28**–C
Immigration [ĭm/ə grā/shən] **114**
immunization [ĭm/yə nə zā/shən] **80** ✦
in [ĭn] **13**–5
  ...fashion [–făsh/ən] **64** ✦
  ...front of [–frŭnt/ əv] **13**–4
  ...love [–lŭv/] **28**–K, **30**–19
  ...pain [–pān/] **30**–12
  ...shock [–shäk/] **82**
inch (in.) [ĭnch] **15**–13
Independence Day [ĭn/də pĕn/dəns dā/] **168**–7
INDIVIDUAL SPORTS [ĭn/də vĭj/oo əl spörts/] **159**
industrial arts [ĭn dŭs/trē əl ärts/] **121**–10
infectious disease [ĭn fĕk/shəs dĭ zēz/] **79** ✦
influenza [ĭn/floo ĕn/zə] **79** ✦
information booth [ĭn/fər mā/shən booth/] **93**–22
ingredients [ĭn grē/dē ənts] **58**–K
INJURIES [ĭn/jə rēz] **78**
ink pad [ĭngk/ păd/] **143**–41
inline [ĭn/līn/]
  ...skates [–skāts/] **161**–10
  ...skating [–skā/tĭng] **159**–9
inquire about the salary [ĭn kwīr/ ə bowt/ dhə săl/ə rē] **141**–K
insect [ĭn/sĕkt]

Index

...bite [–bīt/] **78**–11
...repellent [–rĭ pĕl/ənt] **154**–23
INSECTS [ĭn/sĕkts] **132**
insert [ĭn sürt/] **97**–A
Inside the body [ĭn/sīd/ dhə bäd/ē] **75**
instant coffee [ĭn/stənt kö/fē] **55**–51
instructor [ĭn strŭk/tər] **5** ♦, **139**–58
instrument [ĭn/strə mənt] **120**–A
insulation [ĭn/sə lā/shən] **149**–13
insurance [ĭn shoor/əns]
...card [–kärd/] **84**–4
...form [–förm/] **84**–5
intercom [ĭn/tər käm/] **36**–8
interesting [ĭn/trə stĭng, ĭn/tə rĕs/tĭng] **167**–30
international call [ĭn/tər năsh/ə nəl köl/] **9**–6
internist [ĭn/tür/nĭst] **86**–2
interpreter [ĭn tür/prə tər] **138**–34
INTERSECTION [ĭn/tər sĕk/shən] **90**–**91**
interview [ĭn/tər vyōō/] **141**–H
intestinal parasites [ĭn tĕs/tə nəl păr/ə sīts/] **79**–16
intestines [ĭn tĕs/tənz] **75**–42
into [ĭn/tōō, –tə] **105**–4
introduce [ĭn/trə dōōs/] **8**–D, F
Invention [ĭn vĕn/shən] **115**
invite [ĭn vīt/] **169**–B
iris [ī/rəs] **129**–20
iron [ī/ərn] **72**–G
iron [ī/ərn] **72**–13
ironed shirt [ī/ərnd shürt/] **72**–20
ironing board [ī/ər nĭng börd/] **72**–14
island [ī/lənd] **117**–8
IV (intravenous drip) [ī/vē/] / [ĭn/trə vē/nəs drĭp/] **87**–27
jack [jăk] **109**–51
jack cheese [jăk/ chēz/] **53**–12
jacket [jăk/ət] **66**–7
jack hammer [jăk/ hăm/ər] **149**–9
jack-o'-lantern [jăk/ə lăn/tərn] **168**–11
jam [jăm] **56**–14
janitor [jăn/ə tər] **138**–35
January [jăn/yōō ër/ē] **19**–25
jar [jär(/–)] **56**–2
...of jam [–əv jăm/] **56**–14
jasmine [jăz/mən] **129**–21
jaw [jö] **74**–23
jeans [jēnz] **64**–5
jellyfish [jĕl/ē fĭsh/] **130**–14
jewelry [jōō/əl rē] **69**–8
...store [–stör/] **92**–2
job [jäb(/–)] / [–jäb/]
...board [–börd/] **141**–B
get a... [gĕt/ ə–] **28**–G
JOB SAFETY [jäb/ sāf/tē] **147**
JOB SEARCH [jäb/ sürch/] **141**
JOB SKILLS [jäb/ skĭlz/] **140**
JOBS AND OCCUPATIONS A-H [jäbz/ ən äk/yə pā/shənz]
136–**137**
JOBS AND OCCUPATIONS H-W [jäbz/ ən äk/yə pā/shənz]
138–**139**
jockstrap [jäk/străp/] **67**–14
jog [jäg] **156**–B
join the army [joyn/ dhē är/mē] **28**–F
joystick [joy/stĭk/] **144**–9
judge [jŭj] **99**–6
Judicial [jōō dĭsh/əl] **116**
July [jōō lī/] **19**–31, **168**–7
jump [jŭmp] **156**–J

jumper [jŭm/pər] **65**–18
jumper cables [jŭm/pər kā/bəlz] **109**–52
jump rope [jŭmp/ rōp/] **153**–5
jumpsuit [jŭmp/sōōt/] **65**–16
June [jōōn] **19**–30
junior high school [jōōn/yər hī/ skōōl] **112**–6
Jupiter [jōō/pə tər] **127**–5
jury [joor/ē] **99**–8, **116**
Justices [jŭs/tə səz] **116**–10
kangaroo [kăng/gə rōō/] **135**–44
keep [kēp] **21**–E
ketchup [kĕch/əp, kăch/–] **60**–23
key [kē(/–)] **37**–31
...chain [–chān/] **69**–43
keyboard [kē/börd/] **120**–20, **144**–7
kick [kĭk] **156**–L
kidney [kĭd/nē] **75**–45
kilometers [kĭ läm/ə tərz, kĭl/ə mē/tərz] **15** ♦
kiss [kĭs] **33**–F
KITCHEN [kĭch/ən] **40**
kitchen [kĭch/ən] **63**–10
...timer [–tī/mər] **59**–18
KITCHEN UTENSILS [kĭch/ən yōō tĕn/səlz] **59**
kitten [kĭt/n] **133**–10
knee [nē(/–)] **74**–17
...socks [–säks/] **67**–25
knee-highs [nē/hīz/] **67**–24
knife [(–)nīf(/)] **41**–22, **63**–27
carving... [kär/vĭng–] **59**–12
multi-use... [mŭl/tē yōōs/–, mŭl/tī–] **154**–20
paring... [për/ĭng–] **59**–16
knit [nĭt] **163**–F
knit shirt [nĭt/ shürt/] **65**–20
knitting needles [nĭt/ĭng nēd/lz] **163**–18
koala [kō ä/lə] **135**–45
label [lā/bəl] / [–lā/bəl] **143**–35
prescription... [prĭ skrĭ/shən–] **80**–14
lab technician [lăb/ tĕk nĭsh/ən] **86**–16
ladder [lăd/ər] **149**–2
ladle [lād/l] **59**–7
ladybug [lā/dē bŭg/] **132**–27
lake [lāk] **117**–13
lamb [lăm(/–)] **52**–13, 14, 15
...chops [–chäps/] **52**–15
...shanks [–shăngks/] **52**–13
lamp [lămp] **42**–15, **44**–17
lampshade [lămp/shād/] **44**–18
land [lănd] **111**–O
landlord [lănd/lörd/] **37**–32
language [lăng/gwĭj]
English as a second... [ĭng/glĭsh əz ə sĕk/ənd–] **141**–7
foreign... [för/ən–, fär/–] **141**–8
speak another... [spēk/ ə nä/thər] **140**–J
use the new... [yōōz/ thə nū/–] **143** ♦
lantern [lăn/tərn] **154**–22
laptop [lăp/täp/] **144**–14
large [lärj] **70**–4
last [lăst(/–)]
...name [–nām/] **4**–4
...week [–wēk/] **18**–18
late [lāt] **17**–23
latex gloves [lā/tĕks glŭvz/] **87**–33, **147**–17
laugh [lăf] **33**–H
Laundromat [lön/drə măt/] **90**–1
laundry [lön/drē] **72**–1

…basket [–băs/kət] **72**–2
…detergent [–dĭ tür/jənt] **72**–7
…room [–rōōm/] **36**
lawn [lön(/–)] **39**–21
…mower [–mō/ər] **39**–22
lawyer [lö/yər] **99**–B, **138**–36
lay bricks [lā/ brĭks/] **149**–B
leaf [lēf(/–)] **128**–6, **129**–5
…blower [–blō/ər] **39**–4
leaking [lē/kĭng] **48**–3
learn to drive [lürn/ tə drīv/] **28**–E
lease [lēs] **35** ✦
leather [lĕdh/ər]
…boots [–bōōts/] **70**–18
…jacket [–jăk/ət] **66**–3
leave [lēv(/–)] **111**–L
…a message [–ə mĕs/ĭj] **9**–E
…a tip [–ə tĭp/] **62**–J
…work [–würk/] **26**–M
left [lĕft] **13**–1
leg [lĕg(/–)] **74**–6
…of lamb [–əv lăm/] **52**–14
legal [lē/gəl]
…holiday [–häl/ə dā/] **19**–43
…pad [–păd/] **143**–18
LEGAL SYSTEM [lē/gəl sĭs/təm] **99**
leggings [lĕg/ĭngz] **65**–23
Legislative [lĕj/əs lā/tĭv] **116**
lemons [lĕm/ənz] **50**–11
lend [lĕnd] **20** ✦
length [lĕngkth] **15**–16
lengthen [lĕngk/thən] **73**–C
leopard [lĕp/ərd] **135**–25
leotard [lē/ə tärd/] **67**–1
let out [lĕt/ owt/] **73**–F
letter [lĕt/ər] / [–lĕt/ər] **96**–2, **142**–B, D
…carrier [–kăr/ē ər] **96**–6
air… [ër/–] **96**–13
letterhead paper [lĕt/ər hĕd pā/pər] **143**–19
lettuce [lĕt/əs] **51**–1, **60**–17
level [lĕv/əl] **150**–24
librarian [lī brër/ē ən] **98**–1
LIBRARY [lī/brër ē] **98**
library [lī/brër ē] **5**–6, **89**–28, **98**–17, 19, 20
…book [–bōōk/] **98**–20
…card [–kärd/] **98**–19
…clerk [–klürk/] **98**–17
license plate [lī/səns plāt/] **108**–15
lid [lĭd] **59**–24
LIFE EVENTS [līf/ ĭ vĕnts/] **28**–**29**
lifeguard [līf/gärd/] **155**–18
…station [–stā/shən] **155**–20
lifesaving device [līf/sā/vĭng dĭ vīs/] **155**–19
life vest [līf/ vĕst/] **154**–14
light [līt] **169**–H
light [līt] (weight) **11**–14, **71**–40, (color) **12**–3
light (appliance) [līt(/–)] / [–līt/]
…fixture [–fĭks/chər] **41**–5
…switch [–swĭch/] **44**–19
porch… [pörch/–] **38**–9
lightbulb [līt/bŭlb/] **42**–4
lightning [līt/nĭng] **10**–17
lily [lĭl/ē] **129**–24
limb [lĭm] **128**–3
limes [līmz] **50**–12

line [līn(/–)] / [–līn/] **55**–20
…supervisor [–sōō/pər vī zər] **146**–5
assembly… [ə sĕm/blē–] **146**–8
line dry [līn/ drī/] **72** ✦
linen [lĭn/ən] **70**–17
linen closet [lĭn/ən kläz/ət] **43** ✦
Lines [līnz] **118**
lingerie [län/zhə rā/, –jə–] **67** ✦
lion [lī/ən] **135**–36
lip [lĭp] **74**–30
lipstick [lĭp/stĭk/] **77**–37
Liquid measures [lĭk/wəd mĕzh/ərz] **57**
list [lĭst] **6**–L
listen [lĭs/ən] **2**–C, **85**–D
listen for the dial tone [lĭs/ən fər dhə dī/əl tōn/] **9**–B
liters [lē/tərz] **57** ✦
little [lĭt/l] **11**–1
Little League [lĭt/l lēg/] **158** ✦
live [lĭv] **116**–B
liver [lĭv/ər] (food) **52**–7, (body) **75**–39
livestock [līv/stäk/] **148**–13
LIVING ROOM [lĭv/ĭng rōōm/] **42**
lizard [lĭz/ərd] **131**–41
llama [lä/mə] **135**–26
loading dock [lō/dĭng däk/] **146**–16
load the washer [lōd/ dhə wä/shər, –wö/–] **72**–C
loaf [lōf(/–)] **56**–10
…of bread [–əv brĕd/] **56**–22
loafers [lō/fərz] **68**–19
loan [lōn] **35**–I
Lobby [läb/ē] **37**
lobby [läb/ē] **145**–3
lobster [läb/stər] **53**–23
local call [lō/kəl köl/] **9**–4
lock [läk] **101**–E
lock [läk] (house) **37**–29, **48**–6, (car) **109**–34
lockers [läk/ərz] **5**–7
locket [läk/ət] **69**–33
locksmith [läk/smĭth/] **48**–11
logs [lögz, lägz] **42**–12
lonely [lōn/lē] **30**–18
long [löng(/–)] **23**–3, **71**–34
…underwear [–ŭn/dər wër/] **67**–11
long-distance call [löng/dĭs/təns köl/] **9**–5
long-sleeved shirt [löng/slēvd/ shürt/] **71**–31
look at [lōōk/ ăt/, –ət] **111**–K, **141**–B
look for [lōōk/ för/] / [lōōk/ fər]
…a help wanted sign [–ə hĕlp/ wän/təd sīn/, –wön/–] **141**–C
…a new apartment [–ə nōō/ ə pärt/mənt] **35**–A
…the emergency exit
[–dhē ĭ mür/jən sē ĕg/zət, –ĕk/sət] **111**–J
look in [lōōk/ ĭn]
…the classifieds [–dhə kläs/ə fīdz/] **141**–D
…throat [–thrōt/] **85**–E
look up a word [lōōk/ ŭp ə würd/] **6**–A
loose [lōōs] **71**–42
lose [lōōz] **158** ✦
lost child [löst/ chīld/] **102**–1
loud [lowd] **11**–11
loungewear [lownj/wër/] **67** ✦
love [lŭv(/–)] **30**–19
…seat [–sēt/] **42**–25
low [lō] **71**–46
LPN (licensed practical nurse)
[ĕl/pē/ĕn/] / [lī/sənst prăk/tĭ kəl nürs/] **87**–24

Index

luggage [lŭg/ĭj]
...carrier [–kăr/ē ər] **110**–19
...cart [–kärt/] **145**–6
lug wrench [lŭg/ rĕnch/] **109**–50
lumber [lŭm/bər] **149**–17, **151**
lunar eclipse [lōō/nər ĭ klĭps/] **127** ✦
lunch [lŭnch(/–)] **61**
...benches [–bĕn/chəz] **5**–5
lung [lŭng] **75**–37
LVN (licensed vocational nurse)
  [ĕl/vē/ĕn] / [lī/sənst vō kā/shə nəl nürs/] **87**–24
machine [mə shēn/]
...operator [–äp/ə rā tər] **138**–37
...screw [–skrōō/] **150**–27
magazine [măg/ə zēn/, măg/ə zēn/] **98**–7
...holder [–hōl/dər] **42**–22
magnet [măg/nət] **119**–21
magnolia [măg nōl/yə] **128**–9
mailbox [māl/bäks/] **38**–4, **90**–12
mailboxes [māl/bäk/səz] **37**–36
mailer [mā/lər] **143**–32
mailing address [mā/lĭng ə drĕs/, –ă/drĕs] **96**–8
mail [māl/ ĭt] **96**–B
main office [mān/ ö/fəs] **5**–17
make [māk] **106** ✦
make [māk(/–)]
...a deposit [–ə dĭ päz/ət] **97**–C
...an appointment [–ən ə poynt/mənt] **85**–A
...an offer [–ən ö/fər] **35**–H
...a toast [–ə tōst/] **33**–I
...a wish [–ə wĭsh/] **169**–J
...copies [–käp/ēz] **142**–E
...lunch [–lŭnch/] **26**–F
...the bed [–dhə bĕd/] **46**–G
make sure you understand
  [māk/ shōōr/ yōō ŭn/dər stănd/] **8**–E
male [māl] **4**–13
MALL [möl] **92**–93
mallet [măl/ət] **150**–2
MAMMALS [măm/əlz] **134**–135
Mammals, Sea [sē/ măm/əlz] **131**
man [măn] **22**–11
manager [măn/ĭ jər] **35**–B, **36**–12, **54**–8, **143**–25
mane [mān] **135**–49
mangoes [măng/gōz] **50**–21
mantel [măn/təl] **42**–8
manual [măn/yōō əl] **144**–22
manual labor [măn/yōō əl lā/bər] **140**–D
manufacture [măn/yə făk/chər] **146**–B
map [măp] **3**–12
maple [mā/pəl] **128**–13
March [märch] **19**–27
margarine [mär/jər ən] **54**–39
marigold [mär/ə gōld/] **129**–13
MARINE LIFE, AMPHIBIANS, AND REPTILES
  [mə rēn/ līf/ ăm fĭb/ē ənz ən rĕp/tīlz] **130**–131
mark [märk] **7**–T
marker [mär/kər] **3**–19
MARKET [mär/kət] **54**–55
market [mär/kət] **89**–20
marriage license [mär/ĭj lī/səns] **29**–8
married [mär/ēd] **25**–23, **28**–L
Mars [märz] **127**–6
martial arts [mär/shəl ärts/] **159**–10
mascara [mă skăr/ə] **77**–38

mashed potatoes [măsht/ pə tā/tōz] **61**–11
mask [măsk] **168**–12
masking tape [măs/kĭng tāp/] **151**–49
Master's degree [măs/tərz də grē/] **112** ✦
match [măch] **7**–X
matches [măch/əz] **154**–21
maternity dress [mə tür/nə tē drĕs/] **65**–19
maternity shop [mə tür/nə tē shäp/] **93**–17
MATHEMATICS [măth/ə măt/ĭks] **118**
mattress [mă/trəs] **44**–25
May [mā] **19**–29
mayonnaise [mā/ə nāz/, mā/ə nāz/] **60**–25
meadow [mĕd/ō] **117**–20
measles [mē/zəlz] **79**–5
measure [mĕzh/ər] **15** ✦, **149**–C
Measurement [mĕzh/ər mənt] **15**
MEASUREMENTS [mĕzh/ər mənts] **14**–15
MEASURES [mĕzh/ərz] **57**
measure the ingredients [mĕzh/ər dhē ĭn grē/dē ənts] **57**–A
MEAT AND POULTRY [mēt/ n pōl/trē] **52**
meat and poultry section [mēt/ n pōl/trē sĕk/shən] **54**–2
media section [mē/dē ə sĕk/shən] **98**–11
medical [mĕd/ĭ kəl]
...charts [–chärts/] **87**–20
...emergency bracelet [–ĭ mür/jən sē brās/lət] **83**–14
...waste disposal [–wāst/ dĭ spō/zəl] **86**–14
MEDICAL AND DENTAL EXAMS
  [mĕd/ĭ kəl ən dĕn/təl ĭg zămz/] **85**
Medical clinic [mĕd/ĭ kəl klĭn/ĭk] **84**
MEDICAL CONDITIONS [mĕd/ĭ kəl kən dĭsh/ənz] **79**
Medical conditions and serious diseases
  [mĕd/ĭ kəl kən dĭsh/ənz ən sîr/ē əs dĭ zē/zəz] **79**
MEDICAL EMERGENCIES [mĕd/ĭ kəl ĭ mür/jən sēz] **82**
medication [mĕd/ə kā/shən] **80**–11, 12
...tray [–trā/] **87**–23
medicine cabinet [mĕd/ə sən kăb/ə nət] **43**–19
medium [mē/dē əm] **70**–3
meeting room [mē/tĭng rōōm/] **145**–19
memory [mĕm/ə rē] **144** ✦
men's store [mĕnz/ stör/] **90** ✦
menu [mĕn/yōō] **62**–3
MENU, COFFEE SHOP [kö/fē shäp/ mĕn/yōō] **61**
merchandise [mür/chən dīz/, –dīs/] **152**–24
Mercury [mür/kyə rē] **127**–9
messenger [mĕs/ən jər] **138**–38
messy [mĕs/ē] **11**–16
meter [mē/tər] (measurement) **15**, (taxi) **104**–21
meter [mē/tər] / [–mē/tər]
  gas... [găs/–] **48**–14
  parking... [pär/kĭng–] **91**–18
mice [mīs] **49**–26
microcassette transcriber [mī/krō kə sĕt/ trăn skrī/bər] **142**–4
microfilm [mī/krə fĭlm/] **98**–5
microfilm reader [mī/krə fĭlm rē/dər] **98**–4
microphone [mī/krə fōn/] **164**–4
microscope [mī/krə skōp/] **119**–4
microwave oven [mī/krə wāv/ ŭv/ən] **40**–13
middle-aged [mĭd/l ājd/] **22**–14
middle initial [mĭd/l ĭ nĭsh/əl] **4**–3
middle school [mĭd/l skōōl/] **112**–6
midnight [mĭd/nīt/] **17**–21
midsize car [mĭd/sīz/ kär/] **106**–3
mile [mīl] **15** ✦
milk [mĭlk] **148**–C
milk [mĭlk(/–)] **54**–35

...shake [–shāk/] **60**–12
milliliters [mĭl/ə lē/tərz] **57** ✦
million [mĭl/yən] **14**
miniblinds [mĭn/ē blīndz/] **43**–11
minivan [mĭn/ē văn/] **106**–10
minute [mĭn/ət] **16**–2
mirror [mïr/ər] **43**–18, **44**–1
  rearview... [rïr/vyōō/–] **108**–1
  sideview... [sīd/vyōō/–] **108**–8
missing [mĭs/ĭng] **70**–25
miss the bus [mĭs/ dhə bŭs/] **104** ✦
mistake [mĭ stāk/] **7**–2
mittens [mĭt/nz] **66**–9
mix [mĭks] **58**–K
mixing bowl [mĭk/sĭng bōl/] **59**–31
mobile [mō/bēl] **45**–4
mobile home [mō/bəl hōm/] **34**–8
model (occupation) [mäd/l] **138**–39
model (hobby) [mäd/l] **106** ✦
  ...kit [–kĭt/] **162**–7
  ...trains [–trānz/] **163**–32
models [mäd/lz] **162**–C
modem [mō/dəm, –dĕm] **144**–11
moisturizer [moys/chə rī/zər] **76**–8
molecule [mäl/ĭ kyōol/] **119**–18
Monday [mŭn/dā, –dē] **18**–2
MONEY [mŭn/ē] **20**
money order [mŭn/ē ör/dər] **20**–16
monitor [män/ə tər] **144**–6
monitors [män/ə tərs] **110**–4
monkey [mŭng/kē] **135**–27
month [mŭnth] **4**–16, **18**–9
monthly statement [mŭnth/lē stāt/mənt] **97**–10
Months of the year [mŭnths/ əv dhə yïr/] **19**
moon [mōōn] **127**–13, 14, 15, 16
moose [mōōs] **134**–1
mop [mäp] **46**–J
mop [(–)mäp(/)]
  dust... [dŭst/–] **47**–17
  wet... [wĕt/–] **47**–16
MORE SCHOOL SUBJECTS [mör/ skōol/ sŭb/jĭkts] **121**
morning [mör/nĭng] **17**–16
mosque [mäsk] **89**–23
mosquito [mə skē/tō] **132**–23
motel [mō tĕl/] **89**–22
moth [möth] **132**–22
mother [mŭdh/ər] **24**–5, **25**–25
motherboard [mŭdh/ər börd/] **144**–18
mother-in-law [mŭdh/ər ĭn lö/] **24**–13
motorcycle [mō/tər sī/kəl] **91**–19
mountain [mown/tn]
  ...biking [–bī/kĭng] **154**–8
  ...lion [lī/ən] **134**–2
  ...peak [–pēk/] **117**–14
  ...range [–rānj/] **117**–15
  ...time [–tīm/] **17**–27
mouse [mows] (animal) **133**–17, (computer) **144**–8
mouth [mowth] **74**–22
mouthwash [mowth/wäsh/, –wösh/] **77**–23
move [mōōv] **29**–P
move in [mōōv/ ĭn/] **35**–D
Movement [mōōv/mənt] **115**
mover [mōō/vər] **138**–40
movie [mōō/vē] **166**–1
movies [mōō/vēz] **152**–10

movie theater [mōō/vē thē/ə tər] **88**–11
moving van [mōō/vĭng văn/] **106**–14
mow [mō] **39**–C
mudslide [mŭd/slīd/] **102**–6
muffin [mŭf/ən] **60**–14
muffler [mŭf/lər] (clothing) **66**–4, (car part) **108**–11
mug [mŭg] **41**–28
mugging [mŭg/ĭng] **100**–5
multiplication [mŭl/tə plə kā/shən] **118**–3
multi-use knife [mŭl/tē yōos/ nīf/, mŭl/tī–] **154**–20
mumps [mŭmps] **79**–7
murder [mür/dər] **100**–8
muscle [mŭs/əl] **75**–48
mushrooms [mŭsh/rōomz/] **51**–26
MUSIC [myōō/zĭk] **120**
musician [myōō zĭsh/ən] **138**–41
music store [myōō/zĭk stör/] **92**–1
mussel [mŭs/əl] **130**–17
mussels [mŭs/əlz] **53**–26
mustache [mŭs/tăsh] **23**–5
mustard [mŭs/tərd] **60**–24
mystery [mĭs/tə rē] **166**–15
nachos [nä/chōz] **60**–10
nail (hardware) [nāl] **150**–29
nail (body) [nāl(/–)]
  ...clipper [–klĭp/ər] **77**–29
  ...polish [–päl/ĭsh] **77**–31
  ...polish remover [–päl/ĭsh rĭ mōō/vər] **77**–32
  ...salon [–sə län/] **91**–25
name [nām] **4**–1, 2, 3, 4, A, C, D
napkin [năp/kĭn] **41**–19, **63**–23
narrow [năr/ō] **71**–45
nasal congestion [nā/zəl kən jĕs/chən] **78**–7
nasal spray [nā/zəl sprā/] **81**–23
NATURAL DISASTERS
  [năch/rəl dĭ zăs/tərz, năch/ər əl–] **102**–**103**
natural gas [năch/rəl găs/, năch/ər əl–] **126**–3
nature program [nā/chər prō/grăm] **167**–22
near [nïr] **13** ✦
neat [nēt] **11**–15
neck [nĕk] **74**–2
necklaces [nĕk/lə səz] **69**–9
need [nēd] **109**–(54–59)
needle [nēd/l] (sewing) **73**–22, (pine) **128**–12
neighbor [nā/bər] **37**–22
neighborhood [nā/bər hōod/] **90** ✦
Neighborhood Watch
  [nā/bər hōod/ wäch/, –wöch/] **101** ✦
nephew [nĕf/yōō] **24**–18
Neptune [nĕp/tōon] **127**–2
nerve [nürv] **75**–50
nervous [nür/vəs] **30**–11
nest [nĕst] **132**–5
new [nōo(/–)] **71**–32
  ...moon [–mōōn/] **127**–13
Newfoundland time [nōo/fən lənd tīm/, –fənd–] **17**–31
news [nōoz] **167**–17
newspaper [nōoz/pā/pər] **98**–8
newsstand [nōoz/stănd/] **90**–11
newt [nōot] **130**–26
New Year's Day [nōo/ yïrz/ dā/] **168**–1
next to [nĕkst/ tōo, –tə] **13**–1, 2
next week [nĕkst/ wēk/] **18**–20
nickel [nĭk/əl] **20**–2
niece [nēs] **24**–17

Index

night [nīt] **17**–20
nightgown [nīt/gown/] **67**–5
night-light [nīt/līt/] **45**–3
nightshirt [nīt/shürt/] **67**–9
night table [nīt/ tā/bəl] **44**–21
nine [nīn] **14**
nineteen [nīn/tēn/] **14**
nineteenth [nīn/tēnth/] **14**
nineteen-year-old [nīn/tēn/yïr ōld/] **22**–8
ninety [nīn/tē] **14**
ninth [nīnth] **14**
nipple [nĭp/əl] **95**–27
noisy children [noy/zē chĭl/drən] **11**–11
nonfiction [nän/fĭk/shən] **98** ✦
noon [nōōn] **17**–17
no outlet [nō/ owt/lĕt, –lət] **107**–8
no parking [nō/ pär/kĭng] **107**–12
north [nörth] **107, 123, 124**
NORTH AMERICA AND CENTRAL AMERICA
  [nörth/ ə mĕr/ə kə ən sĕn/trəl ə mĕr/ə kə] **122–123**
nose [nōz] **74**–21
not [nät(/–)]
  ...guilty [–gĭl/tē] **99**
  ...ripe [–rīp] **50**–28
notebook [nōt/bŏŏk/] **3**–24
  ...paper [–pā/pər] **3**–25
note pad [nōt/ păd/] **143**–36
November [nō vĕm/bər] **19**–35
nuclear energy [nōō/klē ər ĕn/ər jē] **126**–8
numbers [nŭm/bərz] **3**–31
NUMBERS AND MEASUREMENTS
  [nŭm/bərz ən mĕzh/ər mənts] **14–15**
nurse [nürs] **94**–C
nurse [nürs(/–)] **84**–10, **87**–22, 24, 29, ✦, **138**–42, ✦
  ...midwife [–mĭd/wīf/] **86** ✦
  ...practitioner [–prăk tĭsh/ə nər] **86** ✦
Nurse's station [nür/səz stā/shən] **87**
nursing home [nür/sĭng hōm/] **34**–11
nut (hardware) [nŭt] **150**–31
nuts (food) [nŭts] **50**–23
nylon [nī/län] **70**–19
oak [ōk] **128**–18
obey the law [ō bā/ dhə lö/] **116**–H
oboe [ō/bō] **120**–5
observatory [əb zür/və tör/ē] **127**–19
observe [əb zürv/] **119**–B
obstetrician [äb/stə trĭsh/ən] **86**–1
OCCUPATIONS (A-H) [äk/yə pā/shənz] **136–137**
OCCUPATIONS (H-W) [äk/yə pā/shənz] **138–139**
ocean [ō/shən] **117**–6, **155**–1
o'clock [ə kläk/] **16**–4
October [äk tō/bər] **19**–34
octopus [äk/tə pəs] **130**–4
odometer [ō däm/ə tər] **108**–21
off [öf] **105**–7
OFFICE [ö/fəs] **142–143**
Office [ö/fəs] **37**
office [ö/fəs] **5**–13, 15, 17, **146**–1
  ...building [–bĭl/dĭng] **89**–24
  ...manager [–măn/ĭ jər] **143**–25
official [ə fĭsh/əl] **158**–6
oil (cooking) [oyl] **55**–49, **57**–2
oil (petroleum) [oyl(/–)] **109**–55, **126**–6
  ...gauge [–gāj/] **108**–19
  ...paint [–pānt/] **163**–24

...spill [–spĭl/] **126**–15
ointment [oynt/mənt] **81**–24, **83**–9
old [ōld] **71**–33
on [än, ön] **13**–8
  ...the left [–dhə lĕft/] **13**–1
  ...the right [–dhə rīt/] **13**–2
once a week [wŭns/ə wēk/] **18**–22
one [wŭn(/–)] **14, 15**–1, 2, 3, 4, 5, 11, **16**–4, 15, **20**–1, 12
  ...o'clock [–ə kläk/] **16**–4
  ...way [–wā/] **107**–6
one billion [wŭn/ bĭl/yən] **14**
one-eighth [wŭn/ätth/, –āth/] **15**–1
one-fifteen [wŭn/ fĭf/tēn/] **16**–7
one-fifty [wŭn/ fĭf/tē] **16**–14
one-forty [wŭn/ för/tē] **16**–12
one-fourth [wŭn/ förth/] **15**–2
one-half [wŭn/ hăf/] **15**–4
one-hundred percent [wŭn/ hŭn/drəd pər sĕnt/] **15**–11
one-oh-five [wŭn/ ō fīv/] **16**–5
one-ten [wŭn/ tĕn/] **16**–6
one-third [wŭn/ thürd/] **15**–3
one-thirty [wŭn/ thür/tē] **16**–10
one-twenty [wŭn/ twĕn/tē] **16**–8
onions [ŭn/yənz] **51**–28, **58**–G, H
online catalog [än/līn/ kăt/l ög/, –äg/, ön/–] **98**–9
on time [än/ tīm/, ön/–] **17** ✦
onto [än/tōō, –tə, ön/–] **105**–6
open [ō/pən] **2**–I
  ...the presents [–dhə prĕz/ənts] **169**–L
  don't... [dōnt/–] **101**–F
opera [äp/rə] **166**–8
operate heavy machinery
  [äp/ə rāt/ hĕv/ē mə shē/nə rē] **140**–F
Operating room [äp/ə rā/tĭng rōōm/] **87**
operating table [äp/ə rā/tĭng tā/bəl] **87**–34
Operations (math) [äp/ə rā/shənz] **118**
operator [äp/ə rā/tər] **9**–7
ophthalmologist [äf/thəl mäl/ə jĭst, –thə mäl/–, äp/–] **86**–7
opossum [ə päs/əm, päs/əm] **134**–4
optician [äp tĭsh/ən] **92**–8
optometrist [äp täm/ə trĭst] **81**–34
orange [ör/ənj, är/–] **12**–6
oranges [ör/ən jəz, är/–] **50**–10
orangutan [ə răng/ə tăng/, –tăn/] **135**–40
orbit [ör/bət] **127**–11
orchard [ör/chərd] **148**–16
orchestra [ör/kə strə] **120**–1
orchid [ör/kĭd] **129**–17
order [ör/dər] **62**–D
orderly [ör/dər lē] **87**–18
order puller [ör/dər pŏŏl/ər] **146**–10
Ordinals [ör/dn əlz, örd/nəlz] **14**
organ [ör/gən] **120**–22
organizer [ör/gə nī/zər] **143**–30
ornament [ör/nə mənt] **168**–19
orthodontist [ör/thə dän/tĭst] **84**–23
orthopedist [ör/thə pē/dĭst] **81**–28
Other instruments [ŭdh/ər ĭn/strə mənts] **120**
otter [ät/ər] **131**–35
ounce [owns] **57**–11
out [owt(/–)] **48**–2
  ...of focus [–əv fō/kəs] **165**–33
  ...of the taxi [–əv dhə tăk/sē] **105**–5
OUTDOOR RECREATION [owt/dör rĕk/rē ā/shən] **154**
outfit [owt/fĭt] **64** ✦

outlet [owt/lĕt, –lət] **44**–20, **107**–8, **151**–41
oval [ō/vəl] **118**–9
oven [ŭv/ən] **40**–20, **46**–C, **47**–3
  ...cleaner [–klē/nər] **47**–3
  microwave...[mī/krə wāv/–] **40**–13
over [ō/vər] **105**–2
overalls [ō/vər ölz/] **65**–21
overcoat [ō/vər kōt/] **66**–2
overdose [ō/vər dōs/, ō/vər dōs/] **82**–K
overdrawn account [ō/vər drön/ ə kownt/] **97** ✦
overexposed [ō/vər ĭk spōzd/] **165**–34
overflowing [ō/vər flō/ĭng] **49**–17
overhead [ō/vər hĕd/]
  ...compartment [–kəm pärt/mənt] **110**–10
  ...projector [–prə jĕk/tər] **2**–4
overjoyed [ō/vər joyd/] **30** ✦
overnight mail [ō/vər nīt/ māl/] **96**–15
over-the-counter medication
  [ō/vər dhə kown/tər mĕd/ə kā/shən] **80**–12
owl [owl] **132**–6
owner [ō/nər] **139**–56
oxfords [äks/fərdz] **68**–20
oxygen mask [äk/sĭ jən mäsk/] **110**–14
oysters [oy/stərz] **53**–27
Pacific time [pə sĭf/ĭk tīm/] **17**–26
pacifier [păs/ə fī/ər] **95**–29
package [păk/ĭj] **56**–8, **96**–5
  ...of cookies [–əv kook/ēz] **56**–20
PACKAGED FOODS [păk/ĭjd foodz/] **56**
packer [păk/ər] **146**–13
packing tape [păk/ĭng tāp/] **143**–42
pager [pā/jər] **9**–16
pail [pāl] **45**–13, **47**–20, **155**–22
pain [pān(/–)]
  ...reliever [–rĭ lē/vər] **81**–16
paint [pānt] **149**–A, **163**–E
paint [pānt(/–)] / [–pānt/] **151**–20
  ...pan [–păn/] **151**–45
  ...roller [–rō/lər] **151**–46
  acrylic... [ə krĭl/ĭk–] **162**–47
paintbrush [pānt/brŭsh/] **151**–9, **163**–23
painter [pān/tər] **138**–43
painting [pān/tĭng] **42**–7, **152**–8
pair of scissors [pĕr/ əv sĭz/ərz] **73**–18
paisley [pāz/lē] **70**–13
pajamas [pə jä/məz, –jä/–] **67**–4
palm [päm] (hand) **75**–59, (tree) **128**–15
pan [păn] **40**–24, **59**–5, 13, 26, 28
pancakes [păn/kāks/] **61**–6
pancreas [păng/krē əs] **75**–46
panda [păn/də] **135**–41
panther [păn/thər] **135**–39
panties [păn/tēz] **67**–16
pants [pănts] **64**–8
pantyhose [păn/tē hōz/] **67**–27
papayas [pə pī/əz] **50**–20
paper [pā/pər] (composition) **113**–2
paper [pā/pər] / [–pā/pər]
  ...bag [–băg/] **55**–22
  ...clip [–klĭp/] **143**–44
  ...cutter [–kŭt/ər] **143**–15
  ...doll [–däl/] **163**–30
  ...products [–präd/ŭkts] **55**–14
  ...shredder [–shrĕd/ər] **143**–24
  ...towels [–tow/əlz] **40**–2, **56**–23

notebook... [nōt/book/–] **3**–24, 25, 26
parade [pə rād/] **168**–2
paragraph [păr/ə grăf/] **113**–5
parakeet [păr/ə kēt/] **133**–15
parallel [păr/ə lĕl/] **118**–21
parcel post [pär/səl pōst/] **96**–14
parent [për/ənt] **94**–1
parents [për/ənts] **24**–4
paring knife [për/ĭng nīf/] **59**–16
park [pärk] **91**–D
park [pärk] **88**–8
parka [pär/kə] **66**–8
PARK AND PLAYGROUND [pärk/ ən plā/grownd/] **153**
parking [pär/kĭng]
  ...garage [–gə räzh/, –räj/] **89**–26
  ...meter [–mē/tər] **91**–18
  ...space [–spās/] **36**–15, **90**–5
parochial school [pə rō/kē əl skool/] **112**–3
parsley [pär/slē] **51**–10
part [pärt] **23**–4
partner [pärt/nər] **6**–J
parts [pärts] **146**–7
Parts of a bird [pärts/ əv ə bürd/] **132**
PARTS OF A CAR AND CAR MAINTENANCE
  [pärts/ əv ə kär/ ən kär/ mān/tn əns] **108**–**109**
Parts of a circle [pärts/ əv ə sür/kəl] **118**
Parts of a fish [pärts/ əv ə fĭsh/] **130**
Parts of a flower [pärts/ əv ə flow/ər] **129**
Parts of a square [pärts/ əv ə skwĕr/] **118**
Parts of a tree [pärts/ əv ə trē/] **128**
PARTY [pär/tē] **169**
Party [pär/tē] **33**
pass [păs] **156**–H
passbook [păs/book/] **97**–5
passenger [păs/ən jər] **104**–7, **110**–23
pass out [păs/ owt/] **7**–O
passport [păs/pört/] **29**–9
pasta [päs/tə] **61**–15
  ...salad [–săl/əd] **53**–15
pastrami [pə strä/mē] **53**–6
patient [pā/shənt] **84**–3
Patient's room [pā/shənts room/] **86**
patio [păt/ē ō] **39**–6
  ...furniture [–für/nĭ chər] **39**–5
patron [pā/trən] **62**–5
pattern (clothes) [păt/ərn] **73**–8
pattern maker [păt/ərn mā/kər] **73** ✦
Patterns (fabric) [păt/ərnz] **70**
pause [pöz] **165**–E
paw [pö] **134**–42
pay [pā(/–)]
  ...taxes [–tăk/səz] **116**–E
  ...the check [–dhə chĕk/] **62**–I
  ...the mortgage [–dhə mör/gĭj] **35**–L
  ...the rent [–dhə rĕnt/] **35**–F
pay phone [pā/ fōn] **9**–11
pay back [pā/ băk/] **20** ✦
pay for [pā/ för/, –fər] **21**–C
PE (physical education) [pē/ē/] / [fĭz/ĭ kəl ĕj/ə kā/shən]
  121–11
peaches [pē/chəz] **50**–5
peacock [pē/käk/] **132**–15
peak [pēk] **117**–14
pearls [pürlz] **69**–30
pears [përz] **50**–6

Index

peas [pēz] **51**–19
pedestrian [pə děs**/**trē ən] **90**–7
   ...crossing [–krö**/**sĭng] **107**–10
pediatrician [pē**/**dē ə trĭsh**/**ən] **86**–4
peel [pēl] **58**–N
peephole [pēp**/**hōl**/**] **37**–27
pelvis [pěl**/**vəs] **75**–55
pen [pěn] **3**–18
pencil [pěn**/**səl] **3**–20
   ...eraser [–ĭ rā**/**sər] **3**–21
   ...sharpener [–shär**/**pə nər] **3**–13, **142**–9
penguin [pěng**/**wĭn] **132**–12
peninsula [pə nĭn**/**sə lə] **117**–7
penny [pěn**/**ē] **20**–1
peppers [pěp**/**ərz] **51**–7
pepper shaker [pěp**/**ər shā**/**kər] **41**–15
Percents [pər sěnts**/**] **15**
Percussion [pər kŭsh**/**ən] **120**
perfume [pür**/**fyo͞om**/**, pər fyo͞om**/**] **76**–5
period [pïr**/**ē əd] **113**–6
periodical section [pïr**/**ē äd**/**ĭ kəl sěk**/**shən] **98**–6
perm hair [pürm**/** hër**/**] **23**–B
perpendicular [pür**/**pən dĭk**/**yə lər] **118**–20
personal check [pür**/**sə nəl chěk**/**] **20**–14
PERSONAL HYGIENE [pür**/**sə nəl hī**/**jēn] **76**–77
personal identification number (PIN)
   [pür**/**sə nəl ī děn**/**tə fə kā**/**shən nŭm**/**bər] **97**–B
PERSONAL INFORMATION [pür**/**sə nəl ĭn**/**fər mā**/**shən] **4**
personal radio-cassette player
   [pür**/**sə nəl rā**/**dē ō kə sět**/** plā**/**ər] **164**–15
pesticide [pěs**/**tə sīd**/**] **49** ✦
   ...poisoning [–poy**/**zə nĭng] **126**–14
pet [pět(**/**–)]
   ...food [–fo͞od**/**] **54**–10
   ...store [–stör**/**] **92**–6
petal [pět**/**l] **129**–8
petri dish [pē**/**trē dĭsh**/**] **119**–6
petroleum [pə trō**/**lē əm] **126**–6
Pets [pěts] **133**
pharmacist [fär**/**mə sĭst] **80**–10
pharmacy [fär**/**mə sē] **80**–9, **90**–2
Phillips screwdriver [fĭl**/**ĭps skro͞o**/**drī**/**vər] **150**–26
phone [fōn(**/**–)] **9**–1
   ...card [–kärd**/**] **9**–10
photo [fō**/**tō]
   ...album [–ăl**/**bəm] **165**–32
   ...shop [–shäp**/**] **90**–4
photocopier [fō**/**tə käp**/**ē ər] **142**–14
photograph [fō**/**tə grăf**/**] **44**–7
photographer [fə täg**/**rə fər] **32**–11
PHOTOGRAPHY [fə täg**/**rə fē] **164**–165
PHYSICAL DESCRIPTION [fĭz**/**ĭ kəl dĭ skrĭp**/**shən] **22**
physically challenged [fĭz**/**ĭ klē chăl**/**ənjd] **22**–25
physical therapist [fĭz**/**ĭ kəl thër**/**ə pĭst] **81**–30
physics [fĭz**/**ĭks] **119**–3
pi (π) [pī] **118** ✦
piano [pē ăn**/**ō] **120**–16
pickax [pĭk**/**ăks**/**] **149**–20
pick up [pĭk**/** ŭp**/**] / [pĭk**/** ŭp**/**–] **94**–G
   ...the children [–dhə chĭl**/**drən] **27**–O
   ...the receiver [–dhə rĭ sē**/**vər] **9**–A
pickup truck [pĭk**/**ŭp trŭk**/**] **106**–7
picnic [pĭk**/**nĭk] **153**–D
picnic table [pĭk**/**nĭk tā**/**bəl] **153**–8
picture [pĭk**/**chər]

...book [–bo͞ok**/**] **45**–17
...dictionary [–dĭk**/**shə nër ē] **3**–29
pie [pī(**/**–)] **61**–21
   ...pan [–păn**/**] **59**–28
pier [pïr] **155**–16
pierced earrings [pïrst**/** ïr**/**ĭng] **69**–37
pig [pĭg] **133**–8
pigeon [pĭj**/**ən] **132**–16
pill [pĭl] **81**–26
pillow [pĭl**/**ō] **42**–20, **44**–9
pillowcase [pĭl**/**ō kās**/**] **44**–10
pilot [pī**/**lət] **110**–12
PIN (personal identification number) [pĭn] **97**–B
pin [pĭn] (jewelry) **69**–36, (sewing) **73**–14
pin [pĭn(**/**–)] / [–pĭn**/**]
   ...cushion [–ko͞osh**/**ən] **73**–15
   push... [po͞osh**/**–] **143**–43
pine [pīn] **128**–10
pinecone [pīn**/**kōn**/**] **128**–11
pineapples [pī**/**năp**/**əlz] **50**–2
Ping-Pong [pĭng**/**păng**/**, –pöng**/**] **159**–13
pink [pĭngk] **12**–10
pint [pīnt] **57**–3
pipe [pīp(**/**–)] **151**–16
   ...wrench [–rěnch**/**] **151**–43
pipes [pīps] **49**–19
pitch [pĭch] **156**–F
pizza [pēt**/**sə] **60**–7
place [plās(**/**–)]
   ...mat [–măt**/**] **41**–20
   ...setting [–sět**/**ĭng] **63**–14
place of birth [plās**/** əv bürth**/**] **4**–17
PLACES TO GO [plā**/**səz tə gō**/**] **152**
PLACES TO LIVE [plā**/**səz tə lĭv**/**] **34**
plaid [plăd] **70**–9
plain [plān] **71**–38
plains [plānz] **117**–19
plan [plăn] **169**–A
plane (tool) [plān] **151**–52
PLANE TRIP [plān**/** trĭp**/**] **111**
Planets [plăn**/**əts] **127**
plant [plănt] **39**–D, **148**–A
plant [plănt] **39**–B, **42**–18
PLANTS [plănts] **128**
plastic [plăs**/**tĭk] **70**
   ...bag [–băg**/**] **55**–23
   ...storage container [–stör**/**ĭj kən tā**/**nər] **59**–3
   ...wrap [–răp**/**] **55**–54
plate [plāt] **41**–24, **63**–15, 16, 17
platform [plăt**/**förm**/**] **104**–15
platter [plăt**/**ər] **41**–3
platypus [plăt**/**ĭ pəs, –po͞os**/**] **135**–46
play [plā(**/**–)] **94**–K, **165**–B
   ...an instrument [–ən ĭn**/**strə mənt] **120**–A
   ...cards [–kärdz**/**] **163**–H
   ...games [–gāmz**/**] **162**–C
play [plā] **166**–2
player [plā**/**ər] **158**–5, **164**–2, 14, 15
PLAYGROUND [plā**/**grownd**/**] **153**
playground [plā**/**grownd**/**] **36**–6
playpen [plā**/**pěn**/**] **95**–11
pliers [plī**/**ərz] **150**–7
plug [plŭg] **164**–18
plumber [plŭm**/**ər] **49**–20
plums [plŭmz] **50**–8

plunger [plŭn/jər] **151**–44
Pluto [plōō/tō] **127**–1
plywood [plī/wōōd/] **149**–16
p.m. [pē/ĕm/] **16**
pneumatic drill [nōō mǎt/ĭk drĭl/] **149**–9
pocket [päk/ət] **73**–4
podium [pō/dē əm] **32**–5
poinsettia [poyn sĕt/ē ə, –sĕt/ə] **129**–23
point [poynt] **2**–F
poison [poy/zən] **82**–J, **147**–3
　...ivy [–ī/vē] **128**–25
　...oak [–ōk/] **128**–23
　...sumac [–sōō/mǎk, –shōō/–] **128**–24
police [pə lēs/]
　...officer [–ö/fə sər] **99**–1, **138**–44
　...station [–stā/shən] **89**–19
polish [päl/ĭsh]
　...nails [–nālz/] **77**–O
　...the furniture [–dhə für/nĭ chər] **46**–K
polka-dotted [pō/kə dät/əd] **70**–8
Pollution [pə lōō/shən] **126**
polyester [päl/ē ĕs/tər, päl/ē ĕs/tər] **70**
poncho [pän/chō] **66**–18
pond [pänd] **117**–21, **153**–6
pool (game) [pōōl] **159**–2
pool (swimming) [pōōl(/–)] **37**–16, **145**–16
　...service [–sür/vəs] **145**–17
porch light [pörch/ līt/] **38**–9
porcupine [pör/kyə pīn/] **134**–10
Pork [pörk] **52**
pork chops [pörk/ chäps/] **52**–10
porpoise [pör/pəs] **131**–31
port [pört] **144**–17
portable [pör/tə bəl]
　...radio-cassette player [–rā/dē ō kə sĕt/ plā/ər] **164**–2
　...TV [–tē/vē/] **164**–7
postage [pō/stĭj] **96**–10
postal [pō/stəl]
　...scale [–skāl/] **143**–16
　...worker [–wür/kər] **138**–45
postcard [pōst/kärd/] **96**–3
Post-it notes [pōst/ĭt nōts/] **143**–34
postmark [pōst/märk/] **96**–9
post office [pōst/ ö/fəs] **89**–29
pot [pät(/–)] **40**–16, **59**–6
　...holders [–hōl/dərz] **59**–29
potato [pə tā/tō]
　...chips [–chĭps/] **55**–40
　...salad [–sǎl/əd] **53**–13
potatoes [pə tā/tōz] **51**–21, **61**–11
potty seat [pät/ē sēt/] **95**–10
pouch [powch] **135**–50
POULTRY [pōl/trē] **52**
poultry section [pōl/trē sĕk/shən] **54**–2
pound [pownd] **57**–12
pour [pör(/–)]
　...the eggs into the pan [–dhē ĕgz/ ĭn/tə dhə pǎn/] **58**–D
　...the water [–dhə wö/tər] **62**–C
power [pow/ər] **48**–2
　...sander [–sǎn/dər] **150**–9
　...switch [–swĭch/] **144**–4
prairie dog [prër/ē dög/] **133**–22
pregnant [prĕg/nənt] **22**–19
PREPOSITIONS [prĕp/ə zĭsh/ənz] **13**
PREPOSITIONS OF MOTION [prĕp/ə zĭsh/ənz əv mō/shən] **105**

preschool [prē/skōōl/] **112**–4
prescription [prĭ skrĭp/shən] **80**–13
　...label [–lā/bəl] **80**–14
　...medication [–mĕd/ə kā/shən] **80**–11
President [prĕz/ə dənt] **116**–6
pretend [prĭ tĕnd/] **163**–G
price [prīs(/–)] **21**–6
　...tag [–tǎg/] **21**–1
principal [prĭn/sə pəl] **5**–14
principal's office [prĭn/sə pəlz ö/fəs] **5**–13
print [prĭnt] **4**–C
print [prĭnt] **70**–10
printer [prĭn/tər] (occupation) **138**–46, (computer) **144**–12
print shop [prĭnt/ shäp/] **91**–22
priority mail [prī ör/ə tē māl/, –är/–] **96**–12
prism [prĭz/əm] **119**–20
prison [prĭz/ən] **99**–G
private school [prī/vət skōōl/] **112**–2
Problems (clothing) [präb/ləmz] **70**
PROBLEMS, HOUSEHOLD [hows/hōld/ präb/ləmz] **48**–49
produce section [prō/dōōs sĕk/shən] **54**–11
product [präd/ŭkt] **118** ✦
program (computer) [prō/grǎm] **144**–21
Programs (TV) [prō/grǎmz] **167**
projector [prə jĕk/tər] / [–prə jĕk/tər]
　carousel slide... [kǎr/ə sĕl/ slīd/–] **165**–29
　overhead... [ō/vər hĕd/–] **2**–4
prosecuting attorney [präs/ĭ kyōō/tĭng ə tür/nē] **99**–10
protect your wallet [prə tĕkt/ yər wä/lət, –wö/–] **101**–D
proud [prowd] **31**–22
prunes [prōōnz] **50**–26
pruning shears [prōō/nĭng shïrz/] **39**–15
psychiatrist [sī kī/ə trĭst, sə–] **86**–6
PUBLIC SAFETY [pŭb/lĭk sāf/tē] **101**
public school [pŭb/lĭk skōōl/] **112**–1
public telephone [pŭb/lĭk tĕl/ə fōn/] **91**–21
PUBLIC TRANSPORTATION [pŭb/lĭk trǎns/pər tā/shən] **104**
pudding [pōōd/ĭng] **61**–20
pull [pōōl(/–)]
　...a tooth [–ə tōōth/] **85**–M
　...the wagon [–dhə wǎg/ən] **153**–A
pullover sweater [pōōl/ō/vər swĕt/ər] **64**–11
pumps [pŭmps] **68**–16
Punctuation [pŭngk/chōō ā/shən] **113**
puppet show [pŭp/ət shō/] **152**–14
puppy [pŭp/ē] **133**–12
purple [pür/pəl] **12**–7
purses [pür/səz] **69**–6
push [pōōsh] **153**–B
pushpin [pōōsh/pĭn/] **143**–43
put away [pōōt/ə wā/] / [pōōt/ə wā/–]
　...the toys [–dhə toyz/] **46**–H
　...your pencil [–yər pĕn/səl] **2**–L
put in order [pōōt/ ĭn ör/dər] **7**–W
put on [pōōt/ än/, –ön/] / [pōōt/ än–, –ön–]
　...makeup [–māk/ŭp/] **77**–P
　...sunscreen [–sŭn/skrēn/] **76**–D
puzzle [pŭz/əl] **45**–22
pyramid [pïr/ə mĭd] **118**–13
quart [kwört] **57**–4
quarter [kwör/tər] (time) **16**, (money) **20**–4
quarter cup [kwör/tər kŭp/] **57**–8
quarter moon [kwör/tər mōōn/] **127**–15
question mark [kwĕs/chən märk/] **113**–7

quiet [kwī/ət] **11**–12
quill [kwĭl] **134**–23
quiz show [kwĭz/ shō/] **167**–23
quotation marks [kwō tā/shən märks/] **113**–9
quotient [kwō/shənt] **118** ✦
rabbit [răb/ət] **133**–13
raccoon [ră kōōn/] **134**–13
race [rās] **157**–Y
racquetball [răk/ət böl/] **159**–11
radiation [rā/dē ā/shən] **126**–13
radiator [rā/dē ā/tər] **109**–42, 56
radio [rā/dē ō] **44**–16, **108**–31
   ...program [-prō/grăm] **166**–4
radioactive [rā/dē ō ăk/tĭv] **147**–6
radiologist [rā/dē äl/ə jĭst] **86**–5
radishes [răd/ĭ shəz] **51**–5
radius [rā/dē əs] **118**–16
rafting [răf/tĭng] **154**–4
rags [răgz] **47**–6
railroad crossing [rāl/rōd krö/sĭng] **107**–11
rain boots [rān/ bōōts/] **66**–19
raincoat [rān/kōt/] **66**–17
rain forest [rān/ för/əst, fär/–] **117**–1
raining [rā/nĭng] **10**–8
raise [rāz] **2**–A
raisins [rā/zənz] **50**–27
rake [rāk] **39**–F
rake [rāk] **39**–11
ranch [rănch] **34**–12
rancher [răn/chər] **148**–22
RANCHING [răn/chĭng] **148**
rash [răsh] **78**–10
raspberries [răz/bĕr/ēz] **50**–18
rat [răt] **133**–18
rats [răts] **49**–27
rattle [răt/l] **95**–31
rattlesnake [răt/l snāk/] **131**–38
raw [rö] **52**–24
ray [rā] **130**–6
rayon [rā/än] **70**
razor [rā/zər] **77**–25
   ...blade [–blād/] **77**–26
read [rēd] **6**–B, **27**–V, **94**–F
Realtor [rē/əl tər] **35**
rearview mirror [rĭr/vyōō/ mĭr/ər] **108**–1
receipt [rĭ sēt/] **21**–5
receive [rĭ sēv/] **96**–D
receiver [rĭ sē/vər] **9**–2
receptionist [rĭ sĕp/shə nĭst] **84**–2, **138**–47
recharging [rē chär/jĭng] **109**–58
record [rĕk/ərd] **98**–15
record [rĭ körd/] (science) **119**–C, (cassette player) **165**–A
Recreation room [rĕk/rē ā/shən rōōm/] **36**
rec room [rĕk/ rōōm/] **36** ✦
rectangle [rĕk/tăng/gəl] **118**–8
recycle [rē sī/kəl] **46**–B, **126**–A
recycling bin [rē sī/klĭng bĭn/] **47**–2
red [rĕd(/–)] **12**–13
   ...hair [–hër/] **23**–14
redwood [rĕd/wōōd/] **128**–1
referee [rĕf/ə rē/] **158**–6
reference [rĕf/rəns]
   ...desk [–dĕsk/] **98**–2
   ...librarian [lī brër/ē ən] **98**–1
refrigerator [rĭ frĭj/ə rā/tər] **40**–9

register [rĕj/ə stər] **116**–F
registered [rĕj/ə stərd]
   ...nurse (RN) [–nürs/] **87**–22
regular price [rĕg/yə lər prīs/] **21**–2
relax [rĭ lăks/] **27**–U
relieved [rĭ lēvd/] **30**–16
religious holiday [rĭ lĭj/əs häl/ə dā/] **19**–44
relish [rĕl/ĭsh] **60**–26
remarried [rē măr/ēd] **25**–27
remote control [rĭ mōt/ kən trōl/] **164**–9
remove [rĭ mōōv/] **97**–F
rent [rĕnt] **28**–I
Renting an apartment [rĕn/tĭng ən ə pärt/mənt] **35**
repair [rĭ për/] **140**–G
repair person [rĭ për/ pür/sən] **48**–10, **138**–48
REPAIRS [rĭ përz/] **48**–49
repeat [rĭ pēt/] **6**–D
report crimes [rĭ pört/ krīmz/] **101**–H
reporter [rĭ pör/tər] **99**–12, **139**–49
Reptiles [rĕp/tīlz] **131**
request [rĭ kwĕst/] **111**–M
rescue breathing [rĕs/kyōō brē/dhĭng] **83**–16
Resident Alien card [rĕz/ə dənt ā/lē ən kärd/] **29**–3
respirator [rĕs/pə rā/tər] **147**–12
Responsibilities (of citizenship)
   [rĭ spän/sə bĭl/ə tēz əv sĭt/ə zən shĭp/] **116**
RESTAURANT [rĕs/tə rənt, –ränt/] **62**–63
restaurant [rĕs/tə rənt, –ränt/] **90**–14
rest rooms [rĕst/ rōōmz/] **5**–8
retire [rĭ tīr/] **29** ✦
return [rĭ türn/] **21**–F
return address [rĭ türn/ ə drĕs/, –ă/drĕs] **96**–7
rewind [rē wīnd/] **165**–D
rewrite [rē rīt/] **113**–D
rhinoceros [rī näs/ər əs] **135**–29
rib cage [rĭb/ kāj/] **75**–53
rice [rīs(/–)] **54**–28, **148**–1
   ...pilaf [–pē/läf, –pī läf/] **61**–18
ride [rīd] **91**–E, **157**–W
rides [rīdz] **152**–17
right [rīt(/–)] / [–rīt/]
   ...turn only [–türn/ ōn/lē] **107**–9
   on the... [än dhə–, ön–] **13**–2
right-of-way [rīt/əv wā/] **107** ✦
Rights and responsibilities [rīts/ ən rĭ spän/sə bĭl/ə tēz] **116**
ring [rĭng] **69**–39
rinse [rĭns] **76**–F
rip [rĭp] **70**–23
ripe [rīp] **50**–29
river [rĭv/ər] **117**–3
RN (registered nurse) [är/ĕn/] **87**–22
roast [rōst] **58**–U
roast [rōst(/–)]
   ...beef [–bēf/] **52**–1, **53**–7, **57**–12
   ...chicken [–chĭk/ən] **61**–12
roasting [rō/stĭng]
   ...pan [–păn/] **59**–13
   ...rack [–răk/] **59**–14
robin [räb/ən] **132**–17
rock [räk] **94**–H
rock [räk(/–)] **155**–24
rock band [räk/ bănd/] **120**–2
rocking chair [räk/ĭng chër/] **94**–6
RODENTS [rōd/nts] **133**
roll [rōl(/–)] **56**–11

...of paper towels [–əv pā/pər tow/əlz] **56**–23
roller coaster [rō/lər kō/stər] **152**–15
rollers [rō/lərz] **23**–21
rolling pin [rō/lĭng pĭn/] **59**–30
rolls [rōlz] **54**–30
romance [rō mănz/, rō/mănz] **166**–16
Roman numerals [rō/mən nōō/mər əlz] **14**
roof [rōōf] **38**–20, **48**–3
roofer [rōō/fər] **48**–8
roof garden [rōōf/ gär/dn] **36**–5
room service [rōōm/ sür/vəs] **145**–12
rooster [rōō/stər] **133**–6
root [rōōt] **128**–5, **129**–3
rope [rōp] **154**–19
rose [rōz] **129**–15
rotary card file [rō/tə rē kärd/ fīl/] **143**–17
rotten [rät/n] **50**–30
rouge [rōōzh] **77**–36
route [rōōt, rowt] **104**–2
router [row/tər] **150**–12
rubber [rŭb/ər]
...band [–bănd/] **143**–45
...cement [–sə mĕnt/] **143**–38
...gloves [–glŭvz/] **47**–4
...mat [–măt/] **43**–3
...stamp [–stămp/] **143**–40
rug [rŭg] **44**–23
ruler [rōō/lər] **3**–27
run [rŭn] **156**–C
rural area [rōōr/əl ër/ē ə] **34**–4
rye bread [rī/ brĕd/] **53**–3
sad [săd] **31**–20, **167**–28
safe-deposit box [sāf/dĭ päz/ət bäks/] **97**–13
safety [sāf/tē]
...boot [–bōōt/] **147**–20
...earmuffs [–ïr/mŭfs] **147**–14
...glasses [–glăs/əz] **147**–10
...goggles [–gäg/əlz] **147**–9
...pin [–pĭn/] **73**–24
...seat [–sēt/] **109**–39
...vest [–vĕst/] **147**–15
...visor [–vī/zər] **147**–11
SAFETY, PUBLIC [pŭb/lĭk sāf/tē] **101**
sailboarding [sāl/bör/dĭng] **160**–10
sailboat [sāl/bōt/] **155**–4
sailing [sā/lĭng] **160**–8
salad [săl/əd]
...bar [–bär/] **60**–16
...dressing [–drĕs/ĭng] **60**–18
...fork [–förk/] **63**–24
...plate [–plāt/] **63**–17
salamander [săl/ə măn/dər] **130**–27
salami [sə lä/mē] **53**–5
sale price [sāl/ prīs/] **21**–3
salesclerk [sālz/klürk/] **68**–1, **139**–50
salesperson [sālz/pür/sən] **139**–50
sales tax [sālz/ tăks/] **21**–7
salmon steak [săm/ən stāk/] **53**–19
saltshaker [sölt/shā/kər] **41**–14
sand [sănd(/–)] **155**–23
...castle [–kăs/əl] **155**–10
...dune [–dōōn/] **117**–5
sandals [săn/dlz] **68**–24
sandbox [sănd/bäks/] **153**–15
sandpaper [sănd/pā/pər] **151**–50

sanitation worker [săn/ə tā/shən wür/kər] **139**–51
Saturday [săt/ər dā/, –dē] **18**–7
Saturn [săt/ərn] **127**–4
saucepan [sös/păn/] **59**–25
saucer [sö/sər] **63**–22
sausage [sö/sĭj] **52**–12, **61**–2
sauté [sö tā/, sō–] **58**–H
save [sāv] **126**–B, C
savings account number [sā/vĭngz ə kownt/ nŭm/bər] **97**–6
saxophone [săk/sə fōn/] **120**–7
say [sā] **6**–C
scaffolding [skăf/əl dĭng] **149**–4
scale (weight) [skāl] **43**–26, **84**–7
scales (fish) [skālz] **130**–3
scallions [skăl/yənz] **51**–17
scallop [skăl/əp, skäl/–] **130**–18
scallops [skăl/əps, skäl/–] **53**–25
scanner [skăn/ər] **144**–13
scared [skërd] **31**–24
scarf [skärf] **66**–4, **70**–15
schedule [skĕj/ōōl, –ōō əl] **104**–3
SCHOOL [skōōl] **5**
school **89**–27
...crossing [–krö/sĭng] **107**–13
adult... [ə dŭlt/–, ăd/ŭlt–] **112**–8
elementary... [ĕl/ə mĕn/trē–] **112**–5
high... [hī/–] **112**–7
junior high... [jōōn/yər hī/–] **112**–6
middle... [mĭd/l–] **112**–6
parochial... [pə rō/kē əl–] **112**–3
private... [prī/vət–] **112**–2
trade... [trād/–] **112**–9
vocational... [vō kā/shə nəl–] **112**–9
School Registration Form [skōōl/ rĕj/ə strā/shən förm/] **4**
SCHOOLS, TYPES OF [tīps/ əv skōōlz/] **112**
SCHOOL SUBJECTS, MORE [mör/ skōōl/ sŭb/jĭkts] **121**
SCIENCE [sī/əns] **119**
science fiction story [sī/əns fĭk/shən stör/ē] **166**–12
scissors [sĭz/ərz] **23**–19, **73**–18
score [skör] **158**–1
scorpion [skör/pē ən] **132**–31
scrambled eggs [skrăm/bəld ĕgz/] **58**, **61**–1
scraper [skrā/pər] **151**–48
screen [skrēn] **2**–2, **144**–6, **152**–12, **165**–28
screen door [skrēn/ dör/] **38**–8
screwdriver [skrōō/drī/vər] **150**–25
Phillips... [fĭl/ĭps–] **150**–26
scrub [skrŭb] **46**–L
scrub brush [skrŭb/ brŭsh/] **47**–19
scuba [skōō/bə]
...diving [–dī/vĭng] **160**–12
...tank [–tăngk/] **155**–8
sculpture [skŭlp/chər] **152**–9
sea [sē(/–)]
...anemone [–ə nĕm/ə nē] **130**–21
...horse [–hörs/] **130**–23
...lion [–lī/ən] **131**–34
...urchin [–ür/chən] **130**–20
Sea animals [sē/ ăn/ə məlz] **130**
SEAFOOD [sē/fōōd/] **53**
seal [sēl] **131**–33
seam [sēm(/–)] **73**–11
...ripper [–rĭp/ər] **73**–19
Sea mammals [sē/ măm/əlz] **131**
search and rescue team [sürch/ ən rĕs/kyōō tēm/] **103**–17

Index

seashell [sē/shĕl/] **155**–21
Seasons [sē/zənz] **19**
seat [sēt(/–)] **2**–E, **152**–11
...belt [–bĕlt/] **109**–36
seat [sēt] **62**–B
seaweed [sē/wēd/] **155** ✦
second [sĕk/ənd] **14, 16**–1
...floor [–flör/] **36**–2
secretary [sĕk/rə tër/ē] **139**–52, **142**–3
section [sĕk/shən] / [–sĕk/shən]
    dairy... [dër/ē–] **54**–9
    produce... [prō/dōōs–] **54**–11
security [sĭ kyōor/ə tē] **111**–C
    ...gate [–gāt/] **36**–13
    ...guard [–gärd/] **97**–4
    ...system [–sĭs/təm] **36**–9
see [sē] **75**–A
seed [sēd] **129**–1
seedling [sēd/lĭng] **129**–2
seesaw [sē/sö/] **153**–16
See you [sē/ yə] **8**
Selective Service [sə lĕk/tĭv sür/vəs] **116**–F
sell [sĕl] **21**–B, **140**–H
semi [sĕm/ī] **106**–15
semicolon [sĕm/ē kō/lən] **113**–13
Senate [sĕn/ət] **116**–3
Senator [sĕn/ə tər] **116**–4
send [sĕnd] **96**–B
senior citizen [sēn/yər sĭt/ə zən] **22**–12
Senses [sĕn/səz] **75**
sentence [sĕn/tns] **113**–4
sentence the defendant [sĕn/tns dhə dĭ fĕn/dənt] **99**–F
September [sĕp tĕm/bər] **19**–33
serious [sïr/ē əs] **167**–26
Serious Diseases [sïr/ē əs dĭ zē/zəz] **79**
serve (sports) [sürv] **157**–N
serve on a jury [sürv/ än ə jōōr/ē, –ön–] **116**–G
server [sür/vər] **62**–4, **63**–6, **139**–53
serve the meal [sürv/ dhə mēl/] **62**–F
service elevator [sür/vəs ĕl/ə vā tər] **145** ✦
serviceman [sür/vəs măn/, –mən] **139**–54
servicewoman [sür/vəs wōom/ən] **139**–54
serving dish [sür/vĭng dĭsh/] **41**–6
set [sĕt(/–)]
    ...hair [–hër/] **23**–C
    ...the table [–dhə tā/bəl] **62**–A
set of dishes [sĕt/ əv dĭsh/əz] **41**–2
seven [sĕv/ən] **14**
seventeen [sĕv/ən tēn/] **14**
seventeenth [sĕv/ən tēnth/] **14**
seventh [sĕv/ənth] **14**
seventy [sĕv/ən tē] **14**
sew [sō(/–)]
    ...by hand [–bī hănd/] **73**–A
    ...by machine [–bī mə shēn/] **73**–B
    ...clothes [–klōz/] **140**–L
SEWING AND ALTERATIONS [sō/ĭng ən öl/tə rā/shənz] **73**
sewing machine [sō/ĭng mə shēn/] **73**–10
sex [sĕks] **4**–12
shade [shād] **155**–11
shampoo [shăm pōō/] **76**–9
Shapes [shāps] **118**
share [shër] **6**–I
shark [shärk] **130**–7
shave [shāv] **77**–M

shaving cream [shā/vĭng krēm/] **77**–27
shears [shïrz] **39**–15
sheep [shēp] **133**–7
sheet [shēt] **44**–13, 14
shelf [shĕlf] **40**–8
Shellfish [shĕl/fĭsh/] **53**
shelter [shĕl/tər] **34**–10
shingles [shĭng/gəlz] **149**–19
shin guards [shĭn/ gärdz/] **161**–13
ship [shĭp] **146**–C
shipping clerk [shĭp/ĭng klürk/] **146**–15
shirt [shürt] **64**–4, **65**–20
shock [shäk] **82**–C
shoe [shōō(/–)]
    ...department [–dĭ pärt/mənt] **68**–3
    ...store [–stör/] **92**–10
shoelace [shōō/lās/] **68**–14
SHOES AND ACCESSORIES [shōōz/ ən ĭk sĕs/ə rēz] **68–69**
shoot [shōōt] **156**–I
shop [shäp] **21**–A
shop [shäp] **121**–10
SHOPPING [shäp/ĭng] **21**
shopping [shäp/ĭng]
    ...basket [–băs/kət] **54**–7
    ...cart [–kärt/] **54**–3
    ...program [–prō/grăm] **167**–25
shore [shör] **117**–12
short [shört] **22**–18, **23**–1, **71**–35
shorten [shör/tn] **73**–D
short-sleeved [shört/slēvd/] **71**–30
shorts [shörts] **64**–13, **67**–3, 12
shortwave radio [shört/wāv/ rā/dē ō] **164**–5
shoulder [shōl/dər] **74**–10
    ...bag [–băg/] **69**–27
    ...harness [–här/nəs] **109**–37
    ...pads [–pădz/] **161**–21
shoulder-length [shōl/dər lĕngkth/] **23**–2
shout [showt] **169**–G
shovel [shŭv/əl] **39**–13, **149**–21
show (puppet) [shō] **152**–14
shower cap [show/ər kăp/] **76**–1
showerhead [show/ər hĕd/] **43**–10
shrimp [shrĭmp] **53**–24, **130**–19
shutter [shŭt/ər] **38**–18
sick [sĭk] **30**–14
side [sīd] **118**–22
sideburns [sīd/bürnz/] **23**–7
sideview mirror [sīd/vyōō/ mïr/ər] **108**–8
sidewalk [sīd/wök/] **91**–26
sight impaired [sīt/ ĭm përd/] **22**–26
sign [sīn(/–)]
    ...a rental agreement [–ə rĕn/təl ə grē/mənt] **35**–C
    ...your name [–yər nām/] **4**–D
sign [sīn] **91**–29
signature [sĭg/nə chər] **4**–18
Signs [sīnz] **107**
silk [sĭlk] **70**–15
silk scarves [sĭlk/ skärvz/] **68**–4
silver dollar [sĭl/vər däl/ər] **20**–6
simmer [sĭm/ər] **58**–R
sing [sĭng] **120**–B, **169**–I
single [sĭng/gəl]
    ...father [–fä/dhər] **25**–25
    ...mother [–mŭdh/ər] **25**–26
sink [sĭngk] **40**–6, **43**–22, **49**–17

sister [sĭs′tər] **24**–8, **25**–30, 32
sister-in-law [sĭs′tər ĭn lö′] **24**–15
sitcom [sĭt′käm′] **167**–18
sit down [sĭt′ down′] **2**–E
situation comedy [sĭch′ōō ā′shən käm′ə dē] **167**–18
six [sĭks] **14**
six-pack [sĭks′păk′] **56**–9
six-pack of soda [sĭks′păk′ əv sō′də] **56**–21
sixteen [sĭks′tēn′] **14**
sixteenth [sĭks′tēnth′] **14**
sixth [sĭksth] **14**
sixty [sĭks′tē] **14**
six-year-old [sĭks′yïr ōld′] **22**–4
Sizes [sī′zəz] **70**
skate [skāt] **157**–V
skateboarding [skāt′bör′dĭng] **159**–12
skating [skā′tĭng] **160**–4, 5
Skeleton [skĕl′ə tn] **75**
ski [skē] **157**–V
ski [skē(′–)]
  …boots [–bōōts′] **161**–26
  …cap [–kăp′] **66**–10
  …mask [–măsk′] **66**–14
  …poles [–pōlz′] **161**–25
skiing [skē′ĭng] **160**–1, 3, 7
skin [skĭn] **75**–51
skinless [skĭn′ləs] **52** ✦
skirt [skürt] **64**–10, **65**–25
skis [skēz] **161**–24
skull [skŭl] **75**–52
skunk [skŭngk] **134**–12
skyscraper [skī′skrā′pər] **88** ✦
slacks [slăks] **64**–8
sledding [slĕd′ĭng] **160**–6
sledgehammer [slĕj′hăm′ər] **149**–22
sleeping bag [slē′pĭng băg′] **154**–12
sleepy [slē′pē] **30**–3
sleeve [slēv] **73**–6
sleeveless [slēv′ləs] **71**–29
slice [slīs] **58**–O
slide [slīd] (science) **119**–5, (park) **153**–13
slides [slīdz] **165**–31
slide tray [slīd′ trā′] **165**–30
slim [slĭm] **22**–22
sling [slĭng] **80**–8
slippers [slĭp′ərz] **67**–6
slot [slät] **144**–19
slow [slō] **11**–4
small [smöl(′–)] **70**–2
  …town [–town′] **34**–3
smell [smĕl] **75**–C
smog [smäg(′–), smög(′–)] **126**–10
  …check [–chĕk′] **109**–57
smoggy [smä′gē, smö′–] **10**–14
smoke detector [smōk′ dĭ tĕk′tər] **37**–25, **45**–11
smoked turkey [smōkt′ tür′kē] **53**–4
snack foods [snăk′ fōōdz′] **55**–16
snail [snāl] **130**–24
snake [snāk] **131**–38, 39
sneeze [snēz] **78**–B
snorkeling [snör′kə lĭng] **160**–11
snowboard [snō′börd′] **161**–23
snowboarding [snō′bör′dĭng] **160**–2
snowing [snō′ĭng] **10**–9
snowstorm [snō′störm′] **10**–20

soap [sōp(′–)] **43**–23, **76**–2
  …dish [–dīsh′] **43**–24
  …pads [–pădz′] **47**–5
soap opera [sōp′ äp′rə] **167**–21
soccer [säk′ər] **158**–12
  …ball [–böl′] **161**–12
Social Security card [sō′shəl sĭ kyōōr′ə tē kärd′] **29**–5
Social Security number [sō′shəl sĭ kyōōr′ə tē nŭm′bər] **4**–15
socks [säks] **67**–15
soda [sō′də] **55**–52, **60**–4
sofa [sō′fə] **42**–19
soft [söft] **11**–6
softball [söft′böl′] **158**–10
Software [söft′wër′] **144**
solar [sō′lər]
  …eclipse [–ĭ klĭps′] **127** ✦
  …energy [–ĕn′ər jē] **126**–1
  …system [–sĭs′təm] **127**
sole [sōl] (fish) **53**–21, (shoe) **68**–12
solid [säl′əd] **70**–6
Solids [säl′ədz] **118**
son [sŭn] **24**–22
son-in-law [sŭn′ĭn lö′] **24** ✦
sore throat [sör′ thrōt′] **78**–6
Sorry. [sär′ē, sör′ē] **8**
sort [sört] **72**–A
soup [sōōp(′–)] **54**–24
  …bowl [–bōl′] **63**–18
  …of the day [–əv dhə dā′] **61**–10
soupspoon [sōōp′spōōn′] **63**–29
sour cream [sow′ər krēm′] **54**–37
south [sowth] **107, 123, 124**
soybeans [soy′bēnz′] **148**–3
space [spās(′–)] **127**–22
  …station [–stā′shən] **127**–18
spades [spādz] **163**–28
spaghetti [spə gĕt′ē] **54**–27
spare tire [spër′ tīr′] **109**–53
sparrow [spär′ō] **132**–8
spatula [spăch′ə lə] **59**–19
speak [spēk] **140**–J
speaker [spē′kər] **36**–8
speakers [spē′kərz] **164**–11
specialist [spĕsh′ə lĭst] **86** ✦
speed [spēd(′–)] **144** ✦
  …limit [–lĭm′ət] **107**–5
speedometer [spĭ däm′ə tər] **108**–20
spell [spĕl] **4**–A, **6**–E
sphere [sfïr] **118**–14
spices [spī′səz] **55**–46
spider [spī′dər] **132**–30
spinach [spĭn′ĭch] **51**–11
spinal column [spī′nəl käl′əm] **75**–54
spiral notebook [spī′rəl nōt′bōōk′] **3**–26
splint [splĭnt] **83**–11
split skirt [splĭt′ skürt′] **65**–25
sponge [spŭnj] **47**–24
spool of thread [spōōl′ əv thrĕd′] **73**–17
spoon [spōōn] **41**–23, **59**–9
SPORTS [spörts] **158**–160
sports [spörts(′–)]
  …car [–kär′] **106**–6
  …coat [–kōt′] **64**–6
  …shirt [–shürt′] **65**–26
SPORTS EQUIPMENT [spörts′ ĭ kwĭp′mənt] **161**
SPORTS VERBS [spörts′ vürbz′] **156**–157

sprained ankle [sprānd/ ăng/kəl] **78**–18
spray [sprā(/–)]
  …gun [–gŭn/] **151**–19
  …starch [–stärch/] **72**–12
spring [sprĭng] **19**–37
sprinkler [sprĭng/klər] **39**–8
square [skwër] **118**–6
squash [skwäsh, skwösh] **51**–13
squeegee [skwē/jē] **47**–9
squid [skwĭd] **130**–10
squirrel [skwür/əl] **133**–21
stacking tray [stăk/ĭng trā/] **142**–5
stadium [stā/dē əm] **152**–26
stage [stāj] **32**–4
stain [stān] **70**–22
stairs [stërz] **37**–35, **105**–8, 9
stairway [stër/wā/] **37**–26
stall shower [stöl/ show/ər] **43** ✦
stamp [stămp(/–)] **96**–10
  …collection [–kə lĕk/shən] **162**–12
standard [stăn/dərd]
  …time [–tīm/] **17**–32
  …transmission [–trănz mĭsh/ən, –trăns–] **109**
stand trial [stănd/ trī/əl, –trīl/] **99**–D
stand up [stănd/ ŭp/] **2**–D
stand-up comedy [stănd/ŭp/ kăm/ə dē] **166**–5
staple [stā/pəl] **142**–G
staple [stā/pəl] **143**–29
stapler [stā/plər] **143**–28
star [stär] **127**–23
starfish [stär/fĭsh/] **130**–15
start [stärt(/–)] **157**–X
  …school [–skool/] **28**–B
starving [stär/vĭng] **30** ✦
state [stāt] **4**–8
station wagon [stā/shən wăg/ən] **106**–8
stay [stā] **101**–B
steak [stāk(/–)] **52**–2, **61**–13
  …knife [–nīf/] **63**–26
steam [stēm] **58**–I
steamer [stē/mər] **59**–4
steel-wool soap pads [stēl/wool/ sōp/ pădz/] **47**–5
steering wheel [stïr/ĭng wēl/] **108**–26
steers [stïrz] **148**–21
stem [stĕm] **129**–4
stepbrother [stĕp/brŭdh/ər] **25**–33
stepdaughter [stĕp/dö/tər] **25** ✦
stepfather [stĕp/fä/dhər] **25**–28
stepladder [stĕp/lăd/ər] **47**–7
stepmother [stĕp/mŭdh/ər] **25**–31
steps [stĕps] **38**–13, **48**–7
stepsister [stĕp/sĭs/tər] **25**–32
stereo system [stĕr/ē ō sĭs/təm] **42**–14
sterile pad [stĕr/əl păd/] **83**–4
stethoscope [stĕth/ə skōp/] **84**–8
stewing beef [stoo/ĭng bēf/] **52**–3
stick shift [stĭk/ shĭft/] **109**–48
stir [stür] **58**–E
stir-fry [stür/frī/] **58**–W
stitches [stĭch/əz] **83**–15
stock clerk [stäk/ klürk/] **139**–55
stockings [stäk/ĭngz] **67**–26
stomach [stŭm/ək] **75**–41
stomachache [stŭm/ək āk/] **78**–4
stop [stäp] **165**–F

stop [stäp] **107**–3
stopover [stäp/ō/vər] **111** ✦
stopped up [stäpt/ ŭp/] **49**–18
storage locker [stör/ĭj läk/ər] **36**–14
store [stör(/–)] / [–stör/]
  …owner [–ō/nər] **139**–56
  candy… [kăn/dē–] **92**–3
  card… [kärd/–] **92**–7
  convenience… [kən vēn/yəns–] **90**–3
  department… [dĭ pärt/mənt–] **93**–13
  electronics… [ĭ lĕk trän/ĭks–] **93**–18
  jewelry… [joo/əl rē–] **92**–2
  music… [myoo/zĭk–] **92**–1
  pet… [pĕt/–] **92**–6
  shoe… [shoo/–] **92**–10
  toy… [toy/–] **92**–5
  video… [vĭd/ē ō–] **93**–15
storm [störm] **10**–16, 18, 20, 21
storm door [störm/ dör/] **38**–12
stove [stōv] **40**–18, **154**–16
stow [stō] **111**–H
straight [strāt(/–)]
  …hair [–hër/] **23**–9
  …line [–līn/] **118**–18
strainer [strā/nər] **59**–22
stranger [strān/jər] **101**–F
straw [strö] **60**–20
strawberries [strö/bĕr/ēz] **50**–17
straw hat [strö/ hăt/] **66**–23
stream [strēm] **117** ✦
street [strēt(/–)] **90**–9
  …vendor [–vĕn/dər] **91**–30
streetlight [strēt/līt/] **91**–23
strep throat [strĕp/ thrōt/] **79**–4
stretch [strĕch] **157**–Q
stretcher [strĕch/ər] **87**–28
string beans [strĭng/ bēnz/] **51**–25
string of pearls [strĭng/ əv pürlz/] **69**–30
Strings [strĭngz] **120**
striped [strīpt] **70**–7
stroller [strō/lər] **94**–2
stucco [stŭk/ō] **149**–14
student [stood/nt] **2**–3, **139**–57
STUDYING [stŭd/ē ĭng] **6**–7
stuffed animals [stŭft/ ăn/ə məlz] **45**–23
subcompact [sŭb/käm/păkt] **106**–1
subtraction [səb trăk/shən] **118**–2
suburbs [sŭb/ürbz] **34**–2
subway [sŭb/wā/] **104**–9
sugar [shoog/ər] **55**–48, **60**–21
  …bowl [–bōl/] **41**–12
  …substitute [–sŭb/stə toot/] **60**–22
suit [soot] (clothing) **64**–2, (diving) **155**–7
summer [sŭm/ər] **19**–38
sun [sŭn] **127**–10
sunbather [sŭn/bā/dhər] **155**–17
sunblock [sŭn/bläk/] **155**–13
sunburn [sŭn/bürn/] **78**–14
Sunday [sŭn/dā, –dē] **18**–1
sunflower [sŭn/flow/ər] **129**–10
sunglasses [sŭn/glăs/əz] **66**–21
sunny [sŭn/ē] **10**–6
sunscreen [sŭn/skrēn/] **76**–6, **155**–13
superintendent [soo/prĭn tĕn/dənt, soo/pər ĭn–] **36**–12
supervise people [soo/pər vīz pē/pəl] **140**–K

supply cabinet [sə plī′ kăb′ə nət] **142**–13
Supreme Court [sə prēm′ kört′] **116**–8
surfboard [sürf′börd′] **155**–5
surfing [sür′fĭng] **160**–9
surgeon [sür′jən] **87**–30
surge protector [sürj′ prə tĕk′tər] **144**–10
surgical [sür′jĭ kəl]
　...cap [–kăp′] **87**–31
　...gown [–gown′] **87**–32
　...nurse [–nürs′] **87**–29
surprised [sər prīzd′, sə–] **31**–31
suspect [sŭs′pĕkt] **99**–A
suspenders [sə spĕn′dərz] **68**–2
SUV (sports utility vehicle)
　[ĕs′yoo̅′vē′] / [spörts′ yoo̅ tĭl′ə tē vē′ĭ kəl] **106**–9
swallow [swäl′ō] **82**–J
swap meet [swäp′ mēt′] **152**–22
sweater [swĕt′ər]
　cardigan... [kär′də gən–] **65**–27
　crewneck... [kroo̅′nĕk′–] **71**–26
　pullover... [poo̅l′ō′vər–] **64**–11
　turtleneck... [tür′tl nĕk′–] **71**–28
　V-neck... [vē′nĕk′–] **71**–27
sweatpants [swĕt′pănts′] **64**–15
sweatshirt [swĕt′shürt′] **64**–14
sweep [swēp] **46**–E
sweet peppers [swēt′ pĕp′ərz] **51**–7
swim [swĭm] **157**–T
swimming [swĭm′ĭng]
　...pool [–poo̅l′] **37**–16
　...trunks [–trŭngks′] **66**–22
swimsuit [swĭm′soo̅t′] **66**–26
swing [swĭng] **157**–O
swings [swĭngz] **153**–12
Swiss cheese [swĭs′ chēz′] **53**–11
swivel chair [swĭv′əl chër′] **143**–22
swollen [swō′lən] **78**–16
swordfish [sörd′fĭsh] **130**–12
SYMPTOMS AND INJURIES [sĭmp′təmz ən ĭn′jə rēz] **78**
synagogue [sĭn′ə gäg′] **88**–9
synthetic materials [sĭn thĕt′ĭk mə tïr′ē əlz] **70**
syringe [sə rĭnj′] **84**–14
syrup [sïr′əp, sür′–] **61**–5
table [tā′bəl] / [–tā′bəl]
　dining room... [dī′nĭng roo̅m′–] **41**–17
　night... [nīt′–] **44**–21
　picnic... [pĭk′nĭk–] **153**–8
tablecloth [tā′bəl klöth′] **41**–18
tablespoon [tā′bəl spoo̅n′] **57**–7
tablet [tăb′lət] **81**–25
table tennis [tā′bəl tĕn′əs] **159**–13
tackle [tăk′əl] **156**–M
taco [tä′kō] **60**–9
tail [tāl] **134**–22
taillight [tāl′līt′] **108**–14
tailor [tā′lər] **73**–9
take [tāk(′–)]
　...a bath [–ə băth′] **76**–B
　...a citizenship test [–ə sĭt′ə zən shĭp tĕst′] **116**–C
　...a message [–ə mĕs′ĭj] **142**–A
　...a nap [–ə năp′] **94**–L
　...a picture [–ə pĭk′chər] **32**–D
　...a seat [–ə sēt′] **2**–E
　...a shower [–ə show′ər] **26**–C, **76**–A
　...medicine [–mĕd′ə sən] **80**–F

...ownership [–ō′nər shĭp′] **35**–J
...the bus [–dhə bŭs′] **26**–H, **104** ✦
...the children to school [–dhə chĭl′drən tə skoo̅l′] **26**–G
...the order [–dhē ör′dər] **62**–E
...(your) temperature [–yər tĕm′prə chər] **85**–C
take care of [tāk′ kër′ əv] **140**–L
take in [tāk′ ĭn′] **73**–E
take off [tāk′ öf′] **111**–L
take out [tāk′ owt′] **2**–K, **46**–Q
take out (food) [tāk′ owt′] **62** ✦
talcum powder [tăl′kəm pow′dər] **76**–3
talk [tök] **2**–B, **7**–P, **35**–B, G, **141**–A, I
talk show [tök′ shō′] **167**–20
tall [töl] **22**–16
tambourine [tăm′bə rēn′] **120**–19
tangerines [tăn′jə rēnz′] **50**–13
tank top [tăngk′ täp′] **67**–2
tape [tāp(′–)] **83**–5, **143**–39, 42
　...deck [–dĕk′] **108**–30
　...measure [–mĕzh′ər] **73**–13, **150**–22
target [tär′gət] **161**–8
tartar [tär′tər] **84**–17
taste [tāst] **75**–D
taxi [tăk′sē] **104**–18
　...driver [–drī′vər] **104**–20
　...license [–lī′səns] **104**–22
　...stand [–stănd′] **104**–19
TB (tuberculosis) [tē′bē′] / [too̅ bür′kyə lō′səs] **79**–13
tea [tē] **60**–5, **61**–24
teach [tēch] **140** ✦
teacher [tē′chər] **2**–5, **5**–2, **139**–58
teakettle [tē′kĕt′l] **40**–17
team [tēm] **103**–17, **158**–3
TEAM SPORTS [tēm′ spörts′] **158**
teapot [tē′pät′] **41**–11
tear [tër] **70**–23
teaspoon [tē′spoo̅n′] **57**–6, **63**–28
technician [tĕk nĭsh′ən] **86**–8, 16
teddy bear [tĕd′ē bër′] **45**–10
teenagers [tē′nā′jərz] **22**–6
teeth [tēth] **74**–25, **77**–J, K, **85**–I
teething ring [tē′dhĭng rĭng′] **95**–30
telemarketer [tĕl′ə mär′kə tər] **139**–59
TELEPHONE [tĕl′ə fōn′] **9**
telephone [tĕl′ə fōn′] **9**–1, 15
　...book [–boo̅k′] **9**–15
　...card [–kärd′] **9**–10
　...number [–nŭm′bər] **4**–11
telescope [tĕl′ə skōp′] **127**–21
television (TV) [tĕl′ə vĭzh′ən] **42**–26, **164**–6
　...program [–prō′grăm] **166**–3
teller [tĕl′ər] **97**–1
Temperature (weather) [tĕm′prə chər] **10**
temperature (fever) [tĕm′prə chər] **78**–8
temperature gauge [tĕm′prə chər gāj′] **108**–23
ten [tĕn] **14**, **15**–7, **16**–6, **20**–9
tenant [tĕn′ənt] **37**–33
tennis [tĕn′əs] **159**–14
　...court [–kört′] **153**–7
　...racket [–răk′ət] **161**–2
　...shoes [–shoo̅z′] **68**–22
tent [tĕnt] **154**–10
tenth [tĕnth] **14**
ten-year-old [tĕn′yïr ōld′] **22**–5
termites [tür′mīts] **49**–22

Index

terrified [tĕr/ə fīd/] **30** ✦
test tube [tĕst/ tōōb/] **119**–16
textbook [tĕkst/bŏŏk/, tĕks/–] **3**–22
thank [thăngk] **8**–H
Thanksgiving [thăngks gĭv/ĭng] **168**–15
Thank you [thăngk/ yōō] **8**
theater [thē/ə tər] / [thē/ə tər] **88**–10
...arts [–ärts/] **121**–12
movie... [–mōō/vē–] **88**–11
thermometer [thər măm/ə tər] **84**–15
thick book [thĭk/ bŏŏk/] **11**–7
thigh [thī] **74**–16
thighs [thīz] **52**–21
thimble [thĭm/bəl] **73**–20
thin [thĭn] **11**–8, **22**–22
third [thürd(/–)] **14**
...floor [–flör/] **36**–3
thirsty [thür/stē] **30**–2
thirteen [thür/tēn/] **14**
thirteenth [thür/tēnth/] **14**
thirteen-year-old [thür/tēn/yïr ōld/] **22**–7
thirty [thür/tē] **14**
this week [dhĭs/ wēk/] **18**–19
thorn [thörn] **129**–28
thousand [thow/zənd] **14**
thread [thrĕd] **73**–17
three [thrē(/–)] **14**
...times a week [–tīmz/ ə wēk/] **18**–24
three-fourths [thrē/förths/] **15**–5
three-piece suit [thrē/pēs/ sōōt/] **64**–1
throat [thrōt(/–)] **75**–36
...lozenges [–lăz/ən jəz] **81**–21
through [thrōō] **105**–11
throw [thrō] **156**–D
throw pillow [thrō/ pĭl/ō] **42**–20
throw up [thrō/ ŭp/] **78**–E
thumb [thŭm] **75**–56
thunderstorm [thŭn/dər störm/] **10**–16
Thursday [thürz/dā, –dē] **18**–5
tick [tĭk] **132**–28
ticket [tĭk/ət] **104**–14
tidal wave [tīd/l wāv/] **103**–15
tide [tīd] **155** ✦
tie [tī] **94**–I
tie [tī] (clothing) **69**–40, (sports) **158** ✦
ties [tīz] (clothing) **69**–10
tiger [tī/gər] **135**–37
tight [tīt] **71**–43
tights [tīts] **66**–11
tile [tīl] **43**–9
TIME [tīm] **16**–17
time clock [tīm/ klăk/] **146**–4
Time zones [tīm/ zōnz/] **17**
tire [tīr] **108**–10, **109**–53
tired [tīrd] **31**–33
tires [tīrz] **109**–59
title [tīt/l] **98**–21, **113**–3
toad [tōd] **130**–28
toast [tōst] **33, 61**–3
toaster [tō/stər] **40**–7
...oven [–ŭv/ən] **40**–15
today [tə dā/] **18**–15
toddler [täd/lər] **22**–3
toe [tō(/–)] **68**–15, **75**–63
...guard [–gärd/] **147**–21

toenail [tō/nāl/] **75**–64
toggle bolt [täg/əl bōlt/] **150**–33
toilet [toy/lət] **43**–17, **49**–18
...brush [–brŭsh/] **43**–16
...paper [–pā/pər] **43**–15
token [tō/kən] **104**–11
tomatoes [tə mā/tōz] **51**–23
tomorrow [tə mär/ō, –mör/ō] **18**–16
tongs [tängz, töngz] **59**–23, **119**–15
tongue [tŭng] **74**–26
too big [tōō/ bĭg/] **70**–21
TOOLS AND BUILDING SUPPLIES
[tōōlz/ ən bĭl/dĭng sə plīz/] **150**–**151**
too small [tōō/ smöl/] **70**–20
toothache [tōōth/āk/] **78**–2
toothbrush [tōōth/brŭsh/] **43**–20, **77**–20
...holder [–hōl/dər] **43**–21
toothpaste [tōōth/pāst/] **77**–21
tornado [tör nā/dō] **103**–13
total [tōt/l] **21**–8, **118** ✦
tote bag [tōt/ băg/] **69**–29
touch [tŭch] **75**–E
towel [tow/əl] **43**–8, 12, 13
...rack [–răk/] **43**–8
townhouse [town/hows/] **34**–7
tow truck [tō/ trŭk/] **106**–13
toy [toy(/–)]
...chest [–chĕst/] **45**–24
...store [–stör/] **92**–5
toys [toyz] **46**–H, **94**–5
track [trăk] (athletic) **5**–11, (train) **104**–10
track and field [trăk/ ən fēld/] **159**–17
trackball [trăk/böl/] **144**–15
track lighting [trăk/ lī/tĭng] **42**–3
tractor [trăk/tər] **148**–9
...trailer [–trā/lər] **106**–15
trade school [trād/ skōōl/] **112**–9
traffic light [trăf/ĭk līt/] **90**–6
TRAFFIC SIGNS [trăf/ĭk sīnz/] **107**
tragedy [trăj/ə dē] **166**–11
trailer [trā/lər] **106**–17
train [trān(/–)] **104**–17
...station [–stā/shən] **104**–13
training pants [trā/nĭng pănts/] **95**–24
transcribe [trăn skrīb/] **142**–C
transcriber (medical) [trăn skrī/bər] **142**–4
transfer [trăns für/, trăns/fər] **97**–E
transfer [trăns/fər] **104**–6
translator [trănz/lā/tər, trăns/–] **138**–34
transmission [trănz mĭsh/ən, trăns–]
automatic... [ö/tə măt/ĭk–] **109**
standard... [stăn/dərd–] **109**
TRANSPORTATION, PUBLIC [pŭb/lĭk trăns/pər tā/shən] **104**
trash [trăsh(/–)]
...bags [–băgz/] **47**–12
...bin [–bĭn/] **37**–20
...chute [–shōōt/] **37**–24
travel [trăv/əl] **29**–N
travel [trăv/əl]
...agency [–ā/jən sē] **92**–9
...agent [–ā/jənt] **139**–60
traveler's check [trăv/lərz chĕk/] **20**–17
tray [trā(/–)] **41**–10, **62**–H, **63**–7
...table [–tā/bəl] **110**–16
treatment [trēt/mənt] **80** ✦

TREES AND PLANTS [trēz/ ən plănts/] **128**
trench coat [trĕnch/ kōt/] **66**–20
triangle [trī/ăng/gəl] **118**–7
tricycle [trī/sĭ kəl] **153**–9
trigonometry [trĭg/ə näm/ə trē] **118**–27
trim [trĭm] **39**–E
tripe [trīp] **52**–8
tripod [trī/päd] **165**–20
trombone [träm bōn/] **120**–12
trout [trowt] **53**–16
trowel [trow/əl] **39**–14, **149**–12
truck driver [trŭk/ drī/vər] **139**–61
TRUCKS [trŭks] **106**
trumpet [trŭm/pət] **120**–13
trunk [trŭngk] (car) **109**–49, (tree) **128**–4, (animal) **135**–47
T-shirt [tē/shürt/] **64**–12, **70**–16, **72**–15, 16, 17, 18
tuba [tōō/bə] **120**–14
tube [tōōb(/–)] **56**–12
  …of toothpaste [–əv tōōth/pāst/] **56**–24
Tuesday [tōōz/dā, –dē] **18**–3
tulip [tōō/ləp] **129**–11
tuna [tōō/nə] **54**–25, **130**–9
tuner [tōō/nər] **164**–13
tunic [tōō/nĭk] **65**–22
tunnel [tŭn/əl] **105**–11
turbulence [tür/byə ləns] **111**–N
turkey [tür/kē] **52**–17, **53**–4, **168**–17
turn [türn(/–)]
  …left [–lĕft/] **107**–C
  …right [–rīt/] **107**–B
turn in [türn/ ĭn/] **113**–E
turnips [tür/nəps] **51**–14
turn signal [türn/ sĭg/nəl] **108**–4
turntable [türn/tā/bəl] **164**–12
turquoise [tür/koyz, –kwoyz] **12**–4
turtle [tür/tl] **131**–42
turtleneck [tür/tl nĕk/] **64**–7
  …sweater [–swĕt/ər] **71**–28
tusk [tŭsk] **135**–48
tuxedo [tŭk sē/dō] **65**–28
TV (television) [tē/vē/] **42**–26, **164**–6
  …antenna [–ăn tĕn/ə] **38**–22
tweezers [twē/zərz] **83**–2
twelfth [twĕlfth] **14**
twelve [twĕlv] **14**
twentieth [twĕn/tē əth] **14**
twenty [twĕn/tē] **14**, **16**–8, 9, **20**–10
twenty-five after one [twĕn/tē fīv/ ăf/tər wŭn/] **16**–9
twenty-five to two [twĕn/tē fīv/ tə tōō/] **16**–11
twenty percent [twĕn/tē pər sĕnt/] **15**–8
twenty to two [twĕn/tē tə tōō/] **16**–12
twice a week [twīs/ ə wēk/] **18**–23
twig [twĭg] **128**–1
two [tōō] **14**
two-story house [tōō/stör/ē hows/] **38** ✦
type [tīp] **140**–M, **142**–D
Types of entertainment [tīps/ əv ĕn/tər tān/mənt] **166**
Types of material [tīps/ əv mə tïr/ē əl] **70**
Types of math [tīps/ əv măth/] **118**
TYPES OF SCHOOLS [tīps/ əv skōōlz/] **112**
Types of stories [tīps/ əv stör/ēz] **166**
Types of TV programs [tīps/ əv tē/vē/ prō/grămz] **167**
typewriter [tīp/rī/tər] **142**–2
  …cartridge [–kär/trĭj] **143**–31
ugly [ŭg/lē] **11**–22

umbrella [ŭm brĕl/ə] **66**–16, **155**–9
umpire [ŭm/pīr] **158** ✦
uncle [ŭng/kəl] **24**–11
uncomfortable [ŭn kŭmf/tə bəl, –tər–] **30**–8
under [ŭn/dər] **13**–9, **105**–1
underexposed [ŭn/dər ĭk spōzd/] **165**–35
underline [ŭn/dər līn/] **7**–V
underpants [ŭn/dər pănts/] **67**–17
undershirt [ŭn/dər shürt/] **67**–10
uniform [yōō/nə förm/] **65**–17, **161**–16
UNIVERSE [yōō/nə vürs/] **127**
university [yōō/nə vür/sə tē] **112**–10
unload [ŭn lōd/] **72**–E
unpack [ŭn păk/] **35**–E
unscented [ŭn sĕn/təd] **77** ✦
up [ŭp] **105**–9
upset [ŭp sĕt/] **31**–30
upstairs [ŭp/stërz/] **38** ✦
Uranus [yoor/ə nəs, yoo rā/nəs] **127**–3
urban area [ür/bən ër/ē ə] **34**–1
use [yōōz(/–)] **140**–N
  …deodorant [–dē ō/dər ənt] **76**–C
user's manual [yōō/zərz măn/yōō əl] **144**–22
U.S. GOVERNMENT AND CITIZENSHIP
  [yōō/ĕs/ gŭv/ər mənt ən sĭt/ə zən shĭp/] **116**
U.S. HISTORY [yōō/ĕs/ hĭs/tə rē] **114**–**115**
Using a pay phone [yōō/zĭng ə pā/ fōn/] **9**
Using the ATM machine [yōō/zĭng dhē ā/tē/ĕm/ mə shēn/] **97**
U.S. MAIL [yōō/ĕs/ māl/] **96**
utilities [yoo tĭl/ə tēz] **35** ✦
U-turn OK (sign) [yōō/türn/ ō kā/] **107**–7
vacancy sign [vā/kən sē sīn/] **36**–11
vacation [vā kā/shən] **19**–46
vaccination [văk/sə nā/shən] **80** ✦
vacuum [văk/yōōm] **46**–I
vacuum cleaner [văk/yōōm klē/nər] **47**–13
  …attachments [–ə tăch/mənts] **47**–14
  …bag [–băg/] **47**–15
valedictorian [văl/ə dĭk tör/ē ən] **32**–8
Valentine's Day [văl/ən tīnz dā/] **168**–4
valet parking [văl/ā pär/kĭng] **145**–1
valley [văl/ē] **117**–18
van [văn] **106**–10, 14
vandalism [văn/də lĭz/əm] **100**–1
vase [vās, vāz, väz] **41**–9
vault [völt] **97**–2
VCR (videocassette recorder)
  [vē/sē/är/] / [vĭd/ē ō kə sĕt/ rĭ kör/dər] **164**–8
veal cutlets [vēl/ kŭt/ləts] **52**–6
vegetable [vĕj/tə bəl]
  …casserole [–kăs/ə rōl/] **58**
  …garden [–gär/dn] **148**–12
  …peeler [–pē/lər] **59**–15
VEGETABLES [vĕj/tə bəlz] **51**
vegetables [vĕj/tə bəlz] **55**–43
vegetarian [vĕj/ə tër/ē ən] **52** ✦
vein [vān] **75**–44
vendor [vĕn/dər] **91**–30
Venus [vē/nəs] **127**–8
vest [vĕst] **65**–24, **66**–13
veterinarian [vĕt/ər ə nër/ē ən] **139**–62
Vice President [vīs/ prĕz/ə dənt] **116**–7
victim [vĭk/təm] **100** ✦
video [vĭd/ē ō]
  …camera [–kăm/rə] **165**–19

Index

...game system [–gām/ sĭs/təm] **162**–1
...store [–stör/] **93**–15
videocassette [vĭd/ē ō kə sĕt/] **98**–13, **164**–8, 10
view [vyōō] **11**–21, 22
vine [vīn] **128**–22
vineyard [vĭn/yərd] **148**–14
violet [vī/ə lət, vī/lət] **129**–22
violin [vī/ə lĭn/] **120**–8
vise [vīs] **150**–21
visor [vī/zər] **147**–11
vital signs monitor [vīt/l sīnz/ män/ə tər] **87**–21
vitamins [vī/tə mənz] **81**–19
V-neck sweater [vē/nĕk/ swĕt/ər] **71**–27
vocational school [vō kā/shə nəl skōōl/] **112**–9
volcanic eruption [väl kän/ĭk ĭ rŭp/shən] **103**–14
volleyball [väl/ē böl/] (sport) **158**–14, (equipment) **161**–3
Volume [väl/yəm, –yōōm] **57**
volunteer [väl/ən tïr/] **87**–19
vomit [väm/ət] **78**–E
vote [vōt] **116**–D
waffles [wä/fəlz, wö/–] **61**–4
waist [wāst] **74**–4
waistband [wāst/bănd/] **73**–3
wait [wāt] **90**–B
waiter [wā/tər] **62**–4
waiting room [wā/tĭng rōōm/] **84**–1
wait on customers [wāt/ än kŭs/tə mərz, –ön–] **140**–O
waitress [wā/trəs] **63**–6
wake up [wāk/ ŭp/] **26**–A
walk [wök] **101**–A, **156**–A
walker [wö/kər] **80**–5, **95**–12
wall [wöl/–)] **42**–6, **48**–4
...unit [–yōō/nət] **42**–13
wallet [wä/lət, wö/–] **69**–26
wallpaper [wöl/pā/pər] **45**–5
walrus [wöl/rəs] **131**–32
War [wör] **114**
warehouse [wër/hows/] **146**–9
warm [wörm] **10**–2
warning label [wör/nĭng lā/bəl] **80**–15
wash [wäsh(/–), wösh(/–)]
...hair [–hër/] **76**–E
...the dishes [–dhə dĭsh/əz] **46**–M
...the windows [–dhə wĭn/dōz] **46**–D
washcloth [wäsh/klöth/, wösh/–] **43**–14
washer [wä/shər, wö/–] **72**–3, **150**–32
wasp [wäsp, wösp] **132**–18
wastebasket [wāst/băs/kət] **43**–25, **46**–F
watch [wäch, wöch] **69**–34
watch TV [wäch/ tē/vē/, wöch/–] **27**–5
water [wö/tər] **39**–B
water [wö/tər] **117**, **155**–1
...fountain [–fown/tn] **153**–11
...glass [–glăs/] **63**–19
...pollution [–pə lōō/shən] **126**–12
...polo [–pō/lō] **158**–15
watercolor [wö/tər kŭl/ər] **163**–25
waterfall [wä/tər föl/] **117**–2
watering can [wö/tər ĭng kăn/] **39**–17
watermelons [wö/tər mĕl/ənz] **50**–24
waterskiing [wö/tər skē/ĭng] **160**–7
WATER SPORTS [wö/tər spörts/] **160**
wave [wāv] **155**–6
wavy [wā/vē] **23**–10
Ways to pay [wāz/ tə pā/] **20**

WEATHER [wĕdh/ər] **10**
Wednesday [wĕnz/dā, –dē] **18**–4
weed [wēd] **39**–A
week [wēk] **18**–11
weekdays [wēk/dāz/] **18**–12
weekend [wēk/ĕnd/] **18**–13
weigh [wā] **57**–B
weight [wāt] **22**–21, **57**
weightlifting [wāt/lĭf/tĭng] **159**–15
weights [wāts] **161**–19
WEIGHTS AND MEASURES [wāts/ ən mĕzh/ərz] **57**
welder [wĕl/dər] **139**–63
well [wĕl] **30**–15
west [wĕst] **107, 123, 124**
western [wĕs/tərn] **166**–9
wet [wĕt(/–)] **72**–17
...mop [–mäp/] **47**–16
...suit [–sōōt/] **155**–7
whale [wāl] **131**–29
wheat [wēt(/–)] **148**–2
...bread [–brĕd/] **53**–2
wheelbarrow [wēl/băr/ō] **39**–16
wheelchair [wēl/chër/] **80**–6
whisk [wĭsk] **59**–21
whiskers [wĭs/kərz] **134**–18
white [wīt(/–)] **12**–14
...bread [–brĕd/] **53**–1
White House [wīt/ hows/] **116**–5
whole [hōl(/–)] **15**–6
...salmon [–săm/ən] **53**–18
wide [wīd] **71**–44
widow [wĭd/ō] **29** ✦
widower [wĭd/ō ər] **29** ✦
width [wĭdth, wĭtth] **15**–17
wife [wīf] **24**–20, **25** ✦
wild animals [wīld/ ăn/ə məlz] **133** ✦
willow [wĭl/ō] **128**–14
win [wĭn] **158** ✦
wind [wĭnd] **126**–2
windbreaker [wĭnd/brā/kər] **66**–24
window [wĭn/dō] **38**–17, **42**–17
...pane [–pān/] **149**–15
...shade [–shād/] **44**–6
windshield [wĭnd/shēld/] **108**–2
...wipers [–wī/pərz] **108**–3
windy [wĭn/dē] **10**–10
wine glass [wīn/ glăs/] **63**–20
wing [wĭng] **132**–2
wings [wĭngz] **52**–20
winter [wĭn/tər] **19**–40
WINTER SPORTS AND WATER SPORTS
[wĭn/tər spörts/ ən wö/tər spörts/] **160**
wipes [wīps] **95**–17
wipe the counter [wīp/ dhə kown/tər] **46**–O
wire [wīr(/–)] **151**–13
...stripper [–strĭp/ər] **151**–37
wish [wĭsh] **169**–J
withdraw cash [wĭdh drö/ kăsh/, wĭth–] **97**–D
witness [wĭt/nəs] **99**–11
wolf [wōōlf] **134**–5
woman [wōōm/ən] **22**–10
wood [wōōd(/–)] **149**–17, **151**–18
...screw [–skrōō/] **150**–28
wooden spoon [wōōd/n spōōn/] **59**–9
woodpecker [wōōd/pĕk/ər] **132**–9

Woodwinds [wo͞od′wĭndz′] **120**

woodworking kit [wo͞od′wûr′kĭng kĭt′] **162**–16

wool [wo͞ol(′–)] **70**–14

...scarf [–skärf′] **66**–4

work [wûrk′] **26**–K, **140**–P

workbook [wûrk′bo͞ok′] **3**–23

Work in a group [wûrk′ ĭn ə gro͞op′] **6**

working [wûr′kĭng] **48**–1

work out [wûrk′ owt′] **157**–P

Work with a partner [wûrk′wĭdh′ ə pärt′nər, –wĭth′–] **6**

WORLD [wûrld] **124**–**125**

worm [wûrm] **130**–22

worried [wûr′ēd] **30**–13

wrap [răp] **169**–D

wrench [rĕnch] **109**–50, **151**–42, 43

wrestling [rĕs′lĭng] **159**–16

wrinkled [rĭng′kəld] **72**–19

wrist [rĭst] **69**–34, **75**–60

wristwatch [rĭst′wäch′, –wöch′] **69**–34

write [rīt] **2**–G, **113**–A

writer [rī′tər] **139**–64

writing assignment [rī′tĭng ə sīn′mənt] **113**–1

wrong [röng(′–)]

...number [–nŭm′bər] **9** ✦

...way [–wā′] **107**–4

X-ray [ĕks′rā′]

...technician [–tĕk nĭsh′ən] **86**–8

xylophone [zī′lə fōn′] **120**–17

yams [yămz] **51**–22

YARD [yärd] **39**

yard [(–)yärd(′)]

front... [frŭnt′–] **38**–15

yard (measurement) [yärd] **15** ✦

yardstick [yärd′stĭk′] **151**–15

yarn [yärn] **163**–17

year [yïr] **4**–16, **18**–8

yellow [yĕl′ō] **12**–12

yesterday [yĕs′tər dā′, –dē] **18**–17

yield [yēld] **107** ✦

yogurt [yō′gərt] **54**–33, **60**–11

young [yŭng] **22**–13

zebra [zē′brə] **135**–34

zero [zïr′ō] **14**

ZIP code [zĭp′ kōd′] **4**–9

zipper [zĭp′ər] **73**–16

zoo [zo͞o] **152**–1

zookeeper [zo͞o′kē′pər] **152**–3

zoom lens [zo͞om′ lĕnz′] **165**–25

zucchini [zo͞o kē′nē] **51**–4

Geographical Index

Continents
Africa [ăf′rĭ kə] 125–5
Antarctica [ănt ärk′tĭ kə, –är′tĭ–] 125–7
Asia [ā′zhə] 125–4
Australia [ö strāl′yə] 125–6
Europe [yŏor′əp] 125–3
North America [nörth′ ə mĕr′ə kə] 124–1
South America [sowth′ ə mĕr′ə kə] 124–2

Countries and other locations
Afghanistan [ăf găn′ə stăn′] 124–125
Albania [ăl bā′nē ə] 124–125
Algeria [ăl jïr′ē ə] 124–125125
American Samoa [ə mĕr′ə kən sə mō′ə] 124–125
Andorra [ăn dör′ə] 124–125
Angola [ăng gō′lə] 124–125
Argentina [är′jən tē′nə] 124–125
Armenia [är mē′nē ə] 124–125
Australia [ö strāl′yə] 124–125
Austria [ö′strē ə] 124–125
Azerbaijan [ăz′ər bī jän′] 124–125
Bahamas [bə hä′məz] 122–125
Bahrain [bä rän′] 124–125
Bangladesh [băng′glə dĕsh′, băng′–] 124–125
Barbados [bär bā′dōs] 124–125
Belarus [bē′lə rōōs′, byĕl′ə–] 124–125
Belgium [bĕl′jəm] 124–125
Belize [bə lēz′] 124–125
Benin [bə nĭn′, –nēn′] 124–125
Bermuda [bər myōō′də] 122–125
Bhutan [bōō tän′] 124–125
Bolivia [bə lĭv′ē ə] 124–125
Borneo [bör′nē ō] 124–125
Bosnia-Herzegovina [băz′nē ə hĕr′tsə gō vē′nə] 124–125
Botswana [bät swä′nə] 124–125
Brazil [brə zĭl′] 124–125
Brunei [brōō nī′] 124–125
Bulgaria [bŭl gĕr′ē ə] 124–125
Burkina Faso [bər kē′nə fä′sō] 124–125
Burundi [bōō rōōn′dē] 124–125
Cambodia [kăm bō′dē ə] 124–125
Cameroon [kăm′ə rōōn′] 124–125
Canada [kăn′ə də] 122–125
Cape Verde [kāp′ vürd′] 124–125
Central African Republic [sĕn′trəl ăf′rĭ kən rĭ pŭb′lĭk] 124–125
Chad [chăd] 124–125
Chile [chĭl′ē] 124–125
China [chī′nə] 124–125
Colombia [kə lŭm′bē ə] 124–125
Comoros [käm′ə rōz] 124–125
Congo [käng′gō] 124–125
Costa Rica [kōs′tə rē′kə, käs′–] 122–125
Croatia [krō ā′shə] 124–125
Cuba [kyōō′bə] 122–125
Cyprus [sī′prəs] 124–125
Czech Republic [chĕk′ rĭ pŭb′lĭk] 124–125
Democratic Republic of the Congo [dĕm′ə krăt′ĭk rĭ pŭb′lĭk əv dhə käng′gō] 124–125
Denmark [dĕn′märk] 124–125
Djibouti [jĭ bōō′tē] 124–125
Dominica [däm′ə nē′kə] 124–125
Dominican Republic [də mĭn′ĭ kən rĭ pŭb′lĭk] 122–125
Ecuador [ĕk′wə dör′] 124–125
Egypt [ē′jĭpt] 124–125
El Salvador [ĕl săl′və dör′] 122–125

Equatorial Guinea [ē′kwə tör′ē əl gĭn′ē, ĕk′wə–] 124–125
Eritrea [ĕr′ə trē′ə] 124–125
Estonia [ĕ stō′nē ə] 124–125
Ethiopia [ē′thē ō′pē ə] 124–125
Fiji [fē′jē] 124–125
Finland [fĭn′lənd] 124–125
France [frăns] 124–125
French Guiana [frĕnch′ gē ăn′ə, –ä′nə] 124–125
French Polynesia [frĕnch′ päl′ə nē′zhə] 124–125
Gabon [gă bōn′] 124–125
Georgia [jör′jə] 124–125
Germany [jür′mə nē] 124–125
Ghana [gä′nə] 124–125
Greece [grēs] 124–125
Greenland [grēn′lənd, –lănd′] 122–125
Grenada [grə nā′də] 124–125
Guatemala [gwä′tə mä′lə] 122–125
Guinea [gĭn′ē] 124–125
Guinea-Bissau [gĭn′ē bĭ sow′] 124–125
Guyana [gī ăn′ə] 124–125
Haiti [hā′tē] 122–125
Honduras [hän dŏor′əs] 122–125
Hong Kong [häng′ käng′] 124–125
Hungary [hŭng′gə rē] 124–125
Iceland [īs′lənd] 124–125
India [ĭn′dē ə] 124–125
Indonesia [ĭn′də nē′zhə] 124–125
Iran [ĭ răn′, ī răn′] 124–125
Iraq [ĭ räk′, ī răk′] 124–125
Ireland [īr′lənd] 124–125
Israel [ĭz′rē əl, –rā–] 124–125
Italy [ĭt′l ē] 124–125
Ivory Coast [īv′rē kōst′] 124–125
Jamaica [jə mā′kə] 122–125
Japan [jə păn′] 124–125
Java [jä′və] 124–125
Jordan [jör′dn] 124–125
Kazakhstan [kä′zăk stän′] 124–125
Kenya [kĕn′yə, kēn′–] 124–125
Kiribati [kïr′ə băs′] 124–125
Kuwait [kōō wāt′] 124–125
Kyrgyzstan [kïr′gĭ stän′, –stän′] 124–125
Laos [lows, lä′ōs] 124–125
Latvia [lăt′vē ə] 124–125
Lebanon [lĕb′ə nən, –nän′] 124–125
Lesotho [lə sō′tō, –sōō′tōō] 124–125
Liberia [lī bïr′ē ə] 124–125
Libya [lĭb′ē ə] 124–125
Liechtenstein [lĭk′tən stīn′] 124–125
Lithuania [lĭth′ōō ā′nē ə] 124–125
Luxembourg [lŭk′səm bürg′] 124–125
Macedonia [măs′ə dō′nē ə] 124–125
Madagascar [măd′ə găs′kər] 124–125
Malawi [mə lä′wē] 124–125
Malaysia [mə lā′zhə] 124–125
Maldives [möl′dēvz, –dīvz] 124–125
Mali [mä′lē] 124–125
Malta [möl′tə] 124–125
Marshall Islands [mär′shəl ī′ləndz] 124–125
Mauritania [mör′ə tā′nē ə] 124–125
Mauritius [mö rĭsh′əs] 124–125
Mexico [mĕk′sĭ kō′] 122–125
Micronesia [mī′krə nē′zhə] 124–125
Moldova [mäl dō′və, möl–] 124–125
Monaco [män′ə kō′] 124–125

Mongolia [mäng gō**/**lē ə] **124–125**
Montenegro [män**/**tə nē**/**grō, –nĕ**/**–] **124–125**
Morocco [mə räk**/**ō] **124–125**
Mozambique [mō**/**zəm bēk**/**] **124–125**
Myanmar [myän**/**mär] **124–125**
Namibia [nə mĭb**/**ē ə] **124–125**
Nauru [nä ōō**/**rōō] **124–125**
Nepal [nə pöl**/**, –päl**/**] **124–125**
Netherlands [nĕdh**/**ər ləndz] **124–125**
New Guinea [nōō**/** gĭn**/**ē] **124–125**
New Zealand [nōō**/** zē**/**lənd] **124–125**
Nicaragua [nĭk**/**ə rä**/**gwə] **122–125**
Niger [nī**/**jər, nē zhër**/**] **124–125**
Nigeria [nī jïr**/**ē ə] **124–125**
North Korea [nörth**/** kə rē**/**ə] **124–125**
Norway [nör**/**wā] **124–125**
Oman [ō män**/**] **124–125**
Pakistan [păk**/**ə stän**/**] **124–125**
Palau [pə low**/**] **124–125**
Panama [păn**/**ə mä**/**] **122–125**
Papua New Guinea [păp**/**yōō ə nōō**/** gĭn**/**ē] **124–125**
Paraguay [păr**/**ə gwī**/**, –gwä**/**] **124–125**
Peru [pə rōō**/**] **124–125**
Philippines [fĭl**/**ə pēnz**/**, fĭl**/**ə pēnz**/**] **124–125**
Poland [pō**/**lənd] **124–125**
Portugal [pör**/**chə gəl] **124–125**
Puerto Rico [pwër**/**tə rē**/**kō, pör**/**tə–] **122–125**
Qatar [kä**/**tär, kə tär**/**] **124–125**
Romania [rō mā**/**nē ə, rōō–] **124–125**
Russia [rŭsh**/**ə] **124–125**
Rwanda [rōō än**/**də] **124–125**
Saudi Arabia [sow**/**dē ə rā**/**bē ə, sö**/**dē–] **124–125**
Senegal [sĕn**/**ə göl**/**, –gäl**/**] **124–125**
Serbia [sür**/**bē ə] **124–125**
Seychelles [sā shĕlz**/**, –shĕl**/**] **124–125**
Sierra Leone [sē ĕr**/**ə lē ōn**/**, –lē ō**/**nē] **124–125**
Singapore [sĭng**/**ə pör**/**] **124–125**
Slovakia [slō vä**/**kē ə] **124–125**
Slovenia [slō vē**/**nē ə] **124–125**
Solomon Islands [säl**/**ə mən ī**/**ləndz] **124–125**
Somalia [sə mä**/**lē ə] **124–125**
South Africa [sowth**/** ăf**/**rĭ kə] **124–125**
South Korea [sowth**/** kə rē**/**ə] **124–125**
Spain [spān] **124–125**
Sri Lanka [srē**/** läng**/**kə, shrē**/**–] **124–125**
Sudan [sōō dăn**/**] **124–125**
Sumatra [sōō mä**/**trə] **124–125**
Suriname [sōōr**/**ə nä**/**mə] **124–125**
Swaziland [swä**/**zē lănd**/**] **124–125**
Sweden [swēd**/**n] **124–125**
Switzerland [swĭt**/**sər lənd] **124–125**
Syria [sïr**/**ē ə] **124–125**
Tahiti [tə hē**/**tē] **124–125**
Taiwan [tī**/**wän**/**] **124–125**
Tajikistan [tä jĭk**/**ə stän**/**, –stän**/**] **124–125**
Tanzania [tăn**/**zə nē**/**ə] **124–125**
Tasmania [tăz mā**/**nē ə] **124–125**
Thailand [tī**/**lănd**/**, –lənd] **124–125**
The Gambia [dhə găm**/**bē ə] **124–125**
Togo [tō**/**gō] **124–125**
Tonga [täng**/**gə] **124–125**
Tunisia [tōō nē**/**zhə] **124–125**
Turkey [tür**/**kē] **124–125**
Turkmenistan [türk mĕn**/**ə stän**/**, –stän**/**] **124–125**
Uganda [yōō găn**/**də] **124–125**

Ukraine [yōō**/**krān, yōō krān**/**] **124–125**
United Arab Emirates [yōō nī**/**təd ăr**/**əb ĕm**/**ər əts] **124–125**
United Kingdom [yōō nī**/**təd kĭng**/**dəm] **124–125**
United States of America [yōō nī**/**təd stāts**/** əv ə mĕr**/**ə kə]
  122–125
Uruguay [yōōr**/**ə gwī**/**, –gwä**/**] **124–125**
Uzbekistan [ōōz bĕk**/**ə stän**/**, –stän**/**] **124–125**
Venezuela [vĕn**/**ə zwā**/**lə] **124–125**
Vietnam [vē**/**ĕt näm**/**, –năm**/**] **124–125**
Western Sahara [wĕs**/**tərn sə hăr**/**ə] **124–125**
Western Samoa [wĕs**/**tərn sə mō**/**ə] **124–125**
Yemen [yĕm**/**ən] **124–125**
Zambia [zăm**/**bē ə] **124–125**
Zimbabwe [zĭm bäb**/**wā] **124–125**

Bodies of water

Arabian Sea [ə rā**/**bē ən sē**/**] **124–125**
Arctic Ocean [ärk**/**tĭk ō**/**shən] **122–125**
Baffin Bay [băf**/**ən bā**/**] **122–125**
Baltic Sea [böl**/**tĭk sē**/**] **124–125**
Barents Sea [băr**/**ənts sē**/**] **124–125**
Beaufort Sea [bō**/**fərt sē**/**] **122–125**
Bering Sea [bër**/**ĭng sē**/**, bïr**/**–] **122–125**
Black Sea [blăk**/** sē**/**] **124–125**
Caribbean Sea [kăr**/**ə bē**/**ən sē**/**, kə rĭb**/**ē ən–] **122–125**
Caspian Sea [kăs**/**pē ən sē**/**] **124–125**
Coral Sea [kör**/**əl sē**/**] **124–125**
East China Sea [ēst**/** chī**/**nə sē**/**] **124–125**
Greenland Sea [grēn**/**lənd sē**/**, –lănd**/**–] **124–125**
Gulf of Alaska [gŭlf**/** əv ə lăs**/**kə] **122–125**
Gulf of California [gŭlf**/** əv kăl**/**ə förn**/**yə] **122–125**
Gulf of Honduras [gŭlf**/** əv hän dōōr**/**əs] **122–125**
Gulf of Mexico [gŭlf**/** əv mĕk**/**sĭ kō**/**] **122–125**
Gulf of St. Lawrence [gŭlf**/** əv sänt**/** lör**/**əns, –lär**/**–] **122–125**
Hudson Bay [hŭd**/**sən bā**/**] **122–125**
Indian Ocean [ĭn**/**dē ən ō**/**shən] **124–125**
Labrador Sea [lăb**/**rə dör**/** sē**/**] **122–125**
Mediterranean Sea [mĕd**/**ə tə rā**/**nē ən sē**/**] **124–125**
North Atlantic Ocean [nörth**/** ət lăn**/**tĭk ō**/**shən] **122–125**
North Pacific Ocean [nörth**/** pə sĭf**/**ĭk ō**/**shən] **122–125**
North Sea [nörth**/** sē**/**] **124–125**
Norwegian Sea [nör wē**/**jən sē**/**] **124–125**
Persian Gulf [pür**/**zhən gŭlf**/**] **124–125**
Philippine Sea [fĭl**/**ə pēn**/** sē**/**] **124–125**
Red Sea [rĕd**/** sē**/**] **124–125**
Sea of Japan [sē**/** əv jə păn**/**] **124–125**
Sea of Okhotsk [sē**/** əv ō kätsk**/**] **124–125**
South Atlantic Ocean [sowth**/** ət lăn**/**tĭk ō**/**shən] **124–125**
South China Sea [sowth**/** chī**/**nə sē**/**] **124–125**
Southern Ocean [sŭdh**/**ərn ō**/**shən] **124–125**
South Pacific Ocean [sowth**/** pə sĭf**/**ĭk ō**/**shən] **124–125**

The United States of America
Capital: Washington, D.C. (District Of Columbia)
  [wä**/**shĭng tən dē**/**sē**/**, wö**/**–]

Regions of the United States
Mid-Atlantic States [mĭd**/**ət lăn**/**tĭk stāts**/**] **123–10**
Midwest [mĭd**/**wĕst**/**] **123–9**
New England [nōō**/** ĭng**/**glənd] **123–11**
Pacific States [pə sĭf**/**ĭk stāts**/**] **123–7**
Rocky Mountain States [räk**/**ē mown**/**tn stāts**/**] **123–8**
South [sowth] **123–13**
Southeast [sowth**/**ēst**/**] **123–13**
Southwest [sowth**/**wĕst**/**] **123–12**
West Coast [wĕst**/** kōst**/**] **123–7**

Geographical Index

States of the United States

Alabama [ăl/ə băm/ə] **122–123**
Alaska [ə lăs/kə] **122–125**
Arizona [ăr/ə zō/nə] **122–123**
Arkansas [är/kən sö/] **122–123**
California [kăl/ə förn/yə] **122–123**
Colorado [kăl/ə răd/ō, –ra/dō] **122–123**
Connecticut [kə nĕt/ĭ kət] **122–123**
Delaware [dĕl/ə wër/] **122–123**
Florida [flör/ə də, flär/–] **122–123**
Georgia [jör/jə] **122–123**
Hawaii [hə wī/ē] **122–123**
Idaho [ī/də hō/] **122–123**
Illinois [ĭl/ə noy/] **122–123**
Indiana [ĭn/dē ăn/ə] **122–123**
Iowa [ī/ə wə] **122–123**
Kansas [kăn/zəs] **122–123**
Kentucky [kən tŭk/ē] **122–123**
Louisiana [lōō ē/zē ăn/ə] **122–123**
Maine [mān] **122–123**
Maryland [mër/ə lənd] **122–123**
Massachusetts [măs/ə chōō/səts] **122–123**
Michigan [mĭsh/ĭ gən] **122–123**
Minnesota [mĭn/ə sō/tə] **122–123**
Mississippi [mĭs/ə sĭp/ē] **122–123**
Missouri [mə zōōr/ē, –zōōr/ə] **122–123**
Montana [măn tăn/ə] **122–123**
Nebraska [nə brăs/kə] **122–123**
Nevada [nə văd/ə, –vä/də] **122–123**
New Hampshire [nōō/ hămp/shər] **122–123**
New Jersey [nōō/ jür/zē] **122–123**
New Mexico [nōō/ mĕk/sĭ kō/] **122–123**
New York [nōō/ yörk/] **122–123**
North Carolina [nörth/ kăr/ə lī/nə] **122–123**
North Dakota [nörth/ də kō/tə] **122–123**
Ohio [ō hī/ō] **122–123**
Oklahoma [ō/klə hō/mə] **122–123**
Oregon [ör/ĭ gən, –gän/, är/–] **122–123**
Pennsylvania [pĕn/səl vān/yə] **122–123**
Rhode Island [rōd/ ī/lənd] **122–123**
South Carolina [sowth/ kăr/ə lī/nə] **122–123**
South Dakota [sowth/ də kō/tə] **122–123**
Tennessee [tĕn/ə sē/] **122–123**
Texas [tĕk/səs] **122–123**
Utah [yōō/tö, –tä] **122–123**
Vermont [vər mänt/] **122–123**
Virginia [vər jĭn/yə] **122–123**
Washington [wä/shĭng tən, wö/–] **122–123**
West Virginia [wĕst/ vər jĭn/yə] **122–123**
Wisconsin [wĭs kän/sən] **122–123**
Wyoming [wī ō/mĭng] **122–123**

Canada

Capital: Ottawa [ät/ə wə]

Regions of Canada

Atlantic Provinces [ət lăn/tĭk präv/ən səz] **123 – 6**
British Columbia [brĭt/ĭsh kə lŭm/bē ə] **123 – 2**
Northern Canada [nör/dhərn kăn/ə də] **123 – 1**
Ontario [än tër/ē ō/] **123 – 4**
Prairie Provinces [prë/ē präv/ən səz] **123 – 3**
Quebec [kwĭ bĕk/] **123 – 5**

Provinces of Canada

Alberta [ăl bür/tə] **122–123**
British Columbia [brĭt/ĭsh kə lŭm/bē ə] **122–123**
Manitoba [măn/ə tō/bə] **122–123**

New Brunswick [nōō/ brŭnz/wĭk] **122–123**
Newfoundland [nōō/fən lənd] **122–123**
Northwest Territories [nörth/wĕst/ tĕr/ə tör/ēz] **122–123**
Nova Scotia [nō/və skō/shə] **122–123**
Ontario [än tër/ē ō/] **122–123**
Prince Edward Island [prĭns/ ĕd/wərd ī/lənd] **122–123**
Quebec [kwĭ bĕk/] **122–123**
Saskatchewan [să skăch/ə wən, –wän/] **122–123**
Yukon Territory [yōō/kän tĕr/ə tör/ē] **122–123**

Mexico

Capital: Mexico (City) [mĕk/sĭ kō/ (sĭt/ē)]

Regions of Mexico

Chiapas Highlands [chē ä/pəs hī/ləndz] **123 – 18**
Gulf Coastal Plain [gŭlf/ kō/stəl plān/] **123 – 16**
Pacific Northwest [pə sĭf/ĭk nörth/wĕst] **123 – 14**
Plateau of Mexico [plă tō/ əv mĕk/sĭ kō/] **123 – 15**
Southern Uplands [sŭdh/ərn ŭp/ləndz] **123 – 17**
Yucatan Peninsula [yōō/kə tăn/ pə nĭn/sə lə, yōō/kə tän/–] **123 – 19**

States of Mexico

Aguascalientes [ä/gwəs kăl yĕn/täs] **122–123**
Baja California Norte [bä/hä kăl/ə förn/yə nör/tä] **122–123**
Baja California Sur [bä/hä kăl/ə förn/yə sōōr/] **122–123**
Campeche [käm pā/chä, käm pē/chē] **122–123**
Chiapas [chē ä/pəs] **122–123**
Chihuahua [chĭ wä/wä, –wə] **122–123**
Coahuila [kō/ə wē/lə] **122–123**
Colima [kə lē/mə] **122–123**
Distrito Federal [dĭ strē/tō fĕd/ə räl/] **122–123**
Durango [dōō răng/gō, –räng/–] **122–123**
Guanajuato [gwä/nə hwä/tō] **122–123**
Guerrero [gə rër/ō] **122–123**
Hidalgo [hĭ dăl/gō, ē dhäl/gō] **122–123**
Jalisco [hə lĭs/kō, –lēs/–] **122–123**
México [mĕk/sĭ kō/, mĕ/hē kō] **122–123**
Michoacán [mē/chō ä kän/] **122–123**
Morelos [mö rĕl/ōs] **122–123**
Nayarit [nä/yə rēt/] **122–123**
Nuevo León [nwä/vō lā ōn/] **122–123**
Oaxaca [wə hä/kə, wä–] **122–123**
Puebla [pwĕb/lä] **122–123**
Querétaro [kə rĕt/ə rō/] **122–123**
Quintana Roo [kēn tä/nə rō/] **122–123**
San Luis Potosí [sän/ lōō ēs/ pō/tə sē/] **122–123**
Sinaloa [sē/nə lō/ə] **122–123**
Sonora [sə nör/ə] **122–123**
Tabasco [tə băs/kō] **122–123**
Tamaulipas [tä/mow lē/pəs] **122–123**
Tlaxcala [tlä skä/lə] **122–123**
Veracruz [vĕr/ə krōōz/, –krōōs/] **122–123**
Yucatán [yōō/kə tän/, –tän/] **122–123**
Zacatecas [zä/kə tā/kəs, sä/–] **122–123**

5 cents **20**–2
10 cents **20**–3
25 cents **20**–4
50 cents **20**–5
à carreaux **70**–11
à côté de **13**–1, 2
à droite **13**–2
à gauche **13**–1
à la ferme et au ranch **148**
à la recherche d'un logement **35**
à manches courtes **71**–30
à pois **70**–8
à travers **105**–11
abat-jour **44**–18
abdomen **74**–3
abeille **132**–26
abri **34**–10
abricots **50**–7
accélérateur **109**–47
accessoires **68**–69
accessoires d'aspirateur **47**–14
accessoires de nettoyage **47**
accident **102**–2
accident d'automobile **102**–2
accompagner les enfants à l'école **26**–G
accordéon **120**–21
accusé **99**–5
achards **60**–26
achat d'une maison **35**
acheter une maison **29**–O
acheter votre billet **111**–A
acheter **21**–C
acteur **136**–2
action **166**–13
action de grâce **168**–15
activités en plein air **154**
activités quotidiennes **26**–27
acupuncture **81**–G
adaptateur **164**–18
addition **118**–1
adjoint(e) administratif (ve) **136**–3
adolescent(e)s **22**–6
adresse **4**–5, **96**–7, 8
adresse de retour **96**–7
adresse postale **96**–8
adresser **96**–A
adultes **22**–9
aérogare **110**–1
aérogramme **96**–13
aéroport **110**
affiche de disponibilité **36**–11
âgé(e) **22**–15
âge et description physique **22**
âge moyen **22**–14
agence de voyage **92**–9
agent de maîtrise **146**–5
agent de voyage **139**–60
agent immobilier **35**
agent(e) de bord **110**–13
agneau **52**–13, 14, 15
agrafe **143**–29

agrafe et porte **73**–23
agrafer **142**–G
agrafeuse **143**–28
agression **100**–7
aide familial(e) **137**–31
aide soignant(e) **87**–18
aider **6**–J
aide-serveur **63**–9
aide-serveuse **63**–9
aigle **132**–10
aiguille à coudre **73**–22
aiguille de pin **128**–12
aiguilles à tricoter **163**–18
ail **51**–29
aile **132**–2
ailes **52**–20
aimant **119**–21
air **109**–59
air (pollution) **126**–10
air (purificateur) **80**–4
aire de restauration **93**–14
ajouter **58**–Q, **72**–B
album de photos **165**–32
algèbre **118**–25
aliments emballés **56**
aliments pour animaux **54**–10
aliments pour bébés **95**–28
aliments surgelés **55**–12
allaiter (un bébé) **94**–C
allée **38**–5, **54**–5
aller **101**–B
aller à l'université **28**–J
aller au marché **26**–L
aller chercher les enfants **27**–O
aller chez un chiropracteur **81**–H
aller chez un chiropraticien **81**–H
aller en prison **99**–G
aller se coucher **27**–X
aller tout droit **107**–A
aller travailler **26**–I
allergies **79**–8
alligator **131**–36
allonger **73**–F
allumage **108**–25
allume-cigares **108**–32
allumer **169**–H
allumettes **154**–21
alphabet **3**–30
ambulateur **80**–5, **95**–12
Amérique centrale **122**–123
Amérique du Nord et
    Amérique centrale **122**–123
amidon **72**–12
amoureuse **30**–19, **166**–16
amphibiens **130**–131
ample **71**–42
ampoule **42**–4, **78**–15
analgésique **81**–16
analyse sanguine **86**–17
ananas **50**–2
âne **133**–2

anémone de mer **130**–21
anesthésiste **87**–35
angine streptococcique **79**–4
Anglais en tant que seconde
    langue **121**–7, **141**–7
angle **118**–24
anguille **130**–5
animalerie **92**–6
animaux **152**–2
animaux de compagnie **133**
animaux de la ferme **133**
animaux domestiques **133**
animaux domestiques et rongeurs **133**
animaux en peluche **45**–23
animaux marins **130**
anneau d'astéroïdes **127**–12
anneau de bébé qui perce
    ses dents **95**–30
année **4**–16, **18**–8
anniversaire **19**–41, **169**–I
anniversaire de mariage **19**–42
annonceur **152**–27
annoter **7**–T
annuaire téléphonique **9**–15
antenne de télé **38**–22
antiacide **81**–18
antilope **135**–35
août **19**–32
apostrophe **113**–11
appareil auditif **81**–33
appareil caméra **165**–19, 24, 27
appareil photo **165**–19, 24, 27
appartements **36**–37
appel international **9**–6
appel interurbain **9**–5
appel local **9**–4
appeler **141**–E
applaudir **32**–B
application **144**–21
apprendre à conduire **28**–E
après-midi **16**, **17**–18
après-rasage (lotion) **77**–28
après-shampooing **76**–10
aquarelle **163**–25
araignée **132**–30
arbitre **158**–6
arbre de Noël **168**–20
arbres et plantes **128**
arc **161**–6
architecte **136**–4
argent **20**
argile **162**–14
armoire à pharmacie **43**–19
armoire de rangement des fournitures
    de bureau **142**–13
armoire **40**–1
arracher une dent **85**–M
arrêt **107**–3
arrêt d'autobus **91**–16, **104**–1
arrêter **99**–A, **165**–F
arrière-cour **38**–2

Index

arroser (les plantes) **39**–B
arroseur **39**–8
arrosoir **39**–17
art **121**–1
artère **75**–43
artichauts **51**–20
articles de sport **161**
artiste **136**–5
arts de la scène **121**–12
arts industriels **121**–10
arts martiaux **159**–10
ascenseur **37**–34
asperges **51**–24
aspirateur **47**–13
assembler **140**–A
assiette **41**–24, **63**–15, 16, 17
assiette à pain et beurre **63**–16
assiette à salade **63**–17
assistance annuaire (411) **9**–8
assistant(e) dentaire **84**–19, **137**–19
assister **140**–B
assouplisseur textile en feuilles **72**–5
assoyez-vous **2**–E
asthme **79**–11
astronaute **127**–17
astronome **127**–20
atelier **121**–10
athlétisme **159**–17
atlas **98**–3
atome **119**–17
attacher **94**–I
attelle **83**–11
attendre **90**–B
attendre la tonalité **9**–B
atterrir **111**–O
attraper **156**–E
attrayant(e) **22**–23
aubergines **51**–18
au-dessus **13**–6
audiocassette **98**–12
audiologiste **81**–32
auditoire **32**–10
aujourd'hui **18**–15
auteur **98**–22, **139**–64
autobus **90**–15, **104**–4
automne **19**–39
autour **105**–10
autres matières scolaires **121**
avaler **82**–J
avance rapide **165**–C
aventure (histoire) **166**–13
averse de grêle **10**–18
aveugle **22**–26
avion **110**–9
avocat **99**–4
avocat de la défense **99**–4
avocat(e) **99**–B, **138**–36
avocats **50**–14
avoir besoin **109**–(54–59)
avoir des gelures/engelures **82**–G
avoir faim **30**–5

avoir la nausée **78**–D
avoir le mal du pays **31**–21
avoir mal **30**–12
avoir soif **30**–2
avoir sommeil **30**–3
avoir un bébé **29**–M
avoir un petit-enfant **29**–Q
avoir une crise cardiaque **82**–D
avoir une réaction allergique **82**–E
avril **19**–28
babouin **135**–32
baby-sitter **136**–12
bac **37**–20
bac à ordures **37**–20
bac à peinture **151**–45
bac à sable **153**–15
bac de recyclage **47**–2
bacon **52**–11, **61**–7
bagage à main **111**–H
bagages **111**–B
bague **69**–39
baie **117**–9
baies **128**–20
baignoire **43**–2
bain-marie **59**–8
baladeur **164**–15
balai **47**–10
balance **43**–26, **84**–7
balance (science) **119**–11
balançoires **153**–12
balayer **46**–E
balayette **43**–16
balcon **37**–17
baleine **131**–29
balle **45**–16, **161**–3, 4, 5, 12, 18, 22
balle de base-ball **158**–9, **161**–18
balle de basket-ball **158**–8, **161**–4
ballet **166**–7
ballon **45**–16, **161**–3, 4, 5, 12, 18, 22
ballon de football **161**–12
ballon de football américain **158**–11,
 161–22
bananes **50**–3
banc **153**–10
bancs de déjeuner **5**–5
bandage **83**–3, 12
bandage élastique **83**–12
banlieue **34**–2
bannière **33**–15
banque **88**–3, **97**
barbe **23**–6
barbecue **39**–7, **58**–T
barbier **88**–15
bardeaux **149**–19
barrette **76**–18
barrière de sécurité **36**–13
bas **67**–26
basse (instrument) **120**–10
bassin **75**–55
bassin de lit **86**–13
bassine **86**–13

basson **120**–6
bâtons de ski **161**–25
batte de base-ball **161**–14
batterie **120**–18
batterie de voiture **109**–43
batteur à œufs **59**–20
batteur électrique **40**–25
battre **58**–B
bavette **95**–8
beau-frère **24**–16
beau-père **24**–14
beau-père (adoptif) **25**–28
bébé **22**–2
bec **132**–1
bec Bensen **119**–9
bec (oiseau) **132**–1
bécher **119**–13
beige **12**–9
beignerie **91**–20
beignet **60**–15
belle-mère **24**–13
belle-mère (adoptive) **25**–31
belle-sœur **24**–15
bénévole **87**–19
béquilles **80**–1
berceau **45**–19
berceuse **94**–6
bétail **148**–13, **148**–21
béton **149**–10
betteraves **51**–6
beurre **54**–36
biberon **95**–26
bibliothécaire **98**–17
bibliothécaire des ouvrages
 de référence **98**–1
bibliothèque **3**–8, **5**–6, **42**–1, **89**–28, **98**,
 98–17, 19, 20
bicyclette **153**–4
bidon **154**–24
bien rangé (placard) **11**–15
biffer **7**–U
bifteck **52**–2, **61**–13
bijouterie **92**–2
bijoux **69**–8
billard **159**–2
billet **104**–14
biologie **119**–1
biscuits **54**–31, **56**–20
bison **134**–6
blanc **12**–14
blanchisserie **90**–1
blasé(e) **31**–26
blattes **49**–25
blé **148**–2
blessé(e) **30**–17
blessé(e) (médical) **82**–A
blessures **78**
bleu **12**–1
bleu pâle **12**–1
bleu foncé **12**–3
blizzard **103**–11

bloc format légal **143**–18
bloc-notes **143**–36
bloc-piles **165**–22
blocs **45**–15
blonde **23**–16
blouse **64**–9
blouse de chirurgien(ne) **87**–32
bobine de fil **73**–17
bocal **56**–2
bocal de confiture **56**–14
bœuf **52**
bœuf à ragoût **52**–3
bœuf en conserve **53**–8
bœuf haché **52**–4
bœuf salé **53**–8
bœufs **148**–21
boire **60**–B
boire des liquides **80**–B
bois **134**–16, **149**–17, **151**–18
bois de charpente **149**–17, **151**
boisson gazeuse **55**–52, **60**–4
boissons **55**–15
boîte **56**–6
boîte à fusibles **48**–13
boîte aux lettres **38**–4, **90**–12
boîte de céréales **56**–18
boîte de conserve **56**–3
boîte de Pétri **119**–6
boîte de soupe **56**–15
boîtes aux lettres **37**–36
bol **41**–25
bol à soupe **63**–18
bon **11**–17
bon marché **11**–20
bonbon **55**–41, **168**–14
bonnet de chirurgien(ne) **87**–31
bonnet de douche **76**–1
bord du trottoir **90**–10
bordereau de dépôt **97**–12
bordure de protection **45**–7
bosse **135**–51
botter **156**–L
bottes **68**–18
bottes de cuir **70**–18
bottes de pluie **66**–19
bottes de randonnée **68**–21
bouche **74**–22
bouche d'incendie **91**–28
bouchée **49**–18
boucher (bouchère) **136**–11
boucher une carie **85**–L
boucle **69**–41
boucle de ceinture **69**–41
boucles d'oreilles **69**–37, **69**–38
boucles d'oreilles pour oreilles percées
   69–37
bouillir **58**–P
bouillotte **80**–3
boulanger (boulangère) **136**–8
boulangerie **89**–16
boule de bowling **161**–5

boule roulante **144**–15
bouleau **128**–8
bouleversé(e) **31**–30
boulon **37**–29, **150**–30, 33
boulon de scellement **150**–33
bouquet **129**–27
bourgeon **129**–6
bout **68**–15, **75**–63
bouteille **56**–1
bouteille de boisson gazeuse **56**–13
bouteille de plongée **155**–8
boutique de cadeaux **145**–7
boutique de maternité **93**–17
bouton **73**–21
bouton d'appel **86**–10
bouton de porte **37**–30
boutonnière **73**–12
bowling **159**–3
box **60**–19, **152**–23
bracelet **69**–35, **83**–14
bracelet d'urgence médicale **83**–14
branche **128**–2
Branches du gouvernement **116**
bras **74**–9
break **106**–8
bretelles **68**–2
briques **149**–11
brocoli **51**–15, **58**–I
broderie **163**–19
brosse **23**–18, **76**–14
brosse à dents **43**–20, **77**–20
brosse à récurer **47**–19
brosse feutrée **3**–17
brosser les cheveux **76**–I
brosser les dents **77**–J
brouette **39**–16
broyeur d'ordures **40**–5
brûleur **40**–19
brûleur Bensen **119**–9
brumeux **10**–11
brun **12**–11
bûches **42**–12
buffet **33**–13
buffet de crudités **60**–16
buisson **39**–20
bulbe **129**–9
bulldozer **149**–6
bureau **142**–143
bureau de direction **146**–1
bureau de la conseillère **5**–15
bureau du conseiller **5**–15
bureau du directeur **5**–13
bureau principal **5**–17
burin **151**–51
cabine **104**–18, **106**–16
câble **144**–16
câbles de démarrage **109**–52
cache-maillot **66**–25
cachemire **70**–13
cachet de la poste **96**–9
cactus **128**–21

caddie **54**–3
cadeau **169**–D
cadeaux **33**–18
cadre de lit **44**–27
cafards **49**–25
café **55**–51, **61**–22
café déca **61**–23
café instantané **55**–51
café-restaurant **88**–2
cafétéria **5**–4
cafetière **40**–11
cage à poules **153**–14
cage thoracique **75**–53
cahier **3**–24
cahier d'exercices **3**–23
caisse **55**–18, **140**–N
caissier (caissière) **55**–19, **97**–1, **136**–14
calcul **118**–28
calculatrice **142**–8
caleçon boxeur **67**–12
caleçon-combinaison **67**–11
caleçons **67**–13, 17
calendrier **18**–19
calendrier éphéméride **142**–6
calmar **130**–10
calme (être) **30**–10
cambriolage **100**–6
caméra vidéo **165**–19
caméscope **165**–21
camio semi-remorque **106**–15
camion à benne **106**–12
camion à ordures **91**–27
camion de pompiers **102**–9
camionnette **106**–7
camions **106**
camisole **67**–21
camping **154**–1
camping-car **106**–11
canalisation sanitaire **43**–4
canard **52**–18, **132**–13
cancer **79**–12
cancer du cerveau **79**–12
cane **80**–7
canne à pêche **154**–18
canoë **154**–3
canotage **154**–2
cantaloups **50**–15
canyon **117**–17
cape (de graduation) **32**–3
cape (habit) **66**–6
capot **108**–6
capsule **81**–27
cardigan **65**–27
cardinaux **14**
carie **74**–20
carnaval **152**–16
carnet à spirale **3**–26
carnet de rendez-vous **143**–27
carottes **51**–3
carpette **44**–23

carré **118**–6
carreaux **163**–27
carrefour **90**–91
carrousel **110**–18, **165**–30
carte **3**–12, **96**–4, **168**–5
carte d'abonnement **104**–12
carte d'appel **9**–10
carte d'assurance **84**–4
carte d'assurance maladie **84**
carte d'étranger résidant **29**–3
carte de base-ball **162**–11
carte de bibliothèque **98**–19
carte de crédit **20**–15
carte de mesures de sécurité **111**–K
carte de retrait **97**–9
carte de sécurité sociale **29**–5
carte de vœux **96**–4
carte mère **144**–18
carte postale **96**–3
cartes **163**–H
carton **56**–4
carton d'oeufs **56**–16
cartouche **162**–2
cascade **117**–2
caserne de pompiers **88**–1
casier de rangement **94**–4
casiers **5**–7
casque **147**–19
casque de football américain **161**–20
casquette de base-ball **66**–27
casquette norvégienne **66**–10
cassé(e)(s) **48**–5, 6, 7, **49**–15, **70**–24
casser trois oeufs **58**–A
casserole **40**–16, **59**–6, **59**–25
casse-tête **45**–22
cassette vidéo **98**–13, **164**–8, 10
castor **134**–9
catalogue en ligne **98**–9
catalogue sur fiches **98**–10
causerie **167**–20
causeuse **42**–25
ceinture d'astéroïdes **127**–12
ceinture de sécurité **109**–36
ceinture montée **73**–3
ceintures **69**–11
céleri **51**–9
Celsius **10**
cent **14**, **20**–1
cent pour cent **15**–11
centimètre (cm) **15**–12
centre commercial **92**–93
centre de formation continue
  (permanente) **112**–8
centre de manucure **91**–25
centre de reprographie **91**–22
centre d'éducation (de formation)
  des adultes **112**–8
cents **20**–2, 3, 4, 5
cercle **7**–S, **118**–5
céréale **56**–18
cérémonie **32**

cerf **134**–14
cerises **50**–16
certificat de naissance **29**–1
certificat de naturalisation **29**–6
certificat de publication de bans
  (licence de mariage) **29**–8
cerveau **75**–35
cette semaine **18**–19
chadelles **169**–H, K
chaîne (bijou) **69**–31, **69**–36
chaîne (quincaillerie) **37**–28, **150**–36
chaîne de montage **146**–8
chaîne de montagnes **117**–15
chaîne de sûreté **37**–28
chaîne stéréo **42**–14
chaise **2**–7
chaise de plage **155**–14
chaise de salle à dîner **41**–16
chaise haute **95**–7
chambre **44**, **145**–10
Chambre des représentants **116**–1
chambre du patient **86**
chambre forte **97**–2
chameau **135**–38
champignons **51**–26
chandail à col en v **71**–27
chandail à col rond **71**–26
chandail à col roulé **71**–28
chandail débardeur **67**–2
chandelier **41**–8
chandelle **41**–7
changer **21**–9
changer de régime **80**–C
changer les couches **94**–E
changer les draps **46**–P
chanter **120**–B, **169**–I
chapeau **66**–1
chapeau de paille **66**–23
chapeaux **68**–5
chaque jour **18**–21
charbon **126**–4
charcuterie et fruits de mer **53**
chargeur de piles **165**–23
chariot **54**–3, **91**–31
chariot à bagages **145**–6
chariot à main **146**–11
chariot de ménage **145**–14
chariot élévateur **146**–14
charpentier **48**–12, **136**–13
chasseur **145**–5
chat **133**–9
château de sable **155**–10
chaterton **151**–38
chaton **133**–10
chaud (sensation) **30**–1
chaud (température) **10**, **10**–1
chaudière **48**–1, **49**–15, **108**–29
chauffeur d'autobus **104**–8
chauffeur de taxi **104**–20
chaussettes **67**–15, **67**–25
chaussures athlétiques **68**–23

chaussures de sécurité **147**–20
chaussures de ski **161**–26
chaussures de tennis **68**–22
chaussures et accessoires **68**–69
chauve **23**–12
chauve-souris **134**–7
cheddar américain **53**–9
chef **63**–11
chef chasseur **145**–4
chef de bureau **143**–25
cheminée **38**–21
chemise **64**–4, **65**–20, **142**–11
chemise à mailles **65**–20
chemise à manches longues **71**–31
chemise de nuit **67**–9
chemise de tricot **65**–20
chemise d'hôpital **86**–15
chemise repassée **72**–20
chemise sport **65**–26
chêne **128**–18
chêne vénéneux **128**–23
chenille **132**–21
chèque de voyage **20**–17
chèque personnel **20**–14
chéquier **97**–7
chercher (en faisant des courses) **21**–A
chercher le siège **111**–G
chercher les panneaux offrant des
  emplois **141**–C
chercher un mot **6**–A
chercher un nouvel appartement **35**–A
chercher vos bagages **111**–P
cheval **133**–4
chevalet **163**–21
cheveux **23**, **74**–19
cheveux bruns **23**–17
cheveux gris **23**–13
cheveux noirs **23**–15
cheveux raides **23**–9
cheveux roux **23**–14
cheville **75**–61, **78**–18
chèvre **133**–1
chevreuil **134**–14
chewing-gum **55**–42
chien **11**–17, 18, **133**–11
chien de prairie **133**–22
chiffons **47**–6
chiffres **3**–31
chiffres romains **14**
chimie **119**–2
chimpanzé **135**–28
chiot **133**–12
chips **55**–40
chiropracteur **81**–H
chiropraticien **81**–H
chirurgien(ne) **87**–30
choc **82**–C
choisir (dans le menu) **62**–D
chorale **121**–3
chouette **132**–6
choux **51**–2

choux-fleurs **51**–16
chrysanthème **129**–19
cible **161**–8
cils **74**–34
cinéma **88**–11
cinq **14**–5, 20
cinq façons de faire cuire du poulet **58**
cinquante **14**
cinquante dollars **20**–11
cinquante pour cent **15**–9
cinquième **14**
cintre **72**–11
circonférence **118**–15
cisailles à haie **39**–12
ciseaux **23**–19, **73**–18
citoyenneté **116**
citrons **50**–11
citrons verts **50**–12
civière **87**–28
clair **10**–6, **12**–3
clarinette **120**–4
classer des papiers **142**–H
classeur **3**–24
clavier **120**–20, **144**–7
clavier électrique **120**–20
clé **37**–31, **109**–50, **151**–42, 43
clé à tuyau **151**–43
client(e) **32**–9, **62**–5, **145**–11
clignotant **108**–4
climatiseur **37**–19, **108**–28
clinique dentaire **84**
clinique médicale **84**
cliniques **84**
clôture **38**–3, **148**–19
clou (quincaillerie) **150**–29
clou à dessin **143**–43
club de golf **161**–1
club de (re)mise en forme **89**–21
club de santé **89**–21
club vidéo **93**–15
cobra **131**–40
coccinelle **132**–27
cochon **133**–8
cochon d'Inde **133**–14
cocotte **59**–11
code à barres **21**–4
code ZIP (code postal) **4**–9
coeur **168**–6
coeur (corps) **75**–38, **79**–14
cœurs **163**–29
coffre **109**–49
coffre à gant **108**–33
coffre à jouets **45**–24
coffre-fort **97**–13
coiffeur (coiffeuse) **137**–30
coin **91**–17, **105**–10, **107**–1
col **73**–7
col roulé **64**–7
coléoptère **132**–19
colibri **132**–11
colis postal **96**–14

collaborer à rassembler des idées **6**–K
collant **66**–11, **67**–27
collationner **142**–F
colle **143**–37, **162**–8
colle au caoutchouc **143**–38
collection **162**–12, 13
collection de pièces de monnaie **162**–13
collection de timbres **162**–12
collectionner des objets **162**–A
collège **112**–6, 10
collier de perles **69**–30
colliers **69**–9
collines **117**–16
colonne vertébrale **75**–54
colorer les cheveux **23**–D
combinaison **67**–22
combinaison de plongée **155**–7
combinaison-pantalon **65**–16
combiné **9**–2
combiné radio-lecteur de cassettes
    portatif **164**–2
comédie **166**–10
comédie de situation **167**–18
comète **127**–25
commande de lit **86**–12
commencer **157**–X
commencer l'école **28**–B
commerce de proximité **90**–3
commis **139**–50
commis aux stocks **139**–55
commode **44**–2, **45**–8
composition **113**–2
compacte **106**–2
compartiment à bagages **110**–10
compétences professionnelles **140**
complimenter **8**–G
composer **9**–D
composition **113**–2
composition anglaise **113**
compresse stérile **83**–4
comprimé **81**–25
comprimés contre le rhume **81**–17
comptable **136**–1
comptant **20**–13, **97**–D
compte-gouttes **119**–14
compteur **104**–21
compteur à gaz **48**–14
compteur de vitesse **108**–20
compteur kilométrique **108**–21
comptoir **40**–22, **46**–O, **60**–13, **80**–12,
    110–3
comptoir de caisse **55**–17
comptoir d'enregistrement **98**–16, **110**–3
concepteur **146**–3
conception **146**–A
concert **166**–6
concession d'automobiles **88**–4
concierge **36**–12, **138**–35
concombres **51**–12
condamner l'accusé **99**–F
conditions requises pour une

demande de citoyenneté **116**
conducteur **104**–16
conducteur (conductrice) de
    camions **139**–61
conduire **26**–I, **90**–C, **140**–E
conduire de la machinerie lourde **140**–F
conduite en état d'ivresse **100**–3
cône **118**–11
confectionneur (confectionneuse) de
    vêtements **137**–27
conférencier (conférencière) invité(e)
    32–9
confettis **168**–3
confiserie **92**–3
confiture **56**–14
congélateur **40**–10
congestion **78**–7
congestion nasale **78**–7
conjoint **24**–19
conjointe **24**–20
conseiller **5**–16
conseillère **5**–16
conservation **126**
conserver **126**–B, C
conserves **54**–4
constellation **127**–24
construction **149**
construire des modèles réduits **162**–C
consulter les petites annonces **141**–D
contenant **56**–5, **59**–3
contenant de fromage cottage **56**–17
contenant de plastique **59**–3
contenants et aliments emballés **56**
continents **124**
contreplaqué **149**–16
contrôle de smog **109**–57
conversation courante **8**
convertir les mesures **57**–C
convier **169**–B
copier (un texte) **6**–F
coq **133**–6
coquillage **155**–21
coquille **67**–14
coquille Saint-Jacques **130**–18
cor (musique) **120**–13
cor d'harmonie **120**–15
cor français **120**–15
corbeille à déchets **43**–25, **46**–F
corbeille à pain **63**–8
corbeilles empilables **142**–5
corde **154**–19
corde à linge **72**–9
corde à sauter **153**–5
cordon **9**–3, **151**–14
corne (animal) **134**–21
cornouiller **128**–16
corps **74**–75
corral **148**–17
corriger **113**–B
corriger (les erreurs) **7**–Z
corrosif **147**–4

costaud(e) **22**–20
costume **168**–13
costume de bain **66**–26
costume trois pièces **64**–1
côté **118**–22
côtelettes d'agneau **52**–15
côtelettes de porc **52**–10
côtes de bœuf **52**–5
coton **70**–16, **148**–6
cou **74**–2
couches jetables **95**–20
couches lavables **95**–21
coude **74**–15
coudre à la machine **73**–B
coudre à la main **73**–A
coudre des vêtements **140**–L
cougar **134**–2
coulée de boue **102**–6
couler **48**–3, **49**–16
couleurs **12**
coup de soleil **78**–14
coupe-branches **39**–15
coupe-ongles **77**–29
couper **23**–A, **58**–M, **77**–N
coupe-vent **66**–24
coupure **78**–13
cour **37**–18, **39**, **99**–C
cour avant **38**–15
cour intérieure **5**–3
Cour suprême **116**–8
courant **48**–2
courbe **118**–19
courges **51**–13
courgettes **51**–4
courir **156**–C
courir (en compétition) **157**–Y
Courrier express **96**–15
courrier prioritaire **96**–12
cours de conduite **121**–5
court (talon) **71**–46
court de tennis **153**–7
cousin **24**–12
coussin **42**–20
coussin à épingles **73**–15
coussin gonflable **108**–16
coût **21**–6
couteau **41**–22, **63**–27
couteau à découper **59**–12
couteau à éplucher **59**–16
couteau à viande **63**–26
couteau suisse **154**–20
coûteuse **11**–19
coûteux **11**–19
couture **73**–11
couture et retouches **73**
couturière **73**–2
couvercle **59**–24
couvert **63**–14
couverture **44**–12
couvre-lit **44**–11
couvreur **48**–8

cow-boy **148**–22
coyote **134**–3
crabe **53**–22, **130**–16
craie **3**–16
crâne **75**–52
crapaud **130**–28
cravates (habit) **69**–10
crayon **3**–20
crayon à sourcils **77**–33
crayons **45**–21
crème aigre **54**–37
crème antihistaminique **83**–10
crème de rasage **77**–27
crème glacée **55**–44
crêpes **61**–6
crevette **53**–24, **130**–19
cric **109**–51
cricket **132**–24
crier **169**–G
crime **100**
crinière **135**–49
crochet **150**–34, 35, **163**–20
crochet à œillet **150**–35
crocodile **131**–37
crocus **129**–25
croissant de lune **127**–14
crosse de hockey **161**–11
crotale **131**–38
cru **52**–24
crustacés **53**
cube **118**–10
cuiller **41**–23, **59**–9
cuiller à soupe **63**–29
cuiller de bois **59**–9
cuillère **41**–23, **59**–9
cuillerée à soupe **57**–7
cuire **58**–L
cuire à la vapeur **58**–I
cuisine **40**, **63**–10
cuisiner (nourriture) **27**–P, **58**–F, **140**–C
cuisinier **63**–11, **137**–17
cuisinière **40**–18, **154**–16
cuisse **74**–16
cuisses **52**–21
cuit-vapeur **59**–4
cuivres (musique) **120**
cul-de-sac **107**–8
culottes de propreté **95**–24
cusinière **63**–11, **137**–17
cuvette **43**–17, **49**–18
cyclisme **159**–4
cycliste **153**–3
cylindre **118**–12
cylindre gradué **119**–10
dans **13**–5, **105**–4
danser **33**–J
darne de saumon **53**–19
date **18**–14
date de naissance **4**–16
dates (fruits) **50**–25
dauphin **131**–30

dé à coudre **73**–20
de dix ans **22**–5
de dix-neuf ans **22**–8
de poids moyen **22**–21
de six ans **22**–4
de soirée **71**–36
de taille moyenne **22**–17
de treize ans **22**–7
déballer **35**–E
débarasser (la table) **62**–G
débardeur (chandail) **67**–2
déborder **49**–17
débouchoir à ventouse **151**–44
décapotable **106**–5
décembre **19**–36
déchets dangereux **126**–9
déchirure **70**–23
décoller (en avion) **111**–L
décontracté **71**–37
décorer **169**–C
découseur **73**–19
décrocher le combiné **9**–A
défense **135**–48
degrés **29**–7
degrés Celsius **10**
degrés Fahrenheit **10**
déjeuner **61**
demain **18**–16
demander **111**–M
demander à propos des avantages sociaux **141**–J
demander les heures **141**–F
démarrer **157**–X
déménager **29**–P
déménageur **138**–40
demi **15**–4, **16**–10, **20**–5
demi tasse de raisins secs **57**–9
demi-frère **25**–29, **25**–33
demi-litre **57**–3
demi-sœur **25**–30, **25**–32
demi-tour autorisé **107**–7
démonte-roue **109**–50
dentiste **84**–18, **137**–20
dents **74**–25, **77**–J, K, **85**–I
déodorant **76**–4
dépanneur **90**–3
dépanneuse **106**–13
déposer **9**–C, **94**–A, **97**–C
derrière **13**–3
dés **162**–4
désastres naturels **102**–103
description de choses **11**
description de vêtements **70**–**71**
description des cheveux **23**
description physique **22**
désert **117**–4
désherber **39**–A
désinfectant **95**–19
désordre **11**–16
dessin animé **167**–19
destructeur de documents **143**–24

détecteur de fumée **37**–25, **45**–11
détenu(e) **99**–14
détergent **47**–23
détergent à lessive **72**–7
détergent à vaisselle **47**–21
deux **14**
deux fois par semaine **18**–23
deux heures moins cinq **16**–15
deux heures moins vingt **16**–12
deux heures moins vingt-cinq **16**–11
deux points **113**–12
deuxième étage **36**–3
deuxième initiale **4**–3
devant **13**–4
devoir de rédaction **113**–1
diabète **79**–9
diagonale **118**–23
diamètre **118**–17
diapositives **165**–31
dicter **6**–N
dictionnaire **3**–28
dictionnaire illustré **3**–29
diététicien(ne) **87**–25
difficile **11**–24
dimanche **18**–1
dimensions **15**
dindon **52**–17, **53**–4, **168**–17
dindon fumé **53**–4
dîner **27**–R
dineur **62**–5
diplôme **29**–2, **32**–6, **32**–7
diplôme universitaire **29**–7
dire **6**–C
directeur (directrice) **5**–14
directions et panneaux de circulation **107**
disc-jockey **33**–17
discuter **6**–L
disposer **35**–K
dispositif d'évacuation des déchets médicaux **86**–14
disque compact **98**–14
disque compact ROM **144**–2
disquette **144**–5
dissolvant de vernis à ongles **77**–32
distribuer **7**–O
divan **42**–19
divertissements **166**–167
division **118**–4
divorcé(e) **25**–24
dix **14**, **15**–7, **16**–6, **20**–9
dix-huit **14**
dix-huitième **14**
dixième **14**
dix-neuf **14**
dix-neuvième **14**
dix-sept **14**
dix-septième **14**
docker **137**–21
docteur **84**–6, **137**–22
doigts **75**–57

dollar **20**–7
donner **21**–D
donner à manger **94**–D, **148**–D
donner un baiser **33**–F
donner une injection d'anesthésique **75**–J
dormeuse molletonnée **67**–7
dors-bien ouverture **67**–7
dos **74**–11
douanes **110**–20
douanier (douanière) **110**–21
double porte **38**–12
doux **10**–2
douze **14**
douzième **14**
drame **166**–11
drap **44**–13, 14
drap plat **44**–13
drapeau **168**–9
drap-housse **44**–14
dribbler **156**–K
drogues **100**–4
drogues illégales **100**–4
droits et responsabilités **116**
drôle **167**–27
dune de sable **117**–5
dur **11**–5
eau **117**, **155**–1
eau chaude **43**–5
eau de Cologne **76**–5
eau de javel **72**–8
eau en bouteille **55**–53
eau froide **43**–7
eau oxygénée **83**–8
ébouer **139**–51
écales (poisson) **130**–3
ecchymose **78**–12
échafaudage **149**–4
échalotes **51**–17
échanger **21**–G
écharpe **66**–4, **80**–8, **70**–15
écharpe de laine **66**–4
écharpes de soie **68**–4
échelle **149**–2
échelle d'acuité visuelle **84**–11
école **5**, **89**–27
école de métiers **112**–9
école élémentaire **112**–5
école paroissiale **112**–3
école primaire **112**–5
école privée **112**–2
école professionnelle **112**–9
école publique **112**–1
écoles, types d' **112**
économe **59**–15
économie **121**–6
économie domestique **121**–9
économiser **126**–B, C
écossais **70**–9
écouter **2**–C, **85**–D
écouter le cœur **85**–D

écouteurs **164**–16
écran **2**–2, **144**–6, **152**–12, **165**–28
écran de cheminée **42**–11
écran solaire **76**–6, **155**–13
écrans **110**–4
écrans d'arrivée et de départ **110**–4
écrasement **102**–3
écrasement d'avion **102**–3
écrire **2**–G, **113**–A
écrire en lettre moulée **4**–C
écritoire à pince **143**–26
écrivain **139**–64
écrou (quincaillerie) **150**–31
écureuil **133**–21
édredon **45**–2
éducation physique **121**–11
éducatrice (éducateur) en garderie **94**–3
efface **3**–21
effacer **2**–H
effrayé(e) **31**–24
église **88**–6
égouttoir à vaisselle **40**–3
éjecter **165**–F
élan **134**–1
élastique **143**–45
électricien **48**–9
électrique **151**–38
électronique et photographie **164**–165
éléments **140**–A
éléphant **135**–42
élève qui prononce un discours d'adieu **32**–8
ellipse **118**–9
emballage **56**–8, **96**–5
emballer **169**–D
emballeur **55**–21
emballeur (emballeuse) **146**–13
embarrassé(e) **31**–25
embout protecteur **147**–21
embrayage **109**–45
émission d'enfant **45**
émission de radio **166**–4
émission de télévision **166**–3
émission pour enfants **167**–24
émission radiophonique **166**–4
émission sur le shopping **167**–25
emménager **35**–D
emmener les enfants à l'école **26**–G
emplois et professions **136**–139
en bas **105**–8
en dessous **13**–7
en état de choc **82**
en haut **105**–9
encadrer des personnes **140**–K
encaustique pour meubles **47**–18
enceinte **22**–19
encyclopédie **98**–18
endroits où aller **152**
énergie et environnement **126**
énergie géothermique **126**–7
énergie hydroélectrique **126**–5

énergie nucléaire **126**–8

énergie solaire **126**–1

enfant bruyant **11**–11

enfant perdu **102**–1

enfant qui commence à marcher **22**–3

enfants **11**–11, 12, **22**–1

enflé **78**–16

engager **99**–B

engager (une conversation) **8**–B

engin élévateur à nacelle **149**–5

enjoliveur de roue **108**–9

ennuyeux **167**–29

enregistrer **98**–15, **119**–C

enregistrer (lecteur de cassette) **165**–A

enregistrer vos bagages **111**–B

ensoleillé **10**–6

entendre **75**–B

entier **15**–6

entonnoir **119**–12

entorse **78**–18

entraîneur **158**–2

entre **13**–10

entrepôt **146**–9

entrevue **141**–H

enveloppe **96**–1, **143**–20

environnement **126**

envoi certifié **96**–11

envoyer **96**–B

épais **11**–7, **71**–41

épaule **74**–10

épaulettes **161**–21

épeler **4**–A, **6**–E

épices **55**–46

épinards **51**–11

épine **129**–28

épingle (à coudre) **73**–14

épingle de sûreté **73**–24

épingles à couche **95**–22

éplucher **58**–N

éplucheur **59**–15

éponge **47**–24

épousseter **46**–A

éprouvette **119**–16

éprouvette graduée **119**–10

épuisette **154**–17

équipe **103**–17, **158**–3

équipe de recherche et sauvetage **103**–17

equivalences **15**

érable **128**–13

erreur **7**–2

éruption cutanée **78**–10

éruption volcanique **103**–14

escabeau **47**–7

escalier **37**–26

escalier de secours **36**–7

escalier mécanique **93**–21

escalopes de veau **52**–6

escargot **130**–24

escarpins **68**–16

escrime **159**–5

espace **127**–22

espace de stationnement **90**–5

espadon **130**–12

essence **109**–54

essuie-glaces **108**–3

essuie-mains **43**–13

essuie-tout **40**–2, **56**–23

essuyer la vaisselle **46**–N

essuyer le comptoir **46**–O

estomac **75**–41

établissement préscolaire **112**–4

étang **117**–21, **153**–6

état **4**–8

état médical **79**

état médical et maladies graves **79**

étau **150**–21

été **19**–38

éternuer **78**–B

étiquette **21**–1, **143**–35

étiquette d'avertissement **80**–15

étiquette de prescription **80**–14

étiquette d'ordonnance **80**–14

étoile **127**–23

étoile de mer **130**–15

étranger **101**–F

être à l'aise **30**–7

être à l'école **26**–J

être âgé de 18 ans **116**–A

être amoureux **28**–K, **30**–19

être bien **30**–15

être blessé **82**–A

être dégoûté(e) **30**–9

être en état de choc **82**–C

être engagé **141**–L

être inconscient **82**–B

être inquiet(e) **30**–13

être mal à l'aise **30**–8

être malade **30**–14

être relâché **99**–H

être repu **30**–6

être soulagé(e) **30**–16

étroit(e) **71**–45

étude **6**–7

études commerciales (de commerce) **121**–2

étudiant(e) **2**–3, **139**–57

étui à appareil-photo **165**–27

événements de la vie **28**–29

évier **40**–6, **43**–22, **49**–17

examens dentaires **85**

examens médical et dentaire **85**

examiner **85**–F, **111**–K, **141**–B

examiner la gorge **75**–E

excité(e) **31**–23

expédier **96**–B

expédition **146**–C

exploration **114**

explosion **102**–4

exposition **152**–21

expressions indiquant le mouvement **105**

exterminateur **49**–21

extincteurs **147**–22

eye-liner **77**–35

fabrication **146**–B

fâché(e) **31**–29

facile **11**–23

facteur **96**–6

faire asseoir **2**–E, **152**–11

faire correspondre **7**–X

faire de l'équitation **154**–9

faire de l'exercice **27**–W, **80**–D, **157**–P

faire de la luge **160**–6

faire de la planche à roulettes **159**–12

faire de la planche à voile **160**–10

faire de la radiographie **85**–H

faire de la voile **160**–8

faire des bricolages **162**–D

faire des courses **21**

faire des photocopies **142**–E

faire des travaux manuels **140**–D

faire du jogging **156**–B

faire du patin **157**–V

faire du patiner **157**–V

faire du skateboard **159**–12

faire du surf **160**–9

faire du surf des neiges **160**–2

faire du vélo **159**–4

faire du vélo tout terrain **154**–8

faire faire une radio **85**–H

faire la lessive **72**–2

faire le lit **46**–G

faire mijoter **58**–R

faire sauter (des aliments) **58**–H

faire semblant **163**–G

faire ses devoirs **27**–T

faire un dépôt **97**–C

faire un dessin **6**–M

faire un discours **32**–E

faire un vœu **169**–J

faire une expérice **119**–A

faire une mise en plis **23**–C

faire une offre **35**–H

faire une overdose **82**–K

faire une permanente **23**–B

faire une sieste **94**–L

faire une surdose **82**–K

familiale **106**–8

famille **24**–25

fantaisie **71**–39

fard à cils **77**–38

fard à joue **77**–36

farine **55**–45, **57**–10

fatigué(e) **31**–33

fauteuil roulant **80**–6

faune marine, amphibiens et reptiles **130**–131

fauteuil **42**–24

favoris **23**–7

faxer **142**–B

femme **4**–14, **22**–10

femme d'affaires **136**–10

femme d'intérieur **137**–32

femme de ménage **138**–33, **145**–15

fenêtre **38**–17, **42**–17
fente **144**–19
fer à friser **76**–15
fer à repasser **72**–13
ferme **34**–13
fermer **2**–J
fermeture éclair **73**–16
fermier **148**–15
ferry **104**–23
fesses **74**–12
fête **168**–16
Fête de l'indépendance **168**–7
fête régionale **152**–19
fête religieuse **19**–44
feu **42**–10, **102**–7
feu arrière **108**–14
feu d'artifice **168**–8
feu de camp **154**–11
feu de circulation **90**–6
feu de frein **108**–13
feu de signalisation **90**–6
feu follet **168**–11
feuille **128**–6, **129**–5
feuille de réponse **7**–T
feuilles de cahier **3**–24, 25, 26
feuilleton à l'eau de rose **167**–21
fèves **51**–25, **54**–26
février **19**–26
fiche **164**–18
fiches médicales **87**–20
fichier rotatif **143**–17
fiction **166**–12
fier (fière) **31**–22
fièvre **78**–8
figurine **162**–10, **163**–31
fil **73**–17, **151**–13, **163**–17
filet à cheveux **147**–18
filet de sole **53**–21
fille **24**–21, 8
fillette **22**–5
film **166**–1
film (de caméra) **165**–26
film alimentaire **55**–54
films **152**–10
fils **24**–22
finissants **32**–1
fissuré **48**–4
fixatif capillaire **76**–12
flèche **161**–7
flet **130**–13
flétan **53**–20
fleur **39**–19, **129**–7
fleuri **70**–12
fleuriste **92**–12, **137**–25
fleurs **129**
flou **165**–33
flûte **120**–3
foie **52**–7, **75**–39
foin **148**–18
foire **152**–13
foire régionale **152**–19

fonctionner **48**–1
fond de teint **77**–40
fontaine **92**–11, **153**–11
football **158**–12
forceps **119**–8
forêt **117**–11, **150**–23
forêt pluviale **117**–1
formes **118**
formulaire d'assurance **84**–5
formulaire de déclaration **110**–22
formulaire d'enregistrement **4**
formulaire d'inscription aux cours **4**
formule **119**–19
foudre **10**–17
fouet **59**–21
four **40**–20, **46**–C, **47**–3
four à micro-ondes **40**–13
fourchette **41**–21, **63**–24, 25
fourchette à salade **63**–24
fourchette de table **63**–25
fourgon de déménagement **106**–14
fourgonnette **106**–10, 14
fourmis **49**–24
fournitures pour le bâtiment **150**–151
fourre-tout **69**–29
fourrure **134**–19
foyer **42**–9
fractions **15**
frais **10**–3, **53**–29
fraise **84**–21, **150**–8, 23
fraises **50**–17
framboises **50**–18
frange **23**–8
frapper **156**–G
frapper une balle avec un swing **157**–O
freesbee **159**–6, **161**–27
frein **109**–44
frère **24**–9
friandise **55**–41
frisé **23**–11
frissons **78**–9
frit **61**–17
frites **60**–2
friture **58**–5
froid (sensation) **30**–4
froissé(e) **72**–19
fromage **53**–9, 10, 11, 12, **54**–38
fromage cheddar **53**–10
fromage cottage **56**–17
fromage gruyère **53**–11
fromage jack **53**–12
front **74**–20
frotter **46**–L
fruit **50**
fruits de mer **53**
frustré(e) **31**–28
gaine **67**–18
galaxie **127**–26
gallon **57**–5
gant **161**–17
gant de toilette **43**–14

gants **66**–5
gants de caoutchouc **47**–4
gants de latex **87**–33, **147**–17
garage **36**, **38**–6
garçon **22**–4, 7
garde de sécurité **97**–4
gardénia **129**–16
garderie **94**–95
garder **21**–E
gardien **99**–3
gardien(ne) de zoo **152**–3
gardienne (d'enfants) **136**–12
gare **104**–13
gâteau **54**–32, **61**–19
gauche **13**–1
gaufre **133**–19
gaufres **61**–4
gauphre **133**–19
gaz naturel **126**–3
gaze **83**–6
geai bleu **132**–7
gel cheveux **76**–11
gel (de) **10**–5
gencives **74**–24
genou **74**–17
géographie **117**
géométrie **118**–26
gérant **35**–B, **36**–12, **54**–8, **143**–25
gésiers **52**–23
gigot d'agneau **52**–14
gilet **65**–24, **66**–13
gilet de corps **67**–10
gilet de sauvetage **154**–14
gilet de sécurité **147**–15
gilet débardeur **67**–2
gilet en duvet **66**–13
girafe **135**–33
glacial **10**–13
glacière **155**–11
globe terrestre **3**–9
golf **159**–7
gomme **3**–21
gorge **75**–36
gorille **135**–30
goûter **75**–D
gouttes pour le yeux **81**–22
gouttière **38**–19
gouvernement américain et
    citoyenneté **116**
gradins **5**–10
graine **129**–1
graisser **58**–C
grand **70**–4
grand magasin **93**–13
grand(e) **22**–16
grande assiette **63**–15
grande tasse **41**–28
grand-mère **24**–2
grand-père **24**–3
grands-parents **24**–1
grange **148**–11

graphiste **137**–29
gratte-ciel **89**–25
grattoir **151**–48
greffier de la cour **99**–12
grêle **10**–19
grenouille **130**–25
griffe **132**–4
grignotines **55**–16
grille **59**–14
grillé **58**–V
grille-pain **40**–7
grille-pain four **40**–15
griller **58**–T
grilloir **40**–21
grillon **132**–24
grimper **153**–C
grippe **79**–2
gris **12**–5
gros **11**–2
grosse branche **128**–3
grosse voiture **106**–4
groupe de rock **120**–2
grue **149**–7
guêpe **132**–18
guichet automatique **97**–3
guillemets **113**–9
guitare **120**–11
gymnase **5**–9
gymnastique **159**–8
habiller **94**–J
habitations **34**
hache **150**–3
hacher **58**–G
haie **39**–1
hall **89**–17, **145**–3, 13
Halloween **168**–10
haltères **161**–19
haltérophilie **159**–15
hamac **39**–2
hamburger **60**–1
hamburger au fromage **60**–3
hanche **74**–5
handicapé(e) **22**–25
haricots verts **51**–25
harnais d'épaule **109**–37
hautbois **120**–5
hauteur **15**–14
haut-parleur **36**–8
haut-parleurs **164**–11
hélicoptère **110**–8
herbe à puce **128**–25
heure **16**–3, **16**–4
heure d'été **17**–33
heure d'Hawaï-des Aléoutiennes **17**–24
heure de l'Alaska **17**–25
heure de l'Atlantique **17**–30
heure de l'Est **17**–29
heure de Terre-Neuve **17**–31
heure des Rocheuses **17**–27
heure du centre **17**–28
heure du Pacifique **17**–26

heure normale **17**–32
heureux (heureuse) **31**–32
hibiscus **129**–12
hibou **132**–6
hier **18**–17
hippisme **159**–18
hippocampe **130**–23
hippopotame **135**–43
histoire des E.-U. **114**–**115**
hiver **19**–40
hochet **95**–31
hockey sur glace **158**–13
homard **53**–23
homme **4**–13, **22**–11
homme d'affaires **136**–10
hôpital **88**–7, **86**–**87**
horaire **104**–3
horloge **3**–10
horreur **166**–14
hors du taxi **105**–5
hot-dog **60**–6
hôtel **88**–5, **145**
hôtel de ville **89**–17
hôtesse **62**–1
houx **128**–19
huile (de cuisson) **55**–49, **57**–2
huissier **99**–13
huit **14**
huitième **14**, **15**–1
huîtres **53**–27
humide **10**–12
humidificateur **80**–2
hydratant **76**–8
hyène **135**–31
hygiène personnelle **76**–**77**
hygiéniste **84**–16
hygiéniste dentaire **84**–16
hypertension **79**–15
I.V. (goutte-à-goutte intraveineux) **87**–27
île **117**–8
immeuble **34**–5
immeuble à appartements **34**–5
immeuble de bureaux **89**–24
immeuble de grande hauteur **89**–25
immigration **114**
immigrer **28**–C
imperméable **66**–17
imprimante **144**–12
imprimé **70**–10
imprimeur **138**–46
imprudent **147**–23
indicateur **84**–12, **108**–19, 22, 23
indicateur de pression artérielle **84**–12
indicateur de température du moteur
     108–23
indicatif régional **4**–10
infection de l'oreille **79**–3
infirmier(ière) **84**–10, **87**–22, 24, 29,
     138–42
infirmier(ière) auxiliaire autorisé(e) **77**–24
infirmier(ière) diplômé(e) **87**–22

infirmier(ière) en chirurgie **87**–29
infirmier(ière) professionnell(e) autorisé(e)
     87–24
inflammable **147**–2
informatique **121**–4
ingénieur **137**–23
ingrédients **58**–K
inondation **103**–16
insectes **132**
insectes et animaux nuisibles **49**
instructeur **139**–58
instrument **120**–A
intéressant **167**–30
interne **86**–2
interphone **36**–8
interprète **138**–34
interrupteur **44**–19
interrupteur de tension **144**–4
intestins **75**–42
introduire **97**–A
invités **33**–14, **169**–B
iris **129**–20
isolation **149**–13
jambe **74**–6
jambières **65**–23, **161**–13
jambon **52**–9
janvier **19**–25
jardin botanique **152**–4
jardin potager **148**–12
jardin sur le toit **36**–5
jardin zoologique **152**–1
jardinier (jardinière) **137**–26, **152**–6
jardins botaniques **152**–4
jarrets d'agneau **52**–13
jasmin **129**–21
jauge d'essence **108**–22
jauge d'huile **108**–19
jaune **12**–12
jeans **64**–5
jetée **155**–16
jeton **104**–11
jeu **152**–18
jeu d'échecs **162**–6
jeu de bascule **153**–16
jeu de dames **162**–5
jeu de société **162**–3
jeu-concours **167**–23
jeudi **18**–5
jeune **22**–13
jeu-questionnaire **167**–23
jeux **162**–**163**
jeux vidéos **162**–1
jonquille **129**–26
joue **74**–29
jouer (un jeu/de la musique) **94**–K,
     165–B
jouer à des jeux **162**–C
jouer aux cartes **163**–H
jouer d'un instrument **120**–A
jouets **46**–H, **94**–5
joueur **158**–5, **164**–2, 14, 15

jour **18**–10
jour férié **19**–43, 44
journal **98**–8
journaliste **99**–12, **139**–49
jours de la semaine **18**
jours de semaine **18**–12
jours fériés **168**
joyeux anniversaire **169**
judas **37**–27
juge **99**–6
juges **116**–10
juillet **19**–31, **168**–7
juin **19**–30
jupe **64**–10, **65**–25
jupe avec une fente sur le devant **65**–25
Jupiter **127**–5
jupon **67**–23
jury **99**–8, **116**
jus de pomme **55**–50, **57**–5
justaucorps **67**–1
kangourou **135**–44
kayak **154**–3
ketchup **60**–23
kiosque à journaux **90**–11
kiosque d'information **93**–22
kit de confection de poupée **162**–15
kit de menuisier **162**–16
klaxon (voiture) **108**–24
koala **135**–45
l'heure **16**–**17**
la semaine dernière **18**–18
lac **117**–13
lacet **68**–14
laid **11**–22
laine **70**–14
laisser **111**–L
laisser un message **9**–E
laisser un pourboire **62**–J
lait **54**–35
lait maternisé **95**–25
laitue **51**–1, **60**–17
lama **135**–26
lame **150**–11
lame de rasoir **77**–26
lampe **42**–15, **44**–17
lampe de poche **151**–39
lampe de porte **38**–9
lampe sur pied **42**–15
lancer **156**–D, **156**–F
langue **74**–26
langue étrangère **121**–8
lanterne **154**–22
lapin **133**–13
lard **52**–11, **61**–7
large **71**–44
largeur **15**–17
lave-linge **72**–3, **150**–32
laver (le plancher) **46**–J
laver la vaisselle **46**–M
laver les cheveux **76**–E
laver les fenêtres **46**–D

laveuse **72**–3, **150**–32
lave-vaisselle **40**–4
le préposé (la préposée) **5**–18
lèchefrite **59**–13
lecteur de cassettes **3**–11, **164**–2, 15
lecteur de disques compacts **164**–14
lecteur de microfilm **98**–4
léger **11**–14, **71**–40
légumes **51**, **55**–43
légumes surgelés **55**–43
lent **11**–4
léopard **135**–25
lessive **72**–1
lettre **96**–2, **142**–B, D
lever **2**–A
levez-vous **2**–D
levier de vitesse au plancher **109**–48
levier de vitesses **108**–27
lèvre **74**–30
lézard **131**–41
librairie **92**–4
licence de taxi **104**–22
lieu de naissance **4**–17
ligne droite **118**–18
lignes **118**
lime émeri **77**–30
limite de vitesse **107**–5
lin **70**–17
linge à vaisselle **47**–22
l'intérieur du corps **75**
lion **135**–36
liquide correcteur **143**–33
liquide de refroidissement **109**–56
lire **6**–B, **27**–V, **94**–F, **111**–K, **141**–B
lis **129**–24
liste **6**–L
lit **44**–8
lit d'enfant **45**–6
lit d'hôpital **86**–11
litre **57**–4
livraison le lendemain **96**–15
livre **3**–22
livre (poids) **57**–12
livre à colorier **45**–20
livre d'images **45**–17
livre de bibliothèque **98**–20
livre épais **11**–7
livrer **96**–C
livret **97**–5
livreur (livreuse) **137**–18
locataire **37**–33
location d'un appartement **35**
logiciels **144**
long (longue) **23**–3, **71**–34
longueur **15**–16
lotion pour le corps **76**–7
louche **59**–7
louer **28**–I
loup **134**–5
loutre **131**–35
luminaire **41**–5

lundi **18**–2
lune **127**–13, 14, 15, 16
lunettes **81**–35
lunettes de sécurité **147**–9
lunettes de soleil **66**–21
lunettes de sûreté **147**–10
lutte **159**–16
luzerne **148**–5
lycée **112**–7
machine à coudre **73**–10
machine à écrire **142**–2
machine à glaçons **145**–18
machinerie lourde **140**–F
mâchoire **74**–23
maçon **136**–9
magasin de cartes **92**–7
magasin de chaussures **92**–10
magasin de jouets **92**–5
magasin de meubles **88**–13
magasin de musique **92**–1
magasin de photo **90**–4
magasin d'électronique **93**–18
magazine **98**–7
magnétophone à cassettes **164**–3
magnétoscope **164**–8
magnifique **11**–21
magnolier **128**–9
mai **19**–29
maigre **11**–8, **22**–22
maillet **150**–2
maillot de bain **66**–22
maillot de corps **67**–10
main **2**, **11**, **74**–8
mairie **89**–17
maïs **51**–27, **148**–4
maison **34**–6, **38**
Maison Blanche **116**–5
maison de poupées **45**–14
maison de retraite **34**–11
maison de ville **34**–7
maître nageur **155**–18
mal de dents **78**–2
mal de dos **78**–5
mal de gorge **78**–6
mal de tête **78**–1
mal d'estomac **78**–4
mal d'oreille **78**–3
maladie cardiaque **79**–14
maladies communes et maladies
   de l'enfance **79**
maladies de l'enfance **79**
maladies et état médical **79**
maladies graves **79**
malendantant(e) **22**–27
malvoyant(e) **22**–26
mammifères **134**–**135**
mammifères marins **131**
manche **73**–6
manche à balais **144**–9
mandarines **50**–13
mandat **20**–16

Index

manèges **152**–17
manger **60**–B
mangues **50**–21
maniques **59**–29
mannequin **138**–39
manœuvre de Heimlich **83**–18
manquant **70**–25
manteau **42**–8
manteau (habit) **66, 66**–4
manteau sport **64**–6
manuel de l'utilisateur **144**–22
manuel de premiers soins **83**–7
marchandise **152**–24
marché **54–55, 89**–20
marché aux puces **152**–22
marcher **101**–A, **156**–A
marches **37**–35, **38**–13, **48**–7, **105**–8, 9
marchette **95**–12
mardi **18**–3
mare aux canards **153**–6
marée noire **126**–15
margarine **54**–39
marguerite **129**–14
mari **24**–19
marié(e)(s) **25**–23, **28**–L
marquer **7**–T
marqueur **3**–19
Mars **127**–6
mars **19**–27
marsouin **131**–31
marteau **150**–1
marteau de forgeron **149**–22
marteau pneumatique **149**–9
marteler **149**–D
masque **168**–12
masque d'attrapeur **161**–15
masque de plongée **155**–3
masque de ski **66**–14
masque d'oxygène **110**–14
masque respiratoire **147**–12
massicot **143**–15
match de base-ball **152**–25
matelas **44**–25
matelas de mousse **154**–13
matériel **144, 150**
matériel agricole **148**–10
matériel de sauvetage **155**–19
mathématiques **118**
matières dangereuses **147**–7
matin **17**–16
mauvais **11**–18
mauve **12**–7
mayonnaise **60**–25
mécanicien (mécanicienne) auto **136**–7
médaillon **69**–33
médicament d'ordonnance **70**–11
médicament prescrit **70**–11
médicament sans ordonnance **80**–12
médicaments **80**–11, 12
méduse **130**–14
mélange à gâteaux **55**–47

mélanger **58**–K
membre du congrès **116**–2
menottes **99**–2
menton **74**–31
menu **62**–3
menu de cafétéria **61**
menu de café-restaurant **61**
mercredi **18**–4
Mercure **127**–9
mère **24**–5, **25**–25
mère célibataire **25**–26
merle américain **132**–17
messager **138**–38
messagère **138**–38
mesure **15**
mesurer **149**–C
mesurer les ingrédients **57**–A
mesures **14–15, 57**
mesures de liquides **57**
mesures de matières sèches **57**
mètre **15, 151**–15
mètre à ruban **73**–13, **150**–22
métro **104**–9
mettre de l'écran solaire **76**–D
mettre en ordre **7**–W
mettre fin à la conversation **8**–C
mettre la ceinture de sécurité **111**–I
mettre la table **62**–A
meuble classeur **142**–10
meubles **35**–K
meubles de patio **39**–5
meurtre **100**–8
mi-bas **67**–24
micro **164**–4
microfilm **98**–5
microscope **119**–4
midi **17**–17
mignon(ne) **22**–24
militaire **139**–54
milk-shake **60**–12
mille **14**
milliard **14**
million **14**
mi-long (cheveux) **23**–2
mince **11**–8, **22**–22
mini-fourgonnette **106**–10
minuit **17**–21
minute **16**–2
minuteur **59**–18
miroir **43**–18, **44**–1
mitaines **66**–9
mixeur **40**–12
mobile **45**–4
mobile home **34**–8
mocassins **68**–19
modèle réduit **162**–7
modèles réduits **162**–C
modèles réduits de train **163**–32
modem **144**–11
modes de paiement **20**
moelleux (moelleuse) **11**–6

moineau **132**–8
mois **4**–16, **18**–9
mois de l'année **19**
molécule **119**–18
mollet **74**–18
monde **124–125**
moniteur **144**–6
moniteur de bébé **45**–9
moniteur de contrôle des signes vitaux **87**–21
moniteurs **110**–4
monologue comique **166**–5
monospace **106**–10
montagnes russes **152**–15
monter à bord de l'avion **111**–F
monteur (monteuse) **136**–6
montre **69**–34
montre-bracelet **69**–34
moquette **42**–27
morse **131**–32
morsure d'insecte **78**–11
morue **130**–8
mosquée **89**–23
motel **89**–22
moteur **109**–41
motifs (de tissus) **70**
moto **91**–19
mouche **132**–29
mouchoir **69**–42
mouffette **134**–12
moufles **66**–9
mouillé **72**–17
moule **130**–17
moule à gâteau **59**–26
moule à tarte **59**–28
moules **53**–26
mourir **29**–R
moustache **23**–5
moustaches **134**–18
moustique **132**–23
moutarde **60**–24
mouton **133**–7
moyen **70**–3
muffin **60**–14
multiplication **118**–3
mur **42**–6, **48**–4
mûr **50**–29
muscle **75**–48
musée d'art **152**–7
musicien (musicienne) **138**–41
musique **120**
myrtilles **50**–19
mystère **166**–15
nachos **60**–10
nageoire **130**–1
nager **157**–T
naître **28**–A
nappe **41**–18
napperon **41**–20
navets **51**–14
ne pas boire **101**–G

ne pas boire et conduire **101**–G
ne pas entrer **107**–4
ne pas ouvrir **101**–F
ne pas pouvoir respirer **82**–N
neigeux **10**–9
Neptune **127**–2
nerf **75**–50
nerveux (nerveuse) **30**–11
nettoyage de la piscine **145**–17
nettoyant à four **47**–3
nettoyant à vitres **47**–8
nettoyer (la maison) **27**–N, **46**–C, **72**–D
nettoyer les dents **85**–I
nettoyeur **91**–24
neuf **14**, **71**–32
neuvième **14**
neveu **24**–18
nez **74**–21
nez ensanglanté **78**–17
nez qui saigne **78**–17
nid **132**–5
nièce **24**–17
niveau **150**–24
Noël **168**–18
noeud papillon **69**–40
noir **12**–15
noix (nourriture) **50**–23
noix de coco **50**–22
nom **4**–1, 2, 3, 4, A, C, D
nom de famille **4**–4
nombres et mesures **14**–**15**
nouveau **71**–32
nouvel an **168**–1
nouvelle lune **127**–13
nouvelles **167**–17
novembre **19**–35
nuageux **10**–7
nuit **17**–20
numéro d'appartement **4**–6
numéro de compte de chèque **97**–8
numéro de compte d'épargne **97**–6
numéro de Sécurité Sociale **4**–15
numéro de téléphone **4**–11
nylon **70**–19
obscurci par le smog **10**–14
observatoire **127**–19
observer **119**–B
obstétricien(ne) **86**–1
obtenir sa citoyenneté **28**–H
obtenir un diplôme **28**–D, **32**–A
obtenir un prêt **35**–I
obtention d'un diplôme **32**–**33**
obturation **84**–22
océan **117**–6, **155**–1
octobre **19**–34
oculiste **86**–7
odomètre **108**–21
œil **73**–23, **74**–27
œillet **129**–18
œufs **54**–34
œufs brouillés **58**, **61**–1

officiel **158**–6
oie **132**–14
oignons **51**–28, **58**–G, H
oiseau-mouche **132**–11
oiseaux, insectes et arachnides **132**
ombre **155**–11
ombre à paupières **77**–34
once **57**–11
once liquide **57**–1
oncle **24**–11
ondulé **23**–10
ongle **75**–58
ongle de pied **75**–64
onguent **81**–24, **83**–9
onguent antibactérien **83**–9
onze **14**
onzième **14**
opéra **166**–8
opérateur (opératrice) de machine **138**–37
opérations (mathématiques) **118**
ophtalmologiste **86**–7
ophtalmologue **86**–7
opossum **134**–4
opticien **92**–8
optométriste **81**–34
orage **10**–16
orange **12**–6
oranges **50**–10
orang-outan **135**–40
orbite **127**–11
orchestre **120**–1
orchidée **129**–17
ordinateur **3**–15
ordinateur portatif **144**–14
ordinateurs **144**
ordinaux **14**
ordure **46**–Q
oreille **74**–28
oreiller **42**–20, **44**–9
oreillons **79**–7
organiseur **143**–30
orgue **120**–22
orignal **134**–1
orme **128**–17
ornement **168**–19
ornithorynque **135**–46
orthodontiste **84**–23
orthopédiste **81**–28
os (corps) **75**–49
os brisé **82**–P
otarie **131**–34
ouïes **130**–2
ouragan **103**–12
ourlet **73**–1
ours **134**–11
ours en peluche **45**–10
oursin **130**–20
outils et fournitures pour le bâtiment **150**–**151**
ouvre-boîte **40**–14, **59**–1

ouvre-boîte électrique **40**–14
ouvrier (ouvrière) agricole **148**–8
ouvrier (ouvrière) du bâtiment **149**–1
ouvrier (ouvrière) engagé(e) **148**–20
ouvrir **2**–I
ouvrir la porte **169**–F
ouvrir les cadeaux **169**–L
ovale **118**–9
pack de six **56**–9
paille **60**–20
pain **53**–1, 2, 3, **54**–29, **56**–10, 22
pain à l'ail **61**–16
pain blanc **53**–1
pain de blé **53**–2
pain de seigle **53**–3
palais de justice **89**–18
palmes **155**–2
palmier **128**–15
palourdes **53**–28
palte-bande **39**–A
pamplemousse **50**–9
pancréas **75**–46
panda **135**–41
panier **42**–2
panier à linge **43**–1
panier de lessive **72**–2
panier de provisions **54**–7
panne (de courant) **48**–2
panneau de signalisation **91**–29
panneau offrant des emplois **141**–C
panneaux **107**
panneaux de circulation **107**
pansement **83**–3, 12
pansement adhésif **83**–3
pantalon d'entraînement **64**–15
pantalon **71**–42
pantalons **64**–8
panthère **135**–39
pantoufles **67**–6
paon **132**–15
papayes **50**–20
papier à en-tête **143**–19
papier aluminium **55**–55
papier de verre **151**–50
papier hygiénique **43**–15
papier peint **45**–5
papillon **132**–20
papillon de nuit **132**–22
papillons adhésifs **143**–34
paquet de biscuits **56**–20
parade **168**–2
paragraphe **113**–5
parallèle **118**–21
parapluie **66**–16, **155**–9
parasites intestinaux **79**–16
parasol de plage **155**–9
parasurtenseur **144**–10
parc **88**–8, **95**–11
parc de stationnement **89**–26
parc et terrain de jeux **153**
parc-mètre **91**–18

parcomètre **91**–18
pardessus **66**–2
pare-brise **108**–2
pare-chocs **108**–7
parent **94**–1
parents **24**–4
parfum **76**–5
parka **66**–8
parler **2**–B, **7**–P, **35**–B, G, **140**–J, **141**–A, I
parler une langue étrangère **140**–J
partager **6**–I
partenaire **6**–J
parties d'un arbre **128**
parties d'un carré **118**
parties d'un cercle **118**
parties d'un oiseau **132**
parties d'un poisson **130**
parties d'une fleur **129**
pas mûr **50**–28
passage à niveau **107**–11
passage pour écoliers **107**–13
passage pour piétons **90**–8
passager **104**–7, **110**–23
passages pour piétons **107**–10
passeport **29**–9
passer **156**–H
passer au contrôle de sécurité **111**–C
passer le fil d'arrivée **157**–Z
passer l'aspirateur **46**–I
passer l'examen de citoyenneté **116**–C
passerelle **104**–15
passe-temps et jeux **162–163**
passoire **59**–17
pastèques **50**–24
pastilles pour la gorge **81**–21
pastrami **53**–6
patates douces **51**–22
pâte dentifrice **77**–21
pâté **107**–2
pâtes **61**–15
patient(e) **84**–3
patinage **160**–4, 5
patinage artistique **160**–5
patinage avec patins à roues alignées **159**–9
patinage sur glace **160**–4
patins à glace **161**–9
patins à roues alignées **161**–10
patio **39**–6
patte **134**–42
pattes **23**–7
paume **75**–59
paupière **74**–33
pause **165**–E
payer **21**–C
payer l'addition **62**–I
payer l'emprunt immobilier **35**–L
payer le loyer **35**–F
payer les impôts **116**–E
pays **34**–4
peau **75**–51

pêche **154**–5
pêches **50**–5
pêcheur commercial **136**–15
pédale d'accélérateur **109**–47
pédale de frein **109**–46
pédiatre **86**–4
peigne **23**–22, **76**–13
peigner les cheveux **76**–G
peignoir de bain **67**–8
peindre **149**–A, **151**–20, 47, **163**–23, E
peinée(e) **30**–17
peintre **138**–43
peinture à l'huile **163**–24
peinture acrylique **162**–9, **162**–47
pelle **39**–13, **149**–21
pelle rétrocaveuse **149**–8
pelouse **39**–21
péninsule **117**–7
percer une dent **85**–K
perceuse électrique **150**–8
perche (poisson) **130**–11
percussion **120**
père **24**–6, **25**–26
père célibataire **25**–25
perles **69**–30, **69**–32
permis de conduire **29**–4
perpendiculaire **118**–20
perruche **133**–15
persil **51**–10
personne âgée **22**–12
personne prenant un bain de soleil **155**–17
personnel de l'hôpital **86**
pesant **11**–13, **71**–41
pèse-lettre **143**–16
pèse-personne **43**–26, **84**–7
peser **57**–B
pétale **129**–8
petit **70**–2
petit(e) **11**–1, **22**–18, **23**–1, **71**–35
petit pain **56**–11
petit-déjeuner **61**
petit-enfant **29**–Q
petit-fils **24**–7
petite branche **128**–1
petite cuiller **57**–6, **63**–28
petite culote **67**–17
petite ville **34**–3
petits pains **54**–30
pétoncle **130**–18
pétoncles **53**–25
pétrole **109**–55, **126**–6
phare **108**–5
pharmacie **80**–9, **90**–2
pharmacien **80**–10
pharmacienne **80**–10
phoque **131**–33
photocopieuse **142**–14
photographe **32**–11
photographie **44**–7, **164-165**
physiothérapeute **81**–30

physique **119**–3
piano **120**–16
pic **132**–9
pics **163**–28
pièce de théâtre **166**–2
pièces **20**, **146**–7
pied **74**–7, **75**
pierre **155**–24
piéton **90**–7
pieuvre **130**–4
pigeon **132**–16
pile **151**–40
pilons **52**–22
pilote **110**–12
pilule **81**–26
piments **51**–8
pin **128**–10
pince à cheveux **76**–17
pince à creusets **119**–15
pince à dénuder **151**–37
pince à linge **72**–10
pinceau **151**–9, **163**–23
pince à épiler **83**–2
pinces **59**–23, **119**–15, **150**–7
pinces à cheveux **76**–19
pingouin **132**–12
Ping-Pong™ **159**–13
pioche **149**–20
piquant **134**–23
pique-niquer **153**–D
piscine **37**–16, **145**–16
piste cyclable **153**–2
piste d'athlétisme **5**–11
piste de danse **33**–16
pistolet **100**–9
pistolet à peinture **151**–19
pizza **60**–7
placard **11**–15, 16, **44**–4
placard de rangement **36**–14
place de stationnement (parking) **36**–15
placoplâtre **149**–18
plafond **42**–5
plage **117**–10, **155**
plaines **117**–19
plan d'étage **38**–1
planche à découper **40**–27
planche à repasser **72**–14
planche de surf **155**–5
plancher **44**–24
Planètes **127**
planifier **169**–A
plante **39**–B, **42**–18
plante d'intérieur **129**–29
planter (un arbre/des semences) **39**–D, **148**–A
plantes **128**
plaque d'immatriculation **108**–15
plaquer **156**–M
plastique **70**
plat **41**–3
plateau **41**–10, **62**–H, **63**–7

plateau à desserts **63**–7
plateau à médicaments **87**–23
plateau de service **41**–6
plate-forme de chargement **146**–16
platine-cassettes **108**–30
plâtre **81**–29
plein **11**–9
pleine lune **127**–16
pleurer **32**–C
plier **72**–F
plombier **49**–20
plonge **63**–12
plongée en apnée **160**–11
plongée sous-marine **160**–12
plonger **157**–5
plongeur **63**–13
pluies acides **126**–11
plume **132**–5
plumeau **47**–1
Pluton **127**–1
pluvieux **10**–8
pneu **108**–10, **109**–53
pneu de secours **109**–53
pneus **109**–59
poche **73**–4, **135**–50
poche de glace **83**–13
pochette matelassée **143**–32
podium **32**–5
poêle **40**–24
poêle à frire **59**–5
poêlon **59**–5, 13, 26, 28
poids **22**–21, **57**
poids et mesures **57**
poignées **59**–29
poignet **69**–34, **75**–60
poinsettia **129**–23
point **113**–6
point d'exclamation **113**–7, 8
point virgule **113**–13
pointer **2**–F
pointeuse **146**–4
points de suture **83**–15
poires **50**–6
pois **51**–19
poison **82**–J, **147**–3
poisson **53**, **61**–17, **130**–12, 14, 15
poisson plat **130**–13
poisson rouge **133**–16
poisson surgelé **53**–30
poisson-chat **53**–17
poisson-épée **130**–12
poitrine (corps) **74**–13, 14
poitrines **52**–19
poivrière **41**–15
poivrons **51**–7
policier (policière) **99**–1, **138**–44
polir les meubles **46**–K
pollution **126**
pollution de l'eau **126**–12
pollution par les pesticides **126**–14
polyester **70**

pomme de pin **128**–11
pomme de terre au four **61**–14
pommeau de douche **43**–10
pommes **50**–4
pommes de terre **51**–21, **61**–11
pompier **102**–8, **137**–24
pompiste **137**–28
ponceuse à moteur **150**–9
poncho **66**–18
ponctuation **113**
pont **105**–2
porc **52**
porc-épic **134**–10
porte **36**
porte d'accès **144**–17
porte d'embarquement **110**–5, **111**–D
porte d'entrée **38**–11
porte de garage **38**–7
porte moustiquaire **38**–8
porte savon **43**–24
porte-bagages **110**–19
porte-bébé **95**–14
porte-brosses à dents **43**–21
porte-clé **69**–43
portefeuille **69**–26
porte-jarretelles **67**–19
porte-journaux **42**–22
porte-monnaie **69**–25
porte-serviettes **43**–8
porter **62**–H
porter un toast **33**–I
portier **36**–10, **145**–2
poser des briques **149**–B
poser une question **6**–G
poste **89**–29
poste de pilotage **110**–11
poste de police **89**–19
poste de secours **155**–20
poste de travail informatique **143**–21
poste d'infirmier(ère) **87**
postérieur **74**–12
postier (postière) **138**–45
pot **95**–10
pot à crème **41**–13
pot de fleurs **39**–18
poubelle **39**–3
pouce **75**–56
pouce (po) **15**–13
poudre de bain **76**–3
poudre de talc **76**–3
poudre pour bébés **95**–18
poudre pour le visage **77**–39
poule **133**–5
poulet **52**–16, **61**–12
poulet cuit **52**–25
poulet rôti **61**–12
poulpe **130**–4
poumon **75**–37
poupée **45**–18
poupée de papier **163**–30
pourcentages **15**

pourri **50**–30
pousser **153**–B
poussette **94**–2, **95**–16
poutre **149**–3
poutre en I **149**–3
poutrelle **149**–3
pré **117**–20
prélever du sang **85**–G
premier **14**
premier étage **36**–2
premier prix **152**–20
première place **152**–20
premiers soins **83**
prendre (votre) température **85**–C
prendre l'autobus **26**–H
prendre la commande **62**–E
prendre le petit-déjeuner **26**–E
prendre possession **35**–J
prendre soin de **140**–L
prendre un bain **76**–B
prendre un médicament **80**–F
prendre un message **142**–A
prendre un rendez-vous **85**–A
prendre une douche **26**–C, **76**–A
prendre une injection **80**–E
prendre une photo **32**–D
prenez place **2**–E
prénom **4**–2
préparation des aliments **58**
préparer le déjeuner **26**–F
préposé à l'expédition **146**–15
préposé au classement **142**–12
préposé aux commandes **146**–10
préposé(e) aux soins **87**–18
prépositions **13**
prépositions indiquant le mouvement
105
prescription **80**–13
présenter **8**–D, F
Président **116**–6
président de la Cour Suprême **116**–9
presse-ail **59**–10
pressing **91**–24
prêt **35**–I
prêt-à-manger **60**
preuves **99**–9
printemps **19**–37
prise **44**–20, **107**–8, **151**–41
prisme **119**–20
prison **99**–G
prix **21**–6
prix courant **21**–2
prix de vente **21**–3
problèmes (vêtements) **64**–2, **70**
problèmes et réparations domestiques
48–49
procureur **99**–4, **99**–10
producteur **148**–15
produit anti-insecte **154**–23
produit assouplissant/adoucissant **72**–6
produits cuisinés **54**–6

produits de cuisson **55**–13
produits de papier **55**–14
professeur **2**–5, **5**–2, **139**–58
professions **136–139**
profondeur **15**–15
programme (ordinateur) **144**–21
programme sur la nature **167**–22
programmeur (programmeuse)
   informatique **136**–16
projecteur de diapositives **165**–29
propre **72**–16
propriétaire **37**–32, **139**–56
propriétaire de l'usine **146**–2
propriétaire de magasin **139**–56
protège-oreilles **66**–12
protège-tympans **147**–13
protéger son portefeuille **101**–D
prudent **147**–24
pruneaux **50**–26
prunes **50**–8
psychiatre **86**–6
puces **49**–23
pudding **61**–20
pull à col en v **71**–27
pull à col rond **71**–26
pull à col roulé **71**–28
pullover **64**–11
pulvérisation nasale **81**–23
puma **134**–2
pupitre **2**–6, **142**–1
purée de pommes de terre **61**–11
puzzle **45**–22
pyjama **67**–4
pyjama-couverture **67**–7
pyramide **118**–13
quarante **14**, **16**–12
quart (heure) **16**
quart de lune **127**–15
quart de tasse **57**–8
quatorze **14**
quatorzième **14**
quatre **14**
quatre-ving-dix (nonante) **14**
quatre-vingts **14**, **15**–10
quatrième **14**, **15**–2
queue **55**–20, **134**–22
qui ne comprend pas bien **31**–27
qui s'ennuie **31**–26
quincaillerie **88**–14
quinze **14**
quinzième **14**
quitter **111**–L
quitter (l'autoroute) **105**–7
quitter le travail **26**–M
rabattre **73**–E
rabot **151**–52
raccords **151**–17
raccourcir **73**–D
raccrocher le combiné **9**–F
racine **128**–5, **129**–3
raclette **47**–9

racquetball **159**–11
radiateur **109**–42, 56
radiation **126**–13
radio **44**–16, **108**–31
radio à ondes courtes **164**–5
radiologue **86**–5
radio-réveil **44**–16, **164**–1
radis **51**–5
rafting **154**–4
ragoût de légumes **58**
raie **23**–4, **130**–6
rails **104**–10
raisins **50**–1
raisins secs **50**–27
rallonge (électrique) **151**–14
rallonger **73**–C
ramasse-poussière **47**–11
rampe d'éclairage **42**–3
ramure **134**–16
ranch **34**–12, **148**
randonnées **154**–6
randonnées avec sac à dos **154**–7
ranger **111**–H
ranger les jouets **46**–H
rangez votre crayon **2**–L
râpe **59**–2
râper **58**–J
rapide **11**–3
raquette de tennis **161**–2
rasoir **77**–25
rasoir électrique **77**–24
rat **133**–18
râteau **39**–11
râteler (les feuilles) **39**–F
raton laveur **134**–13
rats **49**–27
rayé **70**–7
rayon **70**, **118**–16
rayon de la volaille **54**–2
rayon des chaussures **68**–3
rayon des fruits et légumes **54**–11
rayon des produits laitiers **54**–9
rayon des viandes et volailles **54**–2
raz-de-marée **103**–15
RCR (réanimation cardio-respiratoire)
   83–17
rebondir **156**–K
réception **33**, **145**–8, **169**
réceptionniste **84**–2, **138**–47, **145**–8, 9
recevoir **96**–D
recevoir des commentaires **113**–C
recevoir une carte d'embarquement
   111–E
recharger **109**–58
réchaud de camping **154**–16
recherche d'emploi **141**
récolter **148**–B
récoltes **148**
rectangle **118**–8
reçu **21**–5
recueillir les devoirs **7**–Q

recycler **46**–B, **126**–A
rédaction **113**–2
rédiger **113**–D
réfrigérateur **40**–9
regarder la télé **27**–5
région **34**–1, 4
règle **3**–27
règle (science) **119**–5
rein **75**–45
relevé mensuel **97**–10
relish **60**–26
remarié(e)(s) **25**–27
rembobiner **165**–D
remercier **8**–H
remorque **106**–17
remplir l'espace blanc **7**–R
remplir le lave-linge/la laveuse **72**–C
remplir une demande d'emploi **141**–G
remplissez un formulaire **4**–B
remuer **58**–E
renard **134**–15
rendez-vous **19**–45, **85**
rendre **113**–E
rendre un verdict **99**–E
renseignements personnels **4**
réparateur **48**–10, **138**–48
réparations **48**–49
réparer **140**–G
repasser **72**–G
repasser (des vêtements) **73**–8
repérer la sortie de secours **111**–J
répéter **6**–D
répondeur **9**–14
répondre à une question **6**–H
représentant de compagnie aérienne
   110–2
reptiles **131**
requin **130**–7
réservoir d'essence **108**–12
résidence universitaire **34**–9
respecter les lois **116**–H
respiration artificielle **83**–16
responsabilités (d'un citoyen) **116**
ressources énergétiques **126**
restaurant **62–63**, **90**–14
restaurant minute **90**–14
rester au lit **80**–A
retirer (la carte) **97**–F
retirer de l'argent **97**–D
retouches (couture) **73**
retour de bouteilles consignées **54**–1
retourner **21**–F
rétroprojecteur **2**–4
rétroviseur **108**–1
rétroviseur extérieur **108**–8
revenir à la maison **27**–Q
réverbère **91**–23
revers **73**–5
rez-de-chaussée **36**–1
rhinocéros **135**–29
rhume **79**–1

rideaux **44**–5
rimmel **77**–38
rince-bouche **77**–23
rincer **76**–F
rire **33**–H
risque biologique **147**–5
risque de radioactivité **147**–6
risque électrique **147**–1
rivage **117**–12
rivière **117**–3
riz **54**–28, **148**–1
riz pilaf **61**–18
robe **64**–3
robe de grossesse **65**–19
robe de nuit **67**–5
robe du soir **65**–29
robe maternité **65**–19
robe-chasuble **65**–18
robinet **43**–6, **49**–16
robot culinaire **40**–26
rongeurs **133**
rosbif **52**–1, **53**–7, **57**–12
rose **12**–10, **129**–15
rôti **58**–U
rôti de bœuf **52**–1, **53**–7, **57**–12
rôtissoire **59**–13
rouge **12**–13, **77**–36
rouge à lèvres **77**–37
rouge-gorge **132**–17
rougeole **79**–5
rouleau **151**–46
rouleau à pâtisserie **59**–30
rouleaux **23**–21
ruban **83**–5, **143**–39, 42
ruban adhésif transparent **143**–39
ruban cartouche de machine à écrire **143**–31
ruban d'emballage **143**–42
rue **90**–9
ruelle **37**–21
rues en ville **88**–89
s'assurer de comprendre **8**–E
s'endormir **27**–Y
s'enquérir à propos des avantages sociaux **141**–J
s'enquérir à propos du salaire **141**–K
s'enrôler dans l'armée **28**–F
s'étirer **157**–Q
s'éveiller **26**–A
s'excuser **8**–I
s'habiller **26**–D
s'inscrire **116**–F
sable **155**–23
sabot **134**–17
sac (à main) **69**–27, 28, 29
sac (de papier, etc) **55**–22, 23 **56**–7, 19
sac à bandoulière **69**–27
sac à dos **69**–28, **95**–15, **154**–15
sac à dos pour bébé **95**–15
sac de couchage **154**–12
sac de farine **56**–19

sac de papier **55**–22
sac de plastique **55**–23
sac vomitoire **110**–15
sacoches **69**–6
sacs à main **69**–6
sacs à ordures **47**–12
sac d'aspirateur **47**–15
saigner **82**–M
Saint-Valentin **168**–4
saisir le code confidentiel **97**–B
saisons **19**
salade de chou **53**–14
salade de pâtes **53**–15
salade de pommes de terre **53**–13
salade du chef **61**–9
salade verte **60**–8
saladier **59**–31
salamandre **130**–27
salami **53**–5
sale **72**–15
salière **41**–14
salle à dîner **62**–2
salle à manger **41**
salle d'attente **84**–1
salle d'audience **99**–7
salle de bain **43**
salle de classe **2**–3, **5**–1
salle de danse **145**–20
salle de réunion **145**–19
salle d'examen **84**–9
salle d'opération **87**
salle d'urgence **87**
salon **42**
salon de coiffure **88**–15, **93**–16
salopette **65**–21
saluer quelqu'un **8**–A
samedi **18**–7
sandales **68**–24
sandwich au fromage grillé **61**–8
sang **79**–15
sans issue **107**–8
sans manches **71**–29
Saturne **127**–4
saucisses **52**–12, **61**–2
saule **128**–14
saumon entier **53**–18
sauté (légumes) **58**–W
sauter **156**–J
sauterelle **132**–25
savon **43**–23, **76**–2
saxophone **120**–7
scanner **144**–13
scarabée **132**–19
scie à main **150**–4
scie à métaux **150**–5
scie circulaire **150**–10
science **119**
science-fiction **166**–12
score **158**–1
scorpion **132**–31
sculpture **152**–9

se bercer (dans une chaise berçante) **94**–H
se brûler **82**–H
se cacher **169**–E
se casser un os **82**–P
se détendre **27**–U
se gargariser **77**–L
se lever **26**–B
se marier **28**–L
se mettre du maquillage **77**–P
se noyer **82**–I
se pencher **157**–R
se polir les ongles **77**–O
se présenter **111**–D
se présenter à une entrevue **141**–H
se présenter en cour **99**–C
se promener/aller (à pied, en vélo, à cheval, en voiture) **91**–E, **157**–W
se raser **77**–M
se rendre à la maison **27**–Q
se sentir étourdi **78**–C
seau **45**–13, **47**–20, **155**–22
seau à couches **45**–13, **95**–23
sec **72**–18
sèche-linge **72**–4
sécher les cheveux **76**–H
sécheresse **103**–10
sécheuse **72**–4
séchoir **23**–20, **76**–16
seconde **14**, **16**–1
secrétaire **139**–52, **142**–3
section des médias **98**–11
section des périodiques **98**–6
sécurité **111**–C
sécurité au travail **147**
sécurité publique **101**
Sécurité Sociale **4**–15
seize **14**
seizième **14**
semaine **18**–11
semaine prochaine **18**–20
semelle **68**–12
semi-remorque **106**–15
semis **129**–2
Sénat **116**–3
sénateur **116**–4
Sens **75**
sens interdit **107**–4
sensations **30**–31
sentiments **30**–31
sentir **75**–C
sept **14**
septembre **19**–33
septième **14**
séquoia **128**–1
sérieux **167**–26
seringue **84**–14
serpent à sonnettes **131**–38
serpillière **47**–16
serre **132**–4, **152**–5
serré **71**–43

Index

serre-joints en C **150**–6
serre-tête de sécurité **147**–14
serrer dans les bras **33**–G
serrure est cassée **48**–6
serrurier **48**–11
serveur (serveuse) **62**–4, **63**–6, **139**–53
service à l'auto **90**–13
service au volant **90**–13
service aux chambres **145**–12
service d'urgence (911) **9**–9
service de consultation **98**–2
service de courrier des États-Unis **96**
service de garage des voitures **145**–1
service de vaisselle **41**–2
Service Sélectif **116**–F
serviette **41**–19, **43**–8, 12, 13, **63**–23
serviette de bain **43**–12
serviette de plage **155**–15
serviettes humides pour bébés **95**–17
servir (sports) **157**–N
servir des clients **140**–O
servir le repas **62**–F
s'étouffer **82**–L
seul(e) **30**–18
sexe **4**–12
shampooing **76**–9
short **64**–13, **67**–3, 12
shorts de vélo **67**–3
siège **62**–B
siège arrière **109**–38
siège avant **109**–35
siège de sécurité **109**–39
siège de sécurité pour enfant **95**–13,
   109–39
siège pivotant **143**–22
siéger sur un jury **116**–G
signaler les crimes **101**–H
signature **4**–18
signer un contrat de location **35**–C
signez votre nom **4**–D
silencieux (de voiture) **108**–11
simple **71**–38
singe **135**–27
sirop **61**–5
sirop contre la toux **81**–20
situation dangereuse **147**–8
six **14**
sixième **14**
ski **160**–1, 3, 7
ski alpin **160**–1
ski de randonnée **160**–3
ski nautique **160**–7
skier **157**–V
skis **161**–24
slip **67**–16
smog **126**–10
smoking **65**–28
sœur **24**–8, **25**–30, 33
sofa **42**–19
soft-ball **158**–10
soie **70**–15

soie dentaire **77**–22
soie dentaire (passer la) **77**–K
soins de santé **80–81**
soir **17**–19
soixante **14**
soixante-dix (septante) **14**
soja **148**–3
solde (de banque) **97**–11
sole **53**–21
soleil **127**–10
solides **118**
sommet **117**–14
sommet de montagne **117**–14
sommier **44**–26
sonnette **38**–10
sortez votre crayon **2**–K
sortie de secours **37**–23, **111**–J
sortir les ordures **46**–Q
souci **129**–13
soucoupe **63**–22
soudeur (soudeuse) **139**–63
souffler **169**–K
souffleuse à feuilles **39**–4
soulever **94**–G
souliers de ville **68**–20
souliers lacés **68**–20
souligner **7**–V
soupe **54**–24
soupe au poulet **58**
soupe du jour **61**–10
sourcil **74**–32
sourd(e) **22**–27
souris **49**–26, **133**–17
souris d'ordinateur **144**–8
sous **13**–9, **105**–1
sous-compacte **106**–1
sous-exposé **165**–35
sous-main **142**–7
soustraction **118**–2
soutien-gorge **67**–20
spaghetti **54**–27
spatule **59**–19
spectacle de marionnettes **152**–14
sphère **118**–14
sports **158–160**
sports aquatiques **160**
sports d'équipe **158**
sports d'hiver et sports aquatiques **160**
sports individuels **159**
squelette **75**
stade **152**–26
stand de crème glacée **93**–20
standard transmission **109**
station de taxis **104**–19
station d'essence **137**–28
station d'infirmier(ère) **87**
station-service **88**–12
station spatiale **127**–18
stationnement **89**–26
stationnement interdit **107**–12
stationnement pour personnes

handicapées **107**–14
stationner (l'auto) **91**–D
stéthoscope **84**–8
stop **107**–3
store **44**–6
store à lamelles **43**–11
stuc **149**–14
stylo **3**–18
subir un choc électrique **82**–F
subir un procès **99**–D
subir un traitement d'acupuncture **81**–G
succédané de sucre **60**–22
sucette **95**–29
sucre **55**–48, **60**–21
sucrier **41**–12
suivre des instructions **7**
sumac lustré **128**–24
sumac vénéneux **128**–25
superposé (lits) **45**–1
support lombaire **147**–16
supporter **158**–4
sur **13**–8, **105**–2, 6
surexposé **165**–34
surf des neiges **161**–23
surpris(e) **31**–31
survêtement **64**–14
suspect **99**–A
suspendre les vêtements **72**–H
symptômes et blessures **78**
synagogue **88**–9
synthetic materials **70**
syntonisateur **164**–13
système de sécurité **36**–9
système d'injection de carburant **109**–40
système juridique **99**
système solaire **127**
table à langer **45**–12, **95**–9
table basse **42**–23
table de chevet **86**–9
table de nuit **44**–21
table de pique-nique **153**–8
table de salle à dîner **41**–17
table de salon **42**–23
table d'examen **84**–13
table d'extrémité **42**–21
table d'opération **87**–34
tableau **2**–1, **42**–7, **152**–8
tableau d'affichage **3**–14
tableau d'affichage des offres
   d'emploi **141**–B
tableau de bord **108**–17
tableau d'information **9**–8, **93**–19
tablette **40**–8, **110**–16
tache **70**–22
tâches ménagères **46**
taco **60**–9
taie d'oreiller **44**–10
taille **74**–4
taille-crayon **3**–13, **142**–9
taille-crayons électrique **142**–9
tailler **39**–E

tailles **70**
tailleur **73**–9
talon aiguille **68**–17, **71**–47
talon haut **68**–17, **71**–47
talon (pied) **75**–62
talon (soulier) **68**–13
tamanoir **135**–24
tambourine **120**–19
tamia **133**–20
tamis **59**–22
tampon de caoutchouc **143**–40
tampon encreur **143**–41
tampons à récurer **47**–5
tampons à récurer en laine d'acier **47**–5
tante **24**–10
tapageur (enfant) **11**–11
taper (à la machine) **140**–M, **142**–D
tapis **42**–27
tapis de bain **43**–27
tapis de caoutchouc **43**–3
tard **17**–23
tarif **104**–5
tarte **61**–21
tartre **84**–17
tas de compost **39**–10
tasse **63**–21
tasse à café **41**–27
tasse d'huile **57**–2
tasse de farine **57**–10
tatou **134**–8
taxe de vente **21**–7
taxi **104**–18
TB (tuberculose) **79**–13
technicien(ne) **86**–8, 16
technicien de laboratoire **86**–16
technicien d'urgence médicale **87**–26
technicien en radiologie **86**–8
teindre les cheveux **23**–D
teinturerie **91**–24
télé (téléviseur) **42**–26, **164**–6
téléavertisseur **9**–16
télécommande **164**–9
télécopieur **143**–23
téléphone **9**, **9**–1, 15
téléphone cellulaire **9**–13
téléphone public **9**–11, **91**–21
téléphone sans fil **9**–12
téléphoniste **9**–7
télescope **127**–21
télé-vendeur (vendeuse) **139**–59
téléviseur portable **164**–7
témoin **99**–11
température **10**
température (fièvre) **78**–8
tempête **10**–16, 18, 20, 21
tempête de neige **10**–20
tempête de poussière **10**–21
temps froid **10**–4
tenir **94**–B, **101**–C
tennis **159**–14
tennis de table **159**–13

tente **154**–10
tentures **42**–16
termites **49**–22
terrain **5**–12, **148**–7
terrain de base-ball **153**–1
terrain de basket **158**–7
terrain de jeux **36**–6, **153**
terrain de sports **159**–17
terrasse **38**–16
Terre **127**–7
tête **74**–1
tête de lit **44**–15
tétine **95**–27
thamnophis **131**–39
thé **60**–5, **61**–24
thé glacé **60**–5
théâtre **88**–10
théière **40**–17, **41**–11
thermomètre **84**–15
thon **54**–25, **130**–9
tige **129**–4
tigre **135**–37
timbre **96**–10
tique **132**–28
tir à l'arc **159**–1
tirer **156**–I
tirer le wagonnet **153**–A
tiroir **40**–23, **44**–3
titre **98**–21, **113**–3
toasts **33**-I, **61**–3
tobogan **153**–13
toge **32**–2, **65**–29
toile **163**–22
toilettes **5**–8
toit **38**–20, **48**–3
tôle à biscuits **59**–27
tomates **51**–23
tomber (des escaliers) **82**–O
tomber amoureux **28**–K
tonalité **9**–B
tondeuse à gazon **39**–22
tondre **39**–C
tornade **103**–13
tortue **131**–42
tôt **17**–22
total **21**–8
toucher **75**–E
toupie **150**–12
tour de contrôle **110**–7
tourne-disque **164**–12
tourner à droite **107**–B
tourner à droite seulement **107**–9
tourner à gauche **107**–C
tournesol **129**–10
tournevis **150**–25
tournevis Phillips **150**–26
tousser **78**–A
tracteur **148**–9
traducteur **138**–34
train **104**–17
traire **148**–C

traiteur **33**–12
trajet **104**–2, **107**
trancher **58**–O
tranquille **11**–12
transcripteur **142**–4
transcripteur à microcassette **142**–4
transcrire **142**–C
transférer (des fonds) **97**–E
transfert **104**–6
transmission automatique **109**
transport public **104**
transporteur à courroie **146**–12
travail avec un partenaire **6**
travail en classe **7**
travail en groupe **6**
travail manuel **140**–D
travailler **26**–K, **140**–P
travailleur (travailleuse) **146**–6
traversée de **105**–3
traverser la rue **90**–A
traverser une zone de turbulence **111**–N
trèfles **163**–26
treize **14**
treizième **14**
tremblement de terre **102**–5
trench-coat **66**–20
trente **14**
trépied **165**–20
très grand **70**–5
très petit **70**–1
triangle **118**–7
tribunal **89**–18
tribune **32**–4
tricot **64**–11
tricot de corps **67**–10
tricoter **163**–F
tricycle **153**–9
trier **72**–A
trigonométrie **118**–27
tripes **52**–8
triste **31**–20, **167**–28
triton **130**–26
trois **14**
trois fois par semaine **18**–24
trois quarts **15**–5
troisième **14**
troisième étage **36**–4
trombone **120**–12, **143**–44
trompe d'animal **135**–47
trompette **120**–13
tronc d'arbre **128**–4
trop grand **70**–21
trop petit **70**–20
trotte-bébé **95**–12
trottoir **38**–14, **91**–26
trousse à dissection **119**–7
trousse de premiers soins **83**–1
trouver un emploi **28**–G
truelle **39**–14, **149**–12
truite **53**–16
T-shirt **64**–12, **70**–16, **72**–15, 16, 17, 18

tuba **120**–14
tube **56**–12
tube de pâte dentifrice **56**–24
tuile **43**–9
tulipe **129**–11
tunel **105**–11
tunique **65**–22
turbulence **111**–N
turquoise **12**–4
tuyau **151**–16
tuyau d'arrosage **39**–9
tuyaux **49**–19
types d'écoles **112**
types d'histoires **166**
types de divertissement **166**
types de matériaux **70**
types de mathématiques **118**
types de programmes télé **167**
UC (unité centrale) **144**–1
un demi **15**–4
un dollar **20**–6
un huitième **15**–1
un milliard **14**
un pack de six boissons gazeuses **56**–21
un quart **15**–2
un rouleau d'essuie-tout **56**–23
un tiers **15**–3
un(e) **14**, **15**–1, 2, 3, 4, 5, 11, **16**–4, 15, **20**–1, 12
une fois par semaine **18**–22
une heure **16**–4
une heure cinq **16**–5
une heure cinquante **16**–14
une heure dix **16**–6
une heure et demie **16**
une heure quarante **16**–12
une heure quinze **16**–7
une heure trente **16**–10
une heure vingt **16**–8
une heure vingt-cinq **16**–9
uni (couleur) **70**–6
uniforme **65**–17, **161**–16
unité de disque (ordinateur) **144**–3, 20
unité de disque dur **144**–20
unité de disques **144**–3
unité murale **42**–13
univers **127**
université **112**–10
Uranus **127**–3
urgences et désastres naturels **102**–**103**
urgences médicales **82**
usage du dictionnaire **6**
usine **146**
ustensiles de cuisine **59**
utilisation d'un téléphone public **9**
utilisation du guichet automatique **97**
utiliser **140**–N
utiliser un déodorant **76**–C
vacances **19**–46
vache **133**–3
vadrouille **47**–17

vague **155**–6
vague de chaleur **10**–15
vaisselier **41**–1
vallée **117**–18
vandalisme **100**–1
varicelle **79**–6
vase **41**–9
véhicule utilitaire sport **106**–9
veilleuse **45**–3
veine **75**–44
vélo **153**–4
vendeur **68**–1, **91**–30, **139**–50
vendeuse **68**–1
vendeur ambulant **91**–30
vendre **21**–B, **140**–H
vendredi **18**–6
vent **126**–2
venteux **10**–10
ventilateur **41**–4
ventilateur de plafond **41**–4
Vénus **127**–8
ver **130**–22
verbes se rapportant aux sports **156**–**157**
verger **148**–16
vérifier la pression artérielle **85**–B
vérifier votre travail **7**–Y
vernis à ongles **77**–31
verre **11**–9, 10, **41**–26, **63**–19, 20
verre à eau **63**–19
verre à vin **63**–20
verres de contact **81**–36
verrou **37**–29, **101**–E
verrouiller **37**–29 **109**–34
vers le bas **105**–8
verser l'eau **62**–C
verser les oeufs dans le poêlon **58**–D
version préliminaire **113**–A
vert **12**–8
vésicule biliaire **75**–40
vessie **75**–47
veste **66**–7
veste de cuir **66**–3
veste en duvet **66**–15
vêtements I, II, III **64**–**67**
vétérinaire **139**–62
viandes et volailles **52**
vice-président **116**–7
vide **11**–10
vide-ordures **37**–24
vider **72**–E
vider (la corbeille à papier) **46**–F
vieux (vieilles) **71**–33
vigne **128**–22
vignoble **148**–14
VIH (virus de l'immunodéficience humaine) **79**–10
ville **4**–7, **34**–1
vinaigrette **60**–18
vingt **14**, **16**–8, 9, **20**–10
vingt pour cent **15**–8
vingtième **14**

violence des gangs **100**–2
violette **129**–22
violon **120**–8
violoncelle **120**–9
virgule **113**–10
vis à bois **150**–28
vis à métaux **150**–27
Visage **74**, **77**–39
visière de sécurité **147**–11
vitamines **81**–19
vitre **149**–15
vitrine **69**–7
vivre **116**–B
vœu **169**–J
voie à sens unique **107**–6
voiles sèche-linge **72**–5
voilier **155**–4
voir **75**–A
voisin **37**–22
voiture de sport **106**–6
voiture moyenne **106**–3
voiture, pièces et entretien **108**–**109**
voitures et camions **106**
vol et agression **100**–5
volaille **52**
volant **108**–26
volant de lit **44**–22
volet **38**–18
volley-ball (équipement) **161**–3
volley-ball (sport) **158**–14
volume **57**
vomir **78**–E
voter **116**–D
voyage en avion **111**
voyager **29**–N
vue **11**–21, 22
water-polo **158**–15
weekend **18**–13
western **166**–9
xylophone **120**–17
yaourt **54**–33, **60**–11
yogourt **54**–33, **60**–11
yogourt glacé **60**–11
zèbre **135**–34
zéro **14**
zone de récupération des bagages **110**–17
zone d'embarquement **110**–6
zone rurale **34**–4
zone urbaine **34**–1
zoom **165**–25